BEGINNING PHILOSOPHY

BEGINNING PHILOSOPHY

RICHARD DOUBLE

New York Oxford
OXFORD UNIVERSITY PRESS
1999

Oxford University Press

Oxford New York
Athens Auckland Bangkok Bogota Bombay Buenos Aires
Calcutta Cape Town Dar es Salaam Delhi Florence Hong Kong
Istanbul Karachi Kuala Lumpur Madras Madrid Melbourne
Mexico City Nairobi Paris Singapore Taipei Tokyo Toronto Warsaw

and associated companies in
Berlin Ibadan

Published by Oxford University Press, Inc.
198 Madison Avenue, New York, New York 10016

Oxford is a registered trademark of Oxford University Press

Library of Congress Cataloging-in-Publication Data

Double, Richard.
Beginning philosophy / by Richard Double.
p. cm.
Includes bibliographical references and index.
ISBN 0-19-511781-6 (alk. paper)
1. Philosophy. I. Title.
B74.D68 1998
100—dc21 97-40510
CIP

9 8 7 6 5 4 3 2
Printed in the United States of America
on acid-free paper

For Edmund Abegg

Friend and Colleague Extraordinaire

Contents

PREFACE

I have written this book as simply as I can to make it understandable to the complete novice to philosophy. I also want *Beginning Philosophy* to be forceful and provocative reading for students, instructors, and general readers. I provide the best arguments I can for all of the opposing views on the issues I consider, but this is not a neutral book. I reach my own distinctive conclusions about each of the problems. These conclusions often do not represent majority opinions among analytic philosophers, let alone all philosophers.

The text contains eleven chapters. The first chapter introduces the subject of philosophy, and the second provides as much logical methodology as I think is needed to handle the rest of the book. The logic chapter can be skipped, but readers who do so will need to refer back to chapter 2 occasionally. The next eight chapters deal with what I take to be the central issues of Western analytic philosophy—knowledge, existence, and value. Those eight chapters are self-contained and may be read in any order. The eleventh chapter sums up the worldview gotten from the rest of the book.

At the end of each chapter are several addenda that I have found helpful in my own teaching. The *misconceptions* sections expressly warn against errors that introductory students are prone to make. I have found that a good deal of students' difficulties in understanding philosophical reasoning lies in confusions over very basic ideas—ideas that instructors tend to take for granted. For this reason, it is valuable to attack the misconceptions directly. The *guide questions* are specific questions about the text (along with page numbers where the answers are found) that I assign with each reading assignment. Guide questions direct students to the key themes and prompt them to express them in their own words. The *review questions for examinations* are questions that students should master as preparation for tests on the chapters, thus answering the classic question, "What should I study for the exam?" The *discussion questions* require independent judgment, and can serve as essay exam questions, paper topics, in-class discussion material, or issues for readers to ponder on their own. Students who hope to get the most they can from the text will try their hands at the discussion questions. There are also annotated bibliographies of relevant books at the end of each chapter.

At the end of the book there is an appendix of famous philosophical quotes, along with a glossary of philosophical terms and a glossary of the names of the most important historical thinkers cited in the text. The glossary of terms is not meant to take the place of a dictionary—as with any college-level reading, students will need dictionaries.

I have tried to emphasize throughout the interconnections between philosophical problems. Accordingly, the book hangs together best when read straight through. Logical methodology (chapter 2) and theory of knowledge (chapter 3) provide the tools to approach the other philosophical issues. The doctrine of the subjectivism of the commonsense properties of physical objects (scientific realism) introduced in the problem of the external world (chapter 4) helps make the mind/body problem more understandable (chapter 5) and provides a model to understand subjectivism in metaethics (chapter 7). Subjectivism in metaethics links the subjectivism of chapter 4 with the subjectivism about values covered in the chapters on normative ethics (chapter 6) and the free will problem (chapter 8). The existence of God (chapter 9) and the problem of evil (chapter 10)—perhaps the most emotionally charged metaphysical and ethical issues—are treated last so that readers will bring their most developed critical thinking resources to these heart-felt topics. For example, understanding the theory of knowledge and the difficulties of metaphysical theory-construction will help readers appreciate the difficulty of proving the existence of God. Understanding the free will problem helps readers to understand the free will defense in the problem of evil.

Beginning Philosophy contains more material than most instructors will want to cover in one semester. When I teach introduction to philosophy I handle the introductory and logical tools chapters in the first few weeks and then do three more chapters in the rest of the semester. Sometimes I hold a class election to select the chapters we will cover. There are many ways to design the course. Instructors who want to emphasize epistemology and metaphysics might add to the first two chapters, theory of knowledge (chapter 3), the external world (chapter 4), the mind/body problem (chapter 5), and the existence of God (chapter 9). Instructors who want to emphasize value theory might cover chapter 6 (normative ethics), chapter 7 (metaethics), chapter 8 (the free will problem), and chapter 10 (the problem of evil). Instructors who want to cover the topics with the greatest popular appeal might do the mind/body problem, normative ethics, existence of God, and the problem of evil.

I am grateful to many persons for their help. This book results from twenty-five years of teaching introduction to philosophy courses using various texts—James Cornman and Keith Lehrer's *Philosophical Problems and Arguments*, William Alston and Richard Brandt's *The Problems of Philosophy*, William Halverson's *A Concise Introduction to Philosophy*, Thomas Davis's *Philosophy: An Introduction through Original Fiction, Discussion, and Readings*, and Howard Kahane's *Thinking about Basic Beliefs: An Introduction to Philosophy*. These are all excellent texts, and I gladly express my debt to their authors. Not only did I learn much of what I know about philosophy from these texts, but I have derived helpful pedagogic insights from each of them. I thank my Edinboro colleagues Edmund Abegg, Robert Cogan, and Elliott Wreh-Wilson, and four anonymous Oxford University Press readers for helpful suggestions that I have incorporated into the text. Robert Kane made helpful comments on the free will chapter. A special debt is owed to Bruce Waller for massive, valuable aid with the entire manuscript. I am also grateful to Janeen Christ for insightful commentary on each chapter and Diane Harpst and Shannon Fera for meticulous proofreading of the manuscript.

Edinboro, Pennsylvania
April 1998

R. D.

BEGINNING PHILOSOPHY

Chapter 1
INTRODUCTION

Everyone holds philosophical beliefs. If you believe that physical objects exist, that we think with our brains, that there is a difference between right and wrong, that you know that yours is not the only mind, that there is or is no God, or that human beings are often responsible for their actions, then you hold a philosophical belief. Most nonphilosophers do not realize that every philosophical belief has been debated at length and with great precision by philosophers who gave powerful arguments for opposing sides. Philosophical beliefs are disputed beliefs, and disputes exist even if we are unaware of them.

Because we cannot live without holding philosophical beliefs, there is no such thing as avoiding *philosophical questions* about which beliefs are true. The only issue is whether we address the questions directly or whether we assume uncritically that our pre-existing answers to the questions are correct. By studying philosophy, we see that it is possible to think rigorously and fairly about questions that nonphilosophers typically believe cannot be seriously investigated—questions about which most persons throw up their hands and say "That's a matter of one's philosophy!" Not only can *philosophers* perform such a feat, but better still, *philosophy students* can learn to perform the feat also. Because philosophers question so much of what we ordinarily assume, philosophy has the effect of shaking up the complacency of those who study it seriously. In the sense of "radical" meaning "going to the root of things," philosophy is the most radical discipline of all.

WHAT IS PHILOSOPHY?

We begin with a definition of "philosophy." Philosophy is an activity that deals with a particular *subject matter* (what it's about) by using a particular *method* (its way of treating its subject matter). If we can say what the subject matter and the method of philosophy are, we can say what philosophy is.

The *subject matter of philosophy* is *questions*, which have three major characteristics: (1) philosophical questions *have* answers, but the answers remain in dispute; (2) philosophical questions *cannot* be settled by science, common sense, or faith; and (3) philosophical questions are of perennial intellectual interest to human beings.

Condition (1) says that there *are* answers to philosophical questions—philosophical questions are not nonsense questions such as "What color is Tuesday?" The problem is that we do not *know* what the answers are. Condition (2) maintains that philosophical questions cannot be settled by performing experiments or collecting data, by finding out what most persons believe, or by religious faith. Science does not settle philosophical questions because philosophical questions begin where science ends. For example, the question "Does science provide knowledge?" is not a question for scientists. Common sense does not resolve philosophical questions because philosophy asks whether the beliefs of common sense are true. Faith, in the sense of "belief without evidence," cannot settle philosophical questions either. If one side to a philosophical dispute tries to support her answer by saying that she has faith that her answer is correct, the opposite side could just as easily say that *she* has faith in *her* answer. Until someone provides evidence, neither side has supported her position. Finally, according to Condition (3) philosophical questions are questions of such depth and importance that they have always interested thoughtful human beings. Philosophical questions are not here today, gone tomorrow.

The *method* (*methodology*) that philosophers use to address philosophical questions is *critical thinking*. The term "critical thinking" comes from the word "criticize": Critical thinkers criticize the beliefs of everyone, including themselves. Critical thinking has both a *cognitive* (intellectual) and a *temperamental* component. The cognitive component of critical thinking includes these aspects: (1) *Careful attention to the meaning of words, questions, and issues.* Critical thinkers define key terms to clarify what is being said. (2) *A logical mapping out of possible approaches to the issue in question.* We cannot address a question until we understand what its answer might be. (3) *A comprehensive consideration of all the reasons we can think of for and against possible answers in order to find the most likely-to-be-true answer out of all the candidates.* Critical thinkers use the best logical tools they can as carefully as they can to perform these three tasks.

Besides these cognitive skills, critical thinkers need to approach problems with a *critical temperament*. This includes: (1) the desire to understand the issues as clearly as possible; (2) the desire to evaluate all positions fairly, without giving preferential treatment to one's pre-existing beliefs; (3) a willingness to follow complex, sometimes unusual, lines of reasoning; and (4) a willingness to suspend judgment whenever we discover that we have no better evidence for accepting one view instead of another.

The definition of "philosophy" I have just provided corresponds to my view of philosophy as the imperious inquisitor of the most basic beliefs in all areas of thought, including science, common sense, religion, and philosophy itself. No area of belief is given preferential treatment. Philosophers are critical thinkers who use their best intellectual resources to reach the most plausible (worthy of belief) tentative answers they can to questions that cannot be answered conclusively. By answering these questions, philosophers aim to construct a picture of the world that is most likely to be true.

Because every philosophical theory has been criticized and defended by first-rate philosophers, it is usually impossible to know that a philosophical theory is true. The most that philosophers can reasonably hope to do is to show that relative to the other things they think are true, their theories are more likely to be true than competing theories. Philosophers admit their fallibility. For example, the Greek philosopher Socrates (470–399 B.C.) said that although he is ignorant, at least he *realizes* that he is ignorant. Likewise, the Scottish philosopher David Hume (1711–1776) claimed that persons who

> give themselves airs of superior wisdom . . . have a hard task when they encounter persons of inquisitive dispositions, who push them from every corner to which they retreat, and who are sure at last to bring them to some dangerous dilemma. The best expedient to prevent this confusion is to be modest in our pretensions; and even to discover the difficulty ourselves before it is objected to us. By this means, we may make a kind of merit of our very ignorance. (1955, 321–22)

Given the characteristics of the subject matter of philosophical questions I provided above, the main questions in philosophy turn out to be: "What do we know?" (theory of knowledge or epistemology), "What exists?" (metaphysics), and "What is moral?" (ethics). These questions satisfy each condition. When we ask whether we have knowledge, what exists, and how to tell right from wrong, we are asking questions that (1) have answers, (2) cannot be settled in nonphilosophical ways, and (3) have puzzled human beings ever since we have been able to think about abstract issues. The forth major branch of philosophy—logic—constitutes a large part of the critical thinking methodology that philosophy shares with science. I call this way of looking at philosophy "Philosophy as Worldview Construction" (Double, 1996, chap. 2). Philosophy as Worldview Construction tries above all to build the most-likely-to-be-true picture of persons and the cosmos.

Other topics that many philosophers consider to be of equal or greater importance to the issues I emphasize include: investigations of religious language, physical and social sciences, law, political obligation, art, language, mathematics, applied moral problems, and social issues such as race and gender, among others. Differences in emphasis depend in part on personal preferences but also stem from the fact that not all philosophers would agree with my definition of "philosophy." The definition of "philosophy" we provide depends largely on what we think philosophy is for. What we think philosophy is for depends, in turn, on *what we believe philosophy can accomplish* and *what we desire to accomplish by philosophizing*. The definition I provide reveals that I *believe* that philosophy can provide the most-likely-to-be-true answers to unsolvable questions and that I *desire* that philosophy try to do this. Not every philosopher shares these beliefs and desires. Different philosophers have different *metaphilosophies*, that is, *views of what philosophy is and should try to do*. Thus, introduction to philosophy texts written by philosophers who hold other metaphilosophies will be different from this text.

HOW IS PHILOSOPHY POSSIBLE?

So far I have said that philosophy tries to give the best possible answers to questions that cannot be settled by science, common sense, or faith. It is only fair to ask how philosophy can even hope to arrive at answers to philosophical questions if these other methods fail.

The answer is that philosophers construct *theories* to answer philosophical questions. Theory-construction in philosophy is similar to theory-construction in science at those times when scientists deal with very abstract questions that are far removed from observation. For example, although historians do not debate over the dates of the American Civil War, they debate over its causes. Although paleontologists do not debate the existence of dinosaurs, they debate over what led to their extinction. Astrophysicists do not debate over whether the known universe is expanding, but they debate whether it will continue to expand indefinitely or whether it will contract back on itself. In every science, there is a large core of statements that most scientists accept as true and many theoretical questions that are disputed. Just as scientists argue for their theories, philosophers argue for theirs.

An important reasoning device used in science and philosophy is *inference to the best explanation*. In this method of reasoning, we take some group of statements that we believe are true (datum, singular; data, plural), and *hypothesize* (conjecture) that some other fact is true because that hypothesis is the best explanation of the data. For example, suppose we establish that wolves have larger heads relative to their body mass than do domesticated dogs. And suppose we try to come up with a true explanation for (correct theory to explain) this fact. We consider several possible explanations to see if any seems most likely. Here are two. First, perhaps the wolves and the domesticated dogs were both designed by the Martians, and the Martians thought that wolves look better with big heads. That would explain it. (Of course, we have no independent evidence for thinking that the Martians exist, nor why, even if they did exist, they would want to do this.) Second, perhaps after being domesticated from wolves, dogs no longer had to be smart enough to capture their prey in the wild (being fed by humans) and over generations their brains shrank. That would explain it too. (We do have independent evidence that species change over time due to environmental influences.) If either of these explanations is better than the other, then we can say the datum that wolves have larger heads than dogs supports one hypothesis (theory) better than the other. If we can show that one explanation is better than *all others*, we are entitled to call it "the best explanation."

Philosophers often use inference to the best explanation to try to show that their theories provide the most-likely-to-be-true answers to philosophical questions. Several arguments for the existence of God hypothesize God as the best explanation for data we know about the world: that there is motion in the universe, that there is order in the universe, and that the universe exists at all. In the problem of the nature of the external world, *realists* (philosophers who believe that physical objects exist outside of minds) argue that physical objects exist because hypothesizing them best explains the orderliness of our sensations. In the mind/body problem, *materialists* argue that the hypothesis that our minds are our brains best explains why persons with brain injuries suffer mental impairment.

We shall examine inference to the best explanation in greater detail in chapter 2. It suffices at present to understand that philosophy, according to my definition, is not so different from theoretical science. Both philosophers and theoretical scientists want to devise the most-likely-to-be-true theories to explain the facts they think are true. Both rely on inference to the best explanation and other critical thinking methods. Both admit that they cannot *know* that their theories are true. Perhaps most important, both try to achieve consistency across the widest possible domain. Philosophers who see philosophy as I do will try to provide answers to individual philosophical questions that fit together in a plausible way: Our views in epistemology will connect with our answers regarding the external world and metaethics, which will connect with our views on normative ethics, free will, and the existence of God.

A SURVEY OF THE TOPICS COVERED IN THE TEXT

There are 11 chapters in this book. This first chapter is an initial look at what philosophy is. The second chapter covers logic and critical thinking. Chapter 11 sketches the overall worldview one would reach if one accepts the rest of the book. That leaves chapters 3 through 10 to cover eight different problems involving knowledge, existence, and value. In this section I preview the subsequent chapters.

Chapter 2 introduces some of the most basic reasoning devices used by philosophers engaged in critically evaluating philosophical theories. Philosophers examine *arguments* (*lines of reasoning*) for and against various views. To do this, philosophers need to be able to determine when arguments should be accepted. *Logic provides rules that enable us to tell when arguments have structures that are worthy of acceptance.* For example, logic provides an easy way to tell that an argument that goes from the premise "Some philosophers are not PhD's" to the conclusion "Therefore, some PhD's are not philosophers" does not logically follow, even though the premise and the conclusion are both true. Because logic is concerned solely with the structure of arguments rather than their subject matter, logic has application to all reasoning, not just philosophical arguments.

Chapter 3 presents the *theory of knowledge* or *epistemology*. The primary issue in the theory of knowledge is: *Do humans have knowledge, and if so, how is knowledge possible*? Here is an example to illustrate that knowledge may not be as easy to acquire as we ordinarily think. Suppose you buy one raffle ticket (to win a TV set) out of 1,000 tickets that are sold. The odds of your winning the TV—given that you have only one ticket out of 1,000 and assuming that the raffle is fair—are 1 in 1,000. This means that the odds that you are *not* going to win are 999 to 1. So, if you believe that you are *not* going to win the raffle, your belief is 999 to 1 certain. Nonetheless, it seems that you should not say that you *know* that you are not going to win the TV set, but only that you *believe* that you are not going to win. After all, for all you know, yours is the winning ticket. Therefore, even in this case where the odds are 999 to 1 in favor of your belief, you still do not *know* it.

Now, how many things that we *think* we know are less than 999 to 1 certain to be true? It looks as if all of us have *a lot less* knowledge than we ordinarily believe we do. The theory of knowledge examines the possibility that we have *no knowledge* of several important topics: whether we have minds, whether other minds exist, whether physical objects exist, and whether regularities that have held in the past will continue in the future. Philosophers who say that we lack knowledge are *skeptics*, and philosophers who say that we have knowledge are *nonskeptics*.

Chapter 4 considers the metaphysical issue regarding *the nature of the external world*. It is important to see that this is *not* the same issue that is examined in chapter 3. One of the topics in the theory of knowledge chapter is whether we have *knowledge* that the external world exists. In chapter 4 we *ignore* the question of whether we have knowledge and focus on the attempt to paint an accurate picture of what exists.

Here is the problem of the nature of the external world: To what degree, if any, do physical objects match our sensations? If we believe that physical objects exist outside of our sensations of them, we are *realists*. *Direct realists* believe that physical objects have all the sorts of characteristics that we normally think they have—colors, shapes, solid surfaces, sharp edges, tastes, odors, and sounds. *Scientific realists* believe that physical objects are only atoms flying about in mostly empty space. According to scientific realists, these bizarre entities cause perceivers to experience *illusions* of familiar, solid physical objects possessing colors and sharp edges. If we believe that no physical objects exist, we are *phenomenalists*. Phenomenalists believe that there are no physical objects at all, indeed, that space itself does not exist. According to phenomenalists, the only things that exist are nonphysical minds, their contents such as thoughts and sensations, and—for theistic phenomenalists—God, who is also nonphysical.

To understand the *mind/body problem*, covered in chapter 5, we need to know three definitions. "Physical" means "exists in space," "nonphysical" means "existing, but not in space," and "mind" means "thinking thing or consciousness." The mind/body problem asks *whether our minds are physical or nonphysical*. More specifically, the question is whether *our minds are our brains*, as the *materialists* believe or whether *our minds are nonphysical minds* (souls), as the *dualists* and phenomenalists believe.

I borrow from Keith Campbell (1980, ch. 2) a handy way of mapping out the main answers to the mind/body problem. The following four statements each *appear* to be true, but are *logically inconsistent* (*cannot all be true*). Thus, at least one statement has to be false. The problem is that it is difficult to decide which one(s) to reject:

(1) Our minds are nonphysical things.
(2) Our bodies (our brains, in particular) are physical things.
(3) Our minds and our bodies interact.
(4) Nonphysical and physical things cannot interact.

If we accept the first three statements, then we believe that nonphysical minds interact with physical brains and we are *dualistic interactionists*. We, therefore, have to reject the fourth statement. If we accept (1), (2), and (4), then we have to reject (3) and are *dualistic parallelists*, who believe that minds and brains run parallel to each other but do not affect each other. If we accept both (3) and (4), we believe that our minds and our bodies are the same kind of entities, whether both physical or both nonphysical. If we accept (3), (4), and (1), we are *phenomenalists*, who believe that persons' minds and bodies are nonphysical. If we accept (3), (4), and (2), we are *materialists*, who believe that persons are material in body and mind.

The next three chapters deal with value theory. Chapter 6 concerns *normative ethics*, the branch of philosophy that tries to provide ways to determine what actions are morally right and wrong and what activities are most worthwhile. In the theory of moral obligation, philosophers try to arrive at *value judgments* concerning what we owe other beings, morally speaking. The major theories of moral obligation are *utilitarianism* (which holds that morally right actions are those that make the most persons happy) and Kantian ethics (which emphasizes that moral rules must be capable of being adopted by everyone and that persons must be treated with respect).

Chapter 7 covers *metaethics, the higher-level investigation of the claims of normative ethics*. Whereas normative ethics assumes that value questions have answers, metaethics questions that assumption directly and tries to determine whether it is reasonable to believe that value judgments can be true or false. The main opponents in metaethics are the *subjectivists,* who believe that value judgments have no objective validity outside the feelings and attitudes of persons, and the *objectivists,* who believe that some fact outside of persons makes value judgments literally true or false. Subjectivists believe that morality exists only in the eye of the beholder, while objectivists believe that morality exists independently of what anyone thinks is right or wrong.

Metaethics is interesting not only due to its connection with normative ethics, but because it connects metaphysics and value theory. Scientific realism yields *subjectivism* about many of the commonsense properties of physical objects. This metaphysical subjectivism provides a model for subjectivism regarding value. For example, there is a natural inclination for philosophers who think that redness exists only in the consciousness of perceivers to take a similar view toward evaluative properties such as goodness. Thus, subjectivism in metaethics is supported by scientific realism in metaphysics and in turn supports subjectivism in the free will problem.

Chapter 8 presents the *free will problem,* which asks whether persons can have enough freedom in their choices to make them *morally responsible* (*deserving of praise and blame*) for their behavior. The free will problem arises because it is very difficult to understand *how* persons can choose freely enough to make them morally responsible. To see this, consider a dilemma. To say that *persons cause their choices* means that *the choices are physically necessitated to occur by the mental state of the chooser at the time of the choice*. This means that given the mental condition the chooser is in, the choice has to be that way—the choice could not have been otherwise than it is. But if any choice could not have been otherwise, then it seems that we should not hold the chooser morally responsible for the choice. So, we cannot be morally responsible for caused choices.

On the other side of the dilemma, suppose that *persons do not cause their choices*. This means that, *given the mental state of the chooser, the choice might happen AND it might not happen*. Therefore, the mental state of the chooser does not make the difference between the choice occurring and its not occurring. Therefore, it seems that the chooser cannot deserve credit for making the choice, because whether it occurs or not is not up to the chooser. Thus, it seems we cannot be morally responsible for uncaused choices either. Putting together this half of the dilemma with the first half, we conclude that we cannot be morally responsible for choices we cause, and we cannot be morally responsible for choices we do not cause. In the free will problem, philosophers try to produce theories to make sense out of free choice.

Chapter 9 addresses philosophical reasons for including the existence of God—a supreme being existing outside of space and time—in our picture of what exists. *Theists* include God or gods in their picture of reality. *Atheists* say that no gods exist. Here is an example of an argument for theism based on observing order in nature:

(1) Nature is orderly.
(2) Order can arise only through the conscious effort of a being that tries to create order.
(3) The order in nature could not have been produced by any human effort.
(4) Therefore, the order in nature was produced by God.

An example of an argument for atheism looks like this:

(1) If a supreme being exists, then all species of animals are well suited for their environments.
(2) Not all species of animals are well suited for their environments (because many species have become extinct).
(3) Therefore, a supreme being does not exist.

Chapter 10 considers the *problem of evil*, which tries to reconcile the theists' major views about God and the existence of suffering on Earth. Rather than viewing the problem of evil as a difficulty for any particular religion, it is best understood as a logical puzzle: Which of the following inconsistent statements should we reject?

(1) God exists.
(2) God is *omniscient* (knows all truths).
(3) God is *omnipotent* (can do anything that is not logically contradictory).
(4) God is *morally perfect* (which entails that God would not want there to be any unnecessary suffering).
(5) If statements (1), (2), (3), and (4) are true, then there *is no* unnecessary suffering on Earth.
(6) There *is* unnecessary suffering on Earth.

We can avoid the logical contradiction by rejecting one or more of these statements, but which one should we reject? We might give up (1), which would be to adopt atheism. We could give up (2), (3), or (4)—which many religions do—at the cost of seeing God as less than perfect. We could reject (5), but then we would need to explain why a being that is omniscient, omnipotent, and who wanted there to be no unnecessary suffering nonetheless permitted it. Or, we could reject (6) and argue that, contrary to appearances, *all* of the suffering of human beings and animals is really necessary. We would then need to explain how it might be that animal suffering, accidents, famine, diseases, and natural disasters are necessary.

WHY DO PHILOSOPHY?

Philosophical reading can be difficult and philosophical ideas require concentration to be understood. Philosophy raises many questions, provides few answers, and causes doubts where some persons would rather not doubt. So, what drives persons to philosophy?

The first reason is a combination of intellectual curiosity and personal accomplishment. Philosophy addresses the big questions that have always puzzled reflective persons. From the sketch of topics provided in the last section we see that philosophical questions are ones we care about. It may be disappointing to think that we cannot reach a point where we can claim to *know* that the answers we accept are true. But we would be fooling ourselves if we thought that we can know the answers. We *can*, however, do the best job *we* can do with philosophical questions. Although we can never decisively settle philosophical questions, we can say that *relative to our state of information and logical abilities*, a particular theory is most plausible. Just as we cannot guarantee that we will run a four-minute mile but still take satisfaction in running a personal best, in philosophy we can gain satisfaction from doing the best job we can with the extraordinary task of building a plausible worldview. In this sense, philosophy is a personal accomplishment in pursuit of a worthy goal.

A second reason to do philosophy is to enhance our intellectual *autonomy* (independence). The critical thinking skills we develop by doing philosophy make us better reasoners on every issue, not just philosophical questions. By being better reasoners, we liberate ourselves in two ways. First, critical thinking enables us to think things through for ourselves rather than rely on other persons to think for us. By learning what can be said for and against various philosophical theories, we can decide for ourselves what *we* think is true. We do not have to rely on our peer groups, parents, or mass media. Second, we increase our autonomy *over ourselves* when we learn to think logically and impartially about abstract and heartfelt questions. Philosophy liberates us from the trap of deciding what to believe on the basis of our emotions, thus strengthening ourselves against our natural tendency to believe things simply because we want them to be true. Critical thinking in general and philosophy in particular liberate us from others and from ourselves.

Guide Questions

1. Define "philosophy" in terms of its subject matter and method. (1–2)*
2. Describe the temperament of a critical thinker. (2–3)
3. What does it mean to call philosophy "an imperious inquisitor" of science, common sense, faith, and itself? (3)
4. Why do many philosophers believe that philosophical knowledge cannot be achieved? (3)
5. In what important way is the methodology of philosophy similar to that of science? (4–5)
6. What is logic? (6)
7. Explain the point of the example where you believe you will not win the raffle. In other words, what is the example designed to prove? (6)
8. How do realists differ from phenomenalists on the question of the nature of the external world? (6–7)
9. According to my definition of "physical" and "nonphysical," how would physical things differ from nonphysical things? (7) According to these definitions, is air a physical or nonphysical thing?
10. How does normative ethics differ from metaethics. (7–8)
11. Express the free will problem as a logical dilemma. (8–9)
12. How is the term "God" defined by philosophers? (9)
13. Express the problem of evil as a logic problem. (9–10)
14. What are some disadvantages of doing philosophy? (10)
15. What are two advantages to doing philosophy? (10)

Review Questions for Examinations

1. Define: "philosophy," "philosophical subject matter," "critical thinking," "cognitive," "temperament," "metaphysics," "epistemology," "value theory," "logic," "inference to the best explanation," "cause," "omniscient," "omnipotent," "autonomy."
2. Who are the: skeptics, nonskeptics, direct realists, scientific realists, phenomenalists, materialists, dualists, dualistic interactionists, dualistic parallelists, subjectivists, objectivists, theists, and atheists.
3. What are these philosophical issues: the theory of knowledge, the problem of the nature of the external world, the mind/body problem, normative ethics, metaethics, the free will problem, the existence of God, the problem of evil?

*The numbers after the questions indicate the pages where the answers are found.

4. Why can philosophical questions not be settled by science, common sense, or faith?
5. Express these philosophical problems as problems of logical inconsistency: the mind/body problem, the free will problem, and the problem of evil.

Discussion Questions

1. "Metaphysics and the theory of knowledge ask the same question using different words." Is this statement true or false? Explain.
2. Using the definition of "philosophy" provided in this chapter, can you think of another philosophical question that was not mentioned in the text?
3. Demonstrate how Democrats and Republicans might disagree on how to understand some aspect of American society using *inference to the best explanation*.
4. Suggest a moral theory that was not mentioned in this chapter. How might that theory be criticized?
5. Suppose that someday all the foremost physicists of the world agreed that one picture of the universe was entirely accurate. Would that, if it happened, put an end to philosophy? Why or why not?

FOR FURTHER READING

Cornman, James, Keith Lehrer, and George Pappas. 1987. *Philosophical Problems and Arguments*. Indianapolis: Hackett. An excellent, detailed monograph covering epistemology, the mind/body problem, free will, the existence of God, and ethics. Moderately difficult.

Curd, Martin. 1992. *Argument and Analysis: An Introduction to Philosophy*. St. Paul: West Publishing. A detailed combination monograph/anthology covering religious belief, normative ethics, the mind/body problem, the free will problem, and epistemology. Moderately difficult.

Davis, Thomas. 1987. *Philosophy: An Introduction through Original Fiction, Discussion, and Readings*. New York: Random House. A three-part approach to introducing philosophical issues with short stories, text, and readings. Varies in difficulty: The fiction is easy; the readings are difficult.

Halverson, William. 1981. *A Concise Introduction to Philosophy*. New York: Random House. A lively monograph that covers many philosophical topics in dialectical fashion. Each main theory is given its own chapter to argue its case. Readable.

Kahane, Howard. 1983. *Thinking about Basic Beliefs: An Introduction to Philosophy*. Belmont, CA: Wadsworth. A reader-friendly monograph with brief readings from classical philosophers.

Sober, Elliott. 1991. *Core Questions in Philosophy*. New York: Macmillan. An excellent introductory monograph with extensive readings from classical and contemporary philosophers. Moderately difficult.

Chapter 2
SOME METHODOLOGICAL TOOLS

Philosophy's method is critical thinking. Among other things, critical thinking concerns meaning, logic, and the analysis of data. This chapter cannot take the place of courses directly devoted to critical thinking, logic, and scientific method, but we can begin to strengthen our cognitive skills and facilitate our understanding of the rest of the book.

DEFINITION AND MEANING

In "What Pragmatism Means" the American philosopher William James (1842–1910) tells a story about a squirrel that clung to a tree directly opposite a man who "tries to get sight of the squirrel by moving rapidly round the tree, but no matter how fast he goes, the squirrel moves as fast in the opposite direction, and always keeps the tree between himself and the man" (1963, 41).

According to James, a group of campers got into a long debate over whether the man went around the squirrel or not. James settled the debate by offering this bit of linguistic analysis. If by "going round" the squirrel you mean "going from north of the squirrel to its east to its south to west of the squirrel," then the man did go round the squirrel. If you mean "moving from in front of the squirrel to its right side to behind it to its left side," then the man did not. This dispute is, thereby, solved by defining a term. Although philosophical problems are not solved as easily as this one was, providing clear definitions of key terms is the first step in the methodology of critical thinking.

To understand what definitions are, we need to distinguish between *words* and *the objects that words are used to refer to (designate)*. Words are linguistic devices that we pronounce or write on chalkboards. Words contain letters and syllables. Words have *meanings* (*definitions*). When we are talking about a word, we place the word in double quotation marks. For example, the word "Edinboro" has eight letters. *The objects that words refer to are things such as Edinboro, Plato, or free will*. We do not define objects, because only linguistic devices can be given definitions. Instead, we *refer* to objects by their names. If we say that Edinboro is a small town in western Pennsylvania, we refer to the entity Edinboro by naming it.

Here are some examples of correct and incorrect uses of quotation marks to illustrate the difference between words and objects:

(1) "Edinboro" has eight letters. (correct)
(2) Edinboro is a small town. (correct)
(3) "Edinboro" refers to Edinboro. (correct)
(4) Edinboro has eight letters. (incorrect)
(5) "Edinboro" is a small town. (incorrect)
(6) Edinboro refers to "Edinboro." (incorrect)
(7) "Edinboro" refers to "Edinboro." (incorrect)
(8) Edinboro refers to Edinboro. (incorrect)

A *definition of a word or term* is an *alternative form of words that has the same meaning as the original word or term*. To have the same meaning, the original word and its correct definition must pick out exactly the same objects in *all logically possible worlds* (*imaginable situations*). Therefore, a proposed definition fails if we can even imagine how something might satisfy one side of the definition, but not the other. For example, a correct definition of "triangle" is "three-sided plane figure." It is logically impossible to imagine a triangle that is not a three-sided plane figure, and it is logically impossible to imagine a three-sided plane figure that is not a triangle. An incorrect definition of "sibling" would be "a brother or sister who is under 200 years old." It is true that in the real world all siblings are brothers or sisters who are under 200 years old. It is also true that all brothers or sisters who are under 200 years old are siblings. This definition fails, however, because there is a logically possible world where siblings live to be *over* 200 years old. So, being under 200 years old is not part of what we mean by calling someone a "sibling."

Because it is important to make sure that definitions are accurate, philosophers have formalized the method we have just used for testing definitions. *Counterexamples* are *logically possible situations that we imagine to show that a proposed definition is too narrow or too broad.* Suppose someone defined "puppy" as "a small dog." We could provide counterexamples to show that this definition is both too narrow and too broad. One counterexample would be to imagine a six-month-old Great Dane. Relative to most dogs, a Great Dane puppy is not a small dog, so this definition would not count the Great Dane puppy as a puppy. So, the definition excludes too much and is too narrow. The second counterexample would be to imagine an adult Chihuahua. Relative to most dogs, an adult Chihuahua is small, so this definition would count it as a puppy. So, the definition includes too much and is too broad.

Besides being used to show that definitions are defective, counterexamples are sometimes used to criticize theories. For example, suppose someone thought that an infallible moral theory is to always follow one's conscience. A counterexample to this theory would be to imagine a case in which persons' consciences told them to murder strangers. It takes only one successful counterexample to refute a universal claim. Counterexamples are often presented in *thought experiments—often fanciful hypothetical situations that philosophers make up to get us to think about some topic.* A thought experiment that is familiar to nonphilosophers asks if you were to be stranded on a desert island with one person, whom would you pick? It would be irrelevant to respond that you'll never get stranded on an island, because the point of the thought-experiment is not practical but theoretical: This thought experiment is designed to get us to think about our values.

As noted, definition (meaning) is a relationship between words and words. For example, "mother" means "female parent." *Reference* is the relationship by which words designate things. "Mothers" refers to female parents. Not all meaningful words refer to things: "the Loch Ness monster" is a meaningful term, but it does not refer to anything, because there is no Loch Ness monster. We can provide definitions of words without knowing whether what the words try to designate exist. For example, in chapter 9 we shall define "God" before we examine the debate between the theists and atheists over whether God exists.

A final point about meaning is that words can be ambiguous and vague. An *ambiguous* term has *more than one meaning*. For example, "bank" means "financial institution" and "the land beside a body of water." Other ambiguous nonphilosophical words are "club," "field," and "bat." Many philosophical words are ambiguous: "God," "free will," "know," and "mind." When we come across ambiguous words in philosophy, we need to *disambiguate* them, that is, say things like: "If you mean *this* by ambiguous word W, then . . . , but if you mean *that* by W, then. . . ." A *vague* term *has a fuzzy or imprecise meaning*. Some vague words are "good," "many," "middle-class," and "very." Critical thinkers try to tighten up vague words by offering explicit definitions for them or else avoiding them.

LOGIC

We all have a native ability to tell that some arguments (lines of reasoning) are logically better than others. Here are two arguments for the same conclusion with very different logical structures:

ARGUMENT A

(1) My five-year-old brother told me that God exists.
(2) Therefore, God exists.

ARGUMENT B

(1) If God does not exist, then 1 million technological civilizations exist in the Milky Way galaxy.
(2) If 1 million technological civilizations exist in the Milky Way galaxy, then we would have been contacted by one by now.
(3) We have not been contacted by one by now.
(4) Thus, God exists.

A striking difference between arguments A and B lies in the connections between the premises and the conclusions. The premise in A, even if true, would supply no evidence for accepting the conclusion. But if all the premises in B were true, the conclusion would have to be true. We can recognize some facts like this without studying logic, but we will do a much better job if we learn some logic. I begin with the terminology of logic and then present some reasoning devices.

1. Logical Terminology

An *argument* consists of one or more statements (*premises*) that are intended to provide evidence for another statement (the *conclusion*). So, *an argument is a line of reasoning where one or more premises are offered to support a conclusion.* In argument A, (1) is the only premise and (2) is the conclusion. In argument B, (1), (2), and (3) are premises and (4) is the conclusion. *Logic is the branch of philosophy that tells us whether the structure of arguments is strong enough so that IF the premises were true, they would support the conclusion.* Logic—the study of the *structure* of arguments—cannot say whether premises are true, but only whether they would support the conclusion if they were true.

It is important to distinguish between an *argument* and a *conditional statement*. As shown above, an argument makes *three* claims: that its premise (premises) is (are) true, that its conclusion is true, and that its premise or premises support the conclusion. "*Since* it rains today, we cannot play golf" is an argument consisting of one premise ("It rains today"), a conclusion ("We cannot play golf"), and the claim that the premise supports the conclusion. The word "since" serves to indicate that the statement following it is a premise.

A *conditional statement* is an *if-then statement that says that IF one thing is true, THEN another thing is true*. The "if" part is the *antecedent*, and the "then" part is the *consequent*. "*If* it rains today, we cannot play golf" does not say that it rains, nor that we cannot play golf, but only that IF it rains, THEN we cannot play golf. Conditional statements are just statements, not arguments, because a conditional statement makes only one claim, not three. The word "if" is not a premise-indicating word, because conditional statements do not contain premises. Conditional statements can *serve* in arguments as either premises or conclusions. To see this consider:

ARGUMENT C

(1) If persons have high self-esteem, then they have been successful at problem solving in the past and overgeneralize their successes.
(2) If persons have been successful at problem solving in the past and overgeneralize their successes, then they will work harder at solving insoluble problems than persons with low self-esteem.
(3) Hence, if persons have high self-esteem, then they will work harder at solving insoluble problems than persons with low self-esteem.

In this example, the conditionals (1) and (2) are premises and the conditional (3) is the conclusion.

ARGUING DEDUCTIVELY AND ARGUING INDUCTIVELY

Next is the distinction between *arguing deductively* and *arguing inductively*. *When we argue deductively, we INTEND to make the logical structure of our argument so strong that it is logically impossible for our conclusion to be false if all the premises are true*. Using a term I shall define in the next paragraph, when we argue deductively, we *try* to produce a *valid* argument. The importance of the words "intend" and "try" cannot be emphasized strongly enough. *When we argue inductively, we INTEND to produce a strong argument, but we DO NOT INTEND to make the logical structure of our argument so strong that it is logically impossible for our conclusion to be false if all the premises are true*. When we argue inductively, we *try* to produce a strong argument *without trying* to produce a valid argument.

VALIDITY AND INVALIDITY

We next define "valid" and "invalid argument." A *valid argument* is *an argument that has a valid argument form*. A valid argument form is a structure (such as those given below) in which no matter what statements are used to fill in the form, when the form is filled in exactly there can be no instance when all the premises are true and the conclusion is false. Another way to express this is that there can be no counterexamples to a valid argument form. The simplest valid argument form is: A. Therefore, A. Because the premise and the conclusion say the same thing, it is logically impossible that A be filled in with a true premise and A be filled in with a false conclusion.

An *invalid argument* is an argument that does *not* have a valid argument form, that is, where every form it satisfies is an invalid argument form. An invalid argument form is a structure in which there is at least one way of filling it in with all true premises and a false conclusion. For an invalid argument form there will be possible counterexamples. The simplest invalid argument form is: A. Therefore, B. Because the premise and the conclusion are logically unrelated, it is possible to fill in A with a true premise (e.g., "Bill Clinton is a Democrat") and B with a false conclusion (e.g., "Trees are mammals.)

Because arguers try to give valid arguments only when they argue deductively, logicians use the terms "valid" and "invalid" only when evaluating arguments they think are *intended* to be valid, that is, deductive arguments. *If I am arguing inductively* and, thus, not even trying to provide a valid argument, it is inappropriate to remind me that my argument is not valid. After all, by arguing inductively I admit that my argument is not valid, but still think that my argument is strong. *If I am arguing deductively*, however, I am trying to produce a valid argument; here it is appropriate to determine whether my attempt at validity succeeds or fails.

If I have given a valid argument, then the only option for resisting my conclusion is to resist my premises. A critic cannot say that even if all my premises are true, my conclusion still does not follow. Thus, it is desirable to give valid arguments for our conclusions whenever we can. On the other hand, if I am giving an argument that lacks validity—either because I am arguing inductively or because I have tried to give a valid argument and failed—my critic is free to accept all my premises and still reject my conclusion. Thus, arguments that lack validity may be attacked in two ways. A critic can say: (1) One or more of your premises are false; and/or (2) Even if your premises are all true, your conclusion still does not follow.

In sum, when we argue deductively, our arguments are valid or invalid. When we argue inductively, our arguments are strong, weak, or somewhere in-between. Usually we can tell by context whether arguers are arguing deductively or inductively, but it is not important that we determine which. If we follow this procedure for analyzing arguments, it will not matter whether the argument is deductive or inductive:

(1) Analyze the argument into premises and conclusion.
(2) Determine whether the argument is valid or not.

(3) If it is valid we know that we must either resist its premises or accept its conclusion.
(4) If it is not valid (because it is inductive or because it is an invalid deductive argument), we should *still* ask whether its premises would provide strong support for its conclusion *if* they were true.
(5) Whether it is valid or not, we should ask whether its premises *are* true.

2. What Makes a Good Argument?

As noted, a good deductive argument should be valid. Besides being valid, it should also have *all true premises*. We can 'prove' anything by inserting one false premise into a valid argument form. For example, consider the valid argument: "Cats are animals. If cats are animals, then 2 + 2 = 5. Therefore, 2 + 2 = 5." The false second premise allows us to deduce the false conclusion, thereby making this a bad argument despite its validity. Arguments that are both valid and have all true premises are *sound*: *"Sound" = "Valid" + "All true premises."*

It would simplify things if we could say that all sound arguments are good arguments, but, unfortunately, this is not so. Here are some examples of sound arguments that are not very good: (1) "All copper expands when heated. Therefore, all copper expands when heated." (2) "The Earth is more than 4 billion years old. Therefore, either the Earth is more than 4 billion years old or snow is green." (3) "My copy of Carl Sagan's *Broca's Brain* has 398 (Arabic) numbered pages. If my copy of Carl Sagan's *Broca's Brain* has 398 (Arabic) numbered pages, then neon has the atomic number 10. Therefore, neon has the atomic number 10."

Each of these arguments is sound—each has a valid argument form and all true premises. Nonetheless, they look strangely suspicious. They are not *persuasive* to their audiences: In my terminology, each lacks the psychological characteristic of "convincingness." For any argument to be convincing to an audience, it must take the audience on a gradual 'logical journey' *from* premises that the audience accepts *to* a conclusion that the audience finds to be made more believable by the premises. After all, the purpose of giving an argument is to convince one's audience to accept a conclusion they do *not already* believe by showing how that conclusion is supported by facts they already believe. In the three examples, persons would not accept the premises unless they *already* accepted the conclusion. So these arguments are not useful in convincing anyone of their conclusions—despite the fact that they are logically impeccable, sound arguments.

In sum, *a good deductive argument*: (1) *is valid*, (2) *has all true premises*, and (3) *is convincing to its audience*. Because what is convincing to one audience may be unconvincing to another, convincingness is not an objective feature of arguments. For example, an argument may be convincing to you and unconvincing to me simply because it is written in French, which you understand and I do not. Still, we should be aware of the convincingness of arguments.

As noted, in an *inductive argument* the arguer is not even trying to provide a valid argument, so it is inappropriate to call inductive arguments "valid" or "invalid." Rather than talking about validity, we should ask whether inductive arguments are strong or weak. Unfortunately, no one has ever provided rigorous guidelines for distinguishing between inductive arguments that are strong and weak, unlike the case with deductive arguments with their demonstrably valid and invalid argument forms. Nonetheless, in many cases we can distinguish between weak and strong inductive arguments. For example, if I want to prove the conclusion "All the marbles in this jar are red," my argument is stronger if my premise states that I have examined 100 marbles so far and all have been red than if my premise states that I have examined only one. Let us say that *a good inductive argument: (1) is strong, (2) has all true premises, and (3) is convincing to its audience.*

3. Four Valid Argument Forms

A good way to learn some logic is to commit to memory some of the most widely used valid argument forms.

A. *MODUS PONENS* (METHOD OF AFFIRMATION)

In *modus ponens* we assert a conditional statement as one premise and its "if" half (the antecedent) as the other. From these we validly deduce the "then" half (the consequent) as the conclusion. Here is an example. "If we know that other minds exist, then we know with certainty that other minds exist. We know that other minds exist. Therefore, we know with certainty that other minds exist." The argument form is:

(1) If ______________ then _ _ _ _ _ _ _ _ _ _ .
(2) ______________.
(3) Therefore, _ _ _ _ _ _ _ _ _ _ .

The statement we use to substitute into each solid-line location must be word-for-word identical with the statement we substitute into the other solid-line location. Likewise, the statements substituted into the broken-line locations must be identical. If we confuse the order of the statements or use alternative forms of words, we no longer are using modus ponens.

Here is an example of an *invalid misapplication* of modus ponens—the *fallacy of affirming the consequent*. Suppose we were to fill in the first premise of the modus ponens argument form with: "If Abraham Lincoln was vice president of the United States, then Abraham Lincoln was a high government official."

This would be a true statement. Suppose we next filled in the second premise with "Abraham Lincoln was a high government official," which is also true. Finally, suppose we tried to conclude "Therefore, Abraham Lincoln was vice president of the United States." This conclusion is false. What has gone wrong? We incorrectly substituted the consequent of the conditional statement into the second premise where the antecedent was supposed to go. So we have not produced an instance of modus ponens, but instead an instance of an *invalid* argument form (fallacy). Modus ponens has the form: "If A, then B. A. Therefore, B." The *fallacy of affirming the consequent* has the invalid form: "If A then B. B. Therefore, A." The order makes the difference between validity and invalidity.

B. *MODUS TOLLENS* (METHOD OF NEGATION)

In *modus tollens* we assert a conditional statement as one premise and the negation of its consequent as the other. From these we validly deduce the negation of the antecedent as the conclusion. In the examples that follow, I place the negating word "not" at the front of the second premise and the conclusion. I recommend that students do so also, at least until they become very comfortable with modus tollens. In the arguments we will see throughout the text, the negating words will sometimes be contained within the premises and conclusion instead of being placed at the front of the statements.

Here is an example of modus tollens. "If we know that other minds exist, then we know with certainty that other minds exist. Not (We know with certainty that other minds exist). Therefore, not (We know that other minds exist)." The argument form is:

(1) If ______________ then _ _ _ _ _ _ _ _ _ _ .
(2) Not (_ _ _ _ _ _ _ _ _ _).
(3) Therefore, not (______________).

With modus tollens, as with all the argument forms, we must substitute statements exactly according to the form. Here is an example of an invalid misapplication of modus tollens—the *fallacy of denying the antecedent*. Suppose we fill in the first premise of the argument form with the true conditional statement: "If the moon is a planet, then the moon is a heavenly body." Suppose we fill in the second line with the true premise: "Not (The moon is a planet.)" Finally, suppose we tried to conclude from these two premises the false conclusion "Not (The moon is a heavenly body.)" What has gone wrong? We have incorrectly substituted the negation of the antecedent into the second premise, whereas modus tollens requires that we use the negation of the consequent. Modus tollens has the form: If A, then B. Not B. Therefore, not A. The *fallacy of denying the antecedent* has the form: If A, then B. Not A. Therefore, not B.

Modus ponens and modus tollens are equally valid ways to prove a conclusion by adding one premise to a conditional premise. Suppose, for the sake of the example, that Uncle Fred always consumes all the beer in the refrigerator. We can express this information as the conditional statement "If Uncle Fred is home, then there is no beer left in the refrigerator." If this premise is true, then we need add only one more true premise to prove a conclusion. If we add "Uncle Fred is home," then we can validly deduce by modus ponens, "There is no beer left in the refrigerator."

Alternatively, we could reason in a modus tollens fashion if we express the fact about Uncle Fred's drinking habits as a verbally different, but logically equivalent, conditional statement: "If there is beer in the refrigerator, then Uncle Fred is away." If we add to this the premise "Uncle Fred is *not* away," we can validly deduce by modus tollens that "There is no beer left in the refrigerator."

C. DILEMMA

In dilemma we assert two conditional premises and a *disjunctive* (*either/or*) third premise saying that one of the antecedents of the conditionals is true. From these three premises we validly deduce that one of the consequents of the two conditionals must be true. Here is an example. "If the next U.S. president is a Democrat, then the Republicans will be unhappy. If the next U.S. president is a Republican, then the Democrats will be unhappy. Either the next U.S. president will be a Democrat or the next U.S. president will be a Republican. Therefore, either the Republicans will be unhappy or the Democrats will be unhappy." The argument form is:

(1) If ______________ then _ _ _ _ _ _ _ _ _ _ .
(2) If .... then ___ ___ ___ ___ .
(3) Either ______________ or ....
(4) Therefore, either _ _ _ _ _ _ _ _ _ _ or ___ ___ ___ ___ .

Philosophers often use an abridged version of dilemma to prove a nondisjunctive conclusion. Here is an argument we shall examine in the chapter on theory of knowledge: "If human minds are nonphysical minds, then we cannot learn that other persons' minds exist by observing their minds. If human minds are brains, then we cannot learn that other persons' minds exist by observing their minds. But human minds are either nonphysical minds or brains. So, we cannot learn that other persons' minds exist by observing their minds." This is valid, because A follows from the conclusion A or A. Perhaps this is why people sometimes say, "Am I right or am I right?"

D. *REDUCTIO AD ABSURDUM* (REDUCTION TO ABSURDITY)

Reductio ad absurdum is used to demonstrate that a statement is false by showing that if it were true, it would lead to a *logical contradiction* (*the claim that the same statement is both true and false*). Although reductio ad absurdum is similar to modus tollens, it allows us to add additional premises as needed to reach the contradiction, whereas modus tollens is limited to two premises. Here is an example that we shall see in the chapter on the existence of God. "Assume that God never existed to prevent the universe from going out of existence. (This is the assumption to be reduced to absurdity.) Then, on that assumption, over infinite time the universe would have ceased to exist. If so, then we do not exist now. But we do exist now. Therefore, the assumption that God never existed to prevent the universe from going out of existence is false."

Here is a second example taken from the debate between the moral objectivists and moral subjectivists in the metaethics chapter. "Assume that right and wrong are subjective and are not objective facts existing outside of anyone's moral feelings. Then, it is *just a matter of opinion* that it is wrong to kill strangers. But it is *not* just a matter of opinion that it is wrong to kill strangers. Therefore, right and wrong are not subjective."

Here is the form of *reductio ad absurdum*. Be sure you can fill it in with the two examples just provided:

(1) Assume ______________.
(2) Assuming ______________, - - - - - - - - - - is true.
(3) Not (- - - - - - - - - - is true).
(4) Therefore, ______________ is reduced to absurdity.

4. Analogies

Analogies are comparisons that are sometimes used to illustrate a point and sometimes used to prove a conclusion. *Analogies assert that the relationship between two things is similar in some important way to the relationship between two other things*. An example might be: "Sonar is to bats as vision is to humans." The general form of analogies is:

A		X
is to	as	is to
B		Y

Some philosophers use an argument by analogy to argue that, despite the fact that we never directly observe other minds, we can know that other minds exist. Taking the sensation of pain as an example, the argument goes:

(1) My pain-behavior		(3) Your pain-behavior
is to	as	is to
(2) My pain sensation		(4) Your pain sensation

The idea is that we can observe the first three parts of the equation—(1), (2), and (3)—and then infer or deduce the fourth.

5. Logical Analogies

Logical analogies are analogies that are used to demonstrate that deductive arguments are invalid. Logical analogies work only to show that invalid arguments are invalid—logical analogies cannot show valid arguments to be invalid. In a logical analogy, to show that an argument we wish to criticize has an invalid form we compare to it a *clearly invalid* argument that we make up. By giving a second argument that has the same argument form as the original argument—but is itself clearly invalid—we prove by analogy that the original argument is also invalid. Suppose someone reasons invalidly:

- Some basketball players are not college students.
- Therefore, some college students are not basketball players.

This argument's premise and conclusion are both true of the real world. Nonetheless, this argument is *invalid*, because its argument form is invalid. The argument form will accept a substitution-instance with a true premise and a false conclusion. We can demonstrate this by producing a logical analogy as follows.

First, we extract from the original argument its argument form and write it down. To do this, we keep the logical structure of the argument but leave out the specific words:

- Some _______________ are not _ _ _ _ _ _ _ _ _ _ .
- Therefore, some _ _ _ _ _ _ _ _ _ _ are not _______________.

Second, we fill in the blanks and dotted lines with noun terms (not statements) that make the premise clearly true and the conclusion clearly false of the real world. In selecting terms for logical analogies we should use very simple ones whose logical relations are obvious, such as "parents," "fathers," "mothers," "dogs," "cats," "mammals," and so on. The reason is that we want the premises to be *obviously* true and the conclusion *obviously* false. Suppose we fill in the blanks with "animals" and the broken lines with "cats." Then the logical analogy that shows that the original argument is invalid will be:

- Some animals are not cats. (true of the real world)
- Therefore, some cats are not animals. (false of the real world)

By providing this logical analogy we have demonstrated that the original argument is invalid despite the fact that its premise and conclusion are true of the real world. Even if its premise is true, that does not logically guarantee that its conclusion is true.

INFERENCE TO THE BEST EXPLANATION

In noting the similarity between philosophy and science in chapter 1, I claimed that inference to the best explanation is common to both. In logical terms, inference to the best explanation is an inductive way of arguing, but it is significantly different than induction by observation of individual cases ("induction by enumeration"). When we reason by induction by enumeration we conclude that because each member of a known sample of group G has a characteristic C, an unknown member of G will have C also. For example, if all observed golf balls have dimples, we have inductive evidence for thinking that the next golf ball we observe will have dimples.

In *inference to the best explanation* (sometimes called "abduction"), we conclude that an unknown fact is the best explanation for something we think we already know. *If* some unknown fact best explains some datum or data ("datum" is singular, "data" is plural)—if it makes the observed fact less surprising than any other explanation—*then* that datum gives evidence that the explanation is true (Sober, 1991, 26–31). To use inference to the best explanation persuasively, one's audience must accept the datum in question. If the audience denies that the particular datum is really true, one's use of inference to the best explanation will be unconvincing.

Here is an illustration. We go to answer the door when the doorbell rings. Why do we assume that hearing the doorbell ring is evidence that there is someone at the door? In terms of inference to the best explanation, the datum at stake is the fact that the doorbell is ringing. The *hypothesis* (theory) that usually best explains the datum is that the doorbell is ringing *because* there is a person there pushing the button. Thus, we infer the theory—without realizing that it *is* a theory—that someone is pushing the button as the *best explanation* for the *datum* that the bell is ringing. Of course, it may turn out that the ringing is caused by other factors. In this case our theory would be wrong. This shows that inference to the best explanation is fallible.

The following is a scientific example. A psychological experiment studied the conditions under which office workers would grant requests by a stranger who asked to get in line in front of them at a photocopier machine (Zimbardo and Leippe, 1991, 258). The psychologists compared two different ways to make the request. One group of subjects were asked by an experimenter (posing as another office worker) "May I use the copier?" Among this group, 60 percent of the subjects allowed the experimenter to use the machine ahead of them. A second group of subjects were asked "May I use the copier because I have to make some copies?" Among the second group, 93 percent of the subjects agreed to let the experimenter go ahead of them. This is very curious data. Why would subjects be 50 percent more likely to comply with a request when the requester adds the apparently redundant phrase "because I have to make some copies"? Assuming the data were repeatable (they were), psychologists would like to understand what the best (true) explanation is.

The psychologist who ran the experiment, Ellen Langer, offered her explanation. When we hear the word "because," we automatically assume that some justification is being offered, even when it is not. So, the second group of subjects mistakenly thought that some justification for the request had been offered and because of this, they were more likely to comply. But as always, there are other possible explanations. Here is a competing hypothesis. Requests using more words increase the length of time of the interaction between the subjects and the requesters, thereby making it more difficult for the subjects to dismiss the requesters as mere pests. Because there is more personal interaction time (for example, longer eye contact) when the request is longer, subjects are more sensitive about appearing rude to the requesters and are more likely to comply.

A philosophical example comes from an argument for the existence of God. Both theists and atheists accept the datum that much of nature appears to be highly orderly. The question is: What is the best explanation for that orderliness? One of the familiar arguments for the existence of God postulates God as the explanation for orderliness in nature: Nature is orderly *because* God ordered it. Atheists counter by claiming that the theistic hypothesis is not necessary to explain nature's order. Instead, we need only to understand the laws of nature, notably, the laws of physics and biology. To test one's understanding of inference to the best explanation, try to place the three examples just given into the general format below:

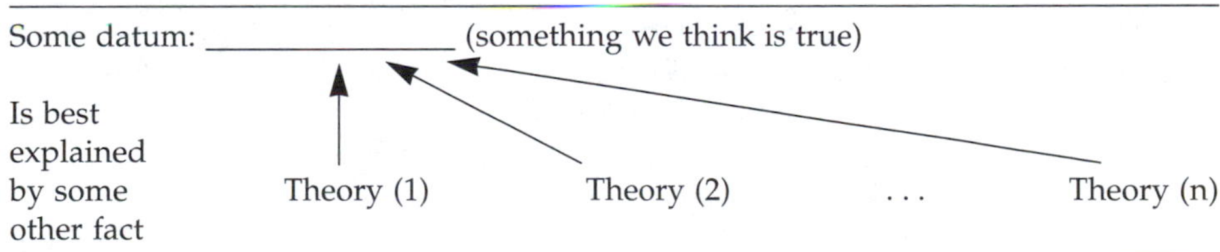

Inference to the best explanation works well with a famous account of scientific theories labeled "conjectures and refutations" by Karl Popper (1965). According to Popper, a genuine scientific theory must have specific, observable consequences. Because genuine theories predict observable outcomes, they always stand in jeopardy of refutation: If those predicted outcomes are not observed, then the theory will be discredited. If nothing we could ever observe could possibly discredit a theory, then the theory is playing the heads-I-win, tails-you-lose game and need not be taken seriously. According to Popper, scientists do *not* typically try to *confirm* their theories on a case-by-case basis by using induction by enumeration. Instead, scientists collect data to be explained, *conjecture* (devise explanatory hypotheses), and then try to *refute* their conjectures by collecting evidence that goes against them. For Popper, it is the fact that scientific theories *stand up against attempts to refute them* rather than that they are *confirmed* by collecting supporting data that warrants their acceptance.

COGNITIVE ERRORS

6. Faulty Data Collection

Historically, many philosophers have been suspicious of inference to the best explanation, because it can be used to postulate the existence of things that are fancifully removed from sense experience. For example, we can explain why copper is a better conductor of heat than iron by citing the difference in the structures of copper and iron atoms. We can also postulate the theory that copper contains *copper gremlins*, who are more irascible than *iron gremlins* and make copper conduct heat more quickly by flying around angrily when stimulated, carrying little bundles of heat with them.

To some extent we can avoid such misuses of inference to the best explanation by postulating theoretical entities only when doing so is absolutely necessary to explain the data in question (*Occam's Razor* named after William of Occam (1285–1349)) *and* to require that the postulated entities have some larger, already-established role to play in scientific explanation. Another way to avoid errors in using inference to the best explanation is *to make sure that what we take to be data really are data*, and not something we falsely believe to be data.

Here is an example. Suppose we go on a picnic twice a week and take Aunt Mildred along much of the time. Further, it seems that almost every time we take Mildred along on our picnics it rains. If we live in a climate where it always rains, it is not surprising that it should rain whenever we take our aunt along. But suppose that where we live it rains only 20 percent of the time. Then if it were true that it rains almost every time we take Aunt Mildred along, that would require some explanation. Perhaps Mildred likes overcast days and joins us only when it looks like it is going to rain. That might explain it. But suppose, for the sake of the example, that this is not true. Rather, we always select nice days for picnics, but, nonetheless, it seems that whenever we take Aunt Mildred along, it rains. What possible hypothesis could explain this?

Well, maybe Aunt Mildred has extraordinary powers and makes it rain whenever she goes on our picnics. Or perhaps the rain gods are angry at Mildred and make it rain out of spite when Mildred goes on picnics. But such explanations seem weak because: (1) We have no independent reason to believe in such powers; and (2) postulating such powers raises other riddles. How did Mildred come to have such powers? What do the rain gods have against Mildred? So, if we adopt such explanations, we are no better off than we would be if we had *no* explanation. Perhaps we should re-examine the assumed data and make sure that they are legitimate. *If there are no real data to be explained, then there is no need to postulate a hypothesis to explain them*!

In this example (it is my thought experiment and I have designed it this way), there *are* no data to explain. True, it *seems* to us that it rains a disproportionate number of times when we take Mildred along, but that impression is in error. What actually happens is that it rains *sometimes* when we take Mildred along, approximately the same percentage of time that it rains in general. But, for whatever reason, we tend to remember the times it rains when we take Mildred along and forget the times we take her and it does not rain. It is a common cognitive trait to focus on the most vivid cases in which two events coincide and wrongly conclude that they coincide more than they do. This is the same sort of error we fall into if we really believe "Every time I sit down to dinner, the phone rings" or "Every time the basketball announcers on television say what a good foul-shooter the basketball player is, they 'jinx' the shooter into missing." To avoid this sort of error, we need to compile a *presence/absence table*.

Consider the table below that records the number of subjects who have a certain symptom and who have a certain disease:

		Disease D	
		Present	Absent
Symptom S	Present	(a) 80	(b) 40
	Absent	(c) 20	(d) 10

In the present/present cell (a), 80 subjects have both the symptom and the disease. In the present/absent cell (b), 40 subjects have the symptom, but do not have the disease. In the absent/present cell (c), 20 subjects fail to have the symptom, but do have the disease. In the absent/absent cell (d), 10 subjects have neither the symptom nor the disease. To what degree does the symptom correlate with the disease?

The most untutored observer would look only to cell (a) and decide that because 80 subjects both have the symptom and the disease, the two are very strongly linked. This conclusion would be extremely naive. A slightly shrewder observer would compare the number in cell (a) with the number in cell (b) and conclude that because 80 is twice as large as 40, the disease correlates highly with the symptom. This is also mistaken. To correctly interpret these data, we need to examine *all four cells* by comparing the ratio between (a) and (b) with the ratio between (c) and (d). In this example, the ratios are each 2 to 1. This means that the subjects are twice as likely to have the disease as not have the disease *whether they have the symptom or not*! Thus, for the subjects described in the table, there is no correlation between having the symptom and the disease. (To see this, suppose "the disease" was being right-handed rather than left-handed, and "the symptom" was having brown hair rather than blonde.) With no correlation, there are no data to explain by inference to the best explanation. (There is no particular need to explain why persons with brown hair tend to be right-handed; so do persons with blond hair.)

The moral of this example is as important for philosophy as it is for science: *We need to be sure that we have statistically significant data before we cast about for an explanation for them*. Persons who understand the need for presence/absence tables will realize that they do not have to postulate theories in cases in which naive persons think they should. *Question*: How shall we explain why our dreams foretell the future? *Answer*: Most of our dreams do not foretell the future. We dwell on the few that come true. *Question*: Why do we tend to win when we wear our lucky sweat socks? *Answer*: We don't. We attend more to the times we win than to the times when we lose.

Here is a rule of thumb. Whenever we are tempted to explain some strange data, ask what the world would have to be like for those data to be true. For example, what would the world have to be like for horoscopes to be accurate? There would have to be some extremely powerful being or beings who *wanted* persons who are born on the same dates to share certain personality types and *governed* human psychological development to produce this effect. Such a view might have made some sense to primitive persons who believed that the heavenly bodies were conscious gods who controlled our lives, but it flies in the face of everything we know today about astronomy and psychology. Because the world would have to be so unlike the way we think it is if horoscopes were accurate, we should question whether the supposed data are true. Once we do, we get a much simpler answer: Horoscopes *seem* accurate because they are couched in vague language that individuals sympathetic to horoscopes interpret to apply to them. This is a lesson we will apply throughout the text. Often the only legitimate data are that things *seem* a certain way, not that things *are* that way.

7. Vividness and the Fallacy of Anecdotal Evidence

A common cognitive error is *to rely on anecdotal evidence (evidence derived from small, vivid samples) and ignore scientifically collected evidence*. We commit the fallacy of anecdotal evidence when we set aside serious evidence in favor of anecdotes. This fallacy is the most extreme case of failing to compile a presence/absence table, because an anecdote is only one item from the present/present cell. The psychologists Richard Nisbett and Lee Ross (1980, 61) call this the "man-who" fallacy. For example, persons often dismiss statistically overwhelming evidence that smoking correlates with lung cancer, by saying things such as "I knew a man who smoked two packs of cigarettes a day for sixty years and never was sick a day in his life." When confronted with evidence that wearing seat belts saves lives, we hear an anecdote about the person who survived the auto accident only because she was not wearing her seat belt and was thrown clear of the resulting fire.

It is easy to see why we like anecdotes. First, anecdotes are easier to understand and explain to other persons than statistics. Second, anecdotes are *vivid* (lively) and make a greater impact on us than do statistics. Third, there is an element in common sense that praises personal experience and is suspicious of carefully collected evidence. To some extent this enhances our egos. Many persons like to think that "seeing things with their own eyes" constitutes a sort of bedrock, forgetting that if a thing does not exist (Bigfoot, space aliens, Elvis being alive), one million firsthand reports of "it" cannot make it exist. Forth, using anecdotes gives us an option to resist genuine evidence and to continue to believe what we want to believe rather than accept unpleasant facts. Using anecdotes increases our ability to believe what we want to believe, even when all the evidence is against us.

8. The Truth-Is-Relative Fallacy

Sometimes a person will say that believing a statement makes it "true for me." This is a misleading way of speaking that risks lapsing into a logical fallacy. Rather than saying that a statement is true relative to its believer, it would be clearer to say the statement is *subjective* (depends for its truth on the person who believes it). In this perfectly sensible sense, many statements are subjective: "Peas taste good," "Blue is prettier than green," "The Beatles sound better than Bach." For example, to say "Peas taste good" is true for me is simply a long-winded way of saying that I like the taste of peas.

The *truth-is-relative-fallacy* occurs when we try to extend this harmless way of talking to include *objective statements*, which are not a matter of anyone's opinions. *Objective statements depend for their truth on the way the world is and not on anyone's beliefs*. Examples of objective statements include statements about mathematics ("2 + 2 = 4"), science ("Peas are legumes"), and most of philosophy ("Minds interact with bodies"). To say "Peas are legumes" is true for me means only that I believe that peas are legumes, and to say "Peas are legumes" is false for me is an equally pretentious way of saying that I do not believe that peas are legumes. The important thing to notice is that *my believing either thing about peas does not make it so*. The biological classification of peas—as opposed to my opinion about their taste—is not dependent on what I think about peas. Therefore, although the truth of subjective statements *is* relative to the subjective opinions of persons, the truth of objective statements is not.

We shall see in this book that philosophers dispute whether certain types of statements in ethics, free will, and theory of knowledge are subjective or objective. But the existence of disputed cases gives no reason to think that *all* statements are subjective. The only way we could prove that all statements are relative would be to prove *solipsism* ('sol-lip-sism), the *doctrine that the only thing that exists is my nonphysical mind*. Needless to say, no one has ever done this.

The confusion between subjective and objective facts is partially caused by mistaking the theory of knowledge question "What can we know?" with the metaphysical question "What exists?" Some persons are tempted to think that all unanswered questions take merely subjective answers. But this is a mistake. The fact that we do not *know* whether a fact is true does not make it subjective. For example, the exact number of hairs that Bill Clinton had on his head at 9 A.M. on January 1, 1976, is an objective fact, even if no one will ever know it. So long as we are talking about an objective issue and not simply expressing our feelings, our statements are not subjective.

METHODOLOGICAL TOOLS AT WORK

I conclude this chapter with three illustrations of how we can use the methods of critical thinking to solve some problems.

9. Are the Golden Rule and Confucius's Rule Equivalent?

According to the *New Testament* Jesus said, "All things whatsoever ye would that men should do to you, do you even so to them" (Matthew 7:12). In the *Analects*, 15:23, Confucius is reported to say, "Do not do unto others that you would not have them do unto you." Suppose someone wondered which moral rule is better. If both say the same thing, then they would be equally good. But do they say the same thing?

We can figure out whether they are equivalent by analyzing their logical structures. The Golden Rule says, "Do unto others what you would have them do unto you." Confucius's Rule says, "Do *not* do unto others what you do *not* want them to do unto you." The Golden Rule is the conditional statement: If A (you would like X done to you), then B (you may do X to others). Confucius's Rule is the conditional statement: If *not* A, then *not* B. We can demonstrate that these conditionals are different by considering the following substitution instances: "If today is Tuesday, then today is a weekday" is not equivalent to: "If today is not Tuesday, then today is not a weekday."

We have thus proved that the Golden Rule and Confucius's Rule are different. The Golden Rule says it is OK to act in any way that you would want persons to act toward you. Confucius's Rule says you must *refrain* from actions if you do not want them done to you. In logical terminology, the Golden Rule provides a *sufficient condition* for moral rightness, whereas Confucius's Rule provides a *necessary condition*. We might now try to decide which rule we think is better by using a thought-experiment. Consider the case in which you wonder whether it is morally right to offend your neighbors by playing loud music in your dormitory room. The Golden Rule would say that it is OK to play loud music in your dorm room if you do not mind your neighbors playing loud music in theirs. Confucius's Rule does not say this: Confucius's Rule says it is not OK to play loud music if you would not like your neighbors to do so, but it does *not* say that it is OK to do so if you do not mind. Nothing in Confucius's Rule gives you the go-ahead. I believe this is one case in which Confucius's Rule is preferable to the Golden Rule.

10. Do Our Psychological Experiences Prove How Things Are Outside Our Minds?

Many persons think that if a psychological feeling is powerful enough, we can count on it as an indicator of truth. Examples include subjects of philosophical dispute: "I can *see* that I have a hand," "I know in my heart of hearts that eating meat is wicked," "I have an ineffable feeling that God communicated with me," "I know intuitively that I have free will." The question, though, is: *How* could our being convinced that something is so *make* it so? There are two categories of things that we can think of: things existing *outside* our minds (for example, physical objects, objective moral truths, or God) and things that exist only in our minds (for example, our sensations that represent physical objects, our moral feelings, or our idea of God). There is no difficulty in saying that our experience proves that something exists *in our minds*, although there always is a small chance that our reports of the contents of our minds might be inaccurate. But if we wish to say that our experience proves that something outside our mind exists, then we are going beyond what is certain—we are making a claim that external reality *matches* what is in our minds—and we cannot issue any guarantees. Individuals are in no position to tell with certainty that external reality matches their psychological states. The most we can do is to try to support our thesis by inference to the best explanation: "I would not have this particular experience if it were not caused in this one way." However, showing this is highly debatable and never certain.

11. Can Wishing for Something Make It True?

In the classic movie *Damn Yankees*, the manager of the last-place Washington Senators baseball team leads his players in a rousing chorus of "You've Gotta Have Heart" to encourage them to be optimistic. Having optimism about our lives helps make us more energetic, happier, and more successful in our endeavors. Should we extend this point to say that wishing can make things *true*?

We can settle this question by making a distinction: It all depends on what you mean by "things." If what you mean is "objective matters that are entirely independent of our opinions," then the answer is "no." Wishing cannot make an objective fact that is true false, or one that is false true. For example, all the wishing in the world will not turn your lottery ticket into a winner. Because philosophical questions involve questions about matters that are independent of our opinions, relying on wishful thinking to support a philosophical theory is always a fallacy. Like the lottery case, all the wishing in the world will not make your favorite philosophical theory true.

If what you mean by "things" is "events that happen in our own lives," then the answer is "sometimes"—but only if the act of wishing has some causal influence on those events. Consider the baseball example again. If thinking optimistically causes the baseball players to try harder and if trying harder increases their chances of success, then wishing for success may help to bring about success. If this happens, though, it is only because the outcome depends to some extent on the state of mind of the person doing the wishing. Philosophical, scientific, and most everyday questions are not like this.

Logical Definitions Chart

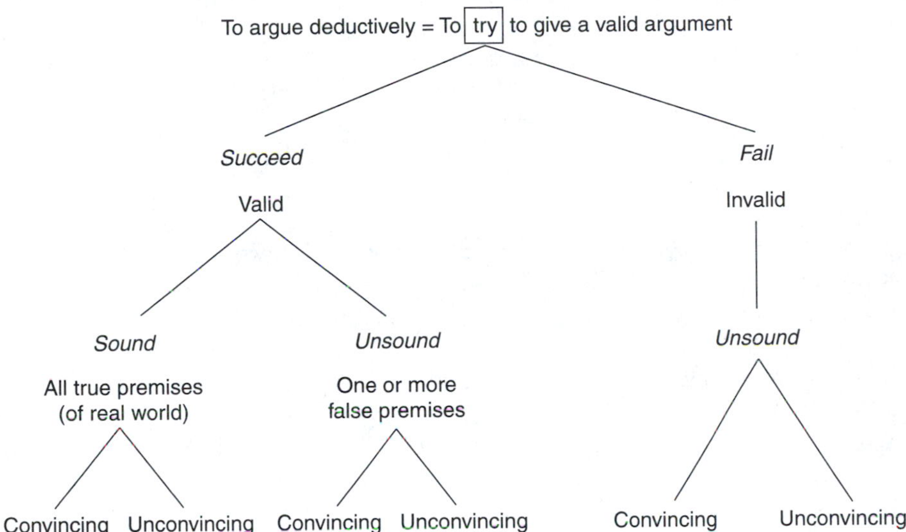

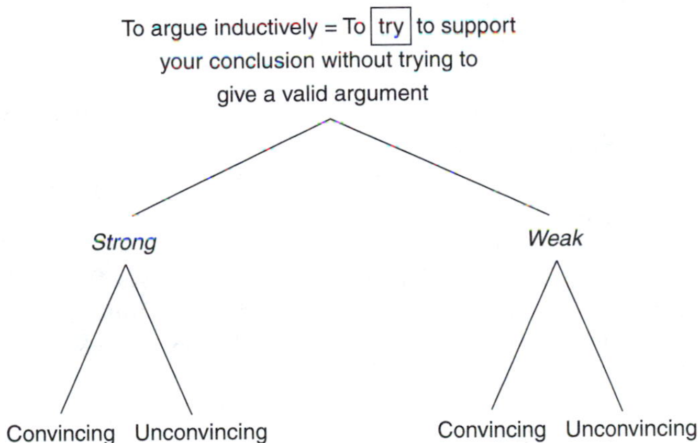

"Argument *A* is valid" means "*A* has a valid argument form (there are *no substitution instances* where all premises are true and the conclusion is false)."

"Argument *A* is invalid" means "*A* has only invalid argument forms (there is *at least one substitution instance* where all premises are true and the conclusion is false)."

"Argument *A* is sound" means "*A* is valid and has all true premises of real world."

"Argument *A* is convincing" means "*A* would convince a nonnegligible number of hearers."

Guide Questions

1. Explain the difference between a word and the thing that the word refers to. (15)
2. What is the definition of "definition"? (15)
3. What is a counterexample? A thought experiment? (16)
4. What is the difference between ambiguity and vagueness? (16–17)
5. Define: "argument," "logic," "conditional statement." (17–18)
6. What is the difference between arguing deductively and arguing inductively? (18)
7. What is the difference between valid and invalid arguments? (18–19)
8. What does "sound" mean? (20) What does "convincing" mean? (20)
9. How does a good deductive argument differ from a good inductive argument? (20–21)
10. In terms of their forms, what is the difference between modus ponens and modus tollens? (21–22)
11. Give your own example of an argument that has the form of *dilemma*. (23) Give an example of reductio ad absurdum. (23–24)
12. Produce a logical analogy to refute this argument: (1) All politicians are elected officials. (2) Therefore, all elected officials are politicians. (25)
13. Express in one sentence the basic idea behind inference to the best explanation. (26)
14. What question was the psychologist Ellen Langer trying to answer in her experiment using the photocopier machine? (26–27)
15. Give two ways by which we can avoid misuses of inference to the best explanation. (28)
16. What was the point of the example comparing the number of subjects who have Disease D and Symptom S? (29–30)
17. What is the fallacy of anecdotal evidence? (30–31)
18. For what sort of matters is truth relative and for what sort is it not? (31–32)
19. Why is the Golden Rule not equivalent to Confucius's Rule? (32–33)
20. What is the problem with taking our psychological feelings as proof about the way the world is? (33)
21. What criterion can we use to distinguish when wishful thinking will work and when it will not work? (34)

Review Questions for Examinations

1. Define these terms: "definition," "possible world," "counterexample," "thought experiment," "ambiguity," "vagueness," "logic," "premise," "conclusion," "argument," "conditional statement," "antecedent," "consequent," "deductive," "inductive," "valid," "invalid," "argument form," "substitution instance," "fallacy," "sound," "convincing."

2. Provide your own examples of these arguments: modus ponens, modus tollens, dilemma, and reductio ad absurdum.
3. Distinguish between modus ponens and the fallacy of affirming the consequent. Distinguish between modus tollens and the fallacy of denying the antecedent.
4. Provide your own examples of: analogies, logical analogies, and inference to the best explanation.
5. How is inference to the best explanation different from induction by enumeration?
6. Give an example of the fallacy of anecdotal evidence. The truth-is-relative fallacy. The fallacy of wishful thinking.

Discussion Questions

1. Can you think of an area outside of academics where the methodology of critical thinking would be helpful? Where it would be harmful? Explain.
2. Can you think of a good inductive argument (one that is strong, has all true premises, and is convincing) that might be made to look *less good* by the addition of more *true* premises?
3. Does wishful thinking have a role to play in our lives? If so, how should we decide where it should and should not be applied?
4. Devise a thought experiment designed to show that happiness is not necessarily the best goal that persons can seek.
5. Using the argument form modus ponens, provide three different substitution instances where the substituting argument has: (1) all true premises and a true conclusion, (2) one or two false premises and a true conclusion, and (3) one or two false premises and a false conclusion. You will not be able to provide a substitution instance with all true premises and a false conclusion. Why not?
6. Here is an example from Daniel Dennett that shows how critical thinking can help avoid preposterous theories based on badly analyzed data. Try to figure out the answer before reading the last paragraph.

   Suppose that prior to the National Football League's Week 1, a betting service mails you a recommendation on which team to bet on in Sunday's game between Atlanta and New Orleans. The betting service predicts that Atlanta will win the game by more than a certain number of points ("cover the point spread") and they do. As a reasonable person, you ignore the letter and do not send the betting service the requested $100 for their prediction for a game on Week 2. Nonetheless, the betting service sends you their prediction for Week 2. They say that Dallas may beat Philadelphia, but they will fail to cover the point spread, so you should bet on Philadelphia. Sure enough, that prediction is also correct. This goes on for nine straight weeks, and each prediction is correct. Finally, before the tenth Sunday of the season the betting service sends you a final letter. The betting service says that they are finished sending you all this valuable information for free: If you want to learn the winning bet for that Sunday, now you must send them $1,000. Should you do so?

As a critical thinker, you try to figure out the best explanation for the success of the betting service's predictions. Could all the games be "fixed," and the gamblers at the betting service have found out or even rigged the games themselves? Possible, but not likely. Could the predictors at the gambling service be very smart? Although choosing winners of some games might be easy (e.g., a team playing at home against a team with a poor record), the factor of the point-spread makes it difficult to decide whether the favored team will win by that number of points. Further, if the predictors at the betting service were so smart, why would they need to make money by soliciting $1,000 fees from persons like you? Why wouldn't they simply bet their own money and become fabulously rich? So, that hypothesis looks unlikely. Maybe the betting service is very lucky in their predictions? But a little knowledge of probability theory counts against that explanation. The probability of two independent events both happening is the product of each individual event's probability. For example, the probability of getting two heads on two consecutive tosses of a fair coin is 0.5×0.5, which is .25. Because the odds of guessing whether a team will cover the point spread are approximately 0.5, the probability of guessing correctly 9 times in a row is 0.5 multiplied by itself 9 times, which amounts to odds of 1 in 512. These are very long odds. So, if we ever face this type of situation, maybe we should say that the betting service *does* have the remarkable ability to see into the future and make accurate predictions about things that we ordinarily cannot predict.

Happily, in Dennett's example there is a simpler explanation that critical thinkers can figure out. The betting service sends out its predictions to thousands of fans at the start of each football season, sending predictions of one outcome to half its audience, and the opposite outcome to the other half. So, the recipients of the incorrect prediction that Atlanta would not cover the point spread on Week 1 never received more predictions. Likewise, the fans who received the correct prediction for Week 1's game, but were mailed an incorrect prediction for Week 2, never received any further predictions, and so on. Thus, the only persons who received the final request for money were fans who had received all nine letters containing winning predictions. But this had nothing to do with precognition; it was a matter of arithmetic.

FOR FURTHER READING

Doyle, Arthur Conan. 1927. *The Complete Sherlock Holmes*. New York: Doubleday. Enjoyable tales of the most famous fictional detective of all time. Holmes calls his method of solving crimes "deduction," but it is mostly inference to the best explanation.

Giere, Ronald. 1994. *Understanding Scientific Reasoning*. Fort Worth: Holt, Rinehart and Winston. An excellent introduction to scientific method, complete with absorbing historical case studies. Easy to read.

Klenk, Virginia. 1994. *Understanding Symbolic Logic*. Englewood Cliffs, NJ: Prentice-Hall. An extremely clear introduction to deductive logic.

Martin, Robert M. 1992. *There are Two Errors in the the Title of this Book: A Sourcebook of Philosophical Puzzles, Paradoxes and Problems*. Peterborough, Ont: Broadview. An engaging invitation to critical thinking and philosophy. Brilliant and amusing.

Moore, Brooke and Richard Parker. 1995. *Critical Thinking*. Mountain View, CA: Mayfield. The most widely used critical thinking text in American universities. Extremely comprehensive.

Schlick, Theodore and Lewis Vaughn. 1995. *How to Think about Weird Things: Critical Thinking for a New Age*. Mountain View, CA: Mayview. An entertaining debunking of popular beliefs such as ESP, astrology, miracle cures, near-death experiences.

Shulman, Max. 1964. *The Many Loves of Dobie Gillis*. New York: Bantam Books. Hilarious short stories about a mid-western college student in the middle of the twentieth century. "Love Is a Fallacy" is especially good.

Sorenson, Roy. 1992. *Thought Experiments*. New York: Oxford University Press. A fascinating study of how philosophers and scientists use thought experiments in constructing their theories. Difficult.

Chapter 3
Theory of Knowledge

INTRODUCTION

In the *theory of knowledge* (*epistemology*) philosophers ask whether persons know things, and if so, how? Unlike *metaphysics*, which tries to provide the most-likely-to-be-true picture of what exists without asking whether we know that our theories are true, epistemology asks the more personal question of whether our efforts at knowing succeed. It is easy to arrive at true beliefs regarding metaphysical questions: Simply guess. But guessing does not provide knowledge. Many persons think they know things when they have done little more than guess—sometimes with comical and sometimes with deplorable results. Studying epistemology enables us to see what knowledge requires and helps us to recognize when we do not have it. This is crucial to educating ourselves, because so long as we falsely think we know things, we are unlikely to try to find out the truth. As Socrates noted, we must acknowledge our ignorance if we are to become wise.

1. The Definition of "Knowledge"

To ask whether we have knowledge, we need to define "knowledge." In epistemology, philosophers concern themselves with *propositional knowledge*. Propositional knowledge is *knowledge that some statement (proposition) is true or false*. Examples of statements include: "Cats like to eat fish," "2 + 2 = 5," and "God exists." Although the word "know" is sometimes used to convey familiarity ("I know Jones") and know-how ("I know how to bake bread"), these are not propositional uses. In this section I provide a list of conditions for propositional knowledge that are intended to be *individually necessary* and *jointly sufficient*: a list of conditions such that each must be satisfied for us to have knowledge and such that if they are all satisfied, then we have knowledge. To do this, we shall complete this formula: Subject S knows proposition *p* if and only if: ______________.

The first condition for knowing some proposition *p* is that *p* is true. I cannot know that *p* is true if *p* is false—at most I can believe (*falsely*) that *p* is true. Medieval thinkers who *believed* that the sun orbits the earth did not *know* that the sun orbits the earth, because the sun does *not* orbit the earth. The second condition is that S believes that *p* is true. Knowledge is a kind of belief; so, if one does not believe *p*, one cannot know *p*. Medievals did not know that the sun is made up of hydrogen, because they did not *believe* that the sun is made up of hydrogen, inasmuch as they lacked the concept "hydrogen." When satisfied together, the first two conditions guarantee that S has a belief that is true. This is called a "true belief." A true belief is simply a belief we have that is true, whether by knowledge or by lucky guess. "True belief" *does not mean* a belief that persons hold with great emotional conviction. True beliefs are not like true loves.

If we stopped our definition of "knowledge" after the first two conditions, we would be saying that any true belief counts as knowledge. But that would be premature, because there are many examples in which we have true beliefs without having knowledge. Here is one. Suppose you buy one lottery ticket among a million that are sold and solely on the basis of wishful thinking convince yourself that you have the winning ticket. Even if you do have the winning ticket, you do not *know* that you do. Here is another example. Suppose you have the true belief that you have two quarters on your person because you examined the contents of your pockets fifteen minutes ago. Suppose, however, that ten minutes ago the two quarters fell through a hole in your pocket onto a carpeted floor without your realizing it. Suppose also that a considerate friend, realizing that you would be embarrassed if you thought anyone noticed that you have holes in your pockets, replaced the two quarters without your being aware of it. Although you hold the true belief "I have two quarters on me," you do not *know* that you have them. So, knowledge must be more than just true beliefs.

What we need to turn true beliefs into knowledge is that we satisfy some extra condition or conditions—conditions that guarantee that our true beliefs qualify as knowledge. The traditional requirement is that knowers be able to *provide adequate evidence* that their belief is true. This is known as being able to *justify* one's belief. Using that idea, here is a standard definition of "knowledge" as *justified, true belief*:

Subject S knows that proposition *p* is true if and only if:

(1) *p* is true. (the truth condition)
(2) S believes that *p* is true. (the belief condition)
(3J) S is able to justify *p* (provide adequate evidence that *p* is true). (the justification condition)

The idea behind the justified, true belief definition of "knowledge" is that having knowledge is an accomplishment. Only those true beliefs that believers can justify to some objective standard of excellence deserve to be called "knowledge." Not only must our beliefs be true, but we must successfully take on all critics who object that our beliefs are not justified. An alternative way to express condition (3J) is:

(3J′) S is able to answer satisfactorily all critics who say that even if S's belief in *p* is true—relative to S's evidence for *p*—*p* is just a matter of luck.

There is a different way to add a third condition to the first two, which produces a second type of definition of "knowledge." Suppose we think that to have knowledge, our true beliefs must be reliably connected to their causal sources. Suppose we also think that it is *not necessary that knowers themselves* be able to provide a justification for their believing *p*. For instance, suppose we believe that a dog can know that there is a bone in front of her if her true belief is caused by the fact that she *is* seeing a bone, despite the fact that she cannot *justify* her belief or *answer satisfactorily* critics' charges. Or suppose we believe that clairvoyant persons who have unfailingly accurate beliefs about unexpected future events without being able to explain how they do it have knowledge. Or suppose we accurately remember things without being able to explain *how* we remember them. In that case, we may require as the third condition in the definition of "knowledge" only that knowers' true beliefs be *causally connected to* the true facts they are about. Philosophers who prefer a causal definition of "knowledge" replace the justification condition with a condition about the appropriate causal connections. Here is a standard version of a *causal definition of "knowledge"*:

Subject S knows that proposition *p* is true if and only if:

(1) *p* is true. (the truth condition)
(2) S believes that *p* is true. (the belief condition)
(3C) S's belief that *p* is causally related to the fact *p* in an appropriate way. (the causal condition)

Some epistemologists disagree whether the justified, truth belief definition or the causal definition of "knowledge" is better, but I think the debate is misguided. Justificatory and causal definitions of knowledge address different issues concerning knowledge. One issue is: "How can you, as a knower, *explain* your knowledge that *p*?" This is the traditional Socratic requirement that knowers must be able to "provide an account" that would prove to other persons that they know what they are talking about. This portrays knowledge as an accomplishment of verbal beings. If this is what we care most about, we will prefer the definition of "knowledge" as justified, true belief. A second, equally important, issue is: "In coming to believe *p*, did S use a reliable mechanism that makes the truth of *p* likely?" We ask this when we care about the likelihood that S's belief is actually true, *regardless of whether S can produce a justification*. If this is the primary issue for us, we care only whether there exists some reliable causal mechanism.

Thus, the different definitions address different issues, and each can be equally "right." They could not both be right if there exists one ideal, true form or definition of knowledge in a Platonic world of Forms (or universals) that any correct definition of "knowledge" must match. But there is no reason to believe as the Greek philosopher Plato (427–347 B.C.) did that Forms exist in this supernatural manner. Because traditional epistemology is concerned most with the justificatory issue, I shall use the justified true belief definition of "knowledge" in this chapter.

2. Three Distinctions

To discuss knowledge we need some additional terminology. This will be the distinctions between statements that are: (1) a priori vs. a posteriori, (2) analytic vs. synthetic, and (3) logically necessary vs. logically contingent.

A PRIORI AND A POSTERIORI JUSTIFICATION

To determine whether a statement is justified, we need to realize that there are two types of justification. If we justify a statement *a posteriori*, we justify it only on the basis of observations and drawing a conclusion from those observations. For example, we might justify or disconfirm the statement "Cats eat fish" by giving cats fish to eat and seeing whether they do. The psychological statement "Rewarding persons for doing things they already like tends to reduce their liking of those things" can be justified or disconfirmed only after observation of the world. An a posteriori statement, thus, is one whose truth or falsity *can* be justified *only after observation* or, "only on the basis of experience." A loose synonym of "a posteriori" is "empirical."

An *a priori* statement can be justified *without relying on observation*. Instead, we can justify an a priori statement by some purely intellectual means. For example, we can justify "Nothing is both totally red and totally blue" not by examining totally red items and recording how many are also totally blue, but by understanding that the statement *must* be true. Likewise with "All bachelors are unmarried" and "10001 is an odd number." This is in contrast to a posteriori statements, which can be shown true or false only after observation.

Here are two possible confusions regarding a priori and a posteriori justification. First, we might object that we can justify arithmetic statements observationally, e.g., we might prove that "$5 \times 5 = 25$" by lining up five rows of five apples and counting them. Therefore, "$5 \times 5 = 25$" might be thought to be both a priori and a posteriori. The confusion here lies in paying insufficient attention to the definition of "a priori." An a priori statement is one that *can* be justified *without* observation—this does *not* mean it *cannot* be justified by observation. The fact that we could justify the claim that bachelors are unmarried by taking a poll at a shopping mall ("Sir, are you a bachelor?" "Yes." "Well, are you unmarried?") does not show that "All bachelors are unmarried" is both a priori and a posteriori.

A second confusion is to think that the fact that we need to have some experience to even understand what an a priori statement means (e.g., "$4 \times 7 = 28$") shows that it is really a posteriori. Granted, we could not justify "$4 \times 7 = 28$" if we did not understand what the numerals, the multiplication sign, and the equal sign mean. We need experience to learn these meanings. But our definition says that a priori statements are ones that can be *justified* without experience, not that they can be *understood* without experience. Learning the meanings of the concepts used in a statement by experience is different than justifying the statement by experience.

ANALYTIC AND SYNTHETIC STATEMENTS

Compare (A) "No bachelors are married" with (B) "No bachelors are over 130 years old." Both statements are true, but there is an obvious difference in *why* they are true. (A) is true simply due to the meaning of the word "bachelor" (is true by definition), whereas (B) is not true by definition. Thus, (A) is an analytic statement, and (B) is synthetic. The truth of (A) can be discovered by analysis of the meaning of "bachelor." The truth of (B) cannot be arrived at by analysis, but must be "synthesized," that is, learned from information not contained in the definition. Compare: (C) "Bodies are not extended" and (D) "Bodies do not have weight." (C) is false because the word "body" means "an entity with spatial extension." (D) is false, but not by definition, because the definition of "body" does not preclude the existence of weightless bodies, e.g., bodies far enough from gravitational forces to be weightless. Thus, (C) is analytic, and (D) is synthetic. An *analytic statement* is a *statement whose truth or falsity depends solely on the meanings of its words*. A *synthetic statement* is a *statement whose truth or falsity does not solely depend on the meanings of its words*.

LOGICALLY NECESSARY AND LOGICALLY CONTINGENT STATEMENTS

Compare: (E) "2 + 2 = 4" and (F) "Bill Clinton won the U.S. presidency in 1996." (E) cannot help but be true. There is no imaginable world where 2 plus 2 do not equal 4, which is not to deny that there are worlds where persons *mean something different* than we do by "2 + 2 = 4." But this possibility does not show that what *we* mean by "2 + 2 = 4" might be false. There are, however, many imaginable worlds where (F) is false—worlds where George Bush or Ronald Reagan won the 1996 election. Thus, (E) is a *logically necessary truth* and (F) is a *logically contingent truth*. Compare: (G) "Squares have five sides" and (H) "Germany won the Second World War." Both are false. (G) has to be false—it is false in every possible world. (H) is in fact false, but it is not false in every possible world. So (G) is a *logically necessary falsehood*, but (H) is a *logically contingent falsehood*. A *logically necessary statement* is a *statement that is true or false in every possible world*. A *logically contingent statement* is a *statement that is true in some possible worlds and false in others*.

I have selected examples to illustrate that these three distinctions deal with different issues. The a priori/a posteriori distinction is *justificatory*, because it deals with how we justify statements. The analytic/synthetic distinction is *semantic*, because it concerns the meanings of statements. The logically necessary/logical contingent distinction deals with necessity and possibility. Many philosophers, including the Scottish skeptic David Hume, have thought that the three distinctions cover exactly the same ground, so that any statement is either a priori, analytic, and logically necessary or a posteriori, synthetic, and logically contingent. Against Hume, it *looks* as if we can find individual statements that belong on both sides of the division. Hume's most famous critic, the German Immanuel Kant (CONT) (1724–1804), built his philosophical system on the notion of necessary, a priori truths that are synthetic rather than analytic. In recent years Saul Kripke (CRIP-KEY) (1972) has argued that claims such as "Water is H_2O" are synthetic and a posteriori, but logically necessary. These debates are too subtle for treatment here, but we should remember that it is not obvious that the three distinctions match each other exactly.

EPISTEMOLOGY AND EPISTEMIC AGENCY

3. The Connection between Epistemology and Epistemic Agency

The question "Why does Smith believe statement *s*?" is ambiguous. It can mean: (1) "What factors led Smith to believe *s*?" This is a *psychological* question that asks how Smith *in fact* came to believe *s*, without raising the issue of whether Smith *should* believe *s*. The question can also mean: (2) "What evidence does Smith have for believing *s*?" This is a *philosophical* question that asks whether Smith believes *s* with justification. Consider an example: "Why does Smith believe that she will win the state lottery tomorrow?" A psychological answer might simply be that Smith always believes that she will win the lottery because she is a very optimistic believer, despite the fact that she has no evidence for her belief. On the other hand, if Smith believes that she will win because a friend who selects the winning number told Smith that she is going to rig the selection in Smith's favor, then she has both a psychological reason *and* some justification for her belief.

Epistemic agents are persons who attempt to know some fact or facts. *Good epistemic agents* believe statements because they have *epistemic reasons* to support them, reject statements when epistemic reasons count against them, and suspend judgment otherwise. The goal of good epistemic agents is to increase the total number of true beliefs they have and also to increase the percentage of true beliefs they hold compared to the false beliefs. *Poor epistemic agents* believe, reject, or suspend belief for *nonepistemic reasons.*

Epistemic reasons for a belief are reasons that increase the probability that one's beliefs are true. For instance, if we wish to increase the likelihood of the truth of our belief that all the jelly beans in a jar are red, we should sample the contents of the jar. With each additional red jelly bean we extract, we contribute evidence to our belief. Any nonred sample will refute it. *Nonepistemic reasons for a belief* are reasons that motivate us to believe without increasing the probability that our beliefs are true. If we think that the more consecutive heads that result from tossing a fair coin, the greater the likelihood that the next toss will be a tails (the gambler's fallacy), we have a psychological reason that provides no evidence for our belief. If we believe the next coin toss will be a tails simply because we want to believe it (wishful thinking), we also have a psychological, nonepistemic reason. *Not all psychological reasons that prompt us to believe are epistemic reasons that increase the probability that our beliefs are true.*

All of us recognize *other* persons whom we regard as poor epistemic agents—persons who fail to base their beliefs on epistemic reasons. These tend to be persons who have different beliefs than we do, but include persons who believe what we do but for different reasons. It is only natural to think that *we* are good epistemic agents, whereas persons who hold different beliefs are crackpots, fools, or are, at least, ill informed. After all, we would not accept a belief unless we thought it is true; thus, we tend to think that someone who rejects our beliefs is wrong. While we tend to allow some latitude regarding aesthetic, moral, religious, or even metaphysical beliefs, we tend to think that persons who get everyday beliefs wrong are defective in some important way.

For example, most of us think that persons who believe the stories in the American supermarket tabloids about aliens reproducing with celebrities are poor epistemic agents—gullible dopes who believe too readily. Poor epistemic agency also occurs in cases in which common opinion is less quick to condemn: beliefs regarding the power of crystals and faith-healing, precognitive dreams and telekinesis, the existence of Bigfoot and the Loch Ness monster, astrology, and other *pseudo (phoney) scientific* folklore.

There is one overall cause of poor epistemic efforts: inattention to whether our beliefs are *justified*, that is, whether we have evidence that makes it likely that our beliefs are true. This inattention to evidence allows us to mistake nonepistemic, nonjustifying reasons for beliefs with epistemic, justifying reasons for beliefs. Good epistemic agents are vitally concerned with justification. Many human beings accept beliefs due to factors that have nothing to do with justification.

4. Factors behind Poor Epistemic Agency

In recent years, psychologists have studied epistemic errors in great detail. One factor is *belief perseverance*, the tendency for beliefs to persist even when we collect evidence that discredits them. Beliefs, once acquired, are very difficult for us to reject, even after we are shown explicit discrediting evidence (Nisbett and Ross, 1980, ch. 8). A second factor behind poor epistemic agency is *ego-defensiveness*, our desire to maintain a high opinion of ourselves. Not only does it require more effort to replace old beliefs with better ones, it often creates *cognitive dissonance*, the ego-threatening psychological discomfort of admitting that one's beliefs are in conflict with each other (Brehm and Cohen, 1962). A closely related third factor is *wishful thinking*. We often prefer to hold beliefs that make us happy, even when all available evidence goes against our beliefs. For example, our tendency to "blame the victim" for suffering misfortunes comes from our desire to believe that the world is basically fair (the "just world hypothesis"). The thought that the world is unjust and that persons suffer for no good reason is very unpleasant for most of us.

A fourth factor is that we often adopt beliefs to conform to those around us and, thus, to avoid conflict. The result is that we believe many things we are told without asking whether they are true. Most persons uncritically absorb their beliefs from their environments, especially television, peer groups, and family. If you want to understand why a person says "X," often the best way is not to ask what good reasons the person has for thinking that "X" is true, but rather to see how the person has been *reinforced* to *say* "X."

A fifth factor involves confusions over epistemic authority. Although experts are more apt to know things about their fields than nonexperts are, we often concede expertise to persons who lack it. In doing so we find persons *credible* (*worthy of belief*) due to epistemically irrelevant factors such as their celebrity status, their confident manner of presenting their points, and even their appearance. As advertisers and salespersons know, the persuasiveness of one's presentation is determined more by the adroitness of the seller than by facts about one's product (Zimbardo and Leippe, 1991).

It is easy to agree in a general way that the above factors are epistemically unacceptable reasons for beliefs, but it is more difficult for us to apply rigorous standards to ourselves. Part of the difficulty is that beliefs serve many functions besides that of representing truths. Beliefs affect our lives in ways that have nothing to do with truth. Some false beliefs can make us happy and energetic, whereas some truths can make us depressed. For example, the illusion that we are better liked than we really are is helpful to us in most circumstances. It is a serious evaluative question whether it is better to have a true belief that makes us sad or a false one that makes us happy. (For a fascinating experiment showing ways that depressed persons see the world more accurately than nondepressed persons, see Lewinsohn et al., 1980.)

There are limits, of course. It was more beneficial for our ancestors who were faced with a charging saber-toothed tiger to believe the unpleasant truth that they were in danger rather than the (temporary) happy falsehood that the tiger was trying to be playful. We need many true beliefs simply to survive, but beyond those, there are times when having false beliefs will not kill us. This means that there are a lot of cases in which we can choose whether to be good epistemic agents or not.

An additional difficulty for our epistemic agency is that few persons can derive full advantage from holding happy, nonepistemically warranted beliefs if they *admit* to themselves that their beliefs are not warranted. If I say "I believe *p* only because it makes me happy," I am less likely to be able to accept *p*. Thus, some persons refuse to consider whether their beliefs are epistemically warranted. In this way they can continue to believe unwarranted things without having to admit to themselves what they are doing. One of the most threatening questions we can ask ourselves is whether our beliefs are epistemically warranted.

5. Characteristics of Good Epistemic Agents: Skills and Temperament

Good epistemic agents believe when their evidence justifies a statement, disbelieve when the evidence disconfirms it, and suspend judgment when the evidence neither justifies nor disconfirms. But how do good epistemic agents go about collecting justification? First, we need to follow truth-tracking methods, such as those discussed in chapter two. We need to learn how to distinguish between real and spurious data, how to analyze data, and how to draw logically acceptable inferences from the data we collect. Good epistemic agents need scientific, mathematical, critical thinking, and logical *skills*. Good epistemic agents also need accurate *information* about statistics, probability, science, and a wide range of subjects.

Second, we need the right temperament—the motivation to use our epistemic skills to be good epistemic agents. Epistemic aptitude in the hands of persons who have no interest in using it is wasted. Good epistemic agents make an evenhanded effort at gathering confirming *and* disconfirming evidence for the beliefs they entertain. This requires not doing what is the most natural thing for us to do: to try to confirm our present beliefs, and ignore or try to disconfirm all beliefs that conflict with ours. A remark by Francis Bacon in 1620 is as insightful today as it was then: "the human understanding when it has once adopted an opinion draws all things else to support . . . it. And though there be a greater number and weight of instances to be found on the other side, yet these it either neglects and despises, or else by some distinction sets aside and rejects." Approximately 350 years later Simon and Garfunkel expressed a similar idea in the lyrics of an anti–Vietnam War song: "A man hears what he wants to hear and disregards the rest."

Good epistemic aptitude is squandered if we use our powers to protect our beliefs from criticism. The epistemic point of acquiring good epistemic skills is *to enable us to move from our present set of beliefs toward the most justified set of beliefs we can*. To move to an improved set of beliefs, we have to admit that our present set of beliefs is not ideal. Such admissions create cognitive dissonance, because we do not like to admit that some of our beliefs are false or unwarranted. Nonetheless, if we are to become better epistemic agents, we need to have enough self-confidence to be willing to endure some psychological distress. Given our natural prejudice for our current beliefs, a good rule of thumb for epistemic agents is this: Try to *disconfirm* one of our beliefs every day.

6. What's So Great about Justifying One's Beliefs?

There are two reasons to care about justification, one *intrinsic* (*valuable in itself*) and one *extrinsic* (*valuable as a means to an end*.) These two reasons correspond to the two questions we noted in section 1 that separate thinkers who adopt a justified, true belief definition of "knowledge" and those who prefer a causal definition. The intrinsic reason to wish to justify one's beliefs is simply that one wants to be able to justify in one's own mind (and to others, if asked) why one believes what one does. For those who prefer the justified, true belief definition of "knowledge," the question "Why should I want my beliefs to be justified?" amounts to "Why should I want to have knowledge?" For someone who cares about knowledge, the answer is simple: "I want to be the kind of person who has knowledge—who can provide justification."

The extrinsic reason for caring about justification is that seeking justification for our beliefs is the best way to increase the probability that they are true. Why? Because collecting justification for our beliefs is the best way to guarantee that we are relying on *causal mechanisms* that maximize the chance that our beliefs are true. If there were a better method of acquiring true beliefs, then justification would have less extrinsic importance. For example, some mystics think that a good way to acquire true beliefs is not by seeking justification, but by putting themselves in a trance in which true beliefs mysteriously come to them. Some religious persons think a good way to acquire true beliefs is to accept religious texts on faith alone. But there is no reason to think that such methods are as effective at increasing the probability that our beliefs are true as seeking to justify our beliefs. Thus, the best way we *in fact* have to arrive at true beliefs is by trying to be good epistemic agents.

THE GENERAL PROBLEM OF SKEPTICISM

7. Skepticism Explained

The definition of "knowledge" and the issue of skepticism are intimately connected. A *skeptic* (also spelled "sceptic") denies that we have knowledge of some individual statement or entire area of belief. A *nonskeptic* asserts that we do have knowledge. We can be skeptical about some areas of beliefs and nonskeptical about others. For example, I might be skeptical about our knowledge of the existence of the physical world, but be nonskeptical about my knowledge of my own mind.

Imagine that a skeptic challenges your claim to know some proposition p. In principle, the skeptic could focus on any of the three conditions that define "knowledge" and argue that you do not satisfy it. The skeptic could argue that you do not know that p because p is false, thereby denying that the truth condition is satisfied. The skeptic could argue that you do not really believe that p is true, thereby denying that the belief condition is satisfied. But arguing in either of these ways would be difficult: To argue that p is false places a burden on the skeptic to show that *p* is false, a burden the skeptic does not want to bear. The skeptic has an even more difficult chore in trying to prove to you that you do not even believe what you *think* you believe. After all, we can generally tell *what* we believe, even if those beliefs turn out to be false.

The most frequent target of the skeptic is the justification condition. Skeptics argue that even if we believe that *p* and our belief is true, we do not have adequate evidence for *p*—we are not justified in believing *p*. According to skeptics, from our perspective as epistemic agents, we are just lucky that our true beliefs turn out to be true—because we are not in a position to show why they are true. For instance, in the case in which my guess that I have a winning lottery ticket turns out to be true, I do not deserve credit for being a knower—I was lucky. According to skeptics, whenever the beliefs that we erroneously think we know turn out to be true, it is a matter of luck, not evidence. Wherever we lack evidence, we cannot meet the justification condition of knowledge, and we cannot know.

Skeptics propose *skeptical hypotheses* and challenge nonskeptics to disprove them. A skeptical hypothesis is *any thought experiment, however bizarre, that a skeptic makes up to challenge our claim to have knowledge*. Skeptics do not claim that their skeptical hypotheses are true; rather they use them primarily to challenge the nonskeptics' claims to have sufficient justification for knowledge.

One of the most famous skeptical hypotheses is that of the *brain-in-a-vat*. Suppose I claim to know that I have a hand because of my sense experience—I can see my hand, feel my hand, and so on. Skeptics ask how I can tell that I am not receiving these sense impressions artificially. Perhaps, for all I can tell, I am a disembodied brain submerged in a vat of liquid with electrodes that stimulate those exact parts of my brain that *would* be stimulated by my sense organs if I really *were* to perceive my hand. Skeptics argue that until nonskeptics can prove that they are not brains-in-vats, nonskeptics do not *know* that they have hands, even if they *do* have hands.

Another way to understand the skeptic's move is through the *principle of deductive closure*. According to this principle, if I know *p*, and I know that *p* logically entails some statement *q*, then I must know *q* also. For example, if I know that 6 is even, and I know that 6's being even entails that 6 is not odd, then I must know that 6 is not odd. Therefore, if I do not know that 6 is not odd, I do not know that 6 is even. Now, apply deductive closure to our attempt to know things solely on the basis of our sense experience. Assume I know I have a hand. I also know that my having a hand logically entails that I am not really a handless brain-in-a-vat. Therefore, I must know that I am not really a handless brain-in-a-vat. But, according to the skeptical hypothesis, I do *not* know that I am not a brain-in-a-vat. Therefore, by modus tollens, I do not know I have a hand.

8. Hume's Skeptical Standard of Justification

Skeptics say our beliefs are unjustified, whereas nonskeptics say our beliefs are justified. As one would expect, skeptics typically have more demanding standards of justification than nonskeptics do. The more demanding one's standards, the more difficult they are to meet. So, the dispute between the skeptics and nonskeptics boils down to the question of who has the correct (or "correct") standards of justification.

A famous skeptical standard of justification is endorsed by *empiricists* such as Hume. Empiricists believe that *all knowledge of the world must be obtained a posteriori*, that is, can be justified only after experience, as discussed in section 2. Hume thinks that *Relations of Ideas*—which do not give knowledge about the world because they can be justified a priori—are merely verbal. Relations of Ideas can be justified simply because their denial is self-contradictory. For example, "$3 \times 5 = {}^{1}/_{2}$ of 30" can be known simply by understanding the meanings of the terms in the statement.

Matters of Fact, according to Hume, which do tell us about the world, are a posteriori, that is, can be justified only after experience. "Water can suffocate us" is a statement that can be justified only after someone has experienced the effects of water. We cannot *deduce* from the meaning of the concept "water" that water will drown us, because it is not a logical contradiction to say that water cannot drown us. Hume regards immediate reports of our sensations (such as "Red sensation now") as justifiable, because such reports do not claim that physical objects are a certain way. Thus, these reports are not subject to being wrong in ways that statements about physical objects are. It is easy to imagine how I could be wrong about whether I actually see a tree, but it is more difficult to see how I could be wrong about whether I *think* that I see a tree or whether I am having tree sensations.

According to Hume, Relations of Ideas and reports of our sensations yield a paltry sort of knowledge. Relations of Ideas are a priori true because they are analytic. Therefore, they do not tell us about what exists. Reports of sensations, which are a posteriori and synthetic, *do* tell us about what exists, but they tell us only about what exists in our minds. But to know that entities exist *outside* our minds, we would have to take something that exists in our minds (our sensations) as evidence for the existence of something outside our minds (physical objects).

Hume's *Empiricist Criterion of Evidence* is his principle for determining when one thing is evidence for another: *One thing (A) is evidence for the existence of another thing (B) only if: either (1) A and B have been observed together (e.g., we ordinarily take the sound of a voice in the dark as evidence that another person is present); or (2) the terms "A" and "B" are connected in meaning (e.g., seeing a square is evidence for seeing a rectangle, because, by definition, all squares are rectangles).* According to Hume's criterion, if "A" and "B" are not related by definition, we can never use A as evidence for B, unless we have observed A and B together.

This criterion yields a powerful skeptical premise for Hume and other empiricists to argue that we cannot have knowledge of anything that we have never observed. For instance, my having tree sensations in my mind can never be evidence for the existence of a tree outside my mind, because I have never observed the tree itself and my tree sensation together. Whenever I *try* to observe the tree, I collect only tree sensations (Veil of Sensations Skepticism). I can never know that past regularities are evidence for their continuance in the future, because I have never observed the past and the future together to see whether they correspond (The Problem of Induction). If we adopt a strict conception of justification such as Hume's, we probably should conclude that we have little knowledge.

9. Descartes's Evil Genius

The French nonskeptic René Descartes provided a famous skeptical hypothesis to challenge the possibility that we have *any* knowledge, whether a priori or a posteriori. Descartes's *Evil Genius hypothesis* is one of the most important thought experiments in the history of philosophy:

> I have long had fixed in my mind the belief that an all-powerful God existed by whom I have been created such as I am. But how do I know that He has not brought it to pass that there is no earth, no heaven, no extended body, no magnitude, no place, and that nevertheless [I possess the perceptions of all these things and that] they seem to me to exist just exactly as I now see them? And, besides, as I sometimes imagine that others deceive themselves in the things which they think they know best, how do I know that I am not deceived every time that I add two and three, or count the sides of a square, or judge things yet simpler, if anything simpler can be imagined? . . . .
>
> I shall . . . suppose, not that God who is supremely good and the fountain of truth, but some evil genius not less powerful than deceitful, has employed his whole energies in deceiving me; I shall consider that the heavens, the earth, colours, figures, sound, and all other external things are nought but the illusions and dreams of which this genius has availed himself in order to lay traps for my credulity; I shall consider myself as having no hands, no eyes, no flesh, no blood, nor any senses, yet falsely believing myself to possess all these things; I shall remain obstinately attached to this idea, and if by this means it is not in my power to arrive at the knowledge of any truth, I may at least do what is in my power [i.e. suspend my judgment], and with firm purpose avoid giving credence to any false thing, or being imposed upon by this arch deceiver, however powerful and deceptive he may be. (Descartes, 1972, Meditation I, 147–48)

Descartes's skeptical argument relies on the justified, true belief definition of "knowledge." If we know any of our a priori or a posteriori beliefs, then we must be able to justify them. We can justify our beliefs only if we can answer all critics who object that even if our beliefs are true, it is only a matter of luck. For example, to know that I have a hand or that two and three equal five, I must be able to show that I am not being deceived into my belief by an all-powerful deceiver. Therefore, until I can refute the Evil Genius hypothesis, I fail to have knowledge, even if I have true beliefs. In the next section, I start with the Evil Genius hypothesis and then examine some other skeptical arguments against different kinds of knowledge.

SPECIFIC SKEPTICAL PROBLEMS

10. Knowledge of Minds: Our Own

Immediately after providing the Evil Genius hypothesis quoted above, Descartes asks whether there is *any* fact that he can know in the face of that hypothesis. After all, if an Evil Genius could deceive Descartes about whether squares have four sides or whether he has a hand, perhaps there is no belief that is immune from the Evil Genius's power to fool us. Descartes concludes that there is at least one belief he could not be wrong about even if an Evil Genius should exist, namely, that he, Descartes, exists. *Recognizing this fact* will provide certain knowledge that he exists:

> [Suppose] there is some deceiver or other, very powerful and very cunning, who ever employs his ingenuity in deceiving me. Then without doubt I exist also if he deceives me, and let him deceive me as much as he will, he can never cause me to be nothing so long as I am something. . . . I am, I exist, is necessarily true each time I pronounce it, or that I mentally conceive it. (Descartes, 1972, Meditation II, 150)

This passage from the Meditations is known as "the *cogito,*" although Descartes does not use here the famous expression he uses elsewhere, "Cogito, ergo sum" ("I think, therefore, I am"). Descartes's point is that so long as he thinks any thought at all, he must exist *as the thinker of that thought*. Descartes does not claim that the *cogito* proves *what* he is—e.g., a nonphysical soul or an embodied brain—but only that he exists as a thinking thing. A thinking thing is a center of consciousness that believes, desires, wills, remembers, and has sensations. This is the ontologically neutral definition of "mind" that I use throughout this text: "mind" means, according to this definition, "a thinking thing." Descartes's point is that we can know that *we* have minds simply by asking whether we exist. If I can ask the question in the first place, then the answer must be "yes," because asking a question is a mental operation, which requires a mind, which proves that my mind exists.

Most philosophers accept Descartes's *cogito*, but some skeptics have disagreed. The most famous objection comes from Hume. Let us ask what knowledge of our own minds amounts to. If our minds are thinking things—centers of consciousness as we have defined them—then they are entities that *have* thoughts. Minds are the things that stand behind our thoughts or are containers that "hold" our thoughts. Our minds are not simply strings of one mental state following another. So, to know we have minds we would have to be aware not only of our mental states, but of the mind itself that *has* the mental states. If we are unaware of any thing standing behind our mental states, then we lack knowledge that we have a mind:

> For my part, when I enter most intimately into what I call *myself*, I always stumble on some particular perception or other, of heat or cold, light or shade, love or hatred, pain or pleasure. I never catch *myself* at any time without a perception, and never can observe any thing but the perception. . . . [M]ankind . . . are nothing but a bundle or collection of different perceptions, which succeed each other with an inconceivable rapidity, and are in a perpetual flux and movement. (Hume, 1968, *Treatise*, bk. 1, pt. 4, 252)

Hume's argument depends on his Empiricist Criterion of Evidence discussed above: A is evidence for B only if either A and B have been observed together or if "A" and "B" are connected by meaning. If we adopt Hume's criterion, then his argument against knowledge of our minds appears very strong. We never *observe* our minds, but only our thoughts. Therefore, we never *observe* our thoughts and our minds together. Nor does it seem that "Here is a sensation now" proves by definition "Here is my mind that has the sensation." It seems conceivable that there might exist a series of mental states, none of which is "owned" by a mind.

We can understand Hume's skeptical argument more fully by seeing how it undermines Descartes's *cogito*. Descartes says it is certain that if he thinks, then he exists as a thinker. Hume would agree that this conditional statement is certain, but deny that Descartes is entitled to claim that he knows that he thinks. According to Hume, if Descartes were fair to his skeptical opponent, all that he would claim to recognize is that *there are thoughts occurring*, but not that he, Descartes-the-thinking-thing, is thinking those thoughts. According to Hume, Descartes is not entitled to use the term "I," because Descartes is only aware of individual thoughts occurring one after another. It is possible—for all that Descartes can prove—that the Evil Genius is not deceiving Descartes-the-thinking-thing, but is creating one *dis*connected thought after another without the presence of any mind that underlies them.

11. Knowledge of Minds: Others'

The definition of the word "mind" I use in this book—"a thinking thing"—is neutral between competing theories of what minds are. Dualists and idealists hold that minds are nonphysical, that is, are not extended in space. By definition, nonphysical minds (souls) have no size, shape, color, mass, or energy. Materialists hold that our minds are our brains. Although no one knows which view is correct, this much is clear: Whether minds are nonphysical minds or physical brains, it is impossible for us to know that other minds exist by *observing* them. If other minds are nonphysical, we cannot tell that they exist by observation, because nonphysical entities cannot be observed. If other minds are the brains of other persons, we *still* cannot tell that they exist by observation, even if we were to remove the skulls of other persons and *look* at their minds. By looking at a brain, even if it is a mind, we would never be able to tell *that* it is a mind—it would simply look like a brain. So, either way, we cannot know by observation that minds besides our own exist. This means that if we are to know that other minds exist, we must know it by some nonobservational method.

The standard nonskeptical solution to our knowledge of other minds is the *argument from analogy*. I observe my own body's behavior that corresponds to my mental states. For instance, I might *observe* what happens when my hand is stuck by a needle and then *feel* the resulting pain. I next *observe* similar behavior in bodies other than my own. When these behaviors are similar to those that accompany my feeling pain, I *infer* or *deduce* that another mind exists and feels pain. The general formula is: My observable bodily behavior is to my mental states as another body's observable behavior is to another mind's mental states.

The weakness of the argument from analogy is that it tries to justify our knowledge of the existence of other minds from only one sample in which we recognize the correspondence of observable behavior and mental states: our own case. This is a *hasty generalization*. Suppose you walk into a factory that has 100 gigantic machines, each so large that you cannot see around it. You walk up to the one closest to the door and observe on the control console a styrofoam coffee cup with an ounce of cold coffee and a cigarette butt floating in it. You would scarcely be justified in concluding that on each of the other 99 machines there would be a similar unappetizing sight. Yet if we use our own case to extrapolate to the existence of other minds, we make a similar unwarranted leap from one observed sample.

The argument from analogy, thus, fails to justify our claim to know other minds exist. It is true that analogical reasoning is the only way for us to *understand* what other minds are *like*. To the extent that we cannot relate another creature's experience to something we have felt ourselves, we cannot even imagine what it is like to be that creature (Nagel, 1979, ch. 12). But this shows only that analogical reasoning enables us to *understand* the hypothesis that other minds exist, not that it *justifies* the hypothesis.

12. Knowledge of the External World

Philosophers use the term "external world" to mean "everything that exists outside my own mind." The part of the external world that philosophers care most about is *physical objects*, including their own bodies and the bodies of other persons. In questioning our knowledge of physical objects, skeptics may have a radical or even more radical question in mind. The radical question asks whether we can know what physical objects are like. The more radical question asks whether we can know that physical objects exist at all.

THE WEATHER VANE EXAMPLE

To appreciate the difficulty in answering these questions, we must discredit the naive answer: "I know that physical objects exist and what they are like because I *observe* them." We can show this answer is unsatisfactory by the *weather vane example*. Suppose we see a weather vane at the top of a building pointing east and conclude that the wind is blowing east. In doing so, we have assumed that the direction of the weather vane and the direction of the wind *covary*: The direction of the weather vane and the direction of the wind correspond so that the vane points in a certain direction if and only if the wind blows in that direction.

What would we say if we realized that the weather vane has been stuck in the same direction for five years? We would retract our claim to be able to determine the direction of the wind by looking at the weather vane. But what if the weather vane is stuck in one direction and we do not realize it? We would continue to assume that the weather vane indicates which way the wind is blowing, but we would be wrong. A weather vane that is going to say the same thing regardless of the direction of the wind cannot show which way the wind is blowing. Even those times when we use the stuck weather vane to conclude that the wind blows east and the wind does blow east, we still would not *know* that the wind blows east. We would be lucky if the wind happens to blow in the direction we believe it blows; but if our only evidence is the stuck weather vane, we lack knowledge because we lack evidence.

I generalize from the weather vane case to a general principle about evidence: *If any thing would tell us the same thing about the world, regardless of the way the world is, then that thing does not provide evidence for the way the world is.* This is a very commonsensical principle. For example, if a person who is careless about truth is going to tell you the same thing whether it is true or false, then that person's testimony is worthless. But *our senses* are going to tell us the same thing about physical objects—that they exist, have colors, sharp edges, and smooth surfaces—whether physical objects are that way or not. Therefore, our senses, by themselves, do not provide evidence regarding the nature of the physical objects.

Let us suppose that you *seem to be* in a classroom right now. That is, you have *classroom sensations*: It looks like a classroom, sounds like a classroom, and feels like a classroom. There are many possible explanations of how these sensations got in your mind. One explanation is that you *are* in a classroom that *is* approximately the way your sensations tell you the classroom is. Another explanation is that you are having a very vivid and unshakable dream of being in a classroom when you are really at home asleep. A third explanation is the skeptical hypothesis that you are a bodiless brain-in-a-vat who is being artificially stimulated to have the identical types of sensations that you would have if you were in a classroom. The point is that your sensations are going to tell you that you are in a classroom whether you are in a classroom, are dreaming that you are in a classroom, or are being artificially stimulated to simulate being in a classroom. In terms of our weather vane principle, your senses would tell you the same thing regardless of the way reality is, so your senses by themselves do not provide evidence about the way reality is.

Some persons find the weather vane example difficult to understand because they hold the *Magical Theory of Perception*. This view ignores the fact that we perceive physical objects only when we rely on a causal process. Instead, the Magical theory thinks that we "mix ourselves" with the physical objects and just know what they are like. Becuase it is unaware of the causal nature of perception, the Magical theory does not recognize general skeptical questions about our senses.

The problem with the Magical theory is that perception *is* a causal process that occurs only when physical objects affect our central nervous systems to produce sensations of (or beliefs about) physical objects. This *Causal Theory of Perception* recognizes that perception involves two entities, what is perceived and the perceiver. As soon as we realize that there are two entities at stake—the cause of our sensations and our sensations themselves—the question immediately arises whether the causes of our sensations resemble our sensations or not.

Some nonskeptics try to avoid this problem by saying that perception does not involve our having *sensations*, but only our acquiring *beliefs* that physical objects are a certain way. This move fails, however. First, even if we quit talking about sensations and talk only about beliefs, perception is still a causal process involving physical objects and perceivers' mental states. The skeptic simply amends the question to ask: Are our *beliefs* that physical objects exist and have colors, sharp edges, and smooth surfaces *made true* by physical objects that are this way?

Second, there are powerful reasons to think that all perception involves the having of sensations. Suppose you are stranded in the desert without water and begin to hallucinate. You look toward the East and see a real oasis, complete with a body of water and green foliage. You turn toward the West and you experience a mirage that is qualitatively indistinguishable from the real oasis. Because we stipulate that the state of your mind in each case is the same, you do not know which way you should travel to reach water. Now, when you face west and experience the mirage, you do not see a real oasis, but there is something sensuous that you experience. These are sensations. But what is in your mind when you face east is exactly like what is in your mind when you face west. Therefore, when you see the real oasis, you must also be experiencing sensations. The only difference is that your oasis-sensations are caused by the real oasis, and your mirage-sensations are caused by your dehydrated state. Generalizing from this example, it seems that whenever we perceive physical objects, we do so by being caused by the physical objects to have sensations. All perception involves having sensations.

VEIL OF SENSATIONS SKEPTICISM

Once we acknowledge the causal nature of perception, the issue of *Veil of Sensations Skepticism* arises. The problem is that our senses give us a familiar picture of the world, but we cannot tell from our senses whether that picture is accurate. Suppose that a piece of chalk really exists, and you wish to determine whether the color of the chalk itself matches the white chalk sensations you experience when you perceive the chalk. How can you find out whether the chalk itself is white as your sensations tell you or whether the chalk is another color, or perhaps no color at all? You cannot find this out by looking at the chalk, because looking at the chalk simply provides more white chalk sensations. No matter how near or far away you hold the chalk, every additional attempt to settle the question by looking at the chalk produces more chalk sensations; you never see whether the chalk itself matches your sensations. You cannot get outside your own mind and determine from a third perspective whether the chalk itself and your chalk sensations match or not. It will do no good to ask other persons, either, because at most you would find out only that *they* have white chalk sensations. But their white chalk sensations exist in *their* minds; you still have no way of finding out whether the chalk *itself* matches what is in their minds.

Consider Veil of Sensations Skepticism in terms of the different theories of the nature of the external world mentioned in the first chapter. Let us grant that most persons see chalk as white, spinach as green, bananas as yellow, and so on. Thus, our data are that most persons have white chalk, green spinach, and yellow banana sensations. Now which theory of the external world best explains these data? *Direct realism* explains the data by saying that the reason why we have these sensations is simply that chalk *is* white, spinach *is* green, and bananas *are* yellow. Now consider *scientific realism*, which holds that physical objects are almost entirely empty space with atoms and parts of atoms flying around at breakneck speeds. Scientific realists explain our sensations this way: When physical objects (which have no colors or sharp edges) affect our perceptual organs (which have no colors or sharp edges), the result in the minds of perceivers is sensations that appear colored and sharp edged, which do not match anything in the physical objects themselves. Finally, consider *phenomenalism*, which holds that no physical objects exist at all. According to phenomenalism, colored sensations in perceivers' nonphysical minds appear without being caused by colored physical objects—there *are no* physical objects. The Irish Bishop George Berkeley ('BAR KLEE) (1685–1753) thought that God places the sensations directly in our minds.

Each of these theories explains why we see the world as we do, but only direct realism holds that physical objects resemble our sensations. Even if direct realism is the theory that accurately describes the physical world, we cannot tell it is simply by observing the world. Observing the world provides only our sensations. For all anyone can tell by having sensations, scientific realism or phenomenalism might be true. If there is any chance, therefore, of *knowing* what physical objects themselves are like, we would have to provide some nonobservational, philosophical proof that one of the theories is *clearly* superior to all its competitors. In the next chapter, we shall see that this is extremely unlikely.

BERKELEY'S ALL-THE-REASON ARGUMENT

Here is a final way to appreciate skeptical arguments about knowledge of the external world. Bishop Berkeley was a nonskeptical phenomenalist who argued that *if* we believe in physical objects, we could never know they exist; but if we accept phenomenalism, we can vanquish skepticism. Here is what I call Berkeley's *all-the-reason argument*, designed to show that belief in physical objects is epistemically unreasonable:

> Suppose—what no one can deny possible—an intelligence, without the help of eternal bodies, to be affected with the same train of sensations or ideas that you are imprinted in the same order and with like vividness in his mind. I ask whether that intelligence hath not all the reason to believe the existence of Corporeal Substances . . . that you can possibly have for believing the same thing? Of this there can be no question. (Berkeley, 1965, Principle 20)

I interpret Berkeley's argument this way:

(1) Consider two minds that have exactly the same sensations, one whose sensations are caused by physical objects and the other that exists in a world that has no physical objects.
(2) The two minds would have exactly the same reason to believe that physical objects exist (because their sensations would be identical).

(3) The mind who receives sensations *not* caused by physical objects has no good reason to believe in physical objects.
(4) Therefore, by analogy, the mind who receives sensations from physical objects has no good reason to believe in physical objects.
(5) Therefore, even if there are physical objects, we have no good reason to believe in them.

13. The Problem of Induction

Induction is the reasoning process by which we take observed states of affairs to be evidence for unobserved states of affairs of the same type. The standard form of induction says that *if A's have always been observed to be followed by B's in the past, then A's probably will be followed by B's in the future*. Examples are our expectation that the sun will rise tomorrow because it has risen in the past, and our conclusion that because all objects thrown into the air have fallen toward Earth, the same will hold true of the next thrown object.

The *problem of induction* is raised by the skeptic who thinks that *our belief in induction is not epistemologically justified*. The skeptic admits that induction has held in the past and agrees that we ought to continue to use induction in our lives. Because our every act presupposes that the future will resemble the past, a call *to quit using induction* would be a call for us to quit acting altogether. (I would not type the next letter on my word processor if I thought that doing so might turn me into a beagle.) The skeptic's point regarding induction—as with the other issues in this chapter—concerns knowledge, not practice: Can we justify our belief that induction will hold in the future or at most do we have only a lucky true belief?

Here is a way to see the problem. Consider a covered, opaque jelly bean jar with a large paddle inside attached to an external crank that allows us to shuffle its contents. We blindfold ourselves, remove the lid, select a jelly bean from the jar, and then close the lid. We remove the blindfold, observe the color of the jelly bean, write it down, put the blindfold back on, return the jelly bean to the jar, and turn the paddle. Suppose we follow this procedure for 99 trials, and each time the jelly bean we remove is red. This would provide very strong evidence that the 100th jelly bean we select will also be red. Suppose, however, that we extract the 100th jelly bean not from the same jar from which we have extracted the first 99, but from a second jar. In that case we have no reliable way to figure out the probability that the jelly bean will be red. The 99 trials taken from the first jar would provide no evidence on what we should expect to extract from the second jar.

The skeptic regarding our knowledge of induction labels the first jelly bean jar "the past" and the second, unsampled jar "the future." According to the skeptic, our projection of the results from past experience to the future is just as unjustified as projecting the results from examining the first jelly bean jar to a conclusion about the second jar. After all, the future is like the unsampled, second jar in this way: We have no experience of it. When we try to support induction by experience, we find that the "supporting evidence" tells us only what happened in the past, not what will happen in the future.

Relying on the terminology introduced in section 2, Hume (1955) provides the classic statement of the problem of induction. For Hume there are only two kinds of statements, *Relations of Ideas* and *Matters of Fact*. If a statement is a *Relation of Ideas*, it is necessarily true or false and can be known to be true or false a priori, because it merely expresses a meaning connection between the terms in it. Now, the statement "The future will resemble the past" is *not* a Relation of Ideas. This means that "The future will resemble the past" is neither logically necessary, true by definition, nor a priori. Therefore, it must be a *Matter of Fact* statement. Now, matter of fact statements are logically contingent, synthetic, and—*if* justifiable at all—are justifiable only a posteriori. Therefore, *if* induction can be justified, it must be justifiable only after experience.

But obviously we can never justify a posteriori the statement that the future will resemble the past. Hume acknowledges that bread nourished us in the past. Hume says, though, that we cannot know a posteriori that bread will nourish us in the future, because a posteriori justification occurs only after experience, and the future can never be experienced. It follows that we can never justify our belief in induction.

INFERENCE TO THE BEST EXPLANATION

Induction (sometimes called "induction by enumeration") counts observed entities as evidence for unobserved entities *of the same type*. There is another reasoning device that is similar to induction, but is importantly different, already mentioned in chapters 1 and 2: *inference to the best explanation*. In inference to the best explanation we reason from observed instances of *one type of entity* to unobserved entities of *another type of entity*. The format is this: We generate competing explanations of *why* some data, which are accepted by all sides, are true. If one explanation is better than all competitors, then that explanation (theory) is most supported by the data.

Suppose you have one set of data, *d*, and two competing explanations for it, *Theory 1*, and *Theory 2*. If Theory 1 makes the data unsurprising, but Theory 2 makes the data surprising, then the data give more evidence for Theory 1 than they do Theory 2. (Sober, 1991, calls this the "surprise principle"). Consider an example taken from the design argument for the existence of God. Let *d* = "There is a watch lying in a field," let Theory 1 = "The watch was designed by a conscious being," and let Theory 2 = "The watch came to exist by accident." Theory 2 would make the data look more surprising than Theory 1 does; so, the data support Theory 1 more than Theory 2. This does not guarantee that

Theory 1 is true, because the data may turn out to be faulty, or other data might be collected that make Theory 1 less attractive than Theory 2. And sometimes even the more surprising explanation will be the true one. Nonetheless, inference to the best explanation is a powerful reasoning device that we use all the time.

Nonskeptics can use inference to the best explanation as an alternative to the Empiricist Criterion of Evidence examined in section 8. The Empiricist criterion held that one entity can be evidence for another only if: (1) the two things have been observed together (e.g., seeing dark clouds is evidence that it is going to rain); or (2) there is a definitional connection between them (e.g., knowing that Smith is married is evidence that Smith is not a bachelor). *Inference to the best explanation allows us to infer the existence of entities we have never seen at all, let alone never observed alongside the things we take to be evidence for them.* If we are to know the existence of theoretical entities in science—subatomic particles, Black Holes, the last ice age, the dinosaurs, or the Big Bang—then we can know them only because postulating them is useful in explanations. So nonskeptics who appeal to inference to the best explanation as a way to justify our knowledge seem to have the support of common sense and much of science. The nonskeptic can make this reply to the skeptic who relies on the Empiricist Criterion of Evidence: "Although I have never observed A's and B's together, the postulation of B's is the most plausible explanation of why A's exist. Because I realize this, I have evidence for saying that I *know* B's exist—without having ever seen them."

Here is how nonskeptics can use inference to the best explanation to reply to the four skeptical arguments considered above.

KNOWLEDGE OF OUR OWN MINDS?

Hume objected to Descartes's *cogito* in this way: "You have never seen *yourself*, but only particular mental states. So, you are not entitled to claim that you *know* that you exist as a consciousness that underlies the particular mental states you experience. For all anyone knows, all that 'you' are is a series of mental states—not a conscious mind that has those thoughts."

Descartes could have used inference to the best explanation in the following way. Although Hume's skeptical hypothesis proposing a series of mental states existing without a mind underlying them is *possible*, it is not very *plausible*. The hypothesis that we are minds that underlie and *have* mental states is a better explanation for the orderliness of mental states than the hypothesis that there is nothing underlying the series of states. For example, we might have a sensation of cold from eating ice cream, followed by a memory of a snowball fight we had with our brother ten years ago, followed by a wish that our brother not take the family car that night. If such a series of mental states occurs without belonging to a single mind, a puzzling question arises. Why do these mental states occur just as they would *if* there *were* a mind underlying them that associated one thought with another? In other words, why are they not completely jumbled, without any rhyme or reason? A supernatural answer will hardly do. An Evil Genius or God *could* order them, but what would be the motive? If there are no minds underlying the series of mental states, then there are no persons. If there are no persons, then a malevolent Evil Genius would have no one to delude, and God would have no subjects to test morally. But no natural explanation seems likely either. Therefore, if we use inference to the best explanation, it seems we can support Descartes's *cogito* over Hume's skeptical hypothesis.

KNOWLEDGE OF OTHER MINDS?

The argument from analogy fails to justify knowledge of other minds, because it makes a hasty generalization that relies on one sample in which we observe that mentality and behavior correspond (our own). The inductive base is too small to justify the generalization. Inference to the best explanation avoids that objection by citing facts (data) that can be better explained by the hypothesis that other minds exist than by the hypothesis that mine is the only mind. In other words, inference to the best explanation says: If other minds did *not* exist, how do you explain X? Posed this way, the question becomes: *Can we think of any data that would be better explained by the other-minds hypothesis than by the mine-is-the-only-mind hypothesis*?

Suppose you go to an alien planet. What sort of things could you discover that would justify your belief that beings with minds exist there? What about artifacts and technology? If you found tools or skyscrapers, then it would be a good bet that they were produced by other beings with minds. How about organized-looking behavior? This also would be reason to think that minded creatures exist, even if you could not figure out what the creatures were doing. An alien watching an American football game, with (as columnist George Will puts it) its rule-governed violence punctuated with brief committee meetings, would conclude that it reveals intelligent life. Whether on Earth or another planet, these are also powerful data: Another body producing noises in a language you understand that provides new information to you ("Watch out for that truck!"). Your ability to affect the behavior of other bodies by your speech ("Please pass the potatoes"). The existence of books, plays, computer programs, and musical compositions that you do not remember producing. The disciplines of mathematics, physics, and philosophy. All these cry out for an explanation in terms of mentality besides your own.

KNOWLEDGE OF THE EXTERNAL WORLD?

If we accept the Empiricist Criterion of Evidence cited in section 8, then Veil of Sensations Skepticism will not only prevent our knowing what physical objects are like, it will even prevent us from knowing whether they exist at all.

Because we can never get outside our own minds and compare physical objects with our sensations, we will never have observational evidence that physical objects correspond to our sensations. But if we use inference to the best explanation, the inability to compare physical objects and our sensations may prove not to prevent us from knowing that physical objects exist. Epistemologically, physical objects would be viewed as theoretical entities that we postulate to explain why we have the sensations we do, just as other minds are viewed as theoretical entities we postulate to explain the behavior of other bodies. The English empiricist John Locke (1632–1704) argued in this way, but his view was rejected by Berkeley and Hume, who thought that empiricists should not use inference to the best explanation regarding physical objects.

Consider again the problem of knowing whether realism or phenomenalism is true. *Realists say that our sensations are caused by physical objects existing in space and time*, whereas *phenomenalists deny that physical objects exist*. Both theorists think they can explain why we have the sensations we do. A familiar realist challenge to the phenomenalists is this: If physical objects do not cause our sensations, then how can you explain: (1) Why there is so much agreement between the sensations experienced by *different* minds? (various persons in a classroom hear and see the same things); and (2) Why the sensations from different sense modalities of the *same* individual agree? (I see an apple, feel an apple, and taste an apple.)

Phenomenalists either must reply that these are brute, inexplicable facts that must be accepted without further explanation, or must invoke a supernatural explanation. (Berkeley said that God directly causes our sensations.) But saying that the *interpersonal* (between persons) and *intrapersonal* (within the same person's different senses) agreement of our sensations is just a brute fact makes the data very surprising. It therefore seems to be a worse explanation than saying that physical objects cause the agreement. And to postulate God as the explanation in place of physical objects seems poor theory-construction strategy. The postulation is unnecessary for explaining our sensations, there are no independent grounds for making it, and it raises puzzling questions such as: Why would God want to do this? It seems, therefore, that realism is knowable and phenomenalism is not—*if* we believe that inference to the best explanation provides justification for our beliefs.

KNOWLEDGE OF INDUCTION?

The empiricist rejection of our claim to know induction depends on the irrefutable premise that we cannot collect a sample of the future and the questionable premise that knowing induction will hold requires observing the future. Both skeptics and nonskeptics agree on this much: *We have been able to predict PAST futures on the basis of PAST pasts.* They disagree whether this fact supports the claim that *knowing CURRENT pasts enables us to know what FU-*

TURE futures will be. A nonskeptic can use inference to the best explanation to argue that the fact that induction has held in the past is best explained by *the same fact* that shows that induction will hold in the future: the laws of nature.

Suppose our data are that all observed pieces of chalk that have been dropped in the past (without other forces acting on them) have fallen toward Earth. Two explanations might be offered. The first explanation is that all such pieces of chalk dropped in the past have followed an exceptionless law of nature (gravity) that holds for all pieces of chalk dropped under the same conditions in the past, present, and future. If we find this explanation the best, we can claim to know that similar pieces of chalk dropped in the future will also fall toward Earth. A second explanation is that although all observed dropped pieces of chalk have followed the law of gravity up until now, this law is going to change in the future. This explanation will not support a claim to know that chalk will fall in the future.

Both explanations are consistent with all the observed data, but the first explanation, which supports our knowledge of induction, seems better. The proponent of the second explanation will need to explain *why* we should believe that the law of gravity is going to change. The skeptic will need to constantly explain what there is about each new moment that gives us reason to think that the laws of nature that *have been constant* are going to change. It is not good enough to point out that the laws *could* change—we need a positive reason for thinking they *will* change.

Skeptics might respond that we do not *know* that the laws of nature that permit specific instances of induction to be successful will hold. If so, nonskeptics who rely on inference to the best explanation have a reply: "We *can* know that the laws of nature will hold. Applying our justified, true belief definition of 'knowledge,' we can know that the laws of nature will hold if and only if: (1) the laws of nature will hold, (2) we believe that the laws of nature will hold, and (3) we can justify our belief that the laws of nature will hold. Inference to the best explanation as just sketched provides the justification."

In sum, if all our carefully collected data have supported a generalization in some particular area, then inference to best explanation suggests it is plausible to think that at least *this* part of nature reveals a timeless law of nature. In this way nonskeptics can cite inference to the best explanation to justify their belief that induction will hold.

A CHALLENGE TO THE THEORY OF KNOWLEDGE

PROBLEMS WITH INFERENCE TO THE BEST EXPLANATION

Before we get too excited about using inference to the best explanation to answer the skeptical challenges, we should note some qualifications. First, using inference to the best explanation may open the door to epistemic laziness and even foolishness. Empiricists worry that once we claim to know things we cannot see, we have set ourselves on a slippery slope that will allow us to claim to know the existence of intangible gremlins and fairies and the inscrutable powers of ESP and pyramids. The British philosopher Bertrand Russell (1872–1970) said that postulating unobservable entities has all the advantages of theft over honest toil.

Second, even if we allow ourselves to use inference to the best explanation, it is often unclear in specific cases what explanation is the best. The question of what constitutes a good explanation is one of the most difficult questions in the philosophy of science.

Third, using inference to the best explanation to address the skeptic has limitations. If we try to use inference to the best explanation to show that we know that other minds exists, it may prove only that one mind besides my mind exists. Technology, language, and books may justify the belief that there is *some* other mind, but these data could all have been constructed by one mind, for example, Descartes's Evil Genius. Proving one mind per body is more difficult. Regarding knowledge of the external world, if we claim that inference to the best explanation enables us to know that realism is true rather than phenomenalism, we still will not know *which* variety of realism is most plausible, e.g., direct realism or scientific realism. So, even if inference to the best explanation allows us to know *that* physical objects exist, it may not enable us to know *what they are like.*

Fourth, we need to remember that inference to the best explanation can show (at most) that the nonskeptic is more likely to be correct than the skeptic—*relative to the other things we think are true.* No theory is ever a better theory than any other in isolation from all other facts, but depends on the truth of other facts, including the assumed data. If we are massively deluded about what is true, as we would be if Descartes's Evil Genius fools us, then we cannot tell which is the best explanation for our experiences. Imagine how foolish we would appear to the Evil Genius if we try to use inference to the best explanation to prove that induction will hold in the future!

THE SUBJECTIVITY OF "KNOWLEDGE"

The question remains: Are the resources of inference to the best explanation powerful enough to show that we really have *knowledge*? When a debate depends this much on inflecting a word, we need to return to basics. What exactly do we mean by "knowledge"? Nonskeptics have to admit that even if the existence of our minds, other minds, physical objects, and uniformity in nature are better explanations for the observed data up to now, it is logically possible that these things do not exist at all or are very different than we think they are. (Some contemporary philosophers try to show that skeptical hypotheses are logically impossible, but I believe these attempts fail.) So, does the logical possibility that the skeptical hypotheses are true undermine knowledge? The answer seems to be: *It all depends on what you mean by "knowledge."*

There are two reasons to doubt whether there can be a single, correct definition of "knowledge." First, we apply many possible meanings to the propositional sense of "know." Peter Unger (1975) argues: (1) we cannot know any proposition we are not certain of; and (2) we cannot be certain of any proposition if there is another proposition we are *more* certain of. According to Unger, "certain" is an absolute word like the word "flat." If any physical object (B) is flatter than some physical object (A), then (A) cannot really be *flat*. Likewise, if any of our beliefs is more certain than another of our beliefs, then that latter belief is not *certain*. Accordingly, the only beliefs we are certain of are beliefs about which we are supremely certain. On this view of knowledge, we can know very little.

On the other extreme, psychologists and researchers in artificial intelligence often use "knowledge" to mean "true belief" when they talk about a person's or computer's "knowledge base." According to this usage, knowledge is plentiful. Other thinkers lie somewhere in the middle. Plato thought that knowledge requires that knowers be able to state an explanation; this position gave support to the justified, true belief notion of "knowledge." But philosophers who endorse the causal definition of "knowledge" do not think that knowers need to be able to give such explanations, requiring only that our true beliefs be caused by reliable mechanisms to be knowledge.

Given this spectrum of ways of looking at propositional knowledge, it is unlikely that any one definition is the "right" one to use to settle the debate between the skeptics and nonskeptics. If there is not one uniquely correct definition of "knowledge," then we cannot say that either the skeptics or nonskeptics are right. Instead, we would be forced to relativize our view by saying, "If you mean by 'knowledge' definition 1, then skepticism is right, and if you mean by 'knowledge' definition 2, then nonskepticism is right, and so on."

Here is the second difficulty. "Knowledge" and "justification" are evaluative words. To ask whether persons have knowledge is to ask whether their justification for their beliefs is *good enough* to merit the positive word "knowledge." This is no less an evaluative question than the question whether a work of art is beautiful or whether an action is morally right. Persons who agree on all the facts of the matter could still disagree on the evaluations they make. This raises the issue of *subjectivism*, the view that *there are no objectively right or wrong evaluations, but only our subjective opinions*. I discuss subjectivism in the metaethics chapter.

If our decisions on which justifications are good enough for knowledge are subjective, then *no one definition* of "knowledge" can be correct. If so, the debates between the skeptics and the nonskeptics cannot be answered. Those debates have an answer only if there is one correct definition of knowledge that specifies the degree of justification required for our true beliefs to count as knowledge.

WHAT IS IMPORTANT

In my view, the important thing in the theory of knowledge is that we understand the relevant facts: (1) Not all reasons why persons hold beliefs are *epistemic* reasons that increase the probability that our beliefs are true. (2) Good epistemic agents try to accept only justified beliefs. (3) Perception is a causal process that may or may not yield knowledge; it is not a magical source of knowledge. (4) For any perceptual belief, there are many possible explanations for why we have that belief. (5) Skeptical hypotheses—e.g., Descartes's Evil Genius, the brain-in-a-vat, Hume's no-minds theory, and Hume's hypothesis that the world might cease to follow the patterns it has followed up to now—are logically possible. (6) Whether we are skeptics or nonskeptics depends on whether we adopt stringent or more liberal standards of evidence. (7) The standards of evidence we use depend on what we mean by "knowledge."

Once we get these facts straight—which can be appreciated without having to make the decision on whether knowledge requires stringent or liberal standards of evidence—our verdict on whether we have knowledge is unimportant. For example, we do not have to worry about whether we *really know* that we are not brains-in-vats, once we recognize that the brain-in-a-vat hypothesis is logically possible, but that it is a worse explanation than the brain-in-our-body theory—*if* most of our other beliefs about the world are true.

What is more important than quarreling over the word "know" is that we improve our epistemic agency through careful attention to whether our beliefs are justified. None of us is a perfect epistemic agent. We all need to work on our abilities to apply sound logical, mathematical, and scientific methods. Epistemology is a subject for study; improving our epistemic agency is a lifelong vocation.

Misconceptions about the Theory of Knowledge

Each of the following is a possible confusion about the theory of knowledge. Explain why each is a mistake.

1. The primary question in the theory of knowledge is whether our beliefs are true or false.
2. A true belief is a belief that a person holds with strong conviction.
3. Skeptics say that the propositions we do not know are false.
4. The issue raised by Veil of Sensations Skepticism is that our senses are often unreliable.

5. The problem with knowing whether *we* have minds is that we cannot see our own brains.
6. The problem with knowing whether *other persons* have minds is that we cannot see their brains.
7. The problem with knowing that *other persons* have minds is that minds are nonphysical souls.
8. Hume believes that the statement "The future will resemble the past" is a relation of ideas.
9. Inference to the best explanation settles the skeptical problems about minds, the external world, and induction.

Guide Questions

1. What is the difference between the theory of knowledge and metaphysics? (40)
2. What does it mean to provide a list of conditions for some concept that is *individually necessary and jointly sufficient*? (41)
3. What problem arises if we define "knowledge" as "true belief"? (41–42)
4. Explain in one sentence the justified, true belief definition of "knowledge." (42) The causal definition of "knowledge." (43)
5. What is the difference between a priori and a posteriori justification? (43–44)
6. What is the difference between analytic and synthetic statements? (44–45)
7. What is the difference between logically necessary and logically contingent statements? (45)
8. Provide two meanings to the question "Why does Smith believe statement *s*?" (46)
9. What is the difference between epistemic reasons for a belief and nonepistemic reasons for a belief? (46)
10. Define "cognitive dissonance." (47)
11. What does it mean to say "One of the most threatening questions we can ask ourselves is whether our beliefs are justified"? (48)
12. How does a good epistemic temperament differ from a poor epistemic temperament? (49)
13. Describe the intrinsic and extrinsic reasons for wanting to justify our beliefs. (49–50)
14. Which condition in the justified, true belief definition of "knowledge" does the skeptic usually claim is not met? Why does the skeptic pick this condition rather than either of the others? (50–51)
15. What point is the brain-in-a-vat example designed to show? (51)
16. Express in your own words Hume's Empiricist Criterion of Evidence. (52–53)
17. Describe Descartes's Evil Genius hypothesis. (53)

18. How does Descartes reason that even if the Evil Genius exists, he can still know that he exists? (54–55)
19. How can Hume's point be used to reject Descartes's claim to be certain that he exists? (55)
20. Why can we not tell by observation that other persons have minds if their minds are nonphysical? Why can we not tell by observation that other persons have minds if their minds are their brains? (56)
21. What is the crucial weakness in using the argument from analogy to try to know that other minds exist? (56)
22. Explain in two sentences the point of the weather vane example for the problem of skepticism. (57–58)
23. As philosophers use the term, what does "sensation" mean? (58)
24. What is Veil of Sensations Skepticism? (59–60)
25. Express Berkeley's all-the-reason argument in two sentences. (60–61)
26. Explain the problem of induction using the jelly bean jar analogy. (61–62)
27. There is one crucial difference between induction by enumeration and inference to the best explanation. What is it? (62)
28. How might someone use inference to the best explanation to argue that we know we have minds? (63–64)
29. How might someone use inference to the best explanation to argue that we know other minds exist? (64)
30. How might someone use inference to the best explanation to argue that we know the external world exists? (64–65)
31. How might someone use inference to the best explanation to argue that we know that induction will hold in the future? (65–66)
32. What are some objections to trying to use inference to the best explanation to answer the skeptical objections regarding minds, the external world, and induction? (66–67)
33. What problem is created by the fact that there are several different definitions of "knowledge"? (68)
34. What problem is created by the fact that "justification" is an evaluative word? (68–69)

Review Questions for Examinations

1. Define: "propositional knowledge," "true belief," "justification," "justified, true belief definition of knowledge," "causal definition of knowledge," "epistemic reason for a belief," "nonepistemic reason for a belief," "skepticism," "skeptical hypothesis," "the principle of deductive closure," "empiricist," "Empiricist Criterion of Evidence," "Matters of Fact," "Relations of Ideas," "the argument from analogy," "external world," "Magical Theory of Perception," "Causal Theory of Perception," "induction," "problem of induction," "inference to the best explanation."

2. Using the concepts "a priori"/"a posteriori," "analytic"/"synthetic," and "logically necessary"/"logically contingent," classify the following statements:
   (a) "Gambling is legal in Alabama."
   (b) "If gambling is legal in Alabama, then gambling or driving while drunk is legal in Alabama."
   (c) "California has fewer residents than Rhode Island."
   (d) "If California has fewer residents than Rhode Island, then Rhode Island has more residents than California."
   (e) "The most widely used word that refers (in English) to dogs begins with 'd.' "
   (f) "2 + 2 = 5."
   (g) "Past regularities will hold in the future."
3. In terms of cognitive skills and temperament, what does it take to be a good epistemic agent?
4. Cite several reasons why persons display poor epistemic agency.
5. Provide at least *one* argument for skepticism concerning our knowledge of: our own minds, other minds, the external world, induction. Be sure you can describe at least *one* reason for thinking we have knowledge in these four cases.

Discussion Questions

1. How might having good epistemic skills be helpful? Are there any ways that being a *poor* epistemic agent could be helpful?
2. "Justifying one's beliefs does not guarantee that they are true. Moreover, one can have true beliefs just by guessing. So, having justification is not so important." Do you find this a good argument? Explain.
3. Two famous skeptical hypotheses are Descartes's Evil Genius and the brain-in-a-vat. Does either thought experiment make doubtful more of our everyday beliefs than the other? Explain.
4. If we adopt a causal definition of "knowledge" we might be able to devise a reply to Descartes's Evil Genius hypothesis. Explain how that reply would go. How might the skeptical defender of Descartes's hypothesis respond?
5. (a) Is it better to hold unjustified beliefs that make us happy or justified beliefs that make us sad? (b) What criterion should we use to decide this question?
6. Peter Unger gives the following analysis of a famous argument offered by the nonskeptic G. E. Moore. I call this sort of example "one person's modus ponens is another person's modus tollens." The modus tollens argument from the skeptic is: "(1) If I know I have a hand, then I know there is no Evil Genius deceiving me into falsely believing I have a hand. (2) Not (I know there is no Evil Genius deceiving me into falsely believing I have a hand).

(3) Therefore, not (I know I have a hand.)" The modus ponens argument of the nonskeptic Moore is: "(a) If I know I have a hand, then I know there is no Evil Genius deceiving me into falsely believing I have a hand. (b) I know I have a hand. (c) Therefore, I know there is no Evil Genius deceiving me into falsely believing I have a hand."

Question: Which argument is better? Why?

7. Generally speaking, is it better to have one belief that we know or two beliefs that are true but that we do not know?

FOR FURTHER READING

Baergen, Ralph. 1995. *Contemporary Epistemology*. Fort Worth, TX: Harcourt Brace. A clearly written introductory survey of the main issues in the theory of knowledge. Moderately difficult.

Chisholm, Roderick. 1989. *Theory of Knowledge*. Englewood Cliffs NJ: Prentice-Hall. The definitive introductory monograph on epistemology. Short and easy to read.

Descartes, René. 1972. *Meditations*. In *The Philosophical Works of Descartes*. Especially Meditations 1 and 2. Cambridge: Cambridge University Press. A classic expression of skepticism and one way to try to answer it. Moderately difficult.

Hume, David. 1955. *An Enquiry Concerning Human Understanding*. Indianapolis: Bobbs-Merrill. A forceful short work by philosophy's foremost skeptic. Difficult.

Moser, Paul and Arnold vander Nat, eds. 1995. *Human Knowledge: Classical and Contemporary Approaches*. New York: Oxford University Press. Excellent anthology. Difficult.

Nisbett, Richard and Lee Ross. 1980. *Human Inference: Its Scope and Limits*. Englewood Cliffs, NJ: Prentice-Hall. A famous survey of psychological research on human cognitive failures. Absolutely brilliant. Moderately difficult.

Zimbardo, Philip and Michael Leippe. 1991. *The Psychology of Attitude Change and Social Influence*. New York: McGraw-Hill. A fascinating, readable survey of psychological research on how persons can be persuaded to change their attitudes, beliefs, and behavior through nonepistemic means.

Chapter 4
The Nature of the External World

INTRODUCTION

Everything that exists is either inside minds (thinking things) or outside minds. Things existing inside minds include ideas, mental images, beliefs, desires, emotions, and sensations. Accordingly, our *idea of George Washington* exists in our minds, even though *George Washington, the person*, no longer exists. The idea of Superman exists in our minds, although there never was such a person. Common sense assumes that atoms, trees, tables, human bodies, continents, and solar systems are physical objects that exist outside minds. Thus, common sense holds that carbon atoms, oak trees, and Antarctica would exist even if no one ever had ideas, beliefs, emotions, or sensations of them. Philosophers question these assumptions. The problem of the nature of the external world is: Which apparent characteristics of physical objects exist only inside minds? Which characteristics exist in physical objects themselves outside minds?

1. Key Terms

For each individual, the *external world* is *everything that exists outside that individual's mind*. According to this definition, the external world for me consists of ordinary physical objects—including my own body—but also the minds of other persons and God. But physical objects are the part of the external world that philosophers care most about in the problem of the external world. If *physical objects* exist, then they are *entities that exist in space and time*. The question philosophers ask about trees and tables and continents is: *Which types of the apparent characteristics of physical objects really exist in the physical objects and which exist only in our minds*? This question can be expressed using the concepts of "appearance" and "reality": *To what degree, if any, does the reality of physical objects match their appearance in perceivers' minds*? The possible answers to this question range from "There is an exact match" to "There is a partial match" to "There *are no* physical objects to match our ideas."

Another way to understand the problem of the nature of the external world is by using the concepts "objective" and "subjective." As used in this problem, *to be objective* is *to exist in itself and not exist merely in anyone's perception*. To use a previous example, common sense believes that Antarctica would exist even if no one had ever discovered it. We ordinarily think that continents are objective entities that exist without anyone having to have ideas or sensations of them.

The concept "subjective" is ambiguous, and this ambiguity sometimes causes confusion. According to the first meaning, which we shall use in this chapter, *to be subjective* is *to exist only in the mind of a thinking or perceiving subject*. So we normally think that pains and mirages are subjective in this first sense: Once our minds quit experiencing them, they do not exist. Here are some examples of things that common sense takes to be objective and subjective in the first defined sense:

OBJECTIVE	SUBJECTIVE
Bill Clinton	our idea of Bill Clinton
a hot stove	a sensation of the warmth of a hot stove
a pizza	our fondness for the flavor of pizza
a pit bull	our fear of pit bulls

The second meaning of "subjective" is "idiosyncratic, peculiar, or in the minority opinion." An example would be "It is *not* just my subjective opinion that Hitler was evil." In this second sense, a person's psychological state is subjective if it is different from those of most other persons. It is important to see that although things that are subjective in the first sense *may* be subjective in the second, they *need not be*. For example, the sensation of pain we receive from touching an open flame is subjective in the first sense, but is not subjective in the second sense. If 100 persons with normal nervous systems place their bare hands in an open flame, all 100 will feel the subjective sensation of pain. Therefore, sensations may be both *subjective* (in the sense of existing only in our minds), but *not subjective* (not idiosyncratic). Some mental states are both subjective to the individuals who have them, but universally (or almost universally) felt by individuals.

A natural question to ask is whether an entity is *more real* if it is objective or subjective. On the one hand, anything that exists—whether in minds or outside minds—exists *somewhere*. My *idea* of Bill Clinton exists only so long as I think it; but while I am thinking of the idea, it exists as an idea. The *person* Bill Clinton exists outside my mind whether I think of him or not. Therefore, *both* ideas and the real things that the ideas represent in the external world exist. On the other hand, it is important to decide whether an entity exists in the external world or whether we only have ideas about it in our minds. In everyday life, when we say that something exists, we do not mean to say only that we have an idea of it, but that the entity has *its own* objective existence. In this sense, objective things have "more existence" than subjective ideas in our minds. Which, for example, has more being: $100 in your pocket or $100 imaginary dollars in your mind? Would you rather exist as a person in your own right or exist merely as a figment of someone's imagination? There is no contest here, because if "you" exist only as part of someone else's imagination, then there is no *you* at all. If all there is to "you" is an idea in someone else's mind, then *his or her idea* is a real thing, but it belongs to that person, not you.

This is not to diminish the importance of subjective things to the persons who feel or think them. First, in our everyday lives, pleasure and pain are two of the most important motivators of behavior, not to mention our beliefs, desires, values, and emotions. Conscious mental states constitute the subject matter of much of psychology and literature. Abstract ideas such as the ideas of freedom and equality have influenced the course of history. Second, wherever there are subjective states that are widely shared, we need some explanation for why so many persons share those states. The fact that anesthesiology is a science shows that the nervous systems of humans share important similarities. The fact that most human beings think that cruelty is wrong needs an explanation in terms of heredity, environment, or a combination of both. Things that exist only in our minds are *important*—they simply are *not* part of our external world.

2. Entry Routes into the Problem

Does the external world match the way it appears? This would be a sensible question even if no one ever thought to ask it, but some everyday facts make us aware of it. First, we are routinely reminded that not all characteristics that seem to exist in physical objects can really be in them. When a flash bulb in a camera goes off, for a few seconds we "see" white spots in our visual field that we realize are not part of the physical objects in front of us. If we plunge our hands into a bucket of warm water after having our left hand in ice water and our right hand in hot water, the warm water will feel hot to the left hand and cold to the right. But we do not think that *the water itself* is both hot and cold. The same food that tastes good when we are healthy may seem tasteless when we are sick. Railroad tracks appear to converge in the distance, although we know that they do not. A straight stick placed in a glass of water appears bent. These and countless other examples suggest that appearance and reality sometimes differ.

Second, our appreciation for the problem of the external world is heightened when we consider the causal nature of perception. Perception via any sense—sight, touch, hearing, taste, or odor—occurs only after the external world affects our minds. For example, we see physical objects only after light reflecting off the surfaces of physical objects affects our eyes and produces visual experiences in our minds. This guarantees that sight always involves a time gap that depends on the speed of light and the speed at which we process the light that affects us. If the sun had exploded five minutes ago, we would not yet be aware of it. Moreover, human perceptual systems are capable of detecting only partial ranges of wave lengths of light and sound waves. This raises the question of whether the light and sound waves that we can recognize are accurate to the true nature of physical objects or whether we are receiving only a misleading part of the story. Perhaps creatures with different perceptual systems more accurately detect the real nature of physical objects.

3. Why the Problem Cannot Be Solved by Observation

In the discussion of Veil of Sensations Skepticism in chapter 3, I argued that we cannot *know* what the external world is like by observing or sensing it. Each time we try to find out what the external world is like by having sense experiences, we simply collect more sensations in our own minds—on the inside of the veil. We are never able to step outside our minds and see whether our sensations and the physical objects (if they exist) match, because we can never adopt a perspective outside our own minds from which to perform the comparison. For the same reason, we cannot answer the question of what the external world *is like* by looking, touching, hearing, smelling, or tasting. Physical objects may or may not match our sensations, but we can never find out by examining our sensations. If we are to address the issue at all, we must do so by constructing philosophical arguments that try to show one answer is better than the others.

It is sometimes suggested that one can tell what the characteristics of physical objects are by asking other persons what *they* perceive. This will not work, because at most this shows that other persons have sensations that are similar to one's own. The problem is that other persons are no more able to tell whether physical objects match *their* sensations than you are. For example, if grass seems to be green to humans, that would be a fact about human perceptual systems; it does not prove that grass itself is green. We might arrive at a consensus about humanity's subjective *sensations*, but we would not thereby establish that *grass itself* is green.

Similarly, it will do no good to say that we can settle the question of the nature of the external world by taking a *photograph*. A photograph is only one more thing that *looks colored*. The sensation of color that we receive from looking at the photograph may or may not match the photograph itself. So looking at a photograph provides no more proof that physical objects match our sensations than does looking at other physical objects.

4. Wider Applications

The problem of the nature of the external world stands on its own as one of the major philosophical problems. "What is real?" may be the most basic philosophical problem of all. We think that small children who think that pain exists *in* the hot stove, waiting for them to unwarily touch it, are quaintly mistaken. We would like to think that *we* are not likewise mistaken when we assume that we know what physical objects are like—when we think that physical objects have colors, shapes, sharp edges, and exist in space. We shall see that there are powerful reasons for questioning the assumption that *any* of the apparent characteristics of physical objects are really in physical objects. These reasons are not very different from the reasons we would give the children to correct their mistake about hot stoves.

Beyond the philosophical question about the nature of the external world, it is important to decide in everyday life whether a characteristic is objective or subjective. First, we need to determine whether persons are *claiming* that appearance or reality is a certain way. We are correct to grant more readily persons' claims to know how subjective things *seem* to them than we grant their claims that objective things *are* a certain way. For example, we accept persons' subjective claims to *seem* to see space aliens much more readily than we accept their objective claims to *really see* space aliens.

Second, if a characteristic is merely subjective, then there is often little point in disputing it. For example, it would be foolish for two persons to quarrel over whether peas *really* taste good or whether the Three Stooges *really* are funny. Whether a food tastes good or whether some comics are funny is a merely subjective characteristic in the first defined sense of existing only in us. The fact that other persons may share your subjective opinion does not change its subjectivity in the first sense. On the other hand, if a characteristic is objective, then it makes sense to debate it, even if we cannot know what the correct answer is. To take two examples from chapter 1: What was the cause of the American

Civil War? Will the known universe continue to expand or will it contract on itself?

The distinction between subjective and objective characteristics is also vital to *aesthetics* (the *philosophical examination of art and beauty*). At the expense of some oversimplification, there are two main views of beauty: subjectivism and objectivism. *Aesthetic subjectivists* think that beauty exists only "in the eye of the beholder" and that the beauty of nature or a work of art is not a characteristic of the object itself. For example, when we have the experience we call "seeing a beautiful painting" the following happens: The painting, which itself (objectively) is neither beautiful nor ugly, causes in us a subjective emotional reaction that we mistakenly take to be the characteristic of beauty existing objectively in the painting itself. (The aesthetic subjectivist George Santayana (1863–1952) wrote a famous book called *The Sense of Beauty*.) *Aesthetic objectivists* think that aesthetic characteristics are real qualities of objects that we recognize. So, the beauty of a painting is just as real as the colors of the paints spread on its canvas, although it may require a sophisticated observer to be able to recognize it.

The same debate between subjectivism and objectivism occurs in *metaethics*, the *branch of philosophy in which philosophers ask about the objectivity of our value judgments concerning right and wrong and intrinsic value*. *Moral objectivists* say that the characteristics of moral rightness and wrongness exist in human actions, irrespective of how anyone feels about those actions. Just as everyone could be mistaken about the shape of the earth, so actions could be right even if everyone thought that they are wrong, and actions could be wrong even if everyone thought they are right. *Moral subjectivists* think that rightness and wrongness are not real characteristics of actions, but are only our subjective feelings and opinions about the actions. According to subjectivists, the fact that we have widely shared sentiments about human actions is an important fact about human beings and normative ethics, but it is nonetheless a fact about *our* feelings.

Besides aesthetics and metaethics, the distinction between subjectivism and objectivism is also important in discussing the theory of knowledge (chapter 3) and the free will problem (chapter 8). Having a solid grasp of the debate over the nature of the external world is a great help in understanding many areas of philosophy.

5. A Preview of Three Main Theories and a Fourth

The problem of the nature of the external world asks which apparent characteristics of physical objects really exist in them and which exist only in us. To make the point more vivid, think of some of the different types of characteristics this book seems to have:

> *Category I*: This book appears to have a color. If you flip its pages, you will hear a sound. If you are daring enough to try to taste it, it does not taste too great. Probably, it has only a faint odor. Category I characteristics are sometimes called "secondary qualities." *Category II*: The book appears to have a degree of solidity, to have a shape, a size, a texture, and to be either in motion or at rest. It also has a definite number (one). *Category III*: If you think about physics, although the book does not *appear* to possess atoms consisting of sub-atomic particles flying around in mostly empty space, you probably believe that it has them. *Category IV*: The book seems to be *extended*, that is, *spread out in three-dimensional space*. In philosophical terms, it seems to be an extended physical object existing objectively in the spatio-temporal (space/time) world.

The competing theories in the problem of the external world disagree over which of these four types of characteristics physical objects really possess. The first theory is *Direct (Commonsense, Naive) Realism*. According to this theory, physical objects exist in the external world and possess all the types of characteristics listed in Categories I through IV. Direct realists believe that physical objects have, for example, colors (Category I), shapes (Category II), they are comprised of atoms flying around in empty space (Category III), and they are extended in physical space (Category IV). Direct realists admit that we are sometimes wrong about which *specific* characteristics a physical object has. Red objects may look gray to color-blind persons, and square towers may look round from a distance. Direct realists do not even have to say that perception gives us *any* accurate information about most of the characteristics of physical objects. Because direct realism is a *metaphysical theory about the nature of the external world*, rather than a *theory about our knowledge of the external world*, direct realists do not have to address the question of knowledge. Direct realists are concerned to argue that physical objects *have* characteristics in all four categories, whether we *know* exactly which ones they have or not.

The second theory, *Scientific (Critical) Realism*, agrees that physical objects exist in space, but think that they lack all the Category I characteristics and many of the Category II characteristics. The fifth-century B.C. Greek atomist philosophers such as Democritus (DEM 'MOCK CRITTUS) and Leucippus (LOU 'KIP ISS) and the seventeenth- and eighteenth-century scientists such as Galileo and Newton thought that physical objects were comprised of tiny, indivisible atoms or nuggets of matter that lack the Category I characteristics of color, sound, odor, and taste. (The word "atom" derives from the Greek word meaning "not divisible.") According to these early scientific realists, physical objects are collections of atoms that have the Category II characteristics of solidity, size, shape, and texture, which cause in the minds of perceivers illusions of Category I characteristics.

The physicists of the twentieth century replaced the conception of atoms as indivisible nuggets of matter with the solar system model of the atom, according to which there are no solid pieces at all, but a bizarre combination of mass and energy that defies easy description. According to the twentieth-century view, atoms lack many of the Category II characteristics that the earlier scientific realists ascribed to the atoms, such as definite shapes, solidity, and texture. According to contemporary scientific realists, once we understand the Category III characteristics of atoms, we have to surrender many of our ideas about physical objects possessing Category I and II characteristics.

The third main theory, *Phenomenalism* (*Idealism*), denies the existence of physical objects altogether. According to phenomenalists, physical objects themselves possess none of the characteristics from the four categories. Phenomenalists believe that there is no physical space at all and there can be no physical objects existing in physical space to be comprised of atoms and have shapes, textures, colors, or odors. According to phenomenalists, all that exist are nonphysical minds and their mental contents—sensations, thoughts, beliefs, desires, and so on. If phenomenalists are theists, they take God to be a supreme nonphysical mind. Although not widely held these days, phenomenalism was widely accepted by philosophers in the nineteenth and early twentieth centuries.

Finally, *solipsism* ('sol lip sism) is the view that *the only things that exist are one's own nonphysical mind and its contents*. Solipsism is seldom presented as an alternative to the three major theories, but is used instead as an example of where we end up when we deny physical objects exist. Phenomenalists are sometimes attacked by the *reductio ad absurdum* argument that their theory leads to solipsism.

6. Theories of Perception versus Theories of the External World

To consider the various theories of perception that the realists and phenomenalists might hold, we need to recall from chapter 3 the philosophical concept of "sensation" (sometimes called "sense-datum" or "sensum"). *Sensations* are *conscious mental entities that come into existence in the last step of perception of the external world*. Sensations are those sensuous experiences that perception has in common with dreams and mental imagery. For example, if we see a red apple, we do so by having a red sensation caused in us by the red apple. If we touch a solid table, we are caused to receive sensations of solidity by the solid table.

In the philosophy of perception and the philosophy of mind there is a controversy over whether sensations should be understood to be *objectified mental things* or *nonobjectified events*. The first view takes sensations to be mental objects—little snapshots in the mind—which are themselves capable of having characteristics. For example, an objectified sensation of a speckled hen might have the characteristic of possessing forty speckles. The second view, which is called the "adverbial theory of sensations," takes sensations to be sensory processes, but not objectified things. According to this view, when we see a speckled hen we do *not* have an objectified image in our minds of a speckled hen with a certain number of speckles. Instead, there is only a process or event happening to us that we might use adverbs to call "sensing-speckled-hen-ly." According to the adverbial theorists, there exists no mental image of a speckled hen in our minds, although we mistakenly *think* there is.

The objectified account seems more accurate to the way our sensations seem to us, but the adverbial account seems to make perception easier to understand and easier to fit into a materialistic theory of the mind. For our purposes in this chapter, we do not need to decide between these two competitors. This debate is a technical one in the philosophy of perception and philosophy of mind that goes beyond the problem of the nature of the external world. We shall look at that issue in the next chapter.

There is a third competitor in the theory of perception that we also examined in chapter 3: the *belief-acquisition account of perception*. According to this account, we do not perceive physical objects by having sensations at all. Instead, *accurate perception occurs when physical objects cause us to have true beliefs about the characteristics they really have.* For example, we do not perceive a red apple by having red sensations. Instead, we perceive a red apple when a red apple causes us (via the transmission of light to our nervous systems) to acquire the belief that the apple is red. The belief-acquisition theory of perception is also supported on the grounds that it makes adopting a materialist theory of the mind (Armstrong, 1968) easier. But like the dispute over the objectified vs. adverbial interpretation of sensations, the belief-acquisition theory is not crucial for the problem of the nature of the external world.

There is a final alternative regarding theories of perception. Realists or phenomenalists might refuse to offer *any* account of how perception occurs, and still insist that their theory of the external world is correct. For example, direct realists can say that physical objects really possess all the kinds of characteristics common sense thinks they have: We just know what physical objects are like by observing them, and that's the end of it. In chapter 3 we called this the "magical theory of perception." Although the magical theory of perception is weak from the standpoint of theory of knowledge, that fact is not directly relevant to the problem of the nature of the external world.

The upshot is that realists can hold at least four theories of perception to go along with their metaphysical theory: Perception occurs as having objectified sensations, as adverbial sensing events, as belief-acquisitions, or as a magical process. Phenomenalists also can choose among the first three theories of perception, although they need to be careful how they state their views to avoid presupposing the real existence of physical objects. We shall not address these theories of perception, but direct our attention to the competing metaphysical theories of direct realism, scientific realism, and phenomenalism.

DIRECT REALISM

Direct realism claims that physical objects possess all the characteristics from Categories I–IV. Although physical objects may not match our sensations of them exactly (perhaps only the Alpha Centurions perceive physical objects the way they really are), physical objects possess the *types* of characteristics we observe them to have.

7. Arguments for Direct Realism

Historically, direct realists have offered few positive arguments for their theory, relying instead on attacking the arguments of the scientific realists and phenomenalists. From a debater's point of view, it is good strategy to convince your opponents that the burden of proof lies on them to prove their theories, and that you do not need to prove yours. I have claimed that philosophers can never successfully prove *any* controversial theory. If this is true, then if philosophers can get their opponents to believe that they must prove their views, they have "won" the debate. But such easy victories are unsatisfying—if one realizes that one has not really won. In this chapter, we shall look at what can be said for each theory, without assuming that any theory has a head start over the rest. This approach follows the metaphilosophical position used throughout this book.

So what can be said in behalf of direct realism? First, it is widely endorsed by common sense. Most persons—at least when they do not think about the causal nature of perception—accept direct realism's view that physical objects have all the types of characteristics they seem to have. If you think that philosophy should support, or, at least not disagree with, common sense, this will seem a strong reason to accept direct realism.

Second, when compared to scientific realism and phenomenalism, direct realism may seem to be a simpler theory, and, generally, we think that simple theories are more likely to be true than complicated theories. Against the phenomenalists, direct realism gives a simple explanation of why we observe the world as we do: Physical objects really *are* that way. Against the scientific realists, the direct realists do not have to explain how physical objects lacking in commonsense characteristics such as colors and sharp edges cause in us sensations that make us believe they possess such characteristics. (The trouble is that it may be just as difficult to explain why our sensations correspond to physical objects as it is to explain why they do *not* correspond.)

SCIENTIFIC REALISM

The theory of scientific realism began with the speculations of ancient Greeks who had little scientific knowledge of matter. It was developed during the rise of modern science in the 1600s and 1700s by thinkers such as Galileo, Descartes, John Locke, and Isaac Newton, who had far greater scientific knowledge. It was refined by twentieth-century scientists and philosophers who had vastly more knowledge. The theme common to all scientific realists is the claim that physics provides the most accurate account of the physical world. According to Wilfred Sellars, "[S]cience is the measure of all things, of what is that it is, and of what is not that it is not" (1963, 173). *Scientific realism* maintains: *(1) Physics gives true descriptions of physical objects*; and *(2) these true descriptions of physical objects show that many commonsense descriptions are false*. Scientific realists deny *Scientific Instrumentalism* (the view that physicists' theoretical entities such as atoms do not exist and are merely fictions that are useful in helping us to predict the course of our sensations).

The picture that emerges from scientific realism is this. Physical objects exist in space external to our minds. Physical objects produce in perceivers sensations of—or beliefs about—physical objects. Physical objects possess all and only the characteristics that physicists need to assign to physical objects to produce the best scientific explanation of the facts about the world. In other words, physical objects have only those characteristics that physicists arrive at through using *inference to the best explanation*. These include the atoms, subatomic particles, energy, and mass described by our most accurate physical theories. Excluded are most of the commonsense characteristics of physical objects such as colors, tastes, odors, degree of solidity, texture, and sharp edges.

The twentieth-century British physicist Arthur Eddington expressed his belief in scientific realism by describing his "two tables" this way:

> I have settled down to the task of writing these lectures and have drawn up my chairs to my two tables. Two tables! Yes; there are duplicates of every object about me—two tables, two chairs, two pens. . . .
>
> One of them has been familiar to me from earliest years. It is a commonplace object of the environment which I call the world. How shall I describe it? It has extension; it is comparatively permanent; it is coloured; above all it is *substantial*. By substantial I do not merely mean that it does not collapse when I lean upon it; I mean that it is constituted of "substance" and by that word I am trying to convey to you some conception of its intrinsic nature. It is a *thing*. . . .
>
> Table No. 2 is my scientific table. . . . My scientific table is mostly emptiness. Sparsely scattered in that emptiness are numerous electric charges rushing about with great speed; but their combined bulk amounts to less than a billionth of the bulk of the table itself. Notwithstanding its strange construction it turns out to be an entirely efficient table. It supports my writing paper as satisfactorily as

table No. I; for when I lay the paper on it the little electrical particles with their headlong speed keep on hitting the underside, so that the paper is maintained in shuttlecock fashion at a nearly steady level. If I lean upon this table I shall not go through; or, to be strictly accurate, the chance of my scientific elbow going through my scientific table is so excessively small that it can be neglected in practical life. (1963, xi–xii)

8. Arguments for Scientific Realism

Scientific realism has two main theses: (1) Physical objects possess the characteristics that physics assigns to physical objects; *and* (2) physical objects do not have the Category I characteristics that common sense assigns to physical objects. Combining (1) and (2) yields the view that physical objects possess all and only the characteristics that physics assigns to them. Proof of the first thesis amounts to defense of the reality of the world of the atom. Because atoms are not directly observed, but are inferred as the best explanation of what we observe, the debate over the existence of atoms becomes a debate over inference to the best explanation. Scientific realists argue that only the postulation of atoms explains the behavior of observable physical objects. Such examples include the different rate of thermal conductivity of various metals, why astronauts who land on the moon cannot breathe unaided, and how two relatively small bombs could result in the destruction of vast sections of two Japanese cities in World War II. Ever since the development of electricity, let alone the atomic bomb, it has been difficult to deny the existence of atoms. Nonetheless, when we get to phenomenalism we shall examine the scientific instrumentalist arguments that atoms should be treated as fictions and not assigned a real existence beyond our theories.

Proving the second thesis—that physical objects lack the Category I characteristics—will be much more difficult for scientific realists. The problem is that a direct realist can acknowledge the existence of atoms, but still say that physical objects possess all the Category I characteristics such as color, sound, odor, and smell that they seem to have. Physical objects, after all, could possess characteristics from *all four* categories. Most of the best-known arguments by scientific realists have tried to show that physical objects do not possess the commonsense Category I characteristics.

THE RELATIVITY OF PERCEPTION ARGUMENT

One of the most famous arguments for scientific realism is the *relativity of perception argument*, which was used by John Locke and Bertrand Russell (1872–1970). Suppose that when you wake up tomorrow everything that looks red to you today looks blue. For instance, fire trucks, Mackintosh apples, and the top traffic light all look blue to you. And suppose that everything that looks blue to you today looks red to you tomorrow. If this happens only to you, you might think that you have some strange ailment. But suppose that the same thing happens to half the people on Earth: What used to look red looks blue, and what used to look blue looks red. Suppose next that this change happens to 75 percent of the human race. What would you say then? How about 90 percent or 100 percent?

Let us change the example slightly. Let us suppose that 100 percent of the noncolor blind perceivers on Earth perceive Mackintosh apples to be red and the water in lakes to be blue. But instead of imagining our color sensations changing, let us consider some wider cosmic populations. Suppose that earthlings make up only 1 percent of the intelligent beings within the Milky Way galaxy, and the majority 99 percent of the perceivers in the rest of our galaxy see Mackintosh apples as blue and the water in lakes as red. Wouldn't this make you question whether the earthlings are seeing the true colors? Maybe we should say that the earthlings have the wrong color sensations and that the rest of the beings in the galaxy are correct. But saying *that* would be risky, because—here is the rest of the story—the intelligent beings in the Milky Way galaxy constitute only 1 percent of the total of intelligent beings in *this part* of the universe. The other 99 percent of the beings in this part of the universe perceive Mackintosh apples to be *yellow* and water in lakes to be *brown*. And so on.

These thought experiments are designed to get us to look at things this way:

(1) What colors physical objects *seem* to have depends on the sensory apparatus of perceivers.
(2) Therefore, it would be arbitrary to say that some perceivers are correct and other perceivers are incorrect.
(3) To avoid being arbitrary, we should say that colors exist only in our minds—they do not exist outside us in physical objects themselves.
(4) Finally, extend this sort of reasoning to the other Category I characteristics of sounds, tastes, and odors.

The relativity of perception argument is far from conclusive. One can object that even if it *would* be arbitrary to say *who* is correct and who is incorrect, it does not follow that no one *is* correct. We may be unable to tell whether earthling color sensations match the colors of physical objects, but for all that, physical objects may possess colors. Our color sensations might even turn out to match the colors of physical objects by luck. We should remember that direct realism claims only that physical objects *have* colors; direct realists do not have to say that we *know which* color they are.

Nonetheless, the relativity argument is suggestive. It makes us ask why direct realists *want* to say that physical objects have colors, even if we could never know what they are. At this stage, though, a perfectly satisfactory answer from the direct realist would be: We want to say that physical objects have colors, because we cannot understand how physical objects could *not* have colors. The idea of objects having shapes and sizes but no colors seems strange. So the scientific realist will need to provide more arguments against the direct realist.

THE SEPARABILITY ARGUMENT

The separability argument can be expressed as a series of three questions. First ask: (1) "What characteristics really belong to physical objects themselves?" This can be answered by asking another question: (2) "What qualities are absolutely necessary for objects to exist?" This question, in turn, is answered by asking: (3) "What characteristics cannot—even in one's imagination—be removed from physical objects?" The upshot of believing that (1) is answered by (2) and (2) is answered by (3) is that physical objects possess only those characteristics we *cannot* imagine them *not* having.

The Italian astronomer and physicist Galileo Galilei (1564–1642) used the separability argument to assign quantitative characteristics to physical objects and deny that they possess Category I characteristics:

> [U]pon conceiving of a material or corporeal substance, I immediately feel the need to conceive simultaneously that it is bounded and has this or that shape; that it is in this place or that at a given time; that it moves or stays still; that it does or does not touch another body; and that it is one, few, or many. I cannot separate it from these conditions by any stretch of my imagination. But that it must be white or red, bitter or sweet, noisy or silent, of sweet or foul odor, my mind feels no compulsion to understand as necessary accompaniments. Indeed, without the senses to guide us, reason or imagination alone would perhaps never arrive at such qualities. For that reason I think that tastes, odors, colors, and so forth are no more than mere names so far as pertains to the subject wherein they reside, and that they have their habitation only in the sensorium. Thus, if the living Creature were removed, all these qualities would be removed and annihilated. (1960, 309)

Here is an illustration of Galileo's thought experiment. Suppose we try to determine what types of characteristics really exist in a piece of chalk. We begin by dividing the chalk in half and ask what characteristics it still must have. We divide it again, ask the same question, and so on as long as it is possible to divide the chalk. According to Galileo, eventually we reach a point where we do not have to say that the remnant of chalk has any taste, odor, or color. We can regard these merely as sensations caused in our minds by the real characteristics of the chalk. But according to Galileo, no matter how many times we divide the piece of chalk, we will continue to have to assign it size, shape, motion/rest, number, and extension in space. These characteristics are necessary to physical objects—according to the physics of Galileo's day. For Galileo, physical objects consist of tiny indestructible atoms that possess the mathematically specifiable characteristics of bodies that are extended in and last through time. Although Galileo relied on a different conception of atoms, his motivation was the same as that of twentieth-century scientific realists such as Sellars and Eddington: Physics is seen as giving the most accurate description of the nature of physical objects.

The key to the separability argument is its claim that physical objects have only the characteristics they must possess and that all the other apparent characteristics are best understood as existing only in perceivers' minds. This premise is similar to Occam's Razor, which we have seen throughout this book. Occam's Razor says that we should not postulate entities needlessly. The separability argument says we should assign to physical objects only those characteristics we cannot avoid assigning to them, thereby avoiding the unnecessary duplication of those characteristics in the objects and in our minds. This premise, thus, shares some of the plausibility of Occam's Razor, but it is far from indisputable. There is nothing to prevent us from saying that physical objects possess some characteristics that are necessary and others that are not necessary.

Here is another way to express this criticism of the separability argument. The separability argument is not conclusive, because we can still say that tiny nuggets of matter *do in fact* possess characteristics of Category I, despite the fact that they do not *have* to possess them. The separability argument is not a *refutation* of direct realism, but at most a *recommendation* for constructing our picture of physical objects using different principles than direct realism uses. Viewed this way, we see that the separability argument shades into the third scientific realist argument.

THE SCIENCE-REPLACES-NAIVE-COMMON-SENSE ARGUMENT

Neither the relativity of perception argument nor the separability argument constitutes a convincing *proof* of scientific realism. Realizing this fact, scientific realists might try a more modest line of reasoning. The *science-replaces-naive-common-sense argument* is presented as a reason to think scientific realism is preferable to direct realism and phenomenalism. Against phenomenalism, scientific realists insist that postulating real physical objects is necessary to best explain our sense experience. Against direct realism, scientific realists argue that what we have learned about the nature of physical objects from twentieth-century physics makes direct realism not impossible, but *obsolete*. Science replaces our prescientific conception of physical objects as having characteristics from all four categories by a simpler and more scientific conception of physical objects. According to the science-replaces-naive-common-sense argument, direct realism is naive in the sense that anyone who accepts it would have to be unaware of contemporary physics.

The simplest way to appreciate the science-replaces-naive-common-sense argument is to recall Eddington's two tables. According to Eddington, common sense's conception of the table as solid, colored, and having sharp edges is a perfectly reasonable conception—if and only if we do not realize that the table really consists of electrical charges in mostly empty space. Once we realize that the table that exists in the physical world is the scientific table, we should surrender the belief that the commonsense table also exists in the physical world. It is true that we have *sensations* that lead common sense to believe that physical objects are solid, colored, and have sharp edges. Scientific realists do not deny that these characteristics exist somewhere. Their point is that we should understand where these characteristics are actually located: in the minds of perceivers, or, as Galileo says, "they have their habitation only in the sensorium."

Let me express the science-replaces-naive-common-sense argument more exactly. The first premise is the *law of identity* (sometimes called "Leibniz's Law," after the German philosopher and inventor of calculus Leibniz ('LIBE NITZ) (1646–1716)). The law of identity states that if two labels, "A" and "B," are names for the same entity, then all internal characteristics of A and B must be the same. If A = B, then any internal characteristic that A has, B has "too," because A and B are just the same thing. For example, if Superman can bench-press 5,000 pounds, then Clark Kent can bench press 5,000. We add to the law of identity two premises that say that the commonsense table and the scientific table possess different kinds of characteristics. Therefore, by modus tollens, the commonsense table is not the scientific table. We complete the argument by saying that because the scientific table exists in the physical world and it is different from the commonsense table, the commonsense table must "exist" only in our minds.

Here is the argument:

(1) If A is identical to B, then A and B share all internal characteristics.
(2) The commonsense table is solid, colored, and has sharp edges.
(3) The scientific table is not solid, not colored, and has no sharp edges.
(4) Therefore, the commonsense table is not identical to the scientific table.
(5) The scientific table exists in physical space.
(6) So, where shall we locate the common sense table? The scientific realists propose: in the minds of perceivers.

If we accept this argument we will embrace the two major tenets of scientific realism: that atoms are real (step 5) and that the Category I characteristics of physical objects exist only in perceivers' minds (step 6). But this argument also is far from persuasive. One problem is that the direct realist can object that this argument *begs the question* (*assumes what it should prove*) when it says in step 3 that the scientific table is not colored, solid, or sharp edged. This argument assumes that there are two different tables, but *a direct realist who believes that there is only one table possessing two types of characteristics will reject that assumption.* The direct realist can say that one and the same table possesses both commonsensical and scientific characteristics. Eddington's talk about two tables is a useful way to illustrate the atomic theory of matter, the direct realist maintains, but it should not be taken in the literal way that Eddington does.

This objection is a good one. Just because we can talk as if there are two tables does not *prove* that there is not just one table with two radically different kinds of characteristics. Therefore, the science-replaces-naive-common-sense argument is *not* an indisputable proof of scientific realism. But admitting that, the scientific realist can still insist that this is a good argument: Once we acknowledge the atomic structure of physical objects, it becomes *unscientific* and *needless* to say that physical objects also possess commonsense characteristics such as color, solidity, and sharp edges. As long as we have a reasonable place to locate colors, solidity, and sharp edges (in the sensations or the beliefs of perceivers), it is superfluous to locate those characteristics as mysteriously coexisting alongside the atoms flying around in empty space. This is the meaning of saying that science *replaces* our prescientific view of physical objects: Our old view is not refuted, it simply becomes obsolete.

The following is an analogy to illustrate the point. Before modern medicine understood epilepsy, many societies thought that victims of epileptic seizures were possessed by demons. In the twentieth century it became widely believed that epilepsy was a disorder in the electrical activity in one or both of a patient's cerebral hemispheres. Thus, epilepsy ceased being thought of as demon possession. The scientific, electrical disorder theory of epilepsy replaced the prescientific theory of demon possession.

Now suppose that an opponent resists the replacement of the demon theory: "I am willing to admit that epilepsy is caused by electrical disorders in patients' brains, as medical science has discovered. But why do you think that the electrical disorders occur? Because the demons are causing them! Thus, epilepsy is TWO things: *electrical disturbances in the brain* that are caused by *demons*."

Although this objection is irrefutable, it would be difficult to take seriously. Why? Because once we have an explanation of epilepsy in terms of electrical disturbances, the postulation of demons is needless. Once we have accepted a scientific theory, we would be foolish to try to hold onto the prescientific theory simply because it *could* be true. There seems to be no good reason to retain demon theory after we get a better scientific theory. Likewise, there is no reason to insist that lightning is both electrical disturbances in the atmosphere and thunderbolts thrown by Zeus once we learn the correct scientific theory. By analogy, there is no good philosophical or scientific reason to keep the theory that physical objects possess colors, solidity, and sharp edges once we have an adequate scientific theory that replaces it.

PHENOMENALISM

The debate between the direct realists and the scientific realists is over the "location" of commonsensical characteristics of physical objects such as colors, shapes, and sharp edges. The former placed them in the physical objects themselves, whereas the latter put them only in our minds. But both direct realists and scientific realists agree that physical objects are really out there in physical space. (That's why they are both called "realists.") The last of the major theorists—the phenomenalists—agree with the scientific realists that commonsense characteristics are not in physical objects, but their reason is very dramatic: *Phenomenalists*, unlike realists, *believe that there exist no physical objects.*

Here are the main tenets of phenomenalism. First and foremost, there are no physical objects—there is no spatial world. This means that there are no human bodies, no trees, no plants, no Earth, no universe, and no atoms. Physical space is an *illusion* of our nonphysical minds. Second, the only things that do exist are nonphysical minds and their mental states—sensations, thoughts, beliefs, and so on. Third, physical objects and unobservable scientific entities such as atoms are merely stories we make up to help predict the order in which our sensations will occur. (The doctrine that any scientific theory that postulates unobservable entities is only a useful fiction is called "scientific instrumentalism.") Fourth, if God (a supreme nonphysical mind) exists, then God causes our finite minds to have sensations *as if* they were affected by real physical objects. Thus, God would be the explanation for the order in our sensations. If God does not exist, there is no ultimate explanation for why our sensations are orderly. The orderliness of our sensations would be a brute, inexplicable fact.

Unfortunately, phenomenalists sometimes express their theory in misleading ways. The Irish Bishop George Berkeley, the most famous phenomenalist, may be the worst offender. In the passage below, he expressed his theory by saying that, for physical objects, their *esse* is *percipi* (their existence is to be perceived). What he means is that there are no such things as physical objects existing in three-dimensional space. The problem is that many readers mistake phenomenalism for a weird kind of realism, where physical objects actually exist in physical space, but only because some perceiver is perceiving them. Although such a theory is imaginable, it is not phenomenalism—it is a theory one might find in an episode of Rod Serling's "Twilight Zone." Phenomenalists do not believe, for example, that trees are really there when they are perceived and would pop out of existence if they were ever unperceived. It is a confusion to think that perception can create or sustain real objects existing in physical space, and phenomenalists are not confused on this point. To charge phenomenalism with having physical objects forever popping in and out of existence is incorrect.

Here is a famous passage in his *Principles of Human Knowledge* where Berkeley has to be interpreted carefully to avoid making phenomenalism appear to be a variety of Twilight Zone realism:

> [A]ll the choir of heaven and the furniture of the earth, in a word all those bodies which compose the mighty frame of the world, have not any subsistence without a mind, that their *being* is to be perceived or known; that consequently so long as they are not actually perceived by me, or do not exist in my mind or that of any other created spirit, they must either have no existence at all, or else subsist in the mind of some Eternal Spirit: it being perfectly unintelligible . . . to attribute to any single part of them an existence independent of a spirit. (1965, sec. 6)

Berkeley also has a misleading way of saying what phenomenalism takes physical objects to be. He often wrote that physical objects are *collections of sensations*: "a certain color, taste, smell, figure and consistence having been observed to go together, are accounted one distinct thing, signified by the name *apple*" (*Principles of Human Knowledge*, sect. 1). The trouble with this way of expressing phenomenalism is that it makes it look as if Berkeley is claiming that an apple—a physical object—is at the same time a collection of sensations. This would be to confuse physical objects existing in physical space and the so-called "phenomenal" (apparent) space of our sensations. Sensations, according to Berkeley, exist not in physical space, but in nonphysical minds. Therefore, to say that an apple is a collection of sensations makes it sound as if an object *in* physical space is composed of entities that are *not in* physical space, which is a contradiction. The best way to avoid such confusions is simply to express phenomenalism as the view that there *are no* physical objects. We (our nonphysical minds) believe that there are physical objects, but the only things that exist are minds, including our thoughts and the sensations that we mistake for physical objects.

Phenomenalists have to provide a different account of veridical and illusory perception than realists do. According to realists, we perceive veridically when our sensations or beliefs about physical objects agree with the way the physical objects really are, and we misperceive when our sensations or beliefs about physical objects do *not* agree with the way the physical objects are. Phenomenalists, not believing that there are any physical objects, cannot use the realists' criterion of veridical and illusory perception. Instead they must distinguish between correct and mistaken perception by the consistency of our sensations or beliefs. In veridical perception, our various sensations correspond with each other—for example, we have a visual apple sensation, we experience the tactile sensations of holding an apple, and we receive the gustatory sensation of the taste of an apple. In illusion, the various sensations do not fit together in an orderly way.

This leads to the strongest objection to phenomenalism—how can phenomenalists explain the intrapersonal and interpersonal consistency of our sensations? Our sensations are *intrapersonally consistent* to the extent that our various senses agree with each other. We have sensations of sight, touch, hearing, taste, and smell that seem to converge on the same physical objects. Different persons have sensations that are *interpersonally consistent* to the extent that the sensations of different persons agree. If I tap on a chalkboard, many different minds will experience similar sounds. Both kinds of consistency seem to require an explanation, and the realists think they have the best one: Physical objects existing outside minds *cause* minds to have sensations in consistent ways. This objection to phenomenalism is a standard argument for realism using inference to the best explanation.

In response, phenomenalists have to argue that the realists' postulation of physical objects—when examined carefully—is not a better explanation for the two types of consistency of our sensations than phenomenalism's explanation is. To do this, phenomenalists offer an ingenious interpretation of the debate between the realists and themselves:

- *Realists*: Physical objects existing in physical space *cause* our sensations to be consistent, in single perceivers and between individuals. This is a better explanation than phenomenalists can provide.
- *Phenomenalists*: *Why* do physical objects cause our sensations to be consistent? For example, why does a real Mackintosh apple consistently cause me and other persons to have red sensations?
- *Realists*: The consistency is due to the uniformity of the laws of nature, specifically, the laws that deal with the reflection of light waves from molecular surfaces of physical objects and our nervous systems' processing of light to cause visual sensations.
- *Phenomenalists*: Why do these laws of nature hold uniformly? For example, why doesn't the red apple cause me to have red sensations and you to have blue sensations?
- *Realists*: Either: (1) The laws of nature just do hold uniformly, and no further explanation is possible. It is a brute, inexplicable fact that the laws of nature hold. OR (2) God causes the laws of nature to be uniform, because God wants us to have an orderly world to live in.
- *Phenomenalists*: Aha. I can provide just as good explanations without postulating physical objects. Consider (1). If you realists can say that the *laws of nature* are brute, inexplicable facts about reality, we phenomenalists can say the same thing about the *laws of sensations*. The laws of sensations make it a brute, inexplicable fact that sensations just are orderly within and between persons. Consider (2). If you cite God to ex-

plain why the laws of nature are orderly, we phenomenalists can do the same thing regarding the laws of sensations. *God* makes the laws of sensations orderly because God wants us to have order in our lives. Either way, the postulation of physical objects provides no better explanation for the consistency of sensations than phenomenalism does.

9. Arguments for Phenomenalism

I leave it to the reader to decide who has the better of the debate over the consistency of sensations. But even if the phenomenalists' reply is inadequate, the inference to the best explanation argument for realism does not cinch the case against phenomenalism. Even if physical objects were a better explanation for our sensations than the phenomenalists can provide, phenomenalism still might have other selling points that make it more attractive than realism. We should look at some positive arguments for phenomenalism that might elevate it in our opinion from a *possible* theory to the most *plausible* one.

THE MIND/BODY ARGUMENT FOR PHENOMENALISM

The mind/body argument for phenomenalism was offered by Berkeley and is very similar to the exercise offered in chapter 1 to illustrate the mind/body problem. Here are its premises. First, suppose we think, as most realists and phenomenalists do, that perception involves having sensations. Second, suppose we think, as most dualists and all phenomenalists do, that sensations are nonphysical—that they are not conditions of brains, but exist in nonphysical minds. (We examine reasons for thinking this is true in chapter 5.) Third, suppose we believe, as common sense does, that sensations causally influence human behavior. For example, visual sensations of a charging rhinoceros would cause us to respond in certain ways. Fourth, suppose we are convinced on general philosophical grounds that an entity that is nonphysical (like a sensation) *cannot* causally influence a physical entity. The reason to believe this is that nonphysical things and physical things are so dissimilar that there is no connecting point by which one could affect the other. Specifically, how could an entity that does *not exist* in space affect an entity that *does exist* in physical space?

If we accept these four premises, we are committed to accepting the following argument for phenomenalism. Nonphysical sensations that occur in perception causally influence our behavior (our "bodies") as stated in premises 1, 2, and 3. But a nonphysical entity cannot influence a physical thing (premise 4). Therefore, our "bodies" cannot really be physical. So what are they? Nonphysical. In sum, the fact that sensations influence our behavior shows that our bodies are nonphysical. And because our bodies are just as physical as atoms, trees, and continents, we may generalize to the conclusion that all things that we prephilosophically believe are physical are really nonphysical.

We may resist this argument by rejecting any of its premises, but each looks at least fairly plausible. Materialists (who think only physical things exist) will deny that perception involves having nonphysical sensations. According to materialists, perceiving the world involves physical sensations (objectified or adverbial) or acquiring beliefs—both which are simply brain states. Dualistic parallelists (who think that physical brains and nonphysical minds run parallel without affecting each other) will deny premise 3. Dualistic interactionists (who think that physical brains interact with nonphysical minds) will deny premise 4. The important thing to notice about the mind/body argument for phenomenalism is that it forces us to reject at least one of its premises. If we accept them all, then we are logically committed to phenomenalism, whether we realize it or not.

THE KNOWLEDGE ARGUMENT

It may be surprising to learn that phenomenalists advertise their theory as an answer to epistemological skepticism, but no less a figure than Berkeley did exactly that. Here is the basic idea. When the realists include physical objects in their metaphysical picture of what exists, they include a type of entity that no one observes directly. Thus, realists open the door to skepticism. By denying the existence of physical objects, phenomenalists dismiss the unknowable entities from their world view, replacing them with entities that *are* knowable—sensations. Thus, phenomenalists claim to save us from skepticism about physical objects.

Here is the knowledge argument expressed in a form that is close to reductio ad absurdum:

(1) Suppose we adopt either direct or scientific realism.
(2) Then we believe that physical objects stand behind our sensations (or our perceptual beliefs about them) as the *causes* of our sensations or beliefs.
(3) This leads to Veil of Sensations Skepticism (discussed in chapter 3). We can never tell *by observation* whether physical objects resemble our sensations or whether our perceptual beliefs are true. Indeed, we can never even tell whether physical objects exist at all, because we are always locked inside our own minds.
(4) Nor is there any *other* way for us to know that physical objects are the way we think they are or even whether they exist.
(5) Therefore, if we adopt either direct or scientific realism, we will be committed to skepticism about the nature and existence of physical objects.
(6) Therefore, assuming we want to avoid skepticism, we should reject realism and adopt phenomenalism.

Phenomenalists realize that the knowledge argument does not *prove* their theory; they simply hope that it provides some motivation for accepting phenomenalism. Phenomenalists might even express the knowledge argument as a modest proposal: "Let's build our theory of what exists on a foundation of entities we *know* exist. We know our sensations exist, but we do not know that physical objects exist. So, let's quit assuming the existence of unknowable physical objects when we build our metaphysical picture of the world."

Here are two objections to even this modest version of the knowledge argument. First, realists might object that we *can* know that physical objects exist as the cause of our sensations, because we need to postulate physical objects as the best explanation for our sensations. The knowledge argument relies on the Empiricist Criterion of Evidence elaborated in chapter 3, which says that the only way A can be evidence for B is if A and B are observed to correspond or if "A" and "B" are related by definition. But there is plenty of reason to reject this principle. If we adopt inference to the best explanation, the knowledge argument cannot get started.

Second, even if realists admit that we lack knowledge of physical objects, they can object to the phenomenalists' suggestion to build our theory of what exists only on a foundation of what we experience in our minds. Why *not* include entities that we cannot know exist—if including them provides an overall more plausible worldview than a sparser worldview that may not hold together? After all, the minds of other persons are not observable to us; so, according to the reasoning used by the knowledge argument, we should say that other minds do not exist. This would include God, also. Therefore, a consistent application of the knowledge argument seems to lead the phenomenalist directly to solipsism, the view that the only things that exist are the contents of the individual phenomenalist's own mind. This scarcely seems like the most-likely-to-be-true view of the world.

THE SIMPLICITY ARGUMENT

In the third argument, phenomenalists use two familiar themes of the realists—Occam's Razor and inference to the best explanation—*against* realism. It is also a nice example of the strategy of trying to turn an apparent weakness of one's theory into a strength. Suppose phenomenalists decide to answer realists' objection concerning the consistency of interpersonal and intrapersonal sensations by saying that God makes our sensations orderly. Neutral observers might regard this as a questionable strategy: to try to salvage a problematic theory (phenomenalism) by appealing to an unprovable theory (theism).

But suppose that a phenomenalist is happy to invoke God as the cause of the orderliness of our sensations, because the phenomenalist believes there is a conclusive proof of the existence of God. If the phenomenalist assumes *that*, then the debate between the realists and the phenomenalists changes dramatically. For now the phenomenalist can look at *physical objects* as redundant, useless postulations, just as the scientific realist thinks that the commonsense table is redundant once we accept atomic theory. If we make God the centerpiece of our worldview, then *God* accounts for the order that exists in the cosmos, and physical objects become useless intermediaries ("middlemen") with no necessary role to play.

Look at it this way. If we are theists and realists, then we think that God is responsible for physical objects that, due to the laws of nature, cause sensations in perceivers of the physical world. If we are theists and phenomenalists, we think that God directly causes our sensations without the existence of physical objects. An omnipotent being could do *that* with no problem. Thus, the phenomenalist can argue that if we are going to believe in God, God will do the same job that physical objects obeying the laws of nature do for realists, only more simply. Thus, the phenomenalist uses Occam's Razor and inference to the best explanation to argue that physical objects are unnecessary postulations.

A FINAL REMARK ON THE DEBATE BETWEEN THE REALISTS AND THE PHENOMENALISTS

The debate over the nature of the external world is a paradigm of an unresolvable metaphysical dispute. Each side can provide strong arguments for its position. Because of this, the other theorists cannot *prove* their theories are correct. Probably one of the major theories—direct realism, scientific realism in some form, or phenomenalism—*is* correct, but we should not claim even to *know* that. Perhaps some bizarre fourth theory is true. No side can claim to know that its answer is correct, not even the side that has the correct answer. The task of philosophers is to try to figure out which theory is most likely to be true, given all the intellectual resources they can bring to bear on this question.

Guide Questions

1. Why is *your* external world different from *my* external world? (75)
2. What does it mean to call something "objective"? (75)
3. What are the two definitions of "subjective"? (75–76)
4. How does knowing how perception occurs raise the problem of the nature of the external world? (77)
5. Why can we not settle the problem of the nature of the external world by taking a photograph? (78)
6. What is the difference between saying "X *seems to be* P" and "X *is* P"? (78)
7. How does the debate between subjectivism and objectivism arise in aesthetics? Metaethics? (79)

8. Give one example of a characteristic from each of the four major categories. (80)
9. How did the idea of atoms held by the Greek atomists differ from that of twentieth-century physicists? (80–81)
10. What is the difference between saying that perception is the having of sensations and saying that perception is the acquisition of beliefs? (81–82)
11. What exactly does direct realism say about physical objects? (83)
12. What did Wilfrid Sellars mean when he said that science is the measure of all things? (84)
13. Scientific realism rejects scientific instrumentalism. What does each theory say? (84)
14. Why does Eddington think that his two tables are different? (84–85)
15. Express the relativity of perception argument in two sentences. (85–86)
16. Express the separability argument in two sentences. (87–88)
17. Express the science-replaces-naive-common-sense argument in two sentences. (88–89)
18. What is Twilight Zone realism? Why is it *not* phenomenalism? (91–92)
19. Why is it misleading to say that phenomenalists believe that physical objects are collections of sensations? (92)
20. What is the realists' objection to phenomenalism based on the intrapersonal and interpersonal consistency of our sensations? How do phenomenalists try to answer this objection? (93–94)
21. Express the mind-body argument for phenomenalism in two sentences. How would a dualistic interactionist resist it? (94–95)
22. What is the main idea behind the knowledge argument for phenomenalism? (95)
23. How might realists use inference to the best explanation to resist the knowledge argument? (96)
24. How might phenomenalists argue that their theory is simpler than realist theories? (96–97)

Review Questions for Examinations

1. Define: "minds," "external world," "physical," "nonphysical," "appearance," "reality," "objective," "subjective," "aesthetic subjectivism," "aesthetic objectivism," "moral objectivism," "moral subjectivism," "sensations," "law of identity," "laws of nature," "laws of sensations."
2. What are the main tenets of these theories: direct realism, scientific realism, phenomenalism, solipsism?
3. What is: the Empiricist Criterion of Evidence, Veil of Sensations Skepticism, inference to the best explanation?
4. Explain these arguments for the following theories. For scientific realism: the relativity of perception argument, the separability argument, the science-replaces-naive-common-sense argument. For phenomenalism: the mind-

body argument, the knowledge argument, the simplicity argument. Provide one criticism of each argument.

5. Who was: Galileo, Arthur Eddington, Berkeley?
6. Explain the debate between the realists and phenomenalists over the consistency of our sensations.
7. How can one thing be both subjective and universal?
8. What is the difference between perception involving sensations and perception involving belief acquisition?
9. Why is it a mistake to think that phenomenalists believe that physical objects are forever popping in and out of existence depending on whether they are perceived?

Discussion Questions

1. Realists explain the datum that we share an orderly world of sensations by reference to the laws of nature. The phenomenalists say that orderliness is due to the laws of sensations. Which side has the better of this dispute?
2. According to the definitions of "subjective" and "objective" used in this chapter, classify these statements as subjective or objective:
   1. George Bush was more intelligent than Dan Quayle.
   2. Taco Bell serves *authentic* Mexican food.
   3. Atoms are real.
   4. Honesty is better than dishonesty.
   5. Abortion is legal in Alaska.
   6. Peas taste good.
3. Which of the three arguments for scientific realism—the relativity of perception argument, the separability argument, or the science-replaces-naive-common-sense argument—is the most convincing? Least convincing?
4. Which argument for phenomenalism—the mind/body argument, the knowledge argument, or the simplicity argument—is the most convincing? Least convincing?
5. Consider this argument paraphrased from Berkeley's *Principles of Human Knowledge*, section 23:

   > Try to imagine a physical object existing without anyone perceiving it. You cannot, because in the very act of imagining it, you are perceiving it yourself. Therefore, we cannot even imagine an unperceived physical object. Therefore, the very idea of there being an unperceived physical object makes no sense. Therefore, there can exist no unperceived physical objects.

   Is this a strong argument? Explain.
6. Describe a theory of the external world that is neither: direct realism, scientific realism, phenomenalism, or solipsism. Can you provide any reasons for thinking this theory might be true?

7. Consider this argument paraphrased from Berkeley's *Principles of Human Knowledge*, sections 1–7:

> Physical objects are simply the totality of their sensible qualities, such as the color, taste, and texture of a lemon. But sensible qualities such as color, taste, and texture are only sensations in our minds. Therefore, physical objects are nothing but collections of sensations in our minds.

Is this a strong argument? Explain.

FOR FURTHER READING

Berkeley, George. 1965. *Berkeley's Philosophical Writings*. New York: Macmillan. Contains *Principles of Human Knowledge*, *Three Dialogues Between Hylas and Philonous*, and other Berkeley masterpieces. Useful introduction by David Armstrong. Moderately difficult.

Cornman, James, Keith Lehrer, and George Pappas. 1987. *Philosophical Problems and Arguments*. Indianapolis: Hackett. Chapter 2 of this introductory text treats the nature of the external world and theory of knowledge. Dialectical format. Moderately difficult.

Halverson, William. 1981. *A Concise Introduction to Philosophy*. New York: Random House. Chapters 13–17 are devoted to the nature of the external world. Highly readable with an extensive bibliography.

Levenson, Carl and Jonathan Westphal, eds. 1994. *Reality*. Indianapolis: Hackett. Anthology of twenty-four readings, many dealing with the nature of the external world. Contains selections from Locke, Berkeley, Hume, Russell, and Eddington.

Chapter 5
The Mind/Body Problem

INTRODUCTION

An employee at my university solves mathematical problems. She sits at a desk outside a closed room, takes problems that are brought to her into the room, and always returns with the correct answer. The employee tells everyone that she uses "a calculating device" to solve the problems. Because no one except the woman ever sees inside the room, various theories have sprung up regarding what the calculating device is. Some theorists, emphasizing the difficulty of many of the problems, suggest that the calculating device is a large computer. Others, noting our limited campus budget, believe the calculating device is a powerful pocket calculator. Others, who believe the woman is a mathematical genius, think the calculating device is nothing over and beyond the woman herself; they say she solves the problems by counting very quickly on her fingers and toes. Because we are unable to answer the question directly, we are forced to theorize.

The mind/body problem asks what kind of existence minds have: Are minds physical or nonphysical? This is similar to asking what is the calculating device in that closed room. We cannot look anywhere to determine the answer.

Thus, to address the question, we must do so indirectly by considering what can be said in favor of the various competing theories. This is what we shall do in this chapter.

1. Definitions: "Mind," "Physical," "Nonphysical"

Consider the word "mind." In philosophical debates, as with debates in general, it is wisest to set up things in a way that is fair to all competing sides. The definition of "mind" we shall use is "thinking thing or center of consciousness." This is a *functional definition*, because it defines the word "mind" by citing the main job (function) that minds perform. By defining "mind" in this way we can inquire into the mind/body problem without assuming that we already know the structure of the thing that the word "mind" designates. If we defined "mind" to mean "brain," we would be guilty of *begging the question* (the fallacy of assuming what we need to prove) against persons who think that minds are not brains. It would be dishonest to pretend to be figuring out what we think minds are if we have *already* decided that minds are brains. If we defined "mind" as "nonphysical mind" or "soul," we would beg the question in the other direction by assuming that minds are *not* brains. By using the functional definition of "mind," we can pose the mind/body problem without prejudice to either side: Do "minds" designate (refer to) *brains*? Or do "minds" designate *nonphysical minds*? The question "What are minds?" thereby becomes the question "*What are thinking things*?" This is to ask about the kind of existence had by the thing that "contains" our beliefs, desires, fears, emotions, sensations, and other mental states.

Consider next the word "physical." To be physical is to be extended in space and to possess the characteristics of physical objects. As we saw in chapter 4, philosophers who agree that physical objects exist disagree about their exact nature. Direct realists believe that physical objects possess commonsense characteristics such as shape, sharp edges, and colors. Scientific realists believe physical objects do not have these characteristics, but possess only those characteristics physics says belongs to atoms and smaller particles—characteristics such as energy, mass, charge, and spin. Everyone agrees, though, that if physical objects exist, they exist in space. Spatial extension, therefore, is the defining characteristic of physical things.

Finally, consider "nonphysical." To be nonphysical is to exist, but not in space. Nonphysical things, if any exist, have none of the commonsense or scientific characteristics that the direct and scientific realists believe physical objects have. By definition, nonphysical things lack the shapes, sharp edges, and colors of commonsense physical objects. They also lack the energy, mass, charge, and spin of atoms and particles. Because nonphysical things do not exist in space, they could not be detected by any measuring device. Some theorists argue that our minds (thinking things) are nonphysical minds. Accordingly, they hold that the most important part of persons is *not* part of the natural world.

2. An Overview of Mind/Body Theories

Because of our understandable preoccupation with ourselves (rather than animals or computers), philosophers care most about the mind/body problem when it is specified to persons. The mind/body problem, therefore, can be stated this way: *What is a person*? The three most important overall possibilities are these: (1) Persons are entirely physical. This theory is *materialism. A materialist believes that there are no nonphysical components to persons.* (2) Persons are entirely nonphysical, having nonphysical minds and not having physical bodies at all. This theory is *idealism* or *phenomenalism. Phenomenalists such as Berkeley believe that our minds are nonphysical minds AND that our bodies do not exist in space—our "bodies" are merely so many sensations in the nonphysical minds of perceivers.* (3) Persons consist of both physical bodies and nonphysical minds. This theory is *dualism. Dualists believe that persons are "dual" in the sense of having both nonphysical minds and physical bodies.*

Materialism, phenomenalism, and dualism are only the main categories. In the following *taxonomy* (categorical listing) of mind/body theories we shall see that there are various ways to be a materialist or dualist. The taxonomy will be determined by our answers to these questions:

1. *Do you believe that persons are made up of one kind of basic entity (thing) or two*? If you think that persons consist of only one type of entity—either entirely physical or entirely nonphysical—then you are a *monist* (literally, a one-ist). Monists who believe that persons are entirely physical are *materialists.* Monists who believe that persons are entirely nonphysical are *phenomenalists. Dualists* (two-ists) believe that persons have nonphysical minds and physical bodies.
2. *If you accept materialism, do you believe that minds and mental events exist or not*? If you are a materialist who believes that the mental does not exist, you are an *eliminative materialist*. Eliminative materialists believe there are no minds and no mental events. If you are a materialist who thinks that mental events really exist as physical events in persons' nervous systems, then you are a *noneliminative* or *identity materialist.* This means that you are a materialist who believes in the mental.
3. *If you accept dualism, do you believe that minds and bodies causally affect each other or not*? If you believe nonphysical minds and physical bodies causally (not *casually*!) affect each other, then you are a *dualistic interactionist.* If you believe that nonphysical minds and physical bodies do not interact, you are a *dualistic parallelist*. Dualistic parallelists hold that physical brains and nonphysical minds *appear* to causally affect each other, but they really do not. Brains and minds simply run in parallel sequences. If you believe that nonphysical minds do not affect physical bodies, but physical bodies affect our nonphysical minds, then you are an *epiphenomenalist* ('epi phen nom men al ist).

Here is a chart of the main theories:

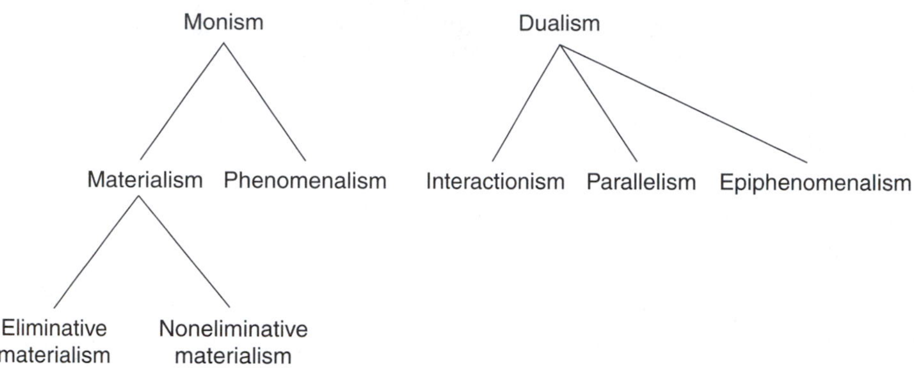

Let me illustrate these six theories. Consider a case in which we would ordinarily say that I have injured my hand, which caused me to feel a sensation of pain, which caused me to take aspirin to try to alleviate the pain. *Eliminative materialists* say that although something is happening to me that leads to my taking the aspirin, it is incorrect to say that I had a *sensation* that possesses the *phenomenal* (felt) *quality* of hurtfulness. Although we have been taught to speak as if there were such things, this is really a mistake—there are no sensations. *Noneliminative materialists* say that the injury to my hand caused another physical event to occur, namely, the sensation of pain that is an event in my brain. That brain event, in turn, caused me to take the aspirin. *Phenomenalists* do not deny that I felt pain in my nonphysical mind, nor that it *seemed to be* caused by the injury to my hand and that the sensation *seems to* cause me to take the aspirin. Phenomenalists deny that I possess a physical hand to be injured and a physical body to grasp an aspirin bottle. Denying that there are *any* physical objects, phenomenalists say that because there are no hands to be injured and no bodies to be moved into action, our pains cannot be caused by injuries nor can pains cause bodily actions.

Dualistic interactionists think that the injury to my physical hand caused my nonphysical mind to have a sensation of pain, which in turn caused my aspirin-seeking behavior. Accordingly, causation occurred between two radically different kinds of things: physical body affects nonphysical mind, which affects physical body. *Dualistic parallelists* believe that the bumping of my physical hand was *followed by* the sensation of pain in my nonphysical mind, which was *followed by* my taking the aspirin. Parallelists differ from interactionists by saying that the injury did not cause the sensation and the sensation did not cause the aspirin-seeking behavior. Instead, physical events and sensations run in noninteracting parallel sequences that create the illusion of causal interaction. Finally, *epiphenomenalists* agree with the dualistic interactionist that the injury to the hand caused the sensation of pain in our nonphysical minds, but agree with the parallelist that the pain did not cause our aspirin-seeking behavior. Epiphenomenalists believe that mental events are like "sparks" that are thrown off by the brain and do not affect the brain's operation.

In the rest of the chapter we examine these theories in detail, what they say, what can be said in favor of them, and what objections they face.

DUALISTIC THEORIES

Phenomenalism holds that: (1) our bodies are nonphysical; and (2) our minds are nonphysical. In this chapter I ignore phenomenalism's first premise and examine only the second for two reasons. First, phenomenalism's claim that there are no physical objects is treated at length in chapter 4, and readers who wish to examine that argument can look there. Second, the phenomenalists' claim that minds are nonphysical—which they share with dualism—is crucial to deciding between dualism and materialism. So, by examining reasons for thinking that minds are nonphysical, we will be addressing a premise that is needed by dualism as well as by phenomenalism. If we deny that minds are nonphysical, we must reject both dualism and phenomenalism.

3. The Basics of Dualism

There are two main tenets to dualism: (1) persons' bodies (including their brains) are physical; and (2) persons' minds (which are sometimes called "souls") are nonphysical. For the reasons given above, I shall skip (1) and focus only on (2). All dualists agree on (1) and (2), whether they are interactionists, parallelists, or epiphenomenalists. For right now, we shall examine reasons for thinking that minds are nonphysical, saving the debate between the three dualistic theories until section 6.

The Greek philosopher Plato (427–347 B.C.) advanced the doctrine of the immortality of the nonphysical soul in many of his writings. Christianity added Plato's view of the soul to its own doctrines. The most famous dualistic interactionist was the French philosopher and inventor of analytical geometry René Descartes, who presented powerful arguments for the existence of the nonphysical mind that we shall examine in the next section.

Let us begin by looking at some reasons that make dualism attractive. First, as is suggested by the fact that Christianity adopted the doctrine of the immortal soul, dualism will appeal to many persons who want to believe in an afterlife. It is possible to have an afterlife without having a nonphysical mind—one's body might be resurrected. Nonetheless, one might like the idea of having an immediate afterlife, rather than having to wait for resurrection to occur. Conversely, it is possible for us to have nonphysical minds and still have no afterlife. Perhaps the nonphysical mind simply loses consciousness upon death. Nonetheless, the idea of an afterlife is a motive for many persons to believe in nonphysical minds.

A second reason why some persons like dualism is the hope that human beings are ontologically different from and "stand above" the rest of the animal kingdom. Medievals portrayed humans as midway between angels and beasts—as having nonphysical souls like angels and physical bodies like animals. Descartes thought that our nonphysical minds set us categorically apart from the rest of the animals. According to Descartes, animals possess no minds and, therefore, are incapable of any mental states, including sensation. The idealist philosopher F. H. Bradley (1846–1924) is reputed to have put Descartes's doctrine into scandalous practice by shooting dogs and cats for sport. After all, Bradley reasoned, animals do not feel pain when we shoot them.

A third reason for believing in nonphysical minds is the desire to secure for us *free will—the ability to choose in a way that makes us morally responsible (deserving of praise and blame) for our actions*. Some philosophers believe that if materialism is true, then, because our bodies' actions would be determined by the laws of nature, we cannot have free will and moral responsibility. But if persons' minds were nonphysical, these philosophers hope, then perhaps our minds could interact with our bodies in ways that are not determined. Maybe nonphysical minds might be able to resist the determinism that is inherent in our bodies. This argument is full of difficulties (see chapter 8 for an examination of the free will problem), but many persons believe that having nonphysical minds would be helpful for free will.

4. The Law of Identity Argument for Dualism

The most important type of argument for dualism holds that our minds (thinking things) and our brains *seem* to have such different characteristics that they cannot *be* the same thing. For instance, when we talk about our brains and the events that occur in our brains, we use a physical vocabulary. We say that our brains weigh three pounds, that they are located in our craniums, and that the events occurring in our brains involve electrical discharges and the release of various chemicals. When we talk about our minds and the mental events that occur in our minds, we use a very different vocabulary. We say that our minds are intelligent or creative, that our thoughts are happy or sad, and that our sensations are painful or itchy. It is clear that we talk about brains and minds in different ways.

If this were *only* a fact about the way we talk, it would not prove anything. (We describe Superman in different ways than we describe Clark Kent, but they are nonetheless the same person.) But often the fact that we talk about things in different ways shows that the things we talk about are different. Suppose we say that Jones is five feet tall, and we also say that the tallest student in the sixth grade is six feet tall. If both these statements are true, it follows that Jones is not the tallest student in sixth grade.

This example illustrates the *law of identity*: *Two APPARENTLY different things, A and B, are really just THE SAME THING going under different names if and only if A and B share all characteristics.* If A and B have all the same characteristics, then "they" are really one and the same thing. If A and B really are the same thing with different names, then A and B have exactly the same characteristics. For example, if Mark Twain and Samuel Clemens have all the same characteristics, they are the same person (they are). If Mark Twain is the same person as Samuel Clemens, then "they" have all the same characteristics.

Dualists use the second half of the law of identity to argue that minds and mental states are not identical to brains and brain states. If dualists can provide even one characteristic that distinguishes minds from brains, they can prove that minds are not identical to brains. As we saw three paragraphs above, dualists think that there are *many* characteristics that distinguish minds and brains. The general format for the *law of identity argument* is this:

(1) Minds and mental states have characteristic C.
(2) Brains and brain states do not have characteristic C.
(3) Therefore, minds and mental states are not identical to brains and brain states.

Here are three specific versions of this general format. One version can be appreciated by closing one's eyes and visualizing an orange elephant:

(A) My mental image is orange and elephant shaped.
(B) No part of my brain is orange and elephant shaped.
(C) Therefore, my mental image is not identical to any part of my brain.
(D) Therefore, probably, my mental image exists in my nonphysical mind.

In this argument we are supposed to be able to prove premise A by inspecting ("introspecting") our mental image. Premise B is held to be true, because brain science has never discovered in persons' brains tiny snapshots of colors and shapes that correspond to their mental images. Step C validly follows from (A) and (B) once we assume the law of identity as a premise. Finally, the conclusion (D) is plausible: If mental images exist (A), and they do not exist in our brains (C), then the most likely place for them to exist would be in our nonphysical minds.

Descartes uses the law of identity to argue for dualism by appealing to what he intuits to be the "essences" (defining characteristics) of minds and bodies:

> because . . . I have a clear and distinct idea of myself inasmuch as I am only a thinking and unextended thing, and . . . I possess a distinct idea of body, inas-

> much as it is only an extended and unthinking thing, it is certain that this I . . . is entirely and absolutely distinct from my body. (1972, 190)

I outline the argument this way:

(i) I am a thinking and unextended thing.
(ii) All bodies (including my body) are nonthinking and extended things.
(iii) Therefore, I am not identical to a body of any kind—including my own body.
(iv) Therefore, dualism is true.

Descartes offers the *divisibility argument*, which also uses the law of identity:

> there is a great difference between mind and body, inasmuch as body is by nature always divisible, and the mind is entirely indivisible. For, as a matter of fact, when I consider the mind, that is to say, myself inasmuch as I am only a thinking thing, I cannot distinguish in myself any parts, but apprehend myself to be clearly one and entire; and although the whole mind seems to be united to the whole body, yet if a foot, or an arm, or some other part, is separated from my body, I am aware that nothing has been taken away from my mind. And the faculties of willing, feeling, conceiving, etc. cannot be properly speaking said to be its parts, for it is one and the same mind which employs itself in willing and in feeling and understanding. But it is quite otherwise with corporeal or extended objects, for there is not one of these imaginable by me which my mind cannot easily divide into parts, and which consequently I do not recognise as being divisible; this [is] sufficient to teach me that the mind or soul of man is entirely different from the body. (1972, 196, Meditation 6)

I outline this argument this way:

(1) Minds (and my mind) cannot be divided into smaller parts.
(2) Bodies (and my body) can be divided into smaller parts.
(3) Therefore, my mind is not identical to my body.

CRITICISMS OF THE THREE VERSIONS OF THE LAW OF IDENTITY ARGUMENT

Critics think that although these dualistic arguments *look* impressive, on closer examination they prove to have false premises or invalid forms. Let us take first the argument concerning mental images. *Eliminative materialists* will deny that persons *are* aware of colored, elephant-shaped images. These theorists believe that although everyday language encourages us to talk this way, mental images do not exist. If images do not exist, then there is no possibility of "locating" them in a nonphysical mind. Thus, eliminative materialists reject the argument, because they believe that the first premise is false.

Noneliminativist or *identity materialists* believe that mental experiences should be understood as *events* that do not contain mental *objects*. Identity materialists say that although we do undergo an experience we call "having an orange, elephant-shaped image," we should not think that there exists a tiny mental object (thing, snapshot) in our consciousness. Instead, identity theorists maintain, we undergo the *mental event or process* of experiencing-an-orange-elephant-shaped-image. The hyphens show that the experience should be understood as an event (like dancing-a-dance), rather than a seeing of a mental thing (like seeing a lemon). Materialists believe that these events turn out to be brain events. Because mental images are actually *processes* or *events* that happen to us rather than objectified snapshots or pictures, there is no need to find a part of the brain that matches the nonexistent snapshots. Therefore, the fact that we cannot locate an orange, elephant-shaped part of our brains gives no reason to locate an image in a nonphysical mind. Thus, identity materialists also reject (A), though on different grounds than do the eliminativist materialists.

Consider next Descartes's argument based on his idea of the essential nature of minds and bodies. Materialist critics think that both of its premises are question begging. In his first premise Descartes claims that he knows that minds are unextended things, but this is exactly what the identity materialist denies. Descartes's only evidence for this premise is to appeal to the way he thinks about minds, but that does not prove anything. The case is likewise with Descartes's second premise that all bodies (including his brain) are incapable of thought. Although Descartes thinks that bodies necessarily lack mentality (he even believes that bodies lack the power of self-movement), this is merely his own dualistic bias. Materialists think that many bodies are *not* unthinking things—namely, the central nervous systems of humans and animals. Therefore, on both premises Descartes has begged the question against identity materialism by assuming premises he needs to prove.

Let us finally consider Descartes's divisibility argument. If we assume, as Descartes did, that minds are by their very essence unextended, then it will seem obvious that minds cannot be divided into simpler parts. But we have seen that this is exactly the point that Descartes needs to prove—it is question begging to assume it. There are two ways to show that Descartes's argument is question begging.

First, if we go along with Descartes and talk about minds as if they are things, then the identity materialist can provide the following argument that minds *are* divisible: (1) Minds are identical to brains. (2) Brains are divisible into smaller parts. (3) Therefore, minds are divisible into smaller parts. Of course, it would be question begging of the materialists to assume (1). But the materialist can reply that one question begging argument deserves another: If both sides beg the question, then neither side wins the argument, and the materialist has thwarted Descartes's argument.

Second, we could quit talking about minds as if they are object-like *things* and talk instead about *mental states* or *events*, as the identity materialist does. If we do, we will need also to shift our discussion to *brain events*. Once we do this, we should reject the divisibility argument, because on this way of reading the argument it will say that mental events are not divisible, but brain events are. The problem is that it makes no clear sense to talk about events as divisible, and perhaps even less sense to say that brain events are divisible and mental events are not.

I do not find arguments for dualism based on the law of identity convincing, because these arguments rely on the fact that we prephilosophically think about minds and brains differently. This fact cuts little ice for anyone who thinks that philosophy should not give special weight to our prephilosophical beliefs. Nonetheless, these objections pose a challenge for materialism. Our mental lives seem to have qualitative, *phenomenological* (experienced) characteristics. For example, it feels a certain way to have a throbbing pain. To use Thomas Nagel's expression, it is *like* something to be a bat (or any conscious being), but it is not like something to be an electron or a chair (1979, ch. 12). Materialists should not ignore this fact. When we get to the debate between eliminative and noneliminative materialists, we shall see this point again.

5. Nonphysical Minds as an Inference to the Best Explanation?

We saw in chapters 1 and 2 that inference to the best explanation is a common denominator underlying philosophy, science, and everyday life. (Why do we think that there is someone at the front door? That hypothesis is the best explanation for why the doorbell is ringing.) Many dualists have argued that supposing that humans possess nonphysical minds is the best explanation for various facts about humans. In this section I examine four attempts to support the existence of nonphysical minds by inference to the best explanation.

DESCARTES ON THE MINDS OF HUMANS

A famous instance of this type of argument was provided by Descartes. Descartes thought that humans possess two traits that distinguish us from animals: We use language and we have a great versatility in our behavior (we can accomplish our goals in many different ways). The best explanation for these differences, according to Descartes, is that humans possess nonphysical minds that produce mentality, whereas animals are only stimulus-response "machines" possessing no mentality at all.

Living in the seventeenth century, Descartes knew little of the remarkable genetic similarities between humans and the rest of the animal kingdom. He also knew nothing about natural selection and evolution. So Descartes missed out on some important facts that bear on his argument. The greatest problem with Descartes's argument, however, is that it commits a simple logical confusion. Although our use of language and our greater behavioral versatility give strong evidence that most humans have greater *mentality* than most animals do, that does not support the conclusion that human mentality requires *non-physical* minds. The greater mentality of language users may be better explained by citing the greater development of the language-processing centers of human brains. Indeed, this is exactly what most psychologists believe occurs in the development of an individual human: Brain development corresponds to language acquisition, because the brain is *responsible for* language. The conclusion Descartes should have reached is that humans minds are generally superior to animal minds in the sense that humans have more advanced *thinking things*. He should not have concluded that humans possess *nonphysical minds*, whereas animals are mere machines.

THE EPISTEMOLOGICAL (KNOWLEDGE) ARGUMENT

Another way to argue that we need to postulate nonphysical minds as an explanatory hypothesis is to claim that we have knowledge of the mental differently than we do the physical. Here is the first version of that argument. Many philosophers believe that our reports of our sensations, beliefs, and desires have a special degree of certainty that our reports about physical objects cannot have. For example, the mental report "*I seem to see a cat*" is more likely to be true than the physical object report "*I see a cat*." I am wrong about the latter if no cat affects my optic nerve; but even if there is no cat, I can be correct in saying that I seem to see a cat. For the same reason, "I feel a tickle" is less likely to be wrong than "I feel a feather." If we acknowledge the greater degree of certainty of mental reports, it is natural to ask: Why are reports of mental states more certain than reports of physical things? The dualists say that our awareness of our mental states is an awareness of a special kind of being—our nonphysical minds.

Two factors reduce the strength of this argument. First, the difference in certainty to be explained may not be so great. The status of physical object beliefs such as my belief that I see my hand is extremely high, even if we can imagine how my belief could be false (for example, if I am deceived by Descartes's Evil Genius as discussed in chapter 3). But I can also be mistaken in my belief that I seem to see my hand. After all, seeming to see my hand is one mental state and *believing* that I seem to see my hand is another. So, there is always a possibility that I can be mistaken. Perhaps many mental reports are slightly more certain than corresponding reports about physical objects, but the difference is not always so great.

The second factor is that to the extent that there is a difference in the certainty of mental reports and physical object reports, saying that minds are nonphysical might not be the best explanation. Mental reports may be less susceptible to being wrong simply because they do not state how things are, but only how things seem. Mental reports are more guarded or careful, and, thus, less likely to be false. This is similar to the way that saying there are *some* persons in the room is less likely to be false than saying the exact number of persons one thinks is in the room. Thus, materialists can reply that it is not *the kind of thing that our mental reports are about* that makes them more likely to be true, but simply *the way we express them*. The hypothesis that mental reports are about nonphysical things seems a more far-fetched explanation.

The second version of the epistemological argument, which is a law of identity argument, claims that we can know our mental states by *introspection*, but we cannot know physical things by introspection. Because we know our minds differently than we know our brains, our minds must be nonphysical. The best reply to this argument is to point out that its second premise is question-begging. If minds are identical to brains, as noneliminative materialists believe, then it logically follows that we *do* introspect our brains whenever we introspect our minds, although we do not *realize* that we are doing so.

PERSONAL IDENTITY

A third dualist use of inference to the best explanation is based on the *problem of personal identity*: What makes an individual the same person over time—over one minute or fifty years? Here is the argument. Suppose that human beings consist entirely of their bodies and have no nonphysical minds. If so, then as the matter in our bodies gradually changes, so do we. Biologists know that living organisms constantly renew themselves as new molecules go into their living cells and replace the old molecules. After twenty years human beings will have almost entirely new molecules in their bodies (the lone exceptions residing in dead cells that have quit functioning). This entails that *if persons are solely material*, as the materialists maintain, then a person cannot literally be the same person after twenty years. This is *not* to claim merely that we will have different beliefs, desires, and values. Rather, we will be *entirely different persons*, in the way that Sylvester Stallone and Arnold Schwarzenegger are entirely different persons. The person who bears your name twenty years from now will not be *you*, but a replacement person who grew out of you—if materialism is true.

This prospect is worrisome. If you think not, consider a thought experiment offered by Derek Parfit (1984, ch. 10). Suppose you are offered money to allow yourself to be "teleported" (as in *Star Trek*) to Mars. The process requires that each of your molecules will be diagrammed, a copy of that diagram will be electronically transmitted to Mars, and the diagram will be used to instantaneously recreate you there. So in three minutes there will be someone on Mars with your exact structure—including beliefs, desires, and memories. The only possible drawback is that the diagramming process on Earth will destroy your molecules. Would such teleportation be a sending of *you* to Mars? Or would it mean *the death of you* and a *copy of you* being made there?

The point of the example is that we normally think that we need to have *the same constitutions* to be *the same persons* over time. If another person who bears your name has none or only a small percentage of your molecules, that person cannot be *you*. But if materialism is true, then because of the way living cells constantly change their matter, we cannot consist of the same matter over time. Our personal identity would be like the identity of a river whose water is constantly changing: merely relative. As Parfit expresses it, we prephilosophically think that there is always a definite answer to the question: Would this individual be *you*? But *if* materialism is true, there is not a definite "yes" or "no" answer possible. Personal identity would be only relative, depending on the degree of similarity that obtains between earlier and later selves.

At this point dualists believe they can come to the rescue: Dualists explain why we are the same persons over time by hypothesizing that persons are not merely physical beings, but have nonphysical minds. Nonphysical minds do not undergo biological change, but remain what (who) they are. Nonphysical minds would be like containers that hold our mental states throughout our existence. The *contents of the container* might change, but the *container* would not. So, nonphysical minds would establish the absolute degree of personal identity that common sense demands and materialism cannot provide.

This personal identity argument suffers from weak data. Why should we believe we are *the same persons* over time, rather than *relatively the same persons*, as materialism maintains? Some of us *like* the idea of absolute personal identity over time, because we find that it provides a more "solid" feeling about ourselves than admitting that who we are is constantly changing. But this is scarcely evidence. Others like absolute personal identity when trying to justify *retribution* (punishment on the grounds of just deserts). For example, it is difficult to justify sentences of life in prison as retribution if you think that personal identity is only relative, and hence, that the prisoner is gradually ceasing to be the criminal who committed the crime. (There are nonretributive, utilitarian grounds for incarceration. See chapter 8.) But if humans are material beings, then their identity *cannot* be absolute in a way that satisfies the retributivist thinkers. Nonetheless, the fact that we want to believe in absolute personal identity to support retribution does not make it true. So, overall, the evidence for absolute personal identity appears shaky. When it comes to using absolute personal identity to argue in favor of nonphysical minds, the dualist has things backward. We need to prove dualism to argue that identity is absolute; we cannot argue the other way around.

PARANORMAL PHENOMENA

Many persons believe in various forms of paranormal (supernatural) experiences: psychokinesis (moving material objects with our minds), precognition (knowing the future), seeing at a distance (clairvoyance), mind reading, communication with the dead, out-of-body experiences, reincarnation, and faith healing. These persons sometimes adopt a version of inference to the best explanation to support dualism: These remarkable events happen, and they can be best explained by the hypothesis that our minds are nonphysical.

Problems lie both with the data and with the theory. First, the data are doubtful, because none of these events have ever been documented. It is a task for critical thinking—the methodology of philosophy as described in chapters 1 and 2—to determine in such cases whether there are any significant data that need to be explained. In the case of paranormal phenomena, the data have always turned out to be nonexistent (Schick and Vaughn, 1995). Without data to be explained, the argument from paranormal phenomena cannot get started.

Second, even if any of the data were real, it is doubtful that the hypothesis of nonphysical minds would explain it any better than saying that our brains have physical powers that we do not fully understand. In Mark Twain's *A Connecticut Yankee in King Arthur's Court*, the time-traveling hero dazzled his medieval captors by starting a fire using a magnifying glass to focus the sun's rays. For persons who did not understand that light rays are physical phenomena that can be refracted by glass, this would seem supernatural, but such a feat would hardly invite a supernatural explanation today. By analogy, if any of the paranormal phenomena ever are shown to be genuine, it is a better bet that its explanation will lie in the physical powers of the brain rather than the nonphysical. After all, we have some understanding of how the brain emits extremely weak electromagnetic waves (Churchland, 1984, 17). It is at least imaginable that when we learn more about the brain we will learn that some of its effects are truly remarkable. On the other hand, we have no idea of how a nonphysical mind could produce strange effects.

6. Interactionism, Parallelism, and Epiphenomenalism

So far we have looked at general reasons for believing that nonphysical minds exist, but we have not addressed the question of whether nonphysical minds interact with our brains (dualistic interactionism), whether there is no interaction in either direction (dualistic parallelism), or whether there is causation only from brains to minds (epiphenomenalism). In this section we consider what can be said for each of the dualistic options: If we believe that minds are nonphysical and bodies are physical, which is the best theory of how they are related?

DUALISTIC INTERACTIONISM

There are two main reasons for thinking that minds (our thinking things) and brains influence each other. First, everyday experience suggests that they do. Intending to scratch my head seems to *cause* me to scratch my head. Putting my hand near a stove seems to *cause* the sensation of warmth in my hand. This does not settle the question: We might be wrong. Nonetheless, it provides at least an initial reason for believing that minds and bodies interact.

Second, even if one doubts the evidential value of our feeling that minds and bodies interact, our everyday experience at least shows that mental and physical events correspond in time. But now we need to ask *why* they correspond in time. Interaction seems to be the simplest explanation. It is difficult to understand why pains follow bumps to our shins and why our bodily movements follow our choices if the relationship between the mental and physical is *not* causal.

Even if we believe that there are strong reasons for believing that *minds* (*thinking things*) interact with our brains, there are important reasons for thinking that dualism's *nonphysical minds* cannot interact with brains. The first falls under the heading of the *problem of interaction*: *How could a nonphysical mind interact with a physical body*? If minds are nonphysical (having no extension in space, no size, no shape, no mass, no force, no charge) and brains are physical (having extension, size, shape, mass, force, and charge), then it is difficult to see *how* they could affect each other. There seems to be no way for the physical brain to latch onto a thing that is not extended in space. And there seems to be no way that a thing that does not exist in space could impart an influence to something that is physical. We can imagine how an ant might push over the Empire State Building, because an ant and the building share physical characteristics: Simply imagine the ant's strength being multiplied one billion times. It is difficult to imagine how a nonphysical thing could influence anything in the physical world—even something as small as a brain cell—because a nonphysical thing would lack the characteristics needed to make the connection.

Probably the best defense for the interactionist regarding the problem of interaction is a good offense. Instead of trying to show that causation between physical and nonphysical things would not be strange, the interactionist should emphasize that *all* causation—even involving two physical events—is strange. (This point about causation owes to Hume, 1955, Section IV.) Consider how causal explanations work. We explain how two *distantly related* events are causally related by citing the links between them. My pressing the button on the doorbell causes an electrical circuit to be completed, which sends current to the ringer, which vibrates to cause sound. When two events are *immediately related*, however, there are no intermediary steps to cite as an explanation. We can say only that one event happened and then the other. Thus, whenever we try to explain an immediate causal connection between *any* two events—

whether they are physical or nonphysical—we will fail. The interactionist can say that when the physical and nonphysical interact, they just do, and no explanation is possible.

The problem of interaction is the puzzle of how interaction could occur. A second objection to interactionism comes from the *principle of conservation of energy*. According to this principle, which has been accepted by physicists since the nineteenth century, whenever events occur in the physical world: (1) There is a transfer of energy from the cause to the effect; and (2) The total amount of energy in the universe remains the same. (When Albert Einstein (1879–1955) discovered that mass is interchangeable with energy, the principle was expanded to include mass.)

Now suppose that an event in a nonphysical mind causes an event to occur in a brain. According to (1), there is a transfer of energy. Therefore, the brain gains energy; but the nonphysical mind, having no physical characteristics, cannot lose energy. So there should be a *gain* in the total amount of energy in the universe, which would violate (2). Going in the other direction, suppose a brain event causes a mental event to occur. According to (1), the brain would lose energy. But the nonphysical mind could not gain energy from the brain, again, because nonphysical minds are incapable of having any energy at all. So there should be a *loss* in energy, also violating (2) of the conservation principle.

Dualistic interactionists sometimes try to resist these objections by saying that when nonphysical minds interact with physical brains there is no transfer of energy. In doing so, they amend (1)—*not all* events involving physical events involve a transfer of energy. *Only events involving two physical things do*. Because there are no energy transfers in *psychophysical* (mind/body) interaction, (2) of the principle is not violated by energy gains and losses. In sum, interactionists say that by amending (1), they can say that (2) is not violated.

We can see that this move is questionable, however, by considering a thought experiment (Cornman, Lehrer, and Pappas, 1987, ch. 4). Suppose we had the psychokinetic ability to affect physical objects with our nonphysical minds without transferring energy to the physical objects. For example, suppose that by "scrunching up" our nonphysical minds we could move a boulder and start it rolling down a hill. In a like manner, suppose we were able to stop a boulder that is already rolling down a hill. When we move the boulder we increase the amount of actual energy in the world. When we stop the boulder, we reduce the amount of actual energy. So, even if we say that there is no *transfer of energy* from our minds to the boulder, the physical world still has its energy disrupted.

Extending the example, it seems that *any* influence nonphysical minds had on physical things would change the amount of energy in the physical world—whether the gains and losses are dramatic such as those involving the boulder, or smaller such as those involving our brain cells. This means that (2) of the conservation principle would be violated *with respect to the physical world alone*.

But we have no reason to believe that (2) is ever violated. So even if interactionists say that the nonphysical influences the physical without a transfer of energy, this will still entail an unsupported belief about the way the physical world is.

DUALISTIC PARALLELISM

Some dualists find the interaction of physical and nonphysical things inconceivable and adopt a bold alternative to interactionism: Mental events and brain events only appear to affect each other, but they really do not. This is known as *dualistic parallelism,* because it holds that minds and bodies run in parallel series without affecting each other. The French philosopher Malebranche (MALL 'BRONCH) (1638–1715) held that God constantly intervenes in the lives of persons to create the *illusion* that the physical and mental are interacting. For example, when I bump my shin God directly causes in my mind a sensation of pain. This theory is known as *occasionalism*, because God is hypothesized to "occasion" or bring about all events on Earth, including even those involving only physical things.

The German philosopher and inventor of calculus Leibniz offered a more famous variety of parallelism: *pre-established harmony*. In starting the universe, God arranged mental and physical events to run in parallel sequences. Thus, bumping your shin is followed by your sensation of pain, because God designed the universe so that these two events would coincide. Imagine two clocks that run at exactly the same rate, the first with no chimes and the second with no hands. When the first clock reaches 12 o'clock, the second clock begins to chime. Although an observer who did not understand that the two clocks are synchronized might think that the movement of the first clock's hands *caused* the chimes to ring, that would be a mistake. Because our nonphysical minds and brains run in perfect harmony, we mistakenly think that there is causal interaction when there is none.

The advantage of any variety of parallelism is that it avoids the problem of interaction. *Question*: How do nonphysical minds and physical brains affect each other? *Answer*: They can't, so they don't. But we need to ask whether the parallelists have a good explanation of why mental events and physical events run in perfect sequence if the connection between them is *not* causal.

The weaknesses of occasionalism and pre-established harmony are clear. First, it is doubtful that the parallelists have gained anything by involving God. Postulating God to avoid the problem of interaction trades one difficulty (Why do minds and bodies run in parallel if they do not interact?) for another (How can we prove God exists?), and adds an additional puzzle (Why would God want to deceive us about something like this?).

Second, parallelists cite God to explain why the nonphysical and the physical run in parallel, because they believe that the physical and nonphysical cannot interact. But God is either physical or nonphysical. (As we see in chapter 9, most philosophical conceptions of God are as nonphysical, but that is not important here.) If God is physical, then the parallelists should say that God cannot affect the nonphysical to make it run parallel to the physical. If God is nonphysical, then the parallelists should say that God cannot affect the physical to make it run parallel to the nonphysical. Therefore, on the parallelist's own principles, God cannot bring about the desired parallel sequence. If the parallelist tries to resist this objection by making an exception for God, then why not simply accept interactionism in the first place and forget about parallelism?

EPIPHENOMENALISM

Epiphenomenalists maintain that our brains affect our minds, but our minds do not affect our brains. Mental states are like the sound a babbling brook makes as it flows downstream or the noise from the whistle on a locomotive. They are caused by the operation of the physical thing, but they do not affect its operation.

The English biologist and early advocate of evolution Thomas Huxley (1825–1895) believed that science supports epiphenomenalism. Huxley noted that in both animals and humans, behavior can often continue despite the loss of mentality. Huxley removed two thirds of a frog's brain and found that it could still swim. A soldier with a serious brain injury who had lost many of his mental functions was still able to sing. Huxley thought that such examples show that mentality is not *necessary for* behavior. Therefore, Huxley surmised, even when mental states are present, they do not *cause* behavior. Huxley also held that epiphenomenalism fits nicely with evolution: Humanity's mentality gradually developed as it was carried along by our evolving nervous systems.

Epiphenomenalism faces two objections. First, epiphenomenalists have no explanation for how the physical could affect the nonphysical—the babbling brook and steam whistle analogies do not help solve the problem of interaction. If we mean by "sound" "vibrations in the air," then the babbling brook's creation of sound is an example of physical-physical causation, and the example sheds no light on the problem. If we mean by "sound" "the sensation of sound in hearers' nonphysical minds," then we have no idea of how the brook can cause sound *in this sense* to come into existence, and the analogy is again uninformative. Either way, the analogy is no help, and we are left with the objection that epiphenomenalism cannot explain how the physical affects the nonphysical. This criticism will be made by parallelists and identity materialists.

There is a second objection. *If* one says that brain events can cause mental events, then why not go all the way to interactionism and say that mental events can cause brain events? After all, by saying that brain events cause mental events epiphenomenalists have already endorsed a causal connection between the physical and the nonphysical. Having made this commitment, why not take advantage of it instead of advocating the counterintuitive view that the mental has no effect on the physical?

MATERIALISM

7. The Basics of Materialism

Materialism holds that persons are entirely physical and have no nonphysical minds or nonphysical mental states. Materialists believe that persons are complex parts of nature: Every component of a person exists both in space and time. Although the majority of contemporary philosophers are materialists, materialists disagree among themselves. The mind/body problem in the twentieth century has been primarily a debate between materialists over which variety is best. *Eliminative materialists* hold that minds and mental states do not exist: Although everyday language suggests that there are mental states such as beliefs, desires, and sensations, there really are none. *Noneliminative* or *identity materialists* hold that mental states do exist and are identical to physical events in our central nervous systems.

Many materialists are determinists who believe that all human choices are causally necessitated by the laws of nature. As discussed in chapter 8, some determinists believe in free will (the soft determinists), and others deny it (the hard determinists). So materialists who believe in determinism can accept free will. On the other hand, some materialists are libertarians who believe that persons make undetermined free choices. So, materialists have at least two ways to believe in free will.

Materialists can also be theists. Probably more materialists are atheists than theists, but many materialists are theists. Most materialists reject the existence of an afterlife, but not all. As noted, one can believe that one has an afterlife in one's resurrected body.

There are several reasons why materialism is attractive. First, materialists say that there is no evidence for the existence of nonphysical minds, and that if there is no evidence for the nonphysical, then we should not postulate it. This is not to say that unknowable things cannot exist, but only that we should not add things to our picture of reality unless we have evidence for their existence. Materialists remind us of the persistent dualist mistake of taking our awareness of our *mentality* as evidence that we have *nonphysical minds*. Even if we are convinced, for example, that we feel pains in our minds (thinking things), this is not evidence that our minds are nonphysical minds. Our minds might be our brains. Consider the following argument that a careless dualist might offer:

(1) I know by introspection that I have a mind.
(2) Minds are nonphysical things.
(3) Therefore, I know I have a nonphysical mind.

For (1) to be true, "mind" must mean "thinking thing." If what one means by "mind" is "nonphysical mind," then one cannot know by introspection that a mind in this sense exists. Therefore, for the argument to be valid, we must also mean "thinking thing" when we use the word "mind" in (2). But then (2) becomes doubtful, because we have no proof that our thinking things are nonphysical. This argument appears sound only because it commits the *fallacy of ambiguity*: "Mind" has one definition in the first premise and a different one in the second premise.

Second, materialism avoids some difficulties that trouble dualism: How do the physical and nonphysical interact? When, where, and how do nonphysical minds show up in a mostly physical world? How can the nonphysical and the physical interact without violating the principle of conservation of energy?

Third, many materialists like to see human beings as more advanced members of the animal kingdom. Doing so makes one's picture of the world *continuous* (smooth flowing), rather than *discrete* (containing sharp breaks). Seeing mentality as nonphysical would create a sharp break in the natural world between the creatures that have minds and those that do not. As science learns to understand the rest of the biological world in terms of the laws governing material processes, it becomes increasingly difficult to think that human beings alone contain a nonphysical component. Materialism provides a view of persons that fits better with what we think we know about the natural world than dualism does. I develop this theme with the next two arguments.

TWO SLIPPERY SLOPE ARGUMENTS FOR MATERIALISM

In a slippery slope argument we argue that because one thing (A1) is clearly X and because there is a smooth gradation of examples (A2, A3 . . .) that are similar to A1, probably each of the other examples is also X. For example, if an iron rod is very hot because of the rapid motion of its component molecules, then it is reasonable to believe that an iron rod that is slightly less hot is made so by slightly less rapid molecular motion, and so on. Slippery slope arguments tend to be sound when they deal with phenomena that are continuous; they tend to be unsound when their subject matter is discrete. For example, if we take the even number *24* and continue to subtract one from it, we do not get numbers that are gradually less and less even, but first an odd number *23*, then an even number *22*, and so on. It is often debatable whether a slippery slope argument correctly applies to a specific case.

The first slippery slope argument concerns the *ontogenesis* (individual development) of humans from their biological origins. *At what time* do nonphysical minds appear as humans develop from fertilized eggs? *How* do nonphysical minds appear as a human develops from egg and sperm? There is no evidence that nonphysical minds are "attached" to the egg and sperm at conception. (One can say this, but saying so is driven by theological doctrine or personal ideology, not evidence.) There is a gradual development of the human brain during fetal development and even through childhood. Materialists think that the correspondence between the development of our mentality and our brains is best explained by saying that our minds *are* our brains. If we say that our minds are nonphysical minds, then when, how, and why do nonphysical minds enter the picture?

A second slippery slope argument is parallel to the one from ontogenesis, but instead involves the location of mentality on the *phylogenetic scale* (the ordering of biological organisms from simple to complex). Just as there is no reason to say that nonphysical minds were attached to fertilized human eggs, there is no reason to assign nonphysical minds to the simplest animals on the phylogenetic scale such as the amoeba or paramecium. There is likewise no reason to assign nonphysical minds to creatures as we gradually ascend the scale to worms, fish, amphibians, reptiles, birds, and mammals. As with ontogenesis, increased mental complexity corresponds with increased nervous system complexity, but there seems to be no plausible place to say: "On this side of the line there are no nonphysical minds, but on that side of the line there are nonphysical minds."

The argument from the phylogenetic scale fits nicely with an evolutionary view of human mentality. Human beings' most distant ancestors—the one-celled animals living in the seas—had no nonphysical minds. Nor did any of the higher forms of life into which these one-celled creatures evolved. As their nervous systems developed, our ancestors began to acquire mentality, but the mentality was always physical: There is no reasonable point in human evolution to say "Nonphysical minds came into existence here." The evolutionary account has ready answers to two questions that are difficult for dualists: *Question*: How did the nonphysical show up on the physical planet Earth? *Answer*: It didn't. *Question*: Why do humans share so much mentality and genetic structure with chimpanzees, orangutans, and gorillas? *Answer*: These are our closest surviving nonhuman relatives—both we and they evolved from common ancestors. Mentality, in animals or humans, always was and always will be physical.

8. Eliminative Materialism

BEHAVIORISM

The first main variety of eliminative materialism, *behaviorism*, claims that humans and animals do not have minds in the functional sense of "thinking things." Instead, behaviorists hold, talk about minds and mental events is a misleading way of talking about intelligent behavior. For instance, a squirrel's desiring to eat an acorn is simply its tendency to try to eat it given the chance. Persons' believing that snow is cold is our tendency to act as if snow is cold.

We confuse ourselves if we think that desiring and believing are anything more than *dispositions* (tendencies) to act in various ways. To say that persons have *minds* understood as centers of consciousness that come between stimuli and responses would be a confusion similar to thinking that because the average American family owns 1.3 cars, there exists some actual family called "the average American family" that mysteriously owns a fractional part of a car (Cornman, Lehrer, and Pappas, 1987, ch. 4).

Behaviorism as a philosophical theory (philosophical behaviorism) achieved moderate popularity in the middle of the twentieth century for two reasons. First, *methodological behaviorism* was an important research strategy in psychology, largely due to the work of Harvard psychologist B. F. Skinner (1904–1990). Skinner claimed that for psychology to be scientific it must explain behavior without referring to unobservable minds and mental events. This meant that psychologists should discover laws that relate publicly observable stimuli to publicly observable responses without citing mental intermediaries. Behaviorists refused to recognize the subjective consciousness that was the subject matter of introspective psychology nor the *explanatory constructs* (postulations) such as the id, ego, and super-ego of the psychoanalytic method of Sigmund Freud (1859–1939). Persons who believed that *psychologists* have no need for the mind in explaining behavior were tempted to think that *philosophers* have no need for the mind for their purpose of painting an accurate picture of reality.

A second reason many philosophers leaned toward behaviorism was their *dis*like of Descartes's dualism. The reasoning of these philosophers may be expressed in a valid argument:

(1) Either there are nonphysical minds, which entails all the difficulties of Cartesian interactionism, *or* there are no minds, in which case behaviorism is true.
(2) Cartesian interactionism is false.
(3) Therefore, behaviorism is true.

If one assumes the (doubtful) first premise of this argument, all one has to do to prove behaviorism is true is to show that Cartesian interactionism is false.

The dominant figure behind this type of argument was the English philosopher Gilbert Ryle (1900–1976), who used the newly popular method of analyzing ordinary language to argue that talk about minds as thinking things involved a "category mistake." According to Ryle, just as it would be a logical confusion to be shown all the buildings of Oxford University and then ask where the university is, it would be a mistake to observe all of a person's intelligent behavior and then ask what the person's mind is. Ryle devoted his influential *The Concept of Mind* (1949) to trying to show how we can understand the whole spectrum of mental language without interpreting it to refer to internal minds or mental events.

Ryle's behaviorism was reinforced by *logical positivists* (scientifically oriented philosophers) such as Rudolf Carnap (1891–1971) and Carl Hempel (1905–). Logical positivists believed that philosophy should reject as meaningless any talk about unobservable entities—whether the subatomic particles of physics or the mental events of psychology. Carnap claimed that "every sentence of psychology may be formulated in physical language. . . . all sentences of psychology describe physical occurrences, namely, the physical behavior of humans and other animals" (Carnap, 1959, 165). Hempel claimed that "All psychological statements which are meaningful . . . are translatable into propositions which do not involve psychological concepts, but only the concepts of physics" (Hempel, 1949, 378).

NEUROPHILIC ELIMINATIVE MATERIALISM

The second main variety of eliminative materialism is generally called "eliminative materialism," but because I am using that term to include behaviorism, I need to find a different term. Because behaviorists get their name from the aspect of human beings they emphasize, an appropriate label for the other school of eliminative materialists would be "neurophiles" (lovers of the brain). Behaviorists say that appreciating the complexity of human behavior allows us to quit seeing humans as having minds; neurophiles say that as we learn how brains work, we will see that we should quit talking about minds and mental states, and replace mental talk with the vocabulary of *neuroscience* (brain science).

Richard Rorty provides an analogy to illustrate neurophilic eliminative materialism. Many persons once believed that epilepsy is caused by demons and that persons suffering epileptic seizures were possessed by demons. As medical science came to understand that epilepsy is caused by electrical disturbances in the brain, persons aware of the scientific picture quit talking about demon possession. Demon theory was discarded once we learned a better theory. Analogously, as brain science discovers what is going on in persons' brains at those times when we *say* that they experience mental events, we should quit talking about mental events and instead adopt the vocabulary of brain science:

> The absurdity of saying "Nobody has ever felt a pain" is no greater than that of saying "Nobody has ever seen a demon," *if* we have a suitable answer to the question "What *was* I reporting when I said I felt a pain?" To this question, the science of the future may reply "You were reporting the occurrence of a certain brain-process, and it would make life simpler for us if you would, in the future, *say* 'My C-fibers are firing' instead of saying 'I'm in pain.'" (1971, 179–80)

Paul Churchland advocates neurophilic eliminative materialism in this way:

> [W]hen neuroscience has matured to the point where the poverty of our current conceptions (of the mind) is apparent to everyone, and the superiority of the new framework is established, we shall then be able to set about *re*conceiving our internal states and activities, within a truly adequate conceptual framework at last. Our explanations of one another's behavior will appeal to such things as our neuropharmacological states, the neural activity in specialized anatomical areas, and whatever other states are deemed relevant by the new theory. (1984, 44–45)

TWO OBJECTIONS TO ELIMINATIVE MATERIALISM

Behaviorists and neurophilic eliminative materialists let their abhorrence of dualism drive them to the conclusion that mental phenomena do not exist. But noneliminative materialism, examined in the next section, is a possible middle ground. Here are two ways to argue that eliminative materialism is too drastic.

The first criticism applies against both behaviorism and neurophilic eliminative materialism. The trouble with denying that mental events exist is not that we prephilosophically believe that we experience mental events. Throughout this book, I have claimed that common sense should not be accepted uncritically. The trouble, instead, is that believing that mental events exists is *itself* a mental event. Therefore, we cannot be wrong in thinking that we have mental states so long as we think we do. (This is similar to Descartes's *cogito* argument examined in chapter 3: If I think I exist, then I must exist. If I think I have mental states, then I must have mental states.)

Imagine the task that eliminative materialists will face in trying to convince persons that they lack mentality. First, the audience will need to *see* or *hear* or otherwise *sense* their message. Second, the audience will need to *recognize* and then *understand* the eliminativists' points. Third, the audience will have to *decide* whether the eliminitivists' points should be accepted. All of the emphasized terms refer to mental (thinking thing) events. This means that the attempt to prove eliminative materialism to an audience appears to be self-defeating. The audience's acceptance of the argument would prove that the argument is unsound.

The second criticism applies only to behaviorism. Behaviorists try to explain the behavior of the most complex known entities in the universe—humans and animals—without referring to intervening variables that lie between stimulus and response. As Jerry Fodor suggests, we cannot even explain the behavior of *inanimate* objects without citing the role that *their* intervening variables—unobservable molecules, atoms, and subatomic particles—play in producing their behavior. For example, we cannot explain the destructive force of an A-bomb without citing its internal states—atomic fission. What chance do we have of explaining the complexities of human behavior without citing the causal roles of humans' internal variables—their mental states?

9. Noneliminative (Identity) Materialism

Noneliminative (identity) materialism holds that mental events exist, that they have most of the characteristics that common sense assigns to them, and that they are brain events. For example, to have a pain is to feel a sensation, which is a brain event or process. Believing, desiring, fearing, hoping, and understanding a language are all real processes that occur in our central nervous systems.

Identity materialism has clear advantages over dualism. By avoiding nonphysical minds and events, identity materialism fits easily into a scientific picture of the world. It avoids the problems about ontogenesis, the phylogenetic scale, and evolution. It also avoids the problem of interaction and does not violate the principle of conservation of energy. By insisting that mental events have both physical causes and physical effects, identity materialism agrees with common sense without buying into the problems of interactionism or epiphenomenalism. Identity materialism also avoids objections to eliminative materialism, because it does not deny that persons have genuine mentality. Identity materialists think we need to take the mind seriously, because the mind is the brain—the most important part of the human organism.

THE CAUSAL ARGUMENT FOR IDENTITY MATERIALISM

Here is a simple, but powerful, argument for identity materialism based on the causal power of minds:

(1) Our minds affect our bodies.
(2) Our bodies are physical things.
(3) Only a physical thing can affect a physical thing.
(4) Therefore, our minds are physical.

This argument is valid and its premises look plausible. The first premise is widely accepted by prephilosophical common sense and dualistic interactionists. Parallelists and epiphenomenalists disagree, but that appears to be a serious weakness in their theories. The second premise is accepted by everyone except the phenomenalists. The third premise is the key to this argument: Interactionists reject it, whereas, phenomenalists, materialists, epiphenomenalists, and parallelists accept it. This puts the interactionist in the minority position but does not mean they are wrong. Nonetheless, if the interactionists are wrong about (3), the argument for identity materialism seems to go through smoothly.

THE LOCALIZATION ARGUMENT AND SPLIT BRAINS

Brain science in the twentieth century has discovered that much of our mental functioning is "localized" to specific parts of the brain. By studying brain injuries it became clear that most persons' language capabilities are dependent on Broca's area—the left frontal lobe of the cerebral cortex. Persons who suffer strokes in the left cortex experience impairment in reading, writing, speaking, and doing arithmetic. Strokes in the right cortex impair three-dimensional vision, pattern recognition, and facial recognition. Injuries to the hippocampus impair our ability to compile new memories. Moreover, persons with psychological disorders such as depression, mania, and schizophrenia display imbalances of certain brain chemicals. Because various types of mental functioning correspond to certain types of brain functioning, it is tempting to think that the mental functioning at stake may be *identical to* the brain functioning at those locations. Thus, localization is a powerful argument for materialism.

Perhaps the most striking demonstration of the localization of brain function is Nobel Prize winner Roger Sperry's experiments on epileptic patients who had the connections between their right and left cerebral hemispheres surgically cut to reduce the transmission of seizures from one hemisphere to the other. These *brain-bisection operations* were largely successful at minimizing or even eliminating the seizures and produced few unwanted side effects. The split-brain patients revealed some remarkable behavior, however, when they were tested by Sperry. Here is one experiment among many.

Patients looked straight ahead at a screen while letters were flashed on the screen so quickly that they did not have time to move their eyes. Thus, the letters shown on the left half of the screen were received only by the patients' right cerebral hemisphere, and the letters shown on the right half of the screen were received only by the patients' left hemisphere. For example, the word HATBAND was flashed on the screen so that the letters HAT were received only by the right hemisphere and the letters BAND were received only by the left hemisphere.

Experimenters then asked the patients what they saw. The patients unanimously replied BAND—but not HAT. Why? Sperry reasoned as follows: The patients' left (linguistic) hemisphere received input only from the right half of the screen. There was no transmission of information from the right (nonlinguistic) hemisphere to the left because the connections had been severed. Therefore, the left hemisphere had no way of knowing that the letters HAT had also been shown on the screen. This result supports the thesis that our speaking ability is localized to the left half of our brains.

The truly remarkable result occurred, however, when patients were given pencils in their left hands (which are controlled by their right cerebral hemispheres) and asked what they had seen. At the same time when patients *said* that the only thing they saw was BAND, they *wrote* with their left hands the letters HAT. The speaking left hemisphere was aware of the letters BAND, and the nonspeaking right hemisphere was aware of the letters HAT, but there seems to be *no single person* who was aware of seeing HATBAND.

This and the other experimental data involving brain bisection prompted brain scientists, psychologists, and philosophers to propose some radical theories about persons. Perhaps disconnecting a human's two cerebral hemispheres *creates* two completely different persons. (This was Sperry's view.) Perhaps two persons *always exist* inside normal humans. That is, maybe in each human cranium there exists a right hemisphere person and a left hemisphere person, who coexist harmoniously unbeknownst to anyone (including themselves). (This is advocated in Puccetti, 1981.) Perhaps the very idea of there existing a countable number of persons per human body is an obsolete concept, and instead, there is just a lot of mental activity connected with parts of human brains (Nagel, 1979, ch. 11).

Whatever the best interpretation of the split-brain experiments is for the issue of personal identity, the experiments seem to support materialism and hurt dualism. If our minds were simple, indivisible, nonphysical minds as the dualists maintain, then how could one mind both believe and not believe that it had seen HAT? How could one and the same mind believe and not believe that it had seen BAND? The most plausible explanation of the split brain experiments seems to be that minds are physical. Strange as it sounds, perhaps when our brains are split in certain ways, so are our minds.

THE SIMPLICITY ARGUMENT FOR IDENTITY MATERIALISM

The law of identity argument for dualism maintains that minds and mental events seem to have characteristics that brain and brain events do not. For example, a mental image is yellow, but it is difficult to see how yellowness can be part of our brain processes. A pain can be acute, but it is difficult to see how brain events can be acute. A thought can be about Brazil or an imaginary mountain made out of gold, but it is difficult to see how brain events can be *about* things.

These apparent differences in the characteristics of mental events and brain events lead dualists to say that mental events are not part of the body. Other thinkers have drawn a more modest conclusion: Although there is only one series of events occurring in persons and their minds, those that occur in persons' minds have two different kinds of characteristics. Mental events have both *physical* characteristics AND *nonphysical* characteristics. For instance, a sensation of pain would have the characteristics of being a certain firing of our neurons, and it would have a completely nonphysical characteristic of being hurtful. Thus, mental events such as thoughts, sensations, and beliefs would be both physical and nonphysical. So materialism would be partly true and partly false.

I think this view is doubtful. First, it makes perfectly good sense to say that our brain events have *mental* characteristics, so long as what we mean by "mental" is "the characteristics of *thinking things*." Indeed, this is what the identity materialist has been saying all along. But it is unclear what it means to say that brain events have mental characteristics in the sense of "*nonphysical* characteristics." In this sense of "mental," a brain event, which exists in the natural world of space and time, would be said to have characteristics that belong to things that *cannot* exist in the natural world. Thus, it is not clear what it means to say that an event is both physical and nonphysical. If we cannot make sense out of a theory, then we cannot know what it is saying. If we cannot know what a theory is saying, then we should not accept it.

Second, once we see the oddness of saying that brain events might have *nonphysical* characteristics, the identity theorist's best reply becomes clear. Identity materialists should respond by saying that mental characteristics *must* be physical. Consider the problem this way:

(1) Suppose that our mental events have real phenomenal characteristics. (Our itches feel itchy, our pains hurt, and our visual images are colored.)
(2) Suppose that our mental events are not nonphysical events, nor do they belong to nonphysical minds.
(3) So, what are the phenomenal characteristics of our mental events?

The simplest answer is that the phenomenal characteristics must be characteristics of the brain. Why? Because there is *nothing else* they can be. Philosophers continue to try to figure out what is the best way to map the mental characteristics of our mental events onto the characteristics of our brains, and there is no consensus regarding the best way. This is one of the ongoing debates in the mind/body problem. But this much seems clear: *If* the phenomenal characteristics are real and *if* there are no nonphysical minds or mental events to have them, then the simplest picture of the world holds that these characteristics belong to the brain. I call this iffy line of reasoning "the simplicity argument."

ARTIFICIAL INTELLIGENCE AS A CHALLENGE FOR MATERIALISM

In recent years computers have performed mathematical calculations on space missions, helped in diagnosing diseases and discovering mineral deposits, and modeled how the human mind works. In 1997 an IBM computer beat the world's best human chess player. It is little wonder that the prospect of building machines that possess genuine mentality has intrigued computer scientists, psychologists, philosophers, novelists, and moviemakers. Let us define *artifi-*

cial intelligence (*AI*) as the building of artifacts that possess genuine mentality, and do not merely simulate mentality.

Among those who think that artificial intelligence is possible, there is a controversy over whether artificially intelligent things would have to be made out of a certain *kind* of matter. Advocates of *AI functionalism* say that *mentality is brought into existence whenever a sufficiently complex computer program is run—regardless of whether the program is run by a biological organism or a nonbiological, artificially constructed machine*. Computer scientists Allen Newell and Herbert Simon endorse the *physical symbol system hypothesis*: "A physical symbol system has the necessary and sufficient means for general intelligent action" (1981, 41). This means that mentality is created by the running of sufficiently complex computer programs, and it does not matter whether the program is run by a human brain, a main frame computer, or an ant farm. According to this view, human brains produce mentality by running their programs, and so can any material thing that is capable of running the right programs.

The most famous opponent of AI functionalism is the materialist philosopher John Searle, who argues that mentality is not simply the satisfaction of the right programs (1984, ch. 2). According to Searle, mentality can be produced only by a physical object that has causal powers equal to that of human and animal brains. So if an artifact such as a computer *did* display mentality (which Searle allows is possible), it would have mentality not simply because it ran a program, but because it was a *substitute brain*. For Searle, the causal powers of biological brains, not the programs they run, create mentality.

Searle supports his view by imagining a person who understands only English who is lodged in a room with an instruction book written in English. When Chinese characters are sent into the room, the English speaker collects them, reads the instruction book that tells him what characters to select as a response, and then sends out of the room the appropriate Chinese characters. Unbeknownst to the English speaker, he is following a Chinese-language program (the same program a native Chinese speaker follows to understand Chinese), and his "replies" are just as good as those that the best native Chinese speaker could provide. To those outside the room, it looks as if there is a Chinese speaker inside the room answering the questions. Despite this appearance, Searle maintains, no understanding of Chinese has been brought into existence. Searle concludes that it takes more than symbol manipulation of the right programs to produce language comprehension. Newell and Simon must be wrong.

The important thing to emphasize in this chapter is that the debate over Newell and Simon's thesis is a debate between materialists. Neither side takes seriously the view that *nonphysical* minds might produce intelligence. Newell and Simon think that a soul cannot run programs, and Searle believes that only material objects with the physical power of brains can have mentality. This suggests that accepting the possibility of AI is a materialist belief and that rejecting the possibility of AI is a dualist belief. This in turn leads to a modus tollens argument that materialists need to answer:

(A) If materialism is true, then it is logically possible to build an artificial being that has genuine mentality.
(B) It is not logically possible to build an artificial being that has genuine mentality.
(C) Therefore, materialism is not true.

Because (A) is true, the key to the argument is (B). On examination, however, the evidence for (B) turns out to be questionable. Here are some popular reasons for thinking (B) is true, followed by materialist objections:

(1) "Computers are not alive, but only living things can have mentality." *Objection*: The computer that beat the world chess champion was not alive, because it is not a biological being. But to say that only biological things can have mentality is question begging.
(2) "Computers have no purposes except those of their designers and programmers." *Objection*: Having one's own purposes is a higher-level mental accomplishment that requires reflection on one's lower-level mental states. So far computers have not been designed to be self-reflective, but there is no reason to suppose they could not.
(3) "Computers merely follow programs, whereas humans are creative." *Objection*: As Daniel Dennett points out (1978, ch. 11), until you understand how a piece of human mentality comes about, you cannot know that it is *not* the result of program following. Nobody knows where *human* creativity comes from: If not by following programs, then perhaps by occasionally being bumped off their programs? Computers can be jostled from their programs. Moreover, how could citing nonphysical minds *explain* creativity instead of simply being a way to punctuate our lack of understanding?
(4) "Computers have no free will, but humans do." *Objection*: Computers can have free will in whatever way humans can, unless having free will requires nonphysical minds. To assume the latter would make (4) question begging.
(5) "Human behavior is flexible, whereas computer behavior is rigid (one of Descartes's tests of mentality)." *Objection*: Most humans are more flexible than most computers, but we need to ask why this is true. So far, we have primarily written programs that enable computers to perform narrowly defined tasks in serial order. Designing machines that would be intelligent in many areas at once—language understanding, pattern recognition, problem solving, locomotion (movement), and writing sonnets would be extremely difficult, prohibitively expensive, and probably

needless. But there is no reason to believe that this is logically impossible.

(6) "Words mean nothing to computers, so they will never *understand* language." *Objection*: How do words mean anything to humans? *We* understand the meanings of words, because we not only respond to them in our behavior but think about them from an abstract point of view. Computers are not designed to do this, but why can't they? And, again, why should the ability to think about words require a nonphysical mind?

(7) "Unlike humans, it would never be morally wrong to dismantle a computer. Therefore, computers can never have genuine mentality." *Objection*: This shows that we do not include existing computers as members of our moral community. This does not show that we could never build an artificial device toward whom we felt moral obligations. If a computer displayed intelligence, then to refuse to give it moral consideration would be chauvinistic. Our present attitudes toward computers reveal only the way computers *are* now, but says nothing about what computers could become.

(8) "Computers are the products of humans." *Objection*: *Humans* are also the products of humans.

CONCLUSION

In retrospect, the motivation that attracts philosophers to materialism was already outlined in the first chapter of this book. This is having a view of philosophy that: (1) tries to paint the most-likely-to-be-true picture of the world, irrespective of what we would like to be true, (2) models itself after scientific theory construction, which aims for simplicity in its explanations and rejects the existence of entities unless there is positive evidence for them, and (3) gives no special place to the beliefs of common sense or religion. As noted, this view of philosophy cannot be proved to be "the best." Hence, the materialist answer to the mind/body problem is not provable. Nonetheless, because this view appeals to many philosophers, materialism is the majority view—at this time, at least.

Discussion in the mind/body problem continues to be driven by developments in biology, neuroscience, computer science, and psychology that need to be integrated into our philosophical theories of the mind. Among materialists, pressing questions remain: Should materialists be eliminativists or noneliminativists? Should we adopt AI functionalism or reject it? What is the best way to think about mental events for the purposes of constructing theories in psychology? What should materialists say about personal identity, split brains, and free will? Moreover, mind/body dualism continues to be given able defenses by each new generation of philosophers.

Misconceptions about the Mind/Body Problem

Each of the following is a possible confusion about the mind/body problem. Explain why each is a mistake.

1. "Mind" means "nonphysical mind" or "soul."
2. "Mind" means "brain."
3. Anything we cannot be aware of with our senses is nonphysical.
4. The only way to believe that persons have nonphysical minds is to believe dualism.
5. The only way to believe that persons have minds is by believing that persons have nonphysical minds.
6. The only way to believe in an afterlife is by believing that persons have nonphysical minds.
7. The only way to believe that persons have free will is by believing that persons have nonphysical minds.
8. The only way to believe in materialism is by believing in eliminative materialism.
9. Noneliminative (identity) materialists believe that persons have nonphysical minds.
10. Noneliminative materialists believe that persons have no thinking things.
11. John Searle believes that computers cannot have minds.

Guide Questions

1. What is the functional definition of the word "mind"? Why is the functional definition a *neutral* definition? (102)
2. What is the single, most important characteristic of *physical* things? Of *nonphysical* things? (102)
3. In what way does dualism agree partly with materialism and partly with idealism (phenomenalism)? (103)
4. What is the difference between *monism* and *dualism*? (103)
5. What is the difference between *eliminative materialism* and *noneliminative (identity) materialism*? (103)
6. In what way does epiphenomenalism agree partly with dualistic interactionism and partly with dualistic parallelism? (104–5)
7. What important thesis does phenomenalism share with dualism? (105)
8. Why might persons who have the following interests like dualism? A belief in an afterlife? (105–6) A desire to see humans as special from all the animals? (106) A hope for free will? (106)
9. Express the *law of identity* in your own words. (106–7)

10. How might dualists use the law of identity to argue that mental images prove their theory? (107)
11. Explain Descartes's two arguments that rely on the law of identity. (107–8)
12. How do *noneliminative materialists* object to the mental image argument? (109)
13. Materialists reply that Descartes *begs the question* against them in his assumption about the essential nature of minds and bodies. What does this mean? (109)
14. How did Descartes argue for the existence of nonphysical minds as an *inference to the best explanation*? How do materialists respond? (110–11)
15. What are the two versions of the *knowledge argument* for nonphysical minds? (111–12)
16. If materialism is true, what problem arises for *personal identity*? (112–13)
17. How do dualists propose to avoid materialism's problem with personal identity? (113)
18. What are the two objections to using *paranormal phenomena* to argue for dualism? (114)
19. What are two reasons for preferring dualistic interactionism to the other dualistic theories? (115)
20. Explain the *problem of interaction* in one sentence. What is the dualistic interactionist's strongest reply? (115–16)
21. Explain the objection to interaction made on the basis of the *principle of conservation of energy*? How do some interactionists reply? (116)
22. Explain the difference between *occasionalism* and *pre-established harmony*. (117)
23. What criticism can be made of both occasionalism and pre-established harmony? (117–18)
24. In what way does *epiphenomenalism* face the problems of both interactionism and parallelism? (118–19)
25. Why is it a fallacy to argue that because we can introspect our minds, we know that dualism is true? (119–20)
26. What is the logical structure of a *slippery slope argument*? (120)
27. In one sentence, explain the argument from: (1) Ontogenesis. (2) The phylogenetic scale. (120–21)
28. What is the difference between *philosophical behaviorism* and *methodological behaviorism*? (121–22)
29. What is the basic tenet of *neurophilic eliminative materialism*? (123)
30. Why would it be paradoxical for eliminative materialists to try to prove their theory to an audience? (124)
31. What are the basic tenets of *noneliminative or identity materialism*? (125)

32. Explain in one sentence the causal argument for identity materialism. (125)
33. What is the argument for identity materialism based on *localization of mental functioning*? (126)
34. Explain the brain bisection ("split brain") experiment described on pages 126–27. Why is this sort of experiment interesting to philosophers? (127)
35. In what sense is it simpler to say that identity materialism is true rather than saying that persons possess both physical and nonphysical characteristics? (128)
36. How does John Searle disagree with Allen Newell and Herbert Simon about the nature of mentality? (129)
37. Explain Searle's Chinese Room thought experiment. (129)
38. In what sense is the logical possibility of artificial intelligence a test for materialism? (129–30)
39. What is the problem with saying that computers can never possess mentality because they are not creative? (130)
40. What is the objection to the possibility of artificial intelligence that is based on morality? (131)

Review Questions for Examinations

1. Define these terms: "mind," "physical," "nonphysical," "nonphysical mind," "the mind/body problem," "interaction."
2. Explain these concepts: "functional definition," "the law of identity," "paranormal phenomena," "personal identity," "the problem of interaction," "the principle of conservation of energy," "introspection," "slippery slope argument," "ontogenesis," "phylogenetic scale," "artificial intelligence."
3. What are these theories: monism, dualism, materialism, phenomenalism, eliminative materialism, noneliminative (identity) materialism, dualistic interactionism, dualistic parallelism, epiphenomenalism, occasionalism, preestablished harmony, behaviorism, neurophilic eliminative materialism.
4. Provide one reason to accept each of the above theories.
5. Provide one reason to reject each of the above theories.
6. What did the following dualists say about interaction of minds and bodies: Descartes, Malebranche, Leibniz, Huxley.
7. Explain how the fact that our sensations possess *phenomenal characteristics* enters into the mind/body problem.
8. Explain how the issue of our knowledge of our mental states enters into the mind/body problem.
9. Explain how the issue of evolution enters into the mind/body problem.
10. Explain how the issue of the localization of mental function in the brain enters into the mind/body problem.

11. Explain how the issue of artificial intelligence enters into the mind/body problem.

Discussion Questions

1. As dualists define "nonphysical minds," such minds could never be detected by any scientific methods. This means that, for instance, when supermarket tabloids report that they have "discovered" that souls weigh two ounces by weighing persons before and after death, we can be sure that they are *not* weighing nonphysical minds in the philosophers' sense.

   This feature might seem to be a drawback for dualism. Can you see how the unobservability of nonphysical minds might be an *advantage* for dualism?
2. Evaluate this argument for materialism: "If our minds were nonphysical as the dualists say, then our brains would be only relay stations that pass signals between our bodies and our minds. If so, our brains would not have to be very large or complex. But our brains contain more than 10 billion neurons. Because they are so big and so complex, our brains must be the source of our mentality."
3. The Canadian brain scientist Wilder Penfield found that by electrically stimulating subjects' brains he could produce in them sensations of colors, odors, butterflies, and even "memories" of things that never happened. Do such findings support dualism or materialism?
4. Evaluate this argument for dualism: "By the age of six, human beings' brains have reached nearly 90 percent of their adult size. By the age of six, human beings' minds have not reached nearly 90 percent of their mental development. Therefore, human minds are probably not brains."
5. Evaluate this argument against dualism: "As Descartes and Leibniz noted, nonphysical minds would be simple, indivisible, and, therefore, indestructible. This means that nonphysical minds would be eternal. But eternal things last *backward in time* as well as forward. Because we have not existed eternally, we must not have nonphysical minds."
6. In our taxonomy of dualistic theories, we listed interactionism, parallelism, and epiphenomenalism. But there seems to be a fourth possibility. What would that fourth theory be? Why do you suppose few philosophers have ever advanced that fourth theory?
7. Evaluate this argument for materialism: "Among humans there is a strong correspondence between brain size and I.Q. So, minds are probably brains."
8. Evaluate this argument for dualism: "Collectively, the brains of women average 150 cubic centimeters smaller than brains of men. But the I.Q. difference between men and women is negligible. Therefore, minds probably are not brains."
9. Evaluate this argument for materialism: "Different animals have different

perceptual abilities. For instance, dogs discriminate smells better than humans do; cats, but not rats, prefer sugar to saccharine. Only materialism can explain such facts."

FOR FURTHER READING

Campbell, Keith. 1980. *Body and Mind.* Notre Dame, IN: University of Notre Dame Press. An easy-to-read, short introduction to the main theories by a prominent epiphenomenalist.

Churchland, Paul. 1984. *Matter and Consciousness.* Cambridge, MA: MIT Press. A short survey of mind/body theories by a foremost eliminative materialist. Contains a wealth of information on biology and brain science. Fairly easy to read.

Cornman, James, Keith Lehrer, and George Pappas. 1987. *Philosophical Problems and Arguments.* Chapter 4. A meticulous examination of the main mind/body theories. Difficult.

Descartes, René. 1972. *Meditations.* In *The Philosophical Works of Descartes.* Especially Meditations 2 and 6. Cambridge: Cambridge University Press. The classic statement of dualistic interactionism by the founder of modern philosophy. Rewards careful reading. Difficult.

Graham, George. 1993. *Philosophy of Mind: An Introduction.* Cambridge, MA: Blackwell. Well-written, reader-friendly discussions of the mind/body problem and related topics such as animal and computer beliefs, life after death, free will, and knowledge of other minds.

Hofstadter, Douglas and Daniel Dennett, eds. 1981. *The Mind's Eye: Fantasies and Reflections of Self and Soul.* Engaging selections from philosophy and literature dealing with the mind/body problem, artificial intelligence, and personal identity. Varies in difficulty.

Sagan, Carl. 1977. *The Dragons of Eden.* New York: Ballantine. Fascinating speculations about minds and biology by a famous astrophysicist. Good chapter on split brains. Fun to read.

Searle, John. 1984. *Minds, Brains, and Science.* Cambridge, MA: Harvard University Press. Enjoyable short book written in plain English advocating noneliminative materialism. Contains Searle's famous Chinese room thought experiment.

Chapter 6
NORMATIVE ETHICS

INTRODUCTION

The basic questions of normative ethics are: (1) What is right and wrong? (2) What things are intrinsically valuable (valuable in themselves)? When we ask the first question, we ask about our moral obligations to others. When we ask the second, we ask what personal characteristics, goals, and ways of living are the most worthy of pursuit. Answers to (1) and (2) are central to creating a normative vision of ourselves—a vision of how we should try to lead our lives—because they answer "Which actions should I perform and which must I avoid?" and "What kind of person should I try to become?" This chapter looks briefly at the question of intrinsic value, while examining moral obligation in detail.

1. Descriptive and Evaluative Statements

Compare two sentences: (A) "Action X is believed to be moral by (some) (many) (most) persons in my group." (B) "Action X is morally right." Sentence (A) talks about *what is believed to be* morally best, while sentence (B) talks about *what is* morally best. We often do not worry much about the difference between statements such as (A) and (B), because we usually do not ask whether what is believed to be right *is* right. Instead, we usually assume the correctness of the moral beliefs of our group: those beliefs held by our families, peer groups, religions, or whatever beliefs we absorb from television, movies, and popular culture generally. Sometimes, though, we do wonder whether what our group believes to be right really *is* right. At such times we ask "Ought I to do that?" or "Is this type of activity truly worthwhile?" To ask such questions is to ask questions in *normative ethics*.

There is an important difference between statements (A) and (B). When we claim that a certain action is believed to be right or approved of, we make a claim that is *descriptive* in the sense that it tries to describe a part of the universe. This "part" of the universe is simply the opinions and attitudes of persons. (A) is a statement about persons' beliefs and belongs to psychology. We sometimes are able to determine whether a descriptive sentence is true or false by observation, and sometimes we cannot. (A statement's *being* true is not the same thing as our *knowing* that it is true.) What makes descriptive statements *descriptive* is not whether we *know* their truth or falsity, but what we have to do to *express* them. To express a descriptive statement, it is never necessary to evaluate as good or bad the thing described. For instance, the statement "Abortion is legal in Alabama" describes a condition of the world that the speaker thinks is a fact. Persons who make this statement are not expressing their approval or disapproval of abortion. A *descriptive statement* is a statement that (1) *is either true or false*, and (2) *requires no evaluation on the part of the person who expresses it*.

Unlike statement (A), when we say or write a statement such as (B), in the very act of expressing the statement we perform an evaluation. To say that an action is moral is to endorse it. In saying that an action is immoral, it is part of the meaning of our statement that we evaluate the action negatively, that is, that we condemn it. Statements in normative ethics that endorse or condemn actions as right or wrong are evaluative statements. An *evaluative statement requires an evaluation on the part of the person who expresses it*. (Notice that this definition leaves open the question whether evaluative statements are either true or false. We examine this question in the metaethics chapter.)

In normative ethics philosophers try to provide theories that show which evaluative statements concerning human well-being we should accept. Alternatively, normative ethics helps us make informed value judgments about human conduct.

2. The Priority of Normative Ethics over Metaethics

The main question in the theory of moral obligation is "How shall we distinguish between right and wrong actions?" The main question in the theory of intrinsic value is "How shall we tell which states of affairs are intrinsically worthwhile?" Neither philosophers nor lay persons have ever reached agreement on either of these questions, and this provides some reason to believe that no agreement will be forthcoming. This suggests the following objection:

> The reason human beings cannot reach agreement on these questions lies in the difference between descriptive and evaluative statements. Although it may be extremely difficult to determine whether some descriptive statements are true or false (for example, "Our solar system will eventually be sucked into a Black Hole"), with descriptive statements there is a truth to the matter. But in the case of statements of normative ethics, there is *no* possibility of ever finding out whether they are true or false. The reason is that evaluations—unlike descriptions—are logically incapable of *being* true or false. When you say that peas taste good and I say that peas taste bad, neither of us is describing a fact about peas; we are simply expressing our different feelings about peas. No consensus is forthcoming because we are expressing our feelings rather than making statements that can be either true or false. And even if consensus does occur, that would not prove that one evaluative view is *better than* another, but only that it is more popular.

This powerful objection to normative ethics is posed from the metaethical theory known as *moral subjectivism*. According to this objection, before we can try to decide what the best normative theories are, we must first establish that normative judgments are capable of being true. From a strictly logical perspective, this point is well-taken. It is reasonable to ask first whether any theory of normative ethics *can be true* before we undertake the task of trying to show which theory *is* true. We shall address at length the challenge from the moral subjectivist in the metaethics chapter. Nonetheless, there are powerful reasons for addressing the questions of normative ethics even if we never address the metaethical problem regarding the objectivity of morals.

First, we can proceed conditionally, even while admitting that we have no answer to the metaethical problem. We might say that *if* moral questions can have objective answers, here are our best answers. After all, the main questions of philosophy are never decisively settled, but remain open to perennial debate. This will prove to be the case in metaethics also. It would be intellectually lazy to refuse to address one philosophical problem until we conclusively settle another: Using that requirement we could avoid addressing *any* philosophical problems, because all philosophical problems depend on others. If we elect to pursue philosophy at all, it must be done conditionally.

Second, we need to be clear about the difference between normative ethics and metaethics. In the former we try to provide the best theory of moral judgments we can. In the latter we decide the place that normative ethics has in our larger philosophical picture. Whatever verdict we reach concerning metaethics, in our everyday lives we will need to make moral decisions. For example, whether we can answer the subjectivist's challenge or not, most of us are going to continue to feel that obvious cases of cruelty and unfairness are wrong. Subjectivism does not change this fact. Everyday life requires us to make normative judgments based on our moral beliefs and feelings when we decide whether to lie to help ourselves out of difficult situations or when we think about the sort of persons we want to become. Because the need to make normative decisions will not go away, we may as well try to make them intelligently, regardless of the metaethical problem.

Third, even if we are convinced by the subjectivist that normative judgments are incapable of being true or false and have no greater justification than the fact that they are widely shared, an understanding of the way humans feel about normative issues is valuable. A sensation of pain is a subjective phenomenon not existing outside those persons who experience it, but learning about the causes of pain enables us to develop the beneficial science of anesthesiology. By analogy, even if moral subjectivism is true, a systematic understanding of human feelings about moral questions may help us understand why persons have the moral disagreements they do. This can provide intellectual insight and practical benefit.

3. How Philosophers Proceed in Normative Ethics: Moral Intuitions and General Principles

The basic tools that philosophers use in trying to develop theories in normative ethics are *moral intuitions*. Moral intuitions are *reflective judgments about normative questions, for instance, judgments about whether a certain action would be morally permissible or whether certain activities are intrinsically worthwhile*. By relying on our intuitions we test various moral ideas to arrive at general moral principles and, eventually, moral theories. Here are two examples of *thought experiments* designed to elicit our moral intuitions.

(1) Suppose you are an artist and have promised to pick up a friend at the airport at 3:00 P.M. You plan to continue working on the most important painting of your life until 2:30 P.M. before making the half-hour trip. But at 2:29 you receive a once-in-a-lifetime insight that, if followed completely nonstop for the next two hours, will lead you to produce the greatest painting in the history of the world. But if you turn your attention away from your insight for even the time it would take to make a phone call to make other arrangements for picking up your friend, the insight will vanish and your painting will be a

worthless piece of junk. Should you focus on your insight and produce the great work or should you attend to your friend and give up the painting?

(2) An immensely talented novelist, you are banished to live alone on a desert island, you will never be retrieved, and you will not die prematurely due to accident or disease. You are given the option of being given all the books of a great library and all the word-processing resources you will ever need to write your novels. If you continue to write, you will write novels greater than those of Dostoevski and Tolstoy. Unfortunately, these will never be known to anyone except you. You are given the option of receiving instead of the word processing programs enough computers games (which you dearly love) so that you can enjoy playing them for the rest of your life. The computer games are so seductive, however, that once you begin playing them you will never be able to write your novels. Which should you select, the word-processing programs or the computer games?

By considering thought experiments such as these, we use our moral intuitions to inform our thinking about moral issues. Here is an analogy to suggest how we might proceed. Suppose that you know how to count and, because of this, have *mathematical intuitions* about arithmetic. If you hear "5 + 7 = 12," it *seems* correct to you, and if you hear "3 × 2 = 9," it *seems* incorrect. You have never learned, however, the rules of addition or multiplication. Suppose you record your mathematical intuitions concerning many arithmetic statements and then begin to devise general formulas that describe how to add and multiply correctly. You continue to test your formulas relying on your mathematical intuitions to verify and disconfirm, and eventually arrive at a fully explicit way to perform addition and multiplication problems. In this case you would have arrived at general principles by relying on your unschooled mathematical intuitions.

Of course, the analogy is not very close, given that we know that there are correct general rules for arithmetic, but it is unclear whether there are correct general moral principles. In addition, some philosophers (Unger, 1996) argue that our everyday moral intuitions need serious revision before they are reliable. The hope remains, however, that the relationship between moral intuitions and moral principles may be similar to the relationship between mathematical intuitions and arithmetic rules so that our moral system-making process is possible. If it is, this would be a great practical aid. In theory, we could use our moral intuitions to work out our moral principles, write the principles down on a three-by-five index card, and carry them around with us. Then, when we face moral decisions, we could pull out the card and use our principles to help us make moral decisions.

Disagreements over moral principles are not the whole story when it comes to moral disputes. Many disagreements stem not from conflicting moral principles, but from disagreements about descriptive facts. For instance, pro- and anti-capital punishment advocates may both hold the *utilitarian principle* that *actions are right if and only if they promote the greatest happiness*, but disagree on whether capital punishment is morally acceptable. They may disagree if the capital punishment proponent believes that capital punishment is a deterrent to capital crime, and, hence, saves lives, while the capital punishment opponent believes that capital punishment is not a deterrent, and, hence, cannot be justified on the grounds of saving lives. A similar disagreement about the facts can occur between pro- and anti-abortion thinkers who both endorse the sanctity of human life. The anti-abortion thinker may believe that the fetus is a person, whereas the pro-abortion thinker may believe that the fetus is not a person.

Most moral philosophers emphasize that moral thinking presupposes general principles that are *universalizable* in the sense that they will yield the same moral answers in all similar cases. Kant argued that moral principles must be ones that we can consistently will that every person follow. Henry Sidgwick (1838–1900) argued that it cannot be right for us to treat persons differently simply because they are different persons: There must be some morally relevant difference to justify differential treatment. The English utilitarians Jeremy Bentham (1748–1832) and John Stuart Mill (1806–1873) argue that we are obligated to maximize the well-being of *all* persons affected by our actions. This insistence on universalization as a test for the rightness of actions seems supported by our moral intuitions. For instance, it seems that for you to be punished more harshly than others who commit the same crime *simply because you are you* would be unfair and immoral. Thus, it seems that moral principles need to be universalizable.

4. Autonomy and Theories of Ethics

Autonomy is self-rule. A country that is autonomous can run its own affairs without control by other countries. A person who is autonomous enjoys greater self-rule than a less autonomous person. Consider the following triple analogy. In the first case you are locked in a house and unable to escape. Here you lack an obvious sort of autonomy, the ability to leave the house if you choose. You are at the mercy of the person who has locked you in the house. In the second case you cannot perform simple arithmetic calculations. Here you lack the autonomy to figure out how much change you should receive at the check-out line. You are at the mercy of the cashiers. In the third case you cannot figure out for yourself the difference between right and wrong. Here you lack a kind of autonomy that is important to reflective persons, moral autonomy, the ability to analyze the moral opinions and actions of other persons and decide whether you find them acceptable or not. Instead, you are at the mercy of others to tell you what is right and wrong.

Philosophy provides a way to increase our moral autonomy: Learn *several* normative theories. In the theory of moral obligation, learn the theories of religious authoritarianism, egoism, and the varieties of utilitarianism and deontologism. Then, when you find yourself in situations calling for normative judgments, you can consider the various theories. You can ask yourself what the philosophical theories would say and then *decide for yourself* which, if any, gives the best answers. If not, you may invent a theory of your own. Either way, learning normative theories gives us the means to develop our own moral thinking. The more options we know about, the more sophisticated our thinking will become, thereby enhancing our moral autonomy.

Learning theories of intrinsic value can also enhance our autonomy. As Kant noted, our autonomy is always at risk of our being pushed and pulled by our various desires. (Kant called the will that is pulled by desires "heteronomous.") Somewhat simplified, Kant's point is that we lose self-governance when we desire things: Our desires take over our lives. This risk is especially great in affluent countries where our economies are based on the creation and satisfaction of desires for new cars, sophisticated electronic gadgetry, and lifestyles devoted to pleasure. It is easy to accept unquestioningly the view that the best thing we can do with our lives is to collect the most affluence possible in exchange for the least effort so that we may devote the largest possible percentage of our lives to having pleasure.

By learning about different theories of intrinsic value, we come to appreciate arguments in behalf of many goals of human life *besides* accumulating pleasure. Although some philosophers have argued that pleasure is the highest goal (the *summum bonum*), other philosophers have placed other things above pleasure: knowledge, the development of our creative abilities, the exercise of power, leading a moral life, serving God, and various combinations of the other values. Learning these theories, as with learning theories of moral obligation, gives us more options and enables us to take a more critical view of our own choices. This makes our decisions more autonomous, *even if* our final judgment is to act solely to maximize our own pleasure. In this case, we understand what we are choosing and what we are rejecting.

SOME PROBLEMATIC THEORIES OF MORAL OBLIGATION

The *truth conditions of statements* are *those parts of reality that make true statements true and false statements false*. The truth condition of the statement "Snow is white" is the color of snow. If the color of snow is white, then "Snow is white" is true, and if the color of snow is not white, then "Snow is white" is false. The truth condition for "Sally likes to eat broccoli" is Sally's liking or not liking to eat broccoli. The truth condition for "$12 \times 8 = 96$" lies in a fact about arithmetic. For each of the theories of moral obligation, we need to understand its account of the truth conditions of moral judgments, that is, its idea of what makes moral judgments true and false.

5. Personal Subjectivism ("Whatever-Your-Conscience-Decides-Is-Right Theory")

Personal subjectivism has two defining theses, one metaphysical and the other epistemological. The *metaphysical thesis* is: *Each person's moral conscience creates the difference between right and wrong for that person.* The *epistemological thesis* is: *The way to find out the difference between right and wrong is by consulting our consciences.* Personal subjectivism does not state the trivial fact that persons' consciences tell them what they *believe* is right and wrong. This is simply what the concept "conscience" means. Rather, personal subjectivism says that whatever our consciences tell us is right, *really is right*. The truth conditions of moral judgments are persons' consciences.

Personal subjectivism has two advantages. First, it takes seriously the claim already noted in this chapter that our *moral intuitions* are the bedrock of moral theorizing. Second, personal subjectivism acknowledges the importance of our individual autonomy in reaching normative judgments. Personal subjectivism recognizes that moral judgments cannot simply be accepted as we might accept facts in an encyclopedia; moral judgments must be questioned, fretted over, and *felt*. Personal subjectivism believes that in making a moral judgment we take personal responsibility for it.

The advantages of personal subjectivism are also its weaknesses. First, our consciences are the products of our environments and need to be informed by careful ethical theorizing before they become a serious way of finding out right and wrong. An individual's conscience varies from time to time and from incident to incident. Consciences are often vague and incomplete. Sometimes it is difficult for us to know *what* our conscience tells us. Worst of all, some persons' consciences tell them to do terribly immoral things. If our consciences were infallible, as personal subjectivism maintains, then, by definition, our consciences could never tell us to do what is wrong.

Second, personal subjectivism destroys interpersonal objectivity in ethics. Suppose two persons have conflicting consciences: Mr. Meat-Eater's conscience says that eating the flesh of mammals is morally permissible, and Ms. Vegetarian's conscience says that eating the flesh of mammals is immoral. Obviously, it is a logical contradiction to say, as personal subjectivism *seems* to say, that eating mammals is both morally permissible and immoral. To avoid this contradiction, subjectivists must say that it is morally permissible for Mr. Meat-Eater to eat mammals and that it is morally wrong for Ms. Vegetarian to eat mammals.

But how can this be? After all, eating mammals is eating mammals, whoever does it. How can the difference in the morality of the action depend on the moral consciences of the eaters? It is true that Mr. Meat-Eater and Ms. Vegetarian *feel* differently about the morality of eating mammals, but how would this make *the activity* right when performed by the former and wrong when performed by the latter? Does the truth of "The Earth is flat" vary depending on whether it is believed or disbelieved? The only way that personal subjectivism can avoid contradiction is by denying the interpersonal nature of morality. If personal subjectivism does this, it surrenders its claim to provide a theory of moral obligation.

6. Religious Authoritarianism

Religious authoritarianism also has a metaphysical and an epistemological thesis. The *metaphysical thesis* is that the *truth conditions of moral judgments are the will of a theological being or beings*. For instance, when we say "Abortion is permissible," our moral judgment is true if God or gods will that abortion is permissible and false if God or gods will that abortion is not permissible. The *epistemological thesis* of religious authoritarianism is that *the way for persons to find out what is right and wrong is by finding out what God or gods will*.

Religious authoritarianism provides more objectivity for ethics than personal subjectivism does, but it is problematic nonetheless. The first difficulty is that religious authoritarianism makes morality depend on the existence of theological beings. According to this theory, if there are no gods, then, because morality simply *is* divine decree, there can be no morality. Although many persons accept this consequence (Dostoevski's character in *The Brothers Karamazov* famously proclaimed that if there is no God, all is permitted), it looks perplexing. Even if there were no theological beings, wouldn't intentional cruelty *still* be wrong?

A second difficulty is our inability to know that theological beings exist. Although we do not examine the specific difficulties of proving the existence of God until chapter 9, knowing the existence of theological beings will pose a daunting problem. And for religious authoritarians who admit that we cannot *know* the existence of God, but must accept it on faith, there is a problem: Many persons will refuse to accept a moral code on faith. So religious authoritarianism has nothing to say to atheists and agnostics.

Let us put aside these first two difficulties. A third difficulty lies in religious authoritarianism's epistemological thesis that we can *find out* what is right and wrong by consulting God's will. There are two ways that religious authoritarians might propose that we find out the will of theological entities. One way would be *internal*: We might consult the contents of our minds. This might include either a *feeling* that God wants us to behave in certain ways or a *direct revelation* from God. A second way would be *external*: We might consult an external source such as a religious expert or a religious text.

The problem with both the internal and external methods is that they run afoul of the *Problem of Representation*: *We can never tell from looking at a representational device whether what it says is true*. Here are some representational devices: a painting, a television commercial, and a spoken sentence such as "There are exactly forty-seven chairs in this classroom." By examining only the representational device, we can never tell whether what it tries to represent is that way: whether any object resembles the painting, whether the claims of the commercial are true, or whether there are forty-seven chairs in this classroom.

The problem of representation shows that we cannot know the will of God by examining the contents of our minds: *We can never tell simply by examining the ideas in our minds whether those ideas accurately represent entities outside our minds.* When religious authoritarians rely on the contents of our minds—assumed direct experiences of theological beings—they assume that these feelings are *effects* that are *caused* by God. But we can never infer from a mental state what its cause is. This is the moral of Veil of Sensations Skepticism discussed in chapter 3. Just as we cannot tell from our sensations alone whether physical objects resemble them, we cannot know that apparently divinely inspired feelings or revelations really have a divine source. The problem of representation also applies to attempts to know the will of God through religious experts or texts. These also are representational devices, which by themselves provide no evidence that what they try to represent is true.

There are other problems concerning religious experts and religious texts. There are great moral differences in the beliefs of Protestantism, Catholicism, Judaism, Islam, Buddhism, Hinduism, Shintoism, Taoism, and Confucianism. And these are only the major current religions. There are thousands of other religions such as Native American religions, the religions of the ancient Greeks and Romans, and prehistoric religions that we do not even have names for. Which religion gives the real moral instructions of the real theological beings? Among all the possible candidates, how are we to decide which religion tells us the will of God? Suppose we say that we will settle this problem by having faith that our religion is the right one. The problem is that other persons who hold different moral beliefs can just as reasonably claim that they have faith that *their* religions or religious experts reveal the will of God. The question will not go away: How can we know that *our* religions tell us God's will?

Suppose the religious authoritarian agrees that it would be dogmatic of us to insist that our religion gives the truth about God's will to the exclusion of other religions. Suppose we say that *all religions* reliably reveal the will of God. Then the religious authoritarian would be landed in the same predicament faced by the personal subjectivist. The same action would be both morally right and morally wrong when done by persons of different religions. For instance, it would be morally permissible for Jews to eat beef, but wrong for Hindus to do so. Here, as with personal subjectivism, morality has lost its universal nature and lapsed into relativism.

There is a general problem that applies to all ways of trying to find out God's will—whether by appealing to our feelings, revelation, religious experts, or religious texts. Assuming that God exists and is morally perfect, it follows that any command given by God must be morally right. So if God commands X, then X is morally right. Now the religious authoritarian mistakenly believes that this definitional truth provides moral knowledge: We simply find out what God commands, and conclude that it is, therefore, morally right. The problem is that for any *supposed* command from God, if the action commanded is not morally right, we can validly deduce that it is *not* a command of God. Therefore, before we can conclude that a supposed command from God really *is* a command from God, we must first decide on independent grounds whether the command is morally right. This makes religious authoritarianism useless as a means of distinguishing between right and wrong.

Let me elaborate. Religious authoritarians rely on a modus ponens argument:

(1) If God commands X, then X is morally right.
(2) My feelings (this revelation, this religious expert, or this religious text) prove(s) that God commands X.
(3) Therefore, X is morally right.

This is a valid argument, and premise (1) is true by definition. Premise (2), however, does all the work, and is highly doubtful. To see this, compare this argument with a modus tollens argument given by an opponent of religious authoritarianism:

(1) If God commands X, then X is morally right.
(2′) My moral intuitions show that X is not morally right.
(3′) Therefore, God does not command X.

The modus ponens argument and the modus tollens argument are both valid, but they arrive at wildly different conclusions. (I call this kind of dispute "one person's modus ponens is another person's modus tollens.") While agreeing that God is morally perfect and would command only morally right actions, the critic of religious authoritarianism shows that to assume that any particular action is commanded by God is to judge that action to be morally right, whether we realize it or not. For if we evaluate that action and decide that it is wrong, then the valid conclusion would be that it is not commanded by God. This objection does not support atheism, agnosticism, or any doubt about God's moral perfection. If we adopt the modus tollens version, the correct conclusion to draw is simply that this supposed command is not the word of God. Maybe God's word has been mistranslated and needs a nonliteral interpretation. Maybe we have taken what we *want to believe* as God's command. The side-by-side comparison of the modus ponens and modus tollens arguments shows that religious authoritarianism cannot make good on its epistemological claim that we can determine right and wrong by finding out God's will—even if the metaphysical claim that right and wrong are constituted by God's commands is true.

This leads to a fourth criticism of religious authoritarianism, which concerns moral autonomy. In using which style of reasoning above, the modus ponens or modus tollens version, does a person display greater moral self-rule? Suppose a voice in your head says that it is God and orders you to kill your sister. Would you assume that this is the word of God and conclude that it is morally right that you kill your sister? Or would you decide that because killing your sister would be immoral, that this voice cannot be a command from God? The same problem arises when we read moral instructions in religious texts or listen to the moral advice of religious experts. Religious authoritarianism gives us a way of distinguishing right and wrong only if we are willing to surrender our reliance on our own moral intuitions, that is, only if we surrender our moral autonomy.

There is one final move by the religious authoritarian to anticipate. Religious authoritarians might say that despite all the problems just cited, religious authoritarianism is the most *prudent* moral theory. We should pick a religion, hope that it is the correct one and that it relays God's will, and follow it despite all the difficulties. Why? Because in this way we at least have *a chance* of selecting the morality God wants us to have, and, thereby, avoid God's punishment for acting contrary to His wishes. This strategy is similar to Pascal's Wager, examined in chapter 9, which says that it is prudent to believe that God exists even if there is no evidence for the belief.

A first reply is that once we admit that we are simply guessing what God's moral views are, a better strategy would be to try to discover on nonreligious grounds the most plausible theory of morals—which will turn out to be God's. For example, given that God is morally perfect, it follows that if utilitarianism is the best moral theory, then God is a utilitarian. Therefore, the best way to find out God's will might be to discover the best moral theory, not the other way around. A second reply is to remember that morality is not the same thing as prudence. If religious authoritarians say that we should follow religious ethics simply to make points with God, then religious authoritarianism becomes a variety of egoism. If egoism is an unacceptable moral theory, then this final defense of religious authoritarianism also fails.

7. Egoism

Egoism is the morality of selfishness. Egoism claims that *we have no moral obligation to act unselfishly*. Some egoists have claimed that human beings, collectively, are made better off when all persons look out only for themselves, but this implausible claim is not essential to egoism. The egoist thinks that we should care only for ourselves, regardless of whether this enhances the well-being of anyone else or not.

The standard argument for egoism has one psychological premise and one philosophical premise:

(1) All persons are built so that the only way they can act is selfishly.
(2) We have no moral duties to act in ways we cannot.
(3) Therefore, we have no moral duties to act unselfishly.

Many psychological facts (and pseudo-facts) are cited to support the psychological premise (1). Psychological hedonism—the view that the motivation of all our actions is the attempt to gain pleasure and avoid pain—is sometimes cited. Premise (1) also benefits from our ability to concoct cynical interpretations of human behavior: Why did your parents change their plans to go out last night and instead help you with your homework? Because they want you to become a rich doctor and support them in their old age!

Regarding the philosophical premise (2), in some sense of the word *can*, it seems that we have moral obligations to do X only if we can do X. If I cannot swim, I am not morally obligated to try to swim to rescue a person drowning fifty yards out to sea, although I am obligated to help however I can. This is known as the doctrine that "ought" implies "can." Because "ought" implies "can," if I cannot do X, then, by modus tollens, I am not obligated to do X.

The weak link in the standard argument for egoism is its first premise. There seems to be too much evidence that persons act in ways they believe are not in their own best interest, but in the interest of other individuals, groups of persons, or even abstract principles. When faced by this rebuttal the egoist sometimes employs a more sophisticated premise called "philosophical egoism" (PHE). This premise is designed to prove the psychological first premise in the standard argument; the new argument can be viewed this way:

(PHE) Persons always choose according to their strongest desires.
  (1) Therefore, all persons are built so that the only way they can act is selfishly.
  (2) We have no moral duties to act in ways we cannot.
  (3) Therefore, we have no moral duties to act unselfishly.

We now need to ask whether (PHE) is true and, if it is, whether it proves (1).

The reason for accepting (PHE) is that it reflects a very plausible way of understanding human behavior that is known as *belief-desire psychology* or *folk psychology*. Our choices, which produce our deliberate behavior, are themselves driven by two broad types of mental states. Our beliefs represent to us the way the world is and suggest strategies for affecting the world. Our desires provide the motivation for us to select the goals we want to reach. Both beliefs and desires are necessary for us to make choices, and together are sufficient for us to make choices, irrespective of the way the world really is.

To see this, let us ask: Under what conditions do you run out of a burning building? It is not necessary for the building to really be on fire, because you may run out of a nonburning building if you mistakenly believe that the building is burning. It is not sufficient that the building really be on fire, because you may not realize that the building is burning. Or you may realize that the building is burning, but desire to stay there because you are trying to commit suicide. The necessary and sufficient conditions for your running out of the burning building are rather that: (1) you believe you will be harmed if you stay in the building *and* (2) you desire not to be harmed.

If belief-desire psychology is true, then all purposive behavior is motivated by our desires to perform actions. In some sense of the word "desire," we desire to do everything we choose; otherwise, we would not choose as we do. In this sense we desire to go to the dentist or else we won't go, although going to the dentist is not something we typically *desire* in the sense of really enjoying it. There is nothing wrong in the egoist dubbing whatever desires that bring about our choices *our strongest desire*. The question remains, however, whether this mundane fact about human choice (PHE) proves the egoistic premise (1).

Here is one objection to trying to conclude (1) from (PHE). The egoist is committed to the claim that all choices that are motivated by our strongest desires are selfish in the sense of being aimed only at our own welfare. Our strongest desires, remember, are defined as whatever desires actually prompt our choices. So the egoist must maintain that all of our motivating desires are self-directed or selfish. But saying this is no more plausible than simply asserting the original argument's premise (1) that all persons are built so that the only way they can act is selfishly. This claim remains just as unsupported after we accept (PHE) as it was when it was asserted as a simple psychological fact. The same counterexamples that defeat psychological egoism defeat the attempt to buttress it with belief-desire psychology: altruistic parents and children, self-sacrificing public servants, and martyrs. Human beings strive for many things for their own sakes that seem not to fit into the egoist's conceptual scheme. These may be common things like doing a good job at washing a car simply for the sake of doing a good job or more important things such as helping a stranger one will never meet again.

A second objection to egoism holds even if philosophical egoism were to prove egoism, which is doubtful. Egoism is not a *moral* theory, but *a rejection of morality*. Remember, we are considering theories of moral obligation—theories of what we owe other beings. But egoism says that we have no moral obligations to anyone except ourselves. Therefore, egoism has nothing to instruct anyone about moral obligations, which means it is not a theory of moral obligation. Instead, egoism claims that theories of moral obligation are null and void.

Consider this example. Suppose there are three persons, A, B, and C, all who have a potentially fatal disease. Only A knows that she possesses three pills that can serve as a probable cure of the fatal disease in the following way: If any person takes all three pills, that person's chance at survival of the disease will be .99. Anyone who takes two of the pills will have a .94 chance of survival. Anyone who takes one of the pills will have a .90 chance of survival. A narrows her options down to three: take all three pills herself, take two herself and give the third to either B or C, or distribute one pill to each person. There are no other reasons that would make it in A's interest to share the pills (such as gratitude from B and C, praise from other persons, or satisfaction from her own conscience). Which option would be morally best for A to select?

Egoism dictates that A should take all three pills herself. If we were in A's situation, *we* might opt for taking all three pills ourselves, but the question concerns which option is *morally right*. As the case is described, from a moral point of view A should share the pills with B and C. This would maximize the prospects for saving lives (a consequentialist theme), and it would treat the most persons as ends in themselves (a deontological theme). Egoism not only does not give the plausible moral answer, it seems not even to be in the moral ball game.

8. Relativism

Relativism maintains that *actions are right and wrong depending on whether they are approved of or rejected by some special group of persons*. That group may be a culture, a society, or a group of religious believers. Relativism is similar to personal subjectivism in that it reduces *morality* to *what is thought to be moral*, but it differs by making the determinant of moral obligation a group, and not simply each individual. As such, relativism takes a less idiosyncratic idea of morality: Individuals can be mistaken in their moral beliefs, provided they are out of sync with the majority who determines right and wrong.

A practical difficulty with relativism is that the idea of "the" morality of a society is largely a fiction. All societies have subcultures in which moral beliefs differ. What is "the" moral opinion of "American society" concerning abortion, affirmative action, animal rights, capital punishment, physician-assisted suicide, or the public funding of expensive life-extending medical care for the terminally ill? Often when we say that something is the moral view of our society we are paying attention only to the part of the society that agrees with our own moral views.

A relativist might try to avoid this problem by identifying the morality of a society with its laws. On this view, the formal laws a society has on the books at any given time determine what is right and wrong within that society. There are several problems with this view. First, formal laws cover only part of what we consider morally important. In the United States there are no laws against lying (except in special cases such as testifying in trials), but lying, in many cases at least, seems to be immoral. Nor do formal laws, because they are *proscriptive* by nature, *prescribe* positive duties of benevolence or even common decency. It would not break any law to refuse to contribute money to save the lives of starving children in foreign lands, but such refusals may well be immoral. (See Unger 1996.)

Second, some laws will inevitably be *immoral*. In an ideal world, all laws would be moral ones, but this is hardly an ideal world. Morality provides a norm against which we evaluate laws for their suitability. If whatever is legal is necessarily moral, then it would be logically impossible to morally evaluate our laws. But legislators revise laws all the time, hoping to make them accord better with what is morally right. Third, if laws determined morality, then a shift in the law due to one vote by a legislator who votes to repeal a law would mean that actions that were previously immoral are now moral or vice versa. This seems to be a reductio ad absurdum of the view that morality depends on the law.

This criticism of equating the moral to the legal points to a general problem with all forms of relativism. Strictly adhered to, relativism destroys the normative character of morality by making the right depend simply on what *is*—the laws, customs, or beliefs of a society. If not strictly adhered to, relativism provides no moral instruction. Consider the following dilemma:

(1) Either we accept the relativists' claim that morality just is whatever a given society believes is moral or we do not.
(2) If we do, then if a society endorses slavery and human sacrifices, we would have to say that slavery and human sacrifices are morally right in that society.
(3) If we do not, then we are relying on some nonrelativist way of determining morality (for example, by consulting our moral intuitions). This means that we have given up relativism as the determinant of morality.

Despite these objections, relativism appeals to many of us when we think about moral differences across cultures: Most persons are hesitant to say that another society is immoral. Part of relativism's appeal probably lies in the *New Testament* injunction "Judge not, that ye be not judged" (Matthew 7:1). We try to avoid criticizing other societies, because we would not like to be criticized ourselves (or be called on to defend our moral views). Thus, many persons say "Who's to say what's right and wrong!" as if that rhetorical question settles the issue. The problem with this move is that, if consistently followed, it destroys the objectivity of morality. Once we adopt it, we cannot criticize the Nazis for the Holocaust, tribes that routinely kill all strangers, slave societies, and cultures whose tradition is to kill, mutilate, or oppress females.

The best answer to the relativist's "who's to say" challenge is to reply "We will" and then provide a plausible method for making the decision. Extrapolating from John Rawls's (1971) *veil of ignorance* method of determining principles of justice, here is a way to distinguish moral and immoral societal practices. Imagine that you have to select the moral rules and practices of the society that you are going to live in immediately after you make your selection. But in making your choice of how that society will operate, you do not know where you will be in that society. You do not know what your race, sex, age, religion, sexual orientation, intelligence, or degree of physical disablement will be once you leave the veil of ignorance and begin to live in that society. What sort of social rules and practices would you select? Most persons would select institutions that do not discriminate against any group simply because they would not like to risk suffering such discrimination themselves. Although Rawls's thought experiment does not tell us everything we need to know about normative thinking, it seems to give at least an initial reply to the relativist's challenge.

TWO MAIN APPROACHES TO MORAL OBLIGATION: CONSEQUENTIALISM AND DEONTOLOGY

The problematic theories just examined—personal subjectivism, religious authoritarianism, egoism, and relativism—fail to take seriously enough the question of what we owe other persons. What must we do to treat persons morally, and what must we avoid doing not to treat persons immorally? The problematic theories avoid this issue by saying that so long as we do X (follow our consciences, the rules of God, or society, or look out for ourselves), we do not really have to *worry about* other persons. The problematic theories see morality as following a formula, but they seem not to take other persons seriously enough. Consequentialism and deontology attempt to remedy this defect.

Moral obligation concerns what we owe other persons in terms of (1) their rights and (2) their well-being apart from their rights. The difference between these two marks a great division between two ways of looking at persons, which translates into two ways of doing normative ethics. To talk about X's *rights* (e.g., rights to life, liberty, the pursuit of happiness) is to talk about things that would be morally wrong for anyone to take away from X. To talk about *well-being apart from rights* is to talk about the states of affairs that are valuable for persons to experience, for instance, pleasure or the development of one's abilities.

One way to construct a theory of moral obligation is to say that right actions are whatever produces results that one thinks are valuable. Such *consequentialist views* make what is morally obligatory entirely a function of whatever has the most valuable consequences. Consequentialist views are also known as *teleological* views of moral obligation, because they hold that rightness depends on the "telos" (goal or end) that our actions produce. Debates over intrinsic value or the *summum bonum* (the highest good) of human action trace as far back as debates over theories of moral obligation. Aristotle thought that the highest good for humans is the exercise of our rational faculties. Epicurus (341–270 B.C.)

and Bentham thought that pleasure and the avoidance of pain is the summum bonum. The ancient Greek and Roman Stoics thought that developing moral virtues such as patience and fortitude was our highest goal. Augustine (353–430) and Thomas Aquinas (1224–1274) thought that devotion to God is our greatest good. The German Friederich Nietzsche ('NEAT CHA) (1844–1900) thought that self-realization—the perfection of one's abilities—is our greatest good. Plato thought that our highest good lies in a mixture of intellectual and moral qualities. Although in its own way this question is as interesting as the search for a theory of moral obligation, in this book I can mention only that consequentialists can choose any intrinsic value as the goal of morally right action.

A second way to construct a theory of moral obligation is to claim that the rightness and wrongness of actions is *not* entirely a function of what produces the most intrinsic value. This is not to say that such theories necessarily hold that consequences are irrelevant to determining rightness, but only that consequences are not the whole story. These views maintain that some factors other than the production of intrinsic value make our actions right and wrong. Typical candidates are the rights of persons or obedience to moral rules whose rightness is not determined by consequences. Such *nonconsequentialist* views are known as *deontological* (*formalist*) theories. The most famous exponent of deontological ethics was Immanuel Kant.

Consequentialist theories have the advantage over deontological theories of reducing by one the number of questions one needs to answer when doing normative ethics. By making the morally right depend entirely on what produces the most intrinsic value, we need first to decide what ends are intrinsically valuable. Once we decide that, we can find out what actions are morally obligatory by determining what maximizes those ends. Deontological theories, on the other hand, do not allow this reduction of the morally obligatory to the valuable. For the deontologist it is one question to ask whether an action produces the most possible intrinsic value, and another to ask whether that action is morally right. The deontologist's response to being told that action X would produce the most value is, "That's nice. But is X right?"

9. The Elements of Utilitarianism

The best-known consequentialist theory is utilitarianism, the view that the balance of pleasure over pain is the criterion of moral rightness. Utilitarianism's most famous exponents were two English philosophers of the 1800s. Jeremy Bentham says the principle of utility "approves or disapproves of every action whatsoever, according to the tendency which it appears to have to augment or diminish the happiness of the party whose interest is in question" (1970, 2)." Bentham's student, John Stuart Mill, expanding Bentham's idea of pleasure to count qualitative distinctions between kinds of pleasures, calls utilitarianism "the greatest happiness principle." Utilitarianism is an egalitarian moral theory that counts every person's utility as valuable as anyone else's, so that the happiness of kings is counted as no more important than the happiness of the poorest peasants. In the nineteenth century, Mill's claim that "each person counts as one, and no one counts as more than one" was politically progressive.

Utilitarianism is *impartial cost-benefit analysis applied to morality*. Utilitarianism is *impartial*, because unlike egoism it requires us to count the welfare of everyone affected by our actions, not just our own welfare. *Cost-benefit analysis* is what we implicitly do whenever we make a purchase or decide to spend our time and effort in an activity: We weigh the expense (in terms of money, time, or effort) against the probable benefit to be gained from the expenditure and decide whether the expected benefit outweighs the cost.

Suppose, for example, that I wish to decide whether playing a state lottery is a prudent financial decision. To do this, I compare the cost-benefit totals of the two options of buying a lottery ticket and not buying a lottery ticket. Suppose a ticket costs one dollar, the jackpot is $1,000,000, and my chance of winning with any one ticket is 1 in 10,000,000. The benefit of one ticket will be $1,000,000 (the jackpot) multiplied by 1/10,000,000 (my odds of winning), which yields a positive ten cents. So we arrive at the overall value of playing the lottery by adding the ten-cent benefit and the $1 cost, which equals a negative ninty cents. Next, I compare this sum with the value of not playing the lottery. In that case, I buy no ticket and there is no cost. There is no benefit either. (As they say in the commercials, you can't win if you don't play.) So the value of not playing the lottery is 0 plus 0, which is 0. The final step is to compare the outcomes of playing vs. not playing. Because not playing has a 0 value, while playing has a value of negative 90 cents, my best financial strategy is to not play.

The above is an example of cost-benefit analysis applied to an instance of *prudential* decision making. To turn this example into a utilitarian example of determining *moral obligations*, we need to count two more factors. First, we need to count in our computations the effect that our actions will have on *other* persons. So, although playing the state lottery is a poor financial strategy for me, if the proceeds from my poor investment are given to needy persons, my playing may be morally right. Notice that utilitarianism's doctrine of counting each person equally requires us to count *our own* utility. Sometimes utilitarianism will prescribe actions that benefit ourselves, and sometimes utilitarianism will prescribe that we sacrifice our own interests to the welfare of others. It all depends on where the most overall utility lies.

Second, instead of using numbers to represent money, utilitarians let numbers represent units of pleasure and pain. Although it is difficult to apply numbers to pleasure and pain, here is an example to illustrate the general idea. Suppose you think that eating a pizza has a positive 10 *hedons* (*pleasure units*) for you, while having your teeth drilled by a dentist for five minutes might be a negative 50 hedons. These numbers say that you find the pain of the dental work five times as disagreeable as you find the eating of the pizza pleasurable. If you were offered a choice, you would be indifferent between enduring the pain of the dentistry as the price you pay to get the enjoyment of five episodes of eating a pizza (not eating five pizzas all at once!). You would not endure the dentistry (negative 50 hedons) in exchange for four pizza eatings (positive 40 hedons), but you would endure it for six (positive 60 hedons).

Utilitarians have considered the sort of factors that contribute to the size of the numbers we assign to various actions. Bentham provided an elaborate "utilitarian calculus" (measuring system) for assigning numbers. Editing down Bentham's list we arrive at five *hedonistic factors*: (a) The *intensity* of the pleasure or pain. (b) The *duration* that the pleasure or pain lasts. (c) The *likelihood* or *probability* that the pleasure or pain will be produced by the action. (We already noted this in the lottery example.) (d) The *purity* of the pleasure or pain, that is, the amount of pain that is mixed with pleasure and the amount of pleasure that is mixed with pain. (e) The *fecundity* of the pleasures and pains, that is, whether pleasures and pain will produce further pleasures or pains. Even if the idea of assigning exact numbers using these variables is far-fetched, the variables seem to be factors that we consider everyday in choosing our actions.

There is a final preliminary. Because utilitarians think that the difference between right and wrong actions is determined by the outcomes of actions, utilitarians maintain that it is possible for us to perform actions rightly or wrongly by mistake. In the former case, we might try *not* to produce the most utility possible (or even try to produce the most pain), fail in our bad intentions, and end up producing the most utility. For instance, we might try to poison someone and mistakenly provide a life-saving drug. In the latter case, we might perform a harmful (hence wrong) act, despite our intention to maximize utility (do the most *utile* act). Utilitarians say that such cases show that the morality of our actions is one issue, and the quality of our moral characters is another. Although the moral quality of persons' characters usually corresponds to the moral quality of their actions, when mistakes occur, the two can differ.

10. Act Utilitarianism (Case-by-Case Utilitarianism)

Act utilitarians believe that the way to determine the rightness of actions is to perform a utilitarian calculation for each individual action: *An act is morally right if and only if it brings about greater utility for everyone affected by the action than any other possible action in that specific situation*. To follow this theory, it is necessary to consider *all* possible actions that might reasonably seem capable of producing the greatest utility. Act utilitarians recognize that this can sometimes be difficult. Therefore, act utilitarians offer two easier formulas: (1)

Between two actions, we determine which is morally better by comparing their respective utilities. (2) For any individual action, we determine whether it is morally permissible by comparing the utility of performing the action with the utility of not performing it.

Here are some examples of act utilitarian moral reasoning.

(1) Your father suffers a heart attack. The fastest way to get medical attention for him is to drive him to a hospital twenty miles down the interstate highway. Although the speed limit is 55 miles an hours, you decide to drive as quickly as you can (without getting into an accident) even though you break the speed limit. (2) A friend with a new haircut that you think borders on self-mutilation asks for your opinion. You believe that your friend's feelings will be hurt if you express your true opinion. Because his hair is shaved, it will not grow back for a month anyway, so nothing can be done at the present time. You decide to delay expressing your real feelings until your friend's hair grows out. You tell a "white lie." (3) A panhandler who looks as if she truly needs money asks you for some and you do.

There is much to like about act utilitarianism. If we perform the utility calculations accurately, act utilitarianism would guarantee that our actions promote the most happiness possible. As such, it appeals to persons of two personality types: (1) persons who love seeing the world in terms of numbers, and (2) soft-hearted persons (sentimentalists), whose highest moral concern lies in increasing pleasure and, especially, in decreasing suffering in the universe. Sentimentalists tend to put aside general moral rules and laws whenever they believe there is a clear payoff in terms of human happiness. For instance, "I know that embezzlers typically should be sent to jail, but Jones is so old that he would die in jail and no other bank would hire him now anyway, so I think we should not prosecute him."

PROBLEMS FOR ACT UTILITARIANISM

There are several familiar objections to act utilitarianism. Some involve practical difficulties. First, act utilitarianism will be difficult to apply whenever it is difficult to determine the probable consequences of our actions. Second, it is often difficult to be sure that we have considered *all* of the possible actions that might produce the most utility. If we overlook the most utile act, then according to act utilitarianism, we have not selected the best moral alternative.

A third objection is that the utilitarian view that morality is determined by the balance of pleasure over pain may seem sleazy. According to Bentham, in calculating the utility of our actions, the enjoyment we receive from pitching pennies counts just as much as the enjoyment we receive from writing poetry. According to Bentham, utilitarians should count the *quantitative*, not the *qualitative*, differences in pleasures. Mill amends Bentham's position by suggesting that utilitarians should take into account qualitatively superior intellectual pleasures:

> Few human creatures would consent to be changed into any of the lower animals for a promise of the fullest allowance of a beast's pleasures. . . . It is better to be . . . Socrates dissatisfied than a fool satisfied. (1981, 12–14)

A problem with Mill's reply is that it undermines utilitarianism's claim to be a quantitative theory, thereby making utilitarianism more difficult to apply. If we allow the *quality* of pleasure ever to overrule *quantity*, then we have relied on a more subjective way to decide which things are most valuable, and hence, right.

A fourth objection is that utilitarianism is too demanding. Suppose morally right actions are those that produce the most utility to humanity at large. Then it seems that it would always be immoral to watch sports on television when one could be gathering money for worthy charities—*unless* watching sports is the best way of rejuvenating ourselves so that we can gather *even more* money for charity. In general, it would seem to be immoral for a middle-class American to enjoy her financial well-being, if she could create more utility for less affluent persons by giving her money to them. So, according to act utilitarianism, for every dollar and possession we own, we should ask whether there is anyone who needs it more than we do. Thus, we seem to be obliged to give away our possessions until we are so poor that we need them more than do the poorest persons to whom we can give them. If act utilitarianism says this, then it makes unrealistic demands. Being entirely impartial between oneself (or loved ones) and strangers may be a noble ideal, but is it morally required?

I want to shift now to criticisms that claim that act utilitarianism recommends morally objectionable actions. If act utilitarianism prescribes immoral actions, that is a serious problem.

A fifth objection involves *distributive justice, the fairness of dividing goods among persons*. Consider two possible ways to distribute pleasure among persons X, Y, and Z. According to Distribution Scheme 1, X gets 7 hedons, Y gets 2, and Z gets 1. According to Distribution Scheme 2, each person gets 3 hedons. (Suppose the cost of administering the equal distribution is 1 hedon.) Distribution Scheme 1 is more utile than Distribution Scheme 2, because it yields 10 rather than 9 hedons, but seems less fair, and, perhaps, less moral.

A sixth objection involves the injustice of scapegoating. Imagine a situation in which an entire city believes that a murder defendant is guilty and will begin to riot that will result in the deaths of 1,000 innocent persons unless the defendant is found guilty. Near the end of the trial the prosecutor discovers a piece of evidence that shows that the defendant is not guilty and that the murder was committed by a person who has died. The evidence, which only the prosecutor knows, would be strong enough to acquit the defendant, but would not convince the angry populace of the defendant's innocence. Should the prosecutor reveal the evidence that will free the defendant and prompt a riot in which 1,000 persons die? Or should the prosecutor withhold the evidence, which will result in the innocent defendant being found guilty? The most utile action seems to be unjust to the innocent defendant. Because act utilitarianism is based on maximizing the number of hedons, it seems unable to safeguard the rights of minorities against the tyranny of the majority.

A seventh objection involves *special duties* and also reminds us of the fourth objection that utilitarianism's demand for complete impartiality may be too strong. Suppose you are a single parent who takes your child camping in a remote area you know may contain snakes that are poisonous only to children. You take along a bottle of snakebite antidote, exactly enough to neutralize the fast-acting snake venom if your 100-pound child should be bitten. After arriving at your campsite, your child goes off playing with two children of strangers. Five minutes later all three children come running to you, all bitten by the type of poisonous snakes for which you have brought the antidote. No one else has any snakebite antidote, and there is no way to save the children except for you to give the life-saving medicine. Here's the problem. The two children of the strangers weigh 50 pounds each. You can divide the antidote between the two 50-pound children, save both of them, and let your child die. Or you can give it all to your child, save her, and let the other children die. Utilitarianism seems to dictate that you must save the two strangers' children, but many persons would urge that you have a *special duty* to save your own child.

An eighth objection involves the idea of immoral pleasures. Suppose that the American Society of Sadists holds its annual convention in the Rose Bowl. After conducting their business meetings and seminars, the group turns to its entertainment. Sergeants-at-arms go into the community and secretly abduct a solitary vagrant and bring him to the fifty-yard line. The sadists then apply to the unwilling victim painful electrical shocks that are nonlethal and leave no ill-effects. The victim experiences an hour of pain, which has the disutility of −1,000 hedons. The 100,000 sadists, who love this sort of entertainment, are gratified by +5 hedons each. So, the utilitarian value of the activity is 100,000 × 5 (500,000 positive hedons) minus 1,000 negative hedons, which yields a result of a positive 499,000 hedons. The victim is given an injection that makes him forget the incident ever occurred, and the sadists never reveal their practice. It seems that the sadists' practice is justified on utilitarian grounds; but it seems morally wrong, because the *immoral* pleasures of the sadists ought not to be counted as factors that make actions *right*. Indeed, because utilitarianism makes utility the determinant of right and wrong, one wonders how utilitarians can distinguish between intrinsically moral and immoral pleasures—e.g., the pleasure of seeing a friend prosper versus the pleasure of seeing an enemy suffer.

HOW THE ACT UTILITARIAN MIGHT REPLY TO THESE OBJECTIONS

Act utilitarians might make concessions to some of the objections, while for others they might dig in their heels and say their theory really does provide the best moral answers. To objections one and two, which say that act utilitarianism makes finding right moral answers difficult, act utilitarians might agree but claim that this is a strong point of their theory rather than a weakness. In many cases it *is* very difficult to figure out what is right and wrong; the best moral theory should recognize that fact. Act utilitarians point out that simple theories of morality that always give pat answers on right and wrong would be *too* simple. To objection four, which complains that utilitarianism is too demanding to be followed in all instances, utilitarians might agree that we cannot always live up to the utilitarian creed but reply that our inability to do so is a failure in us, not in utilitarianism. We can hardly object to a moral theory simply because it says that we are not morally perfect.

To objection seven, which claims that act utilitarianism ignores special duties, act utilitarians can remind us that *they count not just the short-term costs and benefits of our actions, but the long-term effects as well.* It is conceivable that the long-term effects of ignoring special duties to friends and family might harm the institutions of friendship and family so much that it *would* be more utile—all things considered—for us to give preferential treatment to special persons. Applying this theme more generally, we must remember that act utilitarians count the damage that individual transgressions have on the whole of human conduct. For example, act utilitarians count the damage that lying or promise-breaking does to the individual liar or promise-breaker when calculating whether in a particular instance to lie or break a promise.

Act utilitarians might admit that their theory needs some work to deal with the objections from inferior pleasures (3) and immoral pleasures (8). Perhaps there is some way for utilitarians to distinguish between higher and lower pleasures on the one hand and immoral and moral pleasures on the other while keeping their theory basically quantitative. Utilitarians also need to find some way for their theory to deal with the criticism regarding distributive justice (objection 5) and the general problem of guarding minorities against majorities (objection 6).

In other cases, utilitarians might dig in their heels. Regarding the scapegoating issue, they might respond that in some highly contrived thought experiments, but seldom in real life, it *would* be morally obligatory to punish the innocent for the utility of the majority. Being punished for a crime one did not commit is very bad; but so is the badness of 1,000 lives being lost in the riot that would otherwise occur. Utilitarians implore us to look at the whole situation and try not to be *squeamish* (J. C. C. Smart's 1973 word) when we are morally required to do unpleasant acts. As Smart notes, it would not be a virtue for surgeons to be afraid of the sight of blood and refuse to perform surgeries needed to save lives.

11. Rule Utilitarianism (Follow-the-Rules Utilitarianism)

Some utilitarians believe that the way to save utilitarianism from these familiar objections is to make moral rules the determinant of right and wrong. According to *rule utilitarianism*, we should decide what to do in particular cases by following general rules that produce the most utility: *An act is morally right if and only if it follows a rule that would produce the most utility for everyone affected in that type of situation*. Rule utilitarians believe that only in cases in which it is unclear which rule is most utile, such as cases where rules conflict, should we apply the act utilitarian's formula directly.

Rule utilitarians think that their theory avoids some of the strongest objections to act utilitarianism. Instead of calculating utilities each time we make a moral decision, we simply follow the most utile rule. While it is sometimes difficult to perform utility calculations in the case-by-case manner recommended by the act utilitarian, it is easy to appeal to general rules such as "Tell the truth," "Keep your promises," and "Do not punish persons you know to be innocent." This suggests that rule utilitarianism will be easier to apply than act utilitarianism. In addition, following such rules may allow utilitarians to avoid some of the counterexamples designed to show that act utilitarianism gives answers that violate our moral intuitions. In the sadist example, the rule against torturing innocent persons dictates that the sadists are acting immorally, a result that agrees with our moral intuitions. In the snakebite example, following the rule "Look out for the safety of our own children first" would dictate that we should save our own child, again, something that many persons believe is right.

Rule utilitarianism may be easier to apply than act utilitarianism, but is rule utilitarianism an improvement over act utilitarianism? A familiar objection is that rule utilitarianism cannot be *better* than act utilitarianism and remain a utilitarian theory. Consider the following dilemma:

(1) Either rule utilitarianism provides exactly the same moral judgments that act utilitarianism does or it does not.
(2) If rule utilitarianism provides exactly the same moral judgments that act utilitarianism does, then it cannot avoid any counterexamples that act utilitarianism faces. (Both theories would give the same answers.)
(3) If rule utilitarianism provides different moral judgments than act utilitarianism does, then it prescribes actions that produce less than the optimal utility. In this case, it does not rely on utility as the final determinant of moral obligation.
(4) Therefore, either rule utilitarianism cannot avoid any counterexamples that act utilitarianism faces or it does not rely on utility as the final determinant of moral obligation.

Here is a slightly different way to understand this objection. Consider the scapegoating problem from the perspective of three utilitarian theories. As the example was given, *act utilitarianism* tells us to punish the innocent defendant. *An unqualified variety of rule utilitarianism* that says "Never punish persons who you know are innocent" (because punishing innocent persons *usually* produces disutility) tells us not to punish the defendant. *A more exact variety of rule utilitarianism* that says "Never punish persons you know to be innocent, *except* when you know that punishing the innocent person will save 1,000 lives" tells us to punish the defendant.

Now, between the unqualified rule and the more exact rule, which is more faithful to the utilitarian program of determining moral obligation by appealing to utility? Obviously, the more specified rule. Why should *a utilitarian* ever prefer a general rule that produces less utility over a more specific rule that produces more? If we prefer the general rule in this case we would be guilty of *rule worshipping—following a rule simply because it is a rule, not because following it maximizes the end the rule is designed to maximize.* For anyone who really believes that utility is the determinant of moral obligation, moral rules can at most be useful "rules of thumb" that help us to make estimates about which actions will produce the most utility. But as rules of thumb, they should be overridden in every instance when we can perform the actual utility calculation that act utilitarianism requires. If we think we have some other way of telling what actions are right and wrong besides asking what maximizes utility, then we are not utilitarians, but some sort of deontologist.

12. Kant's Deontological Theory

If rule utilitarianism cannot handle the counterexamples to act utilitarianism and remain a utilitarian theory, we should consider nonconsequentialist (formalist or deontological) approaches to moral obligation. Deontological theories maintain that the rightness of our actions depends on following moral rules that are *not* justified by appeal to their consequences. Instead, deontologists think that moral obligation lies in recognizing the rights and the intrinsic value of persons. As such, deontologism is more aware of the rights and importance of individuals than consequentialist theories, which value persons simply as "containers" of intrinsic value. The theory given by Immanuel Kant as the crowning jewel of his complex philosophical system is the most famous deontological theory.

Kant announces two moral principles that by themselves strongly appeal to our moral intuitions. The *Categorical Imperative* prescribes: "*Act only according to that maxim by which you can at the same time will that it should become a universal law*" (Kant, 1959, 39). Kant believes that whenever we act, we reveal our belief in a general principle or "maxim." Suppose that when I give money to a vagrant on the street, my maxim is "Give money to vagrants when I feel like it." To be able to "will" that my maxim become a universal law means that I wish that everyone would do this and that I am able to see that it would be logically possible for *all* persons to act this way. In this case, it seems that there is no logical inconsistency in the maxim that everyone give money to vagrants when they feel like it. So it seems that giving money to vagrants satisfies the categorical imperative.

On the other hand, suppose we find ourselves in a difficult situation and ask ourselves whether it would be right to tell a lie to extricate ourselves. Kant argues that the maxim "All persons shall lie when it suits their purposes" is logically contradictory. If *everyone* followed this rule, everyone would know that everyone else will lie to them when it suits their purposes. But then no one would take anyone's word seriously. Thus, if this maxim were universalized, it would destroy the practice of truth telling, thereby making it logically impossible to lie *or* tell the truth. So, lying is immoral because it is illogical.

Kant's second great moral principle, The *Principle of Ends* maintains: "*Act so that you treat humanity, whether in your own person or in that of another, always as an end and never as a means only*" (Kant, 1959, 47). Here Kant expresses an important part of what we think morality involves—recognizing that persons have their own ends and, therefore, deserve moral respect. Kant thinks that morality demands that we see persons *as persons* who have their own interests, rights, and dignity, and not as mere means to satisfy our own interests. So, for example, in breaking a promise to a person, we are treating that person as a mere means to accomplish the end we have in mind when we break the promise.

One might object that there may be dire situations in which we must treat persons only as means, e.g., in a case when someone must be thrown out of an overcrowded lifeboat to keep it from sinking. Although Kant did not express this qualification himself, a natural addition to Kant's principle is suggested by Robert Kane: "Treat every person as an end and not as a means . . . *whenever possible*. When it is not possible, try to sustain this ideal to the degree possible" (Kane, 1994, 26).

CRITICISMS OF KANTIAN DEONTOLOGY

The first objection to the categorical imperative involves a technical question. Should we take the categorical imperative as providing only *a necessary condition* for actions to be morally permissible or as both *a necessary and sufficient condition*? When Kant says to act *only* in ways we can universalize, he presents universalization as only a necessary condition of right action. This would make universalization a test for immoral actions: If we cannot universalize our actions, then they are not morally permissible. This creates a criterion for *rejecting* actions that are *not* universalizable. It does not follow from this that actions that *are* universalizable are thereby morally permissible. ["If it is not precipitating, then it is not raining" is not equivalent to "If it is precipitating, then it is raining."] If this is the way we interpret the categorical imperative, then the categorical imperative is only a method for rejecting actions, but it does not tell us what we ought to do—it does not provide a sufficient condition. We would then need some other moral principle beyond the categorical imperative to do this.

On the other hand, we could take the categorical imperative as both a necessary and sufficient condition. So understood, the categorical imperative would read: "*An action is morally permissible if and only if it is universalizable.*" Understanding the categorical imperative in this way avoids the difficulty of the previous paragraph, but it has a problem of its own. It seems possible to universalize many immoral rules. Therefore, if we say that universalizability is sufficient for an action to be morally permissible, we would have to conclude that immoral actions pass Kant's test. To use an example from R. M. Hare (1952), it would be possible for a member of group A to will consistently that all members of group B be murdered. All A has to do to make his maxim consistent is to intend it to include *all* members of group B, *including himself* should he turn out to be a member of group B. There is nothing *logically absurd* about A's maxim, even though it is *morally repellant*. This suggests that the categorical imperative cannot be taken as a necessary *and* sufficient condition of moral rightness, but at most as a necessary condition. This throws us back on the first horn of the dilemma: The categorical imperative does not say which actions *are* moral.

A second criticism of Kant's use of the categorical imperative stems from the fact that it cannot be proven, as Kant thought it could, using only the universalization test. Kant argues that committing suicide, making a lying promise, not developing one's talents, and refraining from helping others are logically contradictory in the sense that their maxims are not universalizable. Thus, Kant thought that he could deduce absolute moral rules from reason. The most that Kant proved, however, was that such actions, if universalized, would have objectionable results, that is, would seem contrary to our moral intuitions or prudential interests. The problem is this: Kant asks us to use the test of universalization as a test of the morality of actions. But we can only decide what maxims are universalizable by appealing to our moral intuitions. We have to decide, therefore, whether actions are moral or not *before* we can decide whether they *should* be universalized. So the test of universalization is useless. We cannot tell whether actions are moral until we tell whether we can universalize them, and we cannot tell whether we can universalize them until we determine whether they are moral.

Here is an illustration of this objection. Plato provided a thought experiment in which you store a friend's weapon in your home and promise to return it when he asks for it. Some days later the man quarrels with his wife and runs to you in a rage to retrieve the weapon so that he can attack her with it. You have conflicting duties to keep your promise and to prevent mayhem. Surely, the right thing for you to do is to break your promise and withhold the weapon. So far, this example seems to refute Kant's claim that rules like "Always keep your promises" are unqualified moral truths. It also raises the theoretical problem of how to resolve conflicts of duties without appealing to consequences.

Well, perhaps Kant should say that we test a more specific maxim, for example, "Always keep your promises, except when it would result in someone being seriously hurt." The problem is that this more plausible maxim also cannot be proved by the universalization test. We have to *decide* whether it is an acceptable moral rule before we can decide whether it can be universalized; we cannot decide that it is moral *because* we first find it to be universalizable. Consider other difficult moral cases. For example, we cannot decide whether we can or cannot universalize the maxim to allow abortions within the first trimester of pregnancy until we decide whether such abortions are morally permissible, not the other way around. Inescapably, we have to *make* moral decisions, not *deduce* them from reason.

A third objection concerns the vagueness of the principle of ends. Remember, Kant urges us not to treat persons *merely* as means. He does not make the unrealistic demand that we always treat persons *completely* as ends. (If we did this, we could never enjoy the advantages of living in society, because social interaction involves the mutual use of each other's talents.) Kant says that we are not treating persons as mere means when we enforce capital punishment or execute them for engaging in rebellion. All that the principle of ends requires is that we recognize persons' humanity before we execute them. It seems to follow, then, that so far as the principle of ends goes, we may engage in all sorts of behavior that is harmful to others, so long as we recognize their humanity. This scarcely proscribes us from doing what is morally repugnant. Although it is important to recognize that persons deserve better moral treatment than beings that have no ends of their own, it is difficult to parlay that insight into a satisfactory moral theory.

Fourth, Kant's principles ignore the utility that may be created by actions that violate the categorical imperative or ends principle. Just as utilitarianism faces damaging counterexamples in which the rights of individuals are sacrificed to maximize collective utility, deontological theories face damaging counterexamples because they ignore utility. Suppose that the Martians land on Earth and demonstrate their power by killing 100,000,000 persons worldwide. They then threaten to kill another 100,000,000 persons unless you murder one completely innocent person. If you do so, you treat that person as a mere means to saving the other 100,000,000 persons. It seems that the morally right thing for you to do is to commit the murder, but the principle of ends says that you must not. Any deontological system that endorses losing 999,999,999 lives seems to take insufficient notice of the value of life.

Fifth, Kant's principles stand in conflict with the creation of intrinsic value. Suppose that we can create a tremendous work of art at the cost of breaking a promise or telling a lie. Kant thinks that the categorical imperative and principle of ends may not be set aside regardless of how much intrinsic value could be created by violating them. This means that for Kant moral obligation completely trumps the other things we value in life, with the result that Kantian theory does not tell us what is best—all things considered—for many questions. As a complete normative theory, Kant's view is myopic.

MIXED THEORIES AND WHAT THEY SHOW ABOUT NORMATIVE ETHICS

We have seen that consequentialist theories that make the morally right depend on the creation of intrinsic value (act utilitarianism is the clearest example) have problems with acknowledging individuals' rights and justice. Deontological theories, which ignore the creation of intrinsic value and emphasize individuals' worth as persons, do well on that score but do poorly on nonrights-related well-being. Perhaps some compromise theory that takes account of both utilitarian and deontological aspects of morality is possible.

William Frankena (1973, 47) provides such a theory by suggesting two basic moral principles, the *principle of beneficence* and the *principle of equality*. The former announces the utilitarian claim to avoid doing evil and to increase human happiness. The latter deontological principle forbids us to treat anyone unfairly. Frankena thinks that the principle of equality usually, but not always, takes precedence over the principle of beneficence. The best we can do, according to Frankena, is to use our best judgment to decide moral problems by appealing to these two principles.

James Cornman (Cornman, Lehrer, and Pappas, 1987, 345–50) announces a more explicit combined theory. For Cornman, an act is right if and only if: (a) it treats as few persons as possible as mere means, while treating the most persons as ends; and (b) it promotes the most utility possible that is consistent with condition (a). For Cornman, the Kantian principle of ends overrides the utilitarian second condition.

The problem with mixed theories is the basic conflict between consequentialist and deontological approaches to morality. Frankena admits this and urges us to rely on our moral intuitions in cases when the consequentialist and deontological principles collide. Frankena's view is not as formless as personal subjectivism, but it is not as explicit as philosophers want a theory of moral obligation to be. If we accept Cornman's claim that his condition (a) always overrides (b), we still face one of the difficulties for Kantian ethics already cited: Cornman's theory would say that we cannot sacrifice one person no matter what the payoff in intrinsic value in the universe would be. But if we elect to make Cornman's utilitarian condition (b) count enough to give the intuitively correct answer concerning sacrificing one person to save 100,000,000, then Cornman's theory will be vulnerable to the justice-based criticisms made against act utilitarianism.

This shows that there are at least two major conflicting themes in our thinking about moral obligation. The first is the consequentialist theme that the happiness of persons *counts*, hence we must always be alive to the importance of maximizing intrinsic value. To use a pun, the numbers *count*. The second is that the rights of the individual *count* as well, so we cannot run roughshod over persons by treating them as mere means. The conflict between these two intuitions constitutes a deep fact about how persons *think* about morality, and, thus, a deep fact about morality. It constitutes an inescapable tension at the core of normative theorizing, and it gives support to the theory of moral subjectivism to be examined in the next chapter.

Guide Questions

1. What are the two basic questions of normative ethics? (137)
2. What is a descriptive statement? An evaluative statement? (138)
3. How might a metaethical subjectivist object to normative ethics? (139)
4. Give three ways to reply to the subjectivist's objection. (139–40)
5. What is the relationship between moral intuitions and general moral principles? (140–41)
6. How is it possible for persons who share basic moral principles to disagree about a moral issue? (141–42)
7. What is the basic reason for demanding that moral principles be universalizable? (142)
8. What is the point of the triple analogy regarding being locked in a house, being unable to do arithmetic, and knowing no moral theories? (142–43)
9. Why is personal subjectivism *not* the theory that our consciences tell us what we think is right? (144)
10. How does personal subjectivism undermine ethics? (144–45)
11. What is the metaphysical thesis of religious authoritarianism? The epistemological thesis? (145)
12. Explain how the problem of representation poses a difficulty for religious authoritarianism. (145–46)
13. How does the existence of many religions pose a difficulty for religious authoritarianism? (146)
14. What does it mean to say that one person's modus ponens is another person's modus tollens? (147)
15. Under what conditions would a religious authoritarian be an egoist? (148)
16. What is the psychological premise in the argument for egoism? (148–49)
17. How might someone use *belief-desire* psychology to argue for the psychological premise of egoism? (149–50)

18. How might someone argue that egoism is not really a moral theory? (150–51)
19. What difficulties are there with identifying what is right with what is legal? (151–52)
20. What is the difference between *rights* and *well-being apart from rights*? (153)
21. How does this difference create a distinction between consequentialist and deontological theories of ethics? (153–54)
22. What does it mean to say that utilitarianism is impartial cost-benefit analysis applied to morality? (155)
23. What five factors do utilitarians think contribute to the amount of *hedons* we derive from our actions? (156)
24. How, according to utilitarians, might we do a wrong act, but be morally praiseworthy? (156)
25. Why does act utilitarianism appeal to sentimentalists? (157)
26. What are two practical difficulties in using act utilitarianism? (157)
27. What is the objection to act utilitarianism based on distributive justice? Scapegoating? Special duties? (158–59)
28. How is rule utilitarianism different from act utilitarianism? (161)
29. How is rule utilitarianism supposed to avoid some of the difficulties that act utilitarianism faces? (161)
30. What is the problem with trying to use rule utilitarianism to avoid the objections to act utilitarianism? (161–62)
31. Express the categorical imperative in your own words. (162)
32. Express the principle of ends in your own words. (163)
33. What is the problem with taking the categorical imperative as providing a *sufficient condition* of morality? (164)
34. What is the objection to using Kant's principle of ends to decide what we should do? (165)
35. What does it mean to say that, taken as a complete normative theory, Kant's view is *myopic*? (165–66)
36. What is a mixed deontological/utilitarian moral theory? (166)

Review Questions for Examinations

1. Define these concepts: "descriptive statement," "evaluative statement," "truth-condition," "normative ethics," "metaethics," "statements of moral obligation," "intrinsic value," "instrumental value," "moral intuitions," "moral principles," "moral autonomy," "conscience," "belief-desire psychology," "veil of ignorance," "rights," "well-being apart from rights," "consequentialism," "deontology," "cost-benefit analysis," "hedon," "scapegoating," "categorical imperative," "principle of ends."
2. What are these theories: personal subjectivism, religious authoritarianism,

egoism, relativism, act utilitarianism, rule utilitarianism, Kantian deontology, mixed deontological/utilitarian theories. Provide a reason for accepting each theory. Be able to give at least two criticisms of each of these theories.

3. Classify the following statements as either descriptive or evaluative:
   (a) "The legal drinking age in Pennsylvania is 21."
   (b) "In chess, the bishops may move only diagonally."
   (c) "Cannibalism is right according to certain groups."
   (d) "Cannibalism is right when practiced by certain groups."
   (e) "The moral views of cultures differ significantly."
   (f) "Jane Austin was a greater novelist than Ernest Hemingway."

4. Classify the following statements as examples of either normative ethics or metaethics:
   (a) "Capital punishment is evil."
   (b) "Moral questions have objective answers."
   (c) "Do unto others as you would have them do unto you."
   (d) "There is no good or evil; there are only things people do."
   (e) "Never treat persons as mere means to your ends."

5. Classify the following statements as examples of either consequentialist or deontological reasoning:
   (a) "Act only on principles that you can will everyone to act on."
   (b) "Always act in such a way as to contribute to the most human happiness."
   (c) "Guilty persons must be punished simply because they are guilty."
   (d) "The only sensible reason to punish persons is to modify their subsequent behavior."
   (e) "Actions that contribute to the evolution of the human spirit are right."

6. Classify the following statements as examples of *personal subjectivism*, *religious authoritarianism*, *egoism*, *relativism*, *act utilitarianism*, *rule utilitarianism*, *deontology*, or *mixed deontological/utilitarian theory*:
   (a) "All persons should do whatever actions they think are in their own best interests."
   (b) "For each moral decision we should select the option that produces the greatest balance of pleasure over pain."
   (c) "The way to act morally is to let one's conscience be one's guide."
   (d) "It is always wrong to betray a confidence."
   (e) "We should always follow principles that, if followed by everyone, would produce the greatest balance of pleasure over pain."
   (f) "The best way to determine what is moral is by studying the word of God."
   (g) "To act rightly one should follow the moral rules of one's society."
   (h) "We should try to maximize general happiness, while being sure not to violate anyone's rights."

Discussion Questions

1. Analyze the following moral dilemmas by deciding which of the eight theories of moral obligation gives the *best* answer and which theory gives the *worst* answer. Explain why.
   (a) "You have an auto accident one winter night on a lonely road. The other passengers are badly injured, the car is out of commission, the road is deserted, so you run along it till you find an isolated house. The house turns out to be occupied by an old woman who is looking after her small grandchild. There is no phone, but there is a car in the garage, and you ask desperately to borrow it, and explain the situation. Terrified by your desperation she runs upstairs and locks herself in the bathroom, leaving you alone with the child. You pound ineffectively on the door and search without success for the car keys. Then it occurs to you that she might be persuaded to tell you where they are if you twist the child's arm outside the bathroom door. Should you do it?" (Thomas Nagel, 1986, 176)
   (b) "Jim finds himself in the central square of a small South American town. Tied up against the wall are a row of twenty Indians . . . in front of . . . several armed men in uniform. A heavy man . . . turns out to be the captain in charge and . . . explains that the Indians are a random group of the inhabitants who, after recent acts of protest against the government, are just about to be killed. . . . However, since Jim is an honored visitor from another land, the captain is happy to offer him a guest's privilege of killing one of the Indians himself. If Jim accepts, then as a special mark of the occasion, the other Indians will be let off. Of course, if Jim refuses, then there is no special occasion, and (the soldiers will) kill them all. (Jim realizes that if he takes the gun and tries to rescue the Indians, he and they will all be killed.) What should he do?" (Smart and Williams, 1973, 98–99)
2. Can it ever be morally wrong to act from kindness? Is it possible to be too nice? Explain by reference to the normative theories in the chapter.
3. Which is easier to determine: what is legal or what is moral? Explain.
4. How would the various theories in this chapter answer the question "Is it OK to play dirty if one's opponent does?"
5. How would the theories in this chapter answer the question: "Should we treat persons we like better than persons we do not like?"
6. Which of the theories of moral obligation we examined in this chapter seems to you to explain the largest percentage of nonphilosophers' everyday moral reasoning?
7. Devise a theory of moral obligation that is not one of the eight theories examined in this chapter.

FOR FURTHER READING

Cornman, James, Keith Lehrer, and George Pappas. 1987. *Philosophical Problems and Arguments*. Indianapolis: Hackett. Chapter 6. A comprehensive presentation of normative theories. Moderately difficult.

Dawkins, Richard. 1976. *The Selfish Gene*. New York: Oxford University Press. A fascinating evolutionary account of animal and human morality by a prominent biologist. Contains a wealth of biological information. Moderately difficult.

Frankena, William. 1973. *Ethics*. Englewood Cliffs, NJ: Prentice-Hall. A clear, short, but comprehensive introduction to normative and metaethics.

Kane, Robert. 1994. *Through the Moral Maze: Searching for Absolute Values in a Pluralistic World*. New York: Paragon House. Proposes a combined religious/Kantian approach to dealing with the disintegration of morality in contemporary society. Enjoyable to read.

Mill, John Stuart. 1981. *Utilitarianism*. Indianapolis: Bobbs-Merrill. Mill's classic statement of utilitarianism. Readable.

Pojman, Louis. 1995. *Ethics: Discovering Right and Wrong*. Belmont, CA: Wadsworth. A reader-friendly introductory survey.

Smart, J. J. C. and Bernard Williams. 1973. *Utilitarianism: For and Against*. Cambridge: Cambridge University Press. An erudite debate between a utilitarian (Smart) and a foe (Williams). Difficult. Rewards careful reading.

Unger, Peter. 1996. *Living High and Letting Die: Our Illusion of Innocence*. New York: Oxford University Press. Easy-to-understand thought experiments designed to show that our normal moral consciences are remiss when they tell us it is OK not to save the lives of the world's poor children through charity. Brilliant and sobering.

Chapter 7
METAETHICS

INTRODUCTION

In chapter 6, we examined theories that say what our moral obligations are. I noted in passing a metaethical objection to any attempt to select a best moral theory: Perhaps we should not devise theories of normative ethics until we show *how* such theories can be true. I replied that we do not have to delay considering normative ethics until we address the metaethical issue. Nonetheless, the metaethical question is an important one for anyone who desires a complete philosophical picture of what exists. What is the place of values and moral obligation within our total picture of reality? Are there objective moral truths or only subjective moral feelings, opinions, and attitudes? Addressing this issue is just as necessary for a complete philosophical picture of reality as addressing the nature of the external world or the existence of God. *Metaethics* is *the higher level discussion about normative ethics that asks whether values are objective or subjective.*

1. Key Terms

DESCRIPTIVE STATEMENTS AND EVALUATIVE STATEMENTS

Compare these statements: (A) "Capital punishment reduces the number of capital crimes." (B) "If capital punishment reduces the number of capital crimes, then capital punishment is morally permissible." Statement (A), whether true or false, is a *descriptive statement*, because it attempts to describe a fact about the universe. To state a descriptive statement is not to express a positive or negative evaluation—it is simply to say what one thinks is a fact. *A descriptive statement does not require an evaluation on the part of the person who expresses it.* What makes descriptive statements *descriptive* is not whether we *know* whether they are true or false, but what we have to do to *state* them. Statement (B), despite the fact that it is a conditional, is an expression of what the speaker believes is morally permissible and is, thus, *evaluative. An evaluative statement requires an evaluation on the part of the person who expresses it.* An evaluation is a positive or negative assessment of something.

TRUTH CONDITIONS

To say that a statement has a truth value is to say that it is either true or false. For example, "Hydrogen has the atomic number 1" has a truth value, but "Please pass the salt" does not. *The truth conditions of statements* are those aspects of reality that create truth values; truth conditions make true statements true and false statements false. The truth condition of "The cat is on the mat" is the physical relation between the cat and the mat. If the cat *is* on the mat, then "The cat is on the mat" is true. If the cat *is not* on the mat, then "The cat is on the mat" is false.

Each descriptive statement has a truth condition, whether we know it or not. We do not understand what a descriptive statement *means* until we understand which conditions *would* make it true and which would make it false. For instance, if someone says "Schlugel, schlugel, schlugel," and insists that this is a descriptive statement, we cannot assign a meaning to his utterance until we figure out what conditions of the world would make this statement true or false. The unknowable descriptive statement "The largest diamond in the world lies undiscovered in the middle of the Pacific Ocean" is meaningful, because we understand what facts about the world *would* make it true.

The question: "Do moral statements have truth conditions, and, if so, how?" is the main question in metaethics. When someone says "Promises should be kept" or "Stealing is wrong," what part of reality might serve to make such sentences true or false? *Moral objectivists maintain that moral judgments have truth conditions that lie outside persons' opinions.* Some candidates include: God's will (Religious Authoritarianism), facts about other nonspatio-temporal entities (Nonnaturalism), and facts about the natural world (Naturalism). *Moral subjectivists deny that moral statements have truth conditions that lie beyond persons' opinions.* The major subjectivist theories hold that moral statements either have no truth conditions at all (A. J. Ayer, 1952) or are all false (J. L. Mackie, 1977).

MEANING

The *meanings of words* are their dictionary definitions. For example, the meaning of the word "cat" in my dictionary is "feline mammal." The *referent* of a word is the *thing referred to.* Thus, the referent of my use of the word "cat" is the actual animal I am referring to. Two terms that have different meanings can have the same referent, for example, "The author of *Poor Richard's Almanac*" and "the inventor of bifocals" (Benjamin Franklin). Thus, two statements that have different meanings can have the same truth condition, for example, "The author of *Poor Richard's Almanac* believed in thrift" and "The inventor of bifocals believed in thrift." Each statement is true if and only if Benjamin Franklin believed in thrift. It is possible, therefore, that two *moral statements* that have very different meanings might have the same truth condition. For example, "X is morally right" might have the same truth condition as "X produces the greatest overall pleasure." This is a point that the objectivists will use in their debate against the subjectivists.

2. Definist and Nondefinist Arguments for Metaethical Theories

There are two ways to argue that "two things" that appear to be different are really one and the same thing: definism and nondefinism. *Definist identity theorists* attempt to prove that two apparently different entities are really the same entity by arguing that the *words* that refer to the entity have *the same meaning* (are *synonymous*). If definists could prove that two referring expressions are really equivalent in meaning, then they would succeed in proving that an identity holds between "the two referents" of the terms, because there would be shown to be only *one* referent. For example, some theists argue that God is the greatest possible being, because the word "God" means "the Being than which None Greater can be Conceived."

Nondefinist identity theorists attempt to prove that two apparently different entities are really the same entity, but *not* by saying that the words that refer to the entity have the same meaning. The Morning Star is identical to the Evening Star (actually, the planet Venus) despite the fact that the terms "the Morning Star" and "the Evening Star" have different meanings. "The Morning Star" means "the last star visible in the morning," whereas "the Evening Star" means "the first star visible in the evening." No one could figure out that the Morning Star is the same heavenly body as the Evening Star simply by understanding the meaning of the respective terms: Astronomical theory established the identity.

Here is an example of the difference between definist and nondefinist theories. All proponents of *hedonism* believe that pleasure is the greatest good for human beings (the *summum bonum*). Now there are two ways to try to argue for hedonism. A definist would say that the expression "X is good" just means "X produces pleasure." According to the definist, for anyone who knows the meaning of the term "good," there is no room for doubt. If you know what "good" means, you know that whatever is good produces pleasure, and whatever produces pleasure is good. The nondefinist proponent of hedonism also believes that pleasure is the highest good, but denies that we can know this fact simply by understanding the meaning of "good." Rather, we must prove on nondefinitional grounds (for example, by philosophical reasoning) that pleasure is the highest good.

Here are some points regarding the two views. (1) *If* the definitions offered by the definists were correct, they would prove the identities the definists want to prove. (2) Definism makes a stronger claim than is necessary for the truth of the identity of the referents of the defined terms. A nondefinist identity theory could be true even if its corresponding definist theory fails. Thus, we must be careful not to refute a *straw man* (*a fictional opponent who is weaker than the real foe*) by thinking that to refute definist theories is to refute nondefinist theories. (3) The definists' definitions are almost never acceptable. (We see this when we examine the open-question argument.) Thus, shrewd metaethical theorists usually avoid definist arguments. Nonetheless, we should realize that any individual definist proposal *might* succeed. (4) Because nondefinist arguments have the greatest chance of success, in this chapter we will examine only nondefinist arguments in detail. If the nondefinist arguments fail, the definist arguments will fail also.

3. The Metaphysics of Ethics and the Epistemology of Ethics

In chapter 1 we saw that two questions give rise to two different branches of philosophy. "What exists?" is the fundamental question of metaphysics. "What do we know?" is the fundamental question of epistemology (the theory of knowledge). The same two questions arise in ethics.

In the *metaphysics of ethics* (*metaethics*) we ask "Can any theory of normative ethics be true, and, if so, how?" This asks whether it is reasonable to believe that any theories of normative ethics can be objectively true and brings us directly to the debate between the objectivists and subjectivists. Believing in objectivism or subjectivism does not require that we think we *know* which theory is correct—anymore than thinking that God exists requires that we believe we *know* that God exists. In metaethics, as with metaphysics in general, we sketch theories we think are *likely to be true* and try to argue for them the best we can.

In the *epistemology of ethics* we ask whether we can have moral knowledge, and if we can, how? *Moral skeptics* deny that we have moral knowledge. *Moral nonskeptics* believe that we can have moral knowledge. Knowing that *X* is true requires more than *X*'s being true; knowledge requires that we can justify our true beliefs. Therefore, the moral nonskeptics have a harder task than the moral objectivists do. Even if there are moral truths, we may not be able to know what they are. On the other hand, moral skepticism is a less ambitious theory than moral subjectivism. It is easier to show that *we lack knowledge that X exists* than it is to show that *X does not exist*. [Compare the difficulty of trying to prove: (1) "We do *not* know that Bigfoot exists" and (2) "We know that Bigfoot does *not* exist."] So, even if we cannot *know* which metaethical theory is correct, it would not follow that none *is* correct.

4. Moral Objectivism and Moral Subjectivism

To say that an entity is *objective* is to say that it *exists in itself, and not only in someone's mind*. If an entity is objective, then it exists whether anyone believes it is real or not. For example, if the Loch Ness monster is an objective entity, it exists whether anyone believes it exists or not. If a moral statement is objectively true, it is true whether anyone believes it or not. The definition of "subjective" I use in this book is the opposite of "objective": *to be subjective is to exist only in the mind of a subject*. For example, if we quit having a thought, a pain, or a sensation of heat in our minds, these subjective things cease to exist.

As noted in chapter 4, it is important to be aware of a second definition of "subjective" that means "idiosyncratic" ("unusual," "peculiar," "in the minority opinion"). According to this second definition, widely shared states such as a feeling of pain upon touching a hot stove are *not subjective* even though they exist only in persons' minds and not in the stove. Unfortunately, many persons who think about metaethics, including philosophers who should know better, confuse the two senses of "subjective," and conclude that entities that are nonsubjective in the second sense must be nonsubjective in the first sense.

For example, philosophers sometimes say that because moral opinions are widely shared (nonsubjective in the second sense), they cannot be subjective in the sense of depending entirely on the minds of persons (subjective in the first sense). This is just as mistaken as saying that pain must really exist in hot stoves, because most persons feel pain when they touch hot stoves. The best way to avoid such confusions is to stick with the first definition of "subjective." When we want to emphasize that a subjective opinion or feeling is widely shared, we shall call it "a widely shared subjective state."

Moral objectivism maintains that judgments we make in normative ethics are made true by something beyond the (individual or collective) moral opinions of persons. Moral subjectivism maintains that there is nothing beyond the moral opinions of persons that makes normative judgments true. Objectivists differ over what those objective things might be. Most objectivists say that they are some sort of supernatural or natural *entities*: God's will, a supernatural moral property, or a natural property in the world. Other objectivists such as Kant do not talk about *entities*, but insist that moral judgments can be objectively true, because moral judgments are knowable simply by thinking about them.

We can understand moral objectivism and moral subjectivism by comparing them with theories of the nature of physical objects as described in chapters 1 and 4. *Moral objectivism* is like direct realism. Direct realism holds that physical objects possess all the types of characteristics that common sense assigns to them. Characteristics such as shape, size, solidity, sharply defined edges, color, sound, taste, and odor are said to belong in the physical objects themselves and do not exist merely in the sensations of perceivers. For example, direct realism holds that colors exist spread out on the surfaces of physical objects, and our judgment that a particular physical object is a certain color is true if and only if that object possesses that color. Thus, the truth conditions for our judgments about physical objects' colors exist independently of us in the objects themselves.

Moral objectivism sees moral properties in the same way that direct realism views the commonsense characteristics of physical objects. The objectivity of the judgment "Subject S is wrong to do *X*" or "Action *A* is wrong" depends on the fact that the truth conditions of the judgments reside in facts about either S or *A*. The truth of a moral judgment is determined by objective facts about agents or their actions, *not by the opinions or attitudes of the speaker or other onlookers*. This objective reality may be thought to be part of the natural world (naturalism), the nonnatural world (nonnaturalism), or depend on a priori, intuitable truths, as with Kant. Moral objectivism explains why persons who morally disagree can literally contradict each other: Objective truth can confirm at most one of two contradictory claims about it.

Moral subjectivist theories reject this objectivity claim. Subjectivism's view of moral properties is like the scientific realists' view of commonsense characteristics of physical objects. According to scientific realism, characteristics such as colors, odors, sounds, sharp edges, and commonsense shapes exist *only* in the minds of perceivers. Physical objects, which themselves are mostly empty space with atoms and subatomic particles flying about, cause colored sensations in perceivers as light reflects off the atoms of the objects and causes sensations in perceivers' minds. Scientific realists distinguish between veridical and mistaken perception by saying that veridical perception is having the same type of sensations that normal perceivers would have under standard conditions (eyes open, conscious, white light present, etc.). Misperception is held to be having abnormal sensations.

Moral subjectivists, like the scientific realists regarding the commonsense characteristics of physical objects, deny that moral properties exist independently of what is in our minds. According to subjectivists, statements such as "Action *A* is wrong" do not have truth conditions outside our opinions, feelings, and attitudes. Moral judgments simply express how persons morally feel about actions. Subjectivists think that assigning moral properties to the agents and actions is like our naive talk of physical objects as if they were really colored.

According to subjectivists, moral judgments express attitudes and feelings we social beings have about issues concerning moral issues. For example, our feelings about fairness and benevolence do not point to objective moral truths that exist independently of those feelings, but at most reflect the sort of beings we are. If we were different kinds of creatures with different biological origins, we might have different moral sensitivities (Double, 1991, ch. 7). For instance, if humans reproduced at the rate that insects do and died as quickly, we might feel very differently about the value of human life. These alternative moral sensibilities would be as "right" as the ones we now have, for they would simply reveal the sort of beings we *would* be. This means that, for the subjectivist, there can be no such thing as objective rightness or wrongness, but only subjective sentiments about morality.

Subjectivists disagree over how widely shared persons' moral sentiments are. Some subjectivists believe that basic moral feelings such as benevolence and fairness are almost universally shared by human beings; these feelings help constitute "human nature." This theory is *universal subjectivism*. (If that term sounds like a contradiction, remember the two senses of "subjective." Pains are universal among normal human beings, but are felt subjectively.) Other subjectivists believe that basic moral feelings are *not* shared widely by persons. On this view, basic moral feelings vary greatly from person to person. This theory is *mixed subjectivism*.

Universal subjectivists need to offer an explanation for why moral sentiments are universal (or are as nearly universal as their theory says they are). In my opinion, the most promising explanation is based on natural selection. Just as most perceivers can recognize colors as the result of mechanisms that helped us to evolve, so most "morality perceivers" might have similar moral sentiments because such sentiments were helpful in evolution. For example, genes that predisposed our ancestors toward altruistic or compassionate behavior might have helped our ancestors survive (Dawkins, 1976). If so, these genes might still play a part in human moral sentiments.

If the gap between examples like color sensations on the one hand and moral sentiments on the other seems too large to allow the evolutionary analogy, the universal subjectivist might offer another example. The famous MIT linguist Noam Chomsky's theory of linguistic universals is a linguistic variety of universal subjectivism designed to explain how persons have the ability to learn the grammatical structures of their specific languages. Chomsky suggests that evolution produced structures in human brains that allow us to learn French, or German, or Chinese.

The mixed subjectivist theory, on the other hand, denies that there is anything approaching universal agreement among human moral sentiments. These theorists think there are no biological structures for moral judgment that are analogous to the ones that Chomsky postulates to account for our linguistic abilities. Rather, the mixed subjectivist theory says that our judgments concerning right and wrong are governed by a jumble of conflicting factors—biological, sociological, psychological, contextual, and idiosyncratic. Because these factors affect each person differently, there *are* no universal (or even nearly universal) moral feelings. According to the mixed subjectivist, when it comes to moral feelings, there is no such thing as human nature.

OBJECTIVIST THEORIES OF MORAL JUDGMENTS

5. Religious Authoritarianism

DEFINIST RELIGIOUS AUTHORITARIANISM

As noted in section 2, moral objectivists can use either definist or nondefinist arguments to try to prove their theories. *Definist religious authoritarianism* tries to prove that God creates the objectivity of right and wrong by arguing that moral judgments are definitionally equivalent to (synonymous with) statements about God's commands. Carl F. H. Henry (1957) claims that "I ought" means "the sovereign Lord commands." *Nondefinist religious authoritarianism*, which is more popular, argues that God's commands create the difference between right and wrong, but denies that the meaning of moral judgments can be defined in terms of God's commands.

The objections to definist religious authoritarianism are decisive and perfectly general. Once we understand why definism cannot support religious authoritarianism, we shall see why definism in general cannot support *any* metaethical theory. Definitions are crucial for critical thinking, but they seldom *prove* any substantive theories in philosophy. G. E. Moore (1903) receives the most credit for refuting definism with what is known as the "open-question argument," but many thinkers besides Moore have recognized the idea.

Here is the open-question refutation of definism. Suppose we say that expression "A" is synonymous with expression "B." This is to say that the two expressions have exactly the same meaning. If so, then any person who understands the meanings of both "A" and "B" will recognize that they are synonymous. If so, then for anyone who knows the meanings of "A" and "B," the answer to the question "Is A the same thing as B?" will be obvious: "Yes!" Therefore, if any person who knows the meanings of "A" and "B" can seriously wonder whether A is B—if it is "an open question" for that person whether A is B—then "A" and "B" cannot be synonymous.

Consider an example. Suppose that the name "Superman" means the name "Clark Kent." If they do, then any person who understands the meaning of both names would realize that Superman is the same person as Clark Kent. Many persons know the meanings of "Superman" and "Clark Kent" *without* knowing that Superman *is* Clark Kent. Lois Lane couldn't figure it out for years. Therefore, "Superman" does not mean "Clark Kent." Roughly speaking, "Superman" means "the man of steel from the planet Krypton," and "Clark Kent" means "the mild-mannered reporter for the *Daily Planet*."

Here is how the open question argument applies to definist attempts to define moral terms. Suppose, as Henry says, that "I ought to do X" means "God commands X." Then, for anyone who understands the meaning of both statements, it would *not* be an open question whether what one ought to do is what is commanded by God. But we *can* sensibly ask whether we ought to do what God commands. When we ask the open question "Is what I ought to do what God commands?," we are not asking the same thing as the closed question "Is what I ought to do what I ought to do?" We can be sure, by definition, that the actions we ought to do are the ones we ought to do. But we might be uncertain whether God exists. Maybe what I ought to do is not commanded by God because God does not exist. Or we might wonder, even if we believe God exists, whether God made *any command* regarding the X in question. Or we might wonder whether God might have made the wrong command. The mere fact that we can raise these possibilities shows that "ought" judgments are not synonymous with statements about what God commands.

To reinforce this point, here are Moore's illustrations of how the open-question argument refutes three other definist arguments. If we define *good* as *pleasant*, then we cannot sensibly ask whether a pleasant thing is good. But, of course, we can. If we define *right* as *conducive to the general happiness*, then we cannot sensibly ask whether those things that promote the general happiness are right. But, again, we can. If we define *desirable* as *that which is desired*, we cannot sensibly ask whether the things we desire are desirable (worthy of being desired). But we can.

NONDEFINIST RELIGIOUS AUTHORITARIANISM

Although the open-question argument refutes definist religious authoritarianism, nondefinist religious authoritarianism remains unscathed. That view maintains that God's commands create morality, despite the fact that moral judgments and statements about God's commands are not equivalent in meaning. So we need to consider the nondefinist version of religious authoritarianism.

Although not so easily refuted as its definist counterpart, nondefinist religious authoritarianism has difficulties. *Any* theory—definist or nondefinist—that maintains that actions are right and wrong because they are sanctioned or disapproved by God is puzzling in two ways. First, there is Plato's dilemma in the *Euthyphro*: (1) Are actions right because they are commanded by the gods? (2) Or do the gods command them because they are right? If (1), then morality becomes arbitrary in the sense that, by definition, *anything that God commands (or would command) would have to be right*. So anything God might command, such as not setting female slaves free six years after purchasing them (*Exodus*, ch. 21), would necessarily be right. After all, according to religious authoritarianism, rightness is *nothing but* God's commands. If (2), then God commands actions that are right independently of God's commands, which means that God is *not* the determiner of right and wrong. If God is not the determiner of what actions are right and wrong, then right and wrong exist independently of God's commands. This is not religious authoritarianism at all.

A second problem concerns the very idea of trying to base the *objectivity* of morality on the *subjectivity* of God. Suppose we accept the first horn of Plato's dilemma and say that rightness is entirely (and arbitrarily) dependent on God's will. This creates a kind of nonsubjectivity for morality in the sense that morality would not be determined by the opinions of *persons*, but it is hardly satisfactory. Religious authoritarianism does not address the deeper issue of how morality *can* be nonsubjective, because it leaves unanswered the question: "How could God's moral opinions make morality objective?"

Certainly *you* or *I* cannot create the difference between right or wrong by making a decision. How can God? To say that God must have this sort of ability because God is all powerful is an evasion. We need to understand *how* any entity, even God, could do it. (It is easy to understand how God could make it be in *your best interest* to follow His commands, but this would explain only why following God's commands is prudent, not how God could create morality.) Instead of explaining how morality could be objective, religious authoritarianism pushes the question back one step. Thus, religious authoritarianism does not provide an answer that makes morality understandable. If so, the theistic option is not a strong way to ground the objectivity of morality.

6. Nonnaturalism: Platonic and Non-Platonic Intuitionism

Nonnaturalism maintains that *moral truth is grounded in the supernatural (not existing in space and time) realm.* (On most philosophical and theological views of God, religious authoritarianism is also nonnaturalistic by this definition, but I have followed custom by considering the religious view separately.) The most famous nonnaturalist view was provided by the Greek philosopher Plato with his theory of "Platonic" Forms (ideas, universals). For Plato, Forms are abstract entities (things that exist in neither space nor time) that many general nouns—such as "knowledge," "courage," "temperance," "justice," and "goodness"—refer to. Plato thought that the goodness of individual things depends on *the Form of the Good*, a Platonic universal or idea, that makes all individual good things good.

According to Plato, a character trait or human action is good if and only if it "participates in" the Form of the Good. Specific things are good only because of their connection to the Form of the Good. It is the task of moral education to enable us to "see" the eternal and changeless Forms. (This sort of nonperceptual awareness is known as *intuitionism*.) For example, if we can learn to recognize and appreciate the Forms of the Good and the Just—and this task may take a lifetime—then we can know what individual things are good and just. Moreover, intuiting the Form of the Good is both a cognitive and a motivating experience for Plato: *To know* the Form of the Good is *to be moved to try to be good*.

Non-Platonic Intuitionism is similar to Plato's intuitionism, but avoids Plato's talk about a "third-realm" (nonphysical and nonmental) world of Forms. G. E. Moore (1903) holds that goodness is a nonnatural characteristic of certain entities that we can just recognize or intuit by carefully examining good actions. Moore thinks that goodness cannot be described or verbally analyzed; nonetheless, we recognize it when we confront it. According to Moore, just as we can recognize instances of the simple *natural property of yellow* when we see a banana, we can recognize instances of the simple *nonnatural property of goodness* in good entities.

There are milder forms of intuitionism than that of Plato or Moore. Thomas Reid of Scotland (1978, Essay 3) thinks that we recognize the truth of some very basic moral propositions simply by considering them carefully. For example, the truth of the doctrine "We ought not do to another, what we think wrong to be done to us in like circumstances" is immediately obvious on reflection—at least to a mature perceiver who is capable of understanding moral truth.

W. D. Ross maintains that our moral insights, though not infallible, provide us with accurate information about morality that should be rejected only if it is refuted by *other, clearer* moral insights. Understanding *a prima facie duty* as a duty we have unless a stronger duty overrules it, Ross claims that principles of prima facie duty become intuitively clear to us in the way that "2 + 2 = 4" does: "When we have reached sufficient maturity to think in general terms, we apprehend *prima facie* rightness to belong to the nature of any fulfillment of promise" (Ross, 1930, ch. 2). Thus, the intuitionists Moore, Reid, and Ross claim that there are basic moral truths that we called synthetic a priori judgments (see chapter 3)—judgments whose truth is not simply a matter of definition, but can be known by pure intellectual intuition, without being justified by the senses.

PROBLEMS FOR PLATO

First, there are general difficulties with Plato's theory. Given that Forms are supposed to exist outside space and time, *how* do they exist? How does the Form of the Good *make* particular good things good? Plato said that individual good things "participate" in the Form of the Good, but what does this mean? How do we *know* that we have discerned the Form of the Good (rather than mistaking our own moral opinions for it)? Even if the Form of the Good exists, can it be any *use* to us in our attempt to gain moral knowledge?

Second, suppose we say that morality is objective (that agents and actions are right and wrong) because of Platonic Forms. The question arises: "How *could* an entity's having some relationship to a Form *constitute* the rightness or wrongness of that entity?" I do not know whether any moral realist has an adequate answer to the question of what makes things have objective moral value, but "participates in the Form of the Good" and "resembles the Form of justice" seem to be nonanswers. Merely verbal answers such as Plato's are not going to provide the explanatory insight that we need to answer the question. To use an example from Jerry Fodor (1975, 6–7), if we want to know why Wheaties are the breakfast of champions, we need to be told a story about vitamins, minerals, and carbohydrates. Learning that they are eaten by nonnegligible numbers of champions does not answer our question.

Here is a third difficulty. The Form of the Good—if it were to exist—and individual good things would be distinct entities. Thus, we can imagine them to exist apart, because distinct things always can be separated in different "possible worlds." Thus, there could be these two possible worlds: In *Possible World 1*, good actions and the Form of the Good exist. In *Possible World 2*, exactly similar actions exist, but the Form of the Good does not.

Consider what Plato would have to say about these worlds. In *Possible World 1*, actions that are good in that world are good because of their relationship to the Form of the Good. For example, an act of kindness would be good, because kindness participates in the Form of the Good. In *Possible World 2*, there exist the exact same type of actions that are good in Possible World 1, but, because the Form of the Good does not exist in that possible world, those actions are not good. So the act of kindness would not be good in *Possible World 2*, despite the fact that everything about it except its participation in the Form of the Good is identical to the act of kindness in *Possible World 1*.

This apparent commitment of Platonic intuitionism appears implausible. In my example, no intrinsic characteristics of kind actions are different in *Possible World 1* and *Possible World 2*. Actions in each world share all the characteristics that we ordinarily think are relevant to their moral status, for example, the amount of utility they produce, or whether they are motivated by respect for persons. If so, then we should *not* say—as Plato would have to say—that the moral nature of actions depends on the existence of the Form of the Good. If actions are to be objectively right and wrong, their moral status has to depend on characteristics of the actions themselves, not the existence of a Platonic Form.

PROBLEMS FOR MOORE, REID, AND ROSS

Consider next the non-Platonic intuitionism of Moore. First, Moore's postulation of nonnatural moral properties is puzzling, because it is unclear what nonnatural properties are supposed to be like. One wants to ask: *Where* and *how* do they exist? On this point, intuitionism compares unfavorably with naturalistic objectivism. For example, suppose a naturalist said that the rightness of an action is its tendency to produce happiness. This tendency can be understood as a characteristic of the action itself. This may or may not be an acceptable metaethical theory, but it at least indicates *where* the property of goodness exists. To be told by Moore that an action's goodness does not exist in the natural world makes one wonder *how* it could exist. What sort of thing could moral goodness be?

Let us move on to the less flamboyant intuitionism of Reid and Ross, who do not talk about Platonic forms and Moore's nonnatural property of goodness, but simply claim that we intellectually "intuit" moral truths. The first problem for such views is that Reid and Ross must distinguish between their intuitionism and their opponents' subjectivism. It is not enough for Reid and Ross to say that persons "intuit" moral feelings. Everyone—objectivists and subjectivists—will agree with this. The intuitionists must say that our moral intuitions are not simply our *feelings* about moral topics, as the subjectivists believe, but are *accurate observations of some objective moral truths that lie outside our minds*. Intuitionists must say that our intuitions are like perceptions in that there is some objective *thing* outside our minds that is perceived. If intuitionism does not postulate the recognition of real moral properties outside our moral intuitions, then it becomes a variety of subjectivism, not objectivism.

Therefore, even though Reid and Ross do not explicitly say so, they are committed to saying that we intuit moral properties that exist outside our minds. If these properties are to be nonnatural, what might they be? Platonic forms or Moorean nonnatural properties! But we have already seen that there are serious objections to both Plato's and Moore's views. We must not think that because Reid and Ross appear to make more modest claims than do Plato and Moore that their theories avoid the basic objections to intuitionism. If Reid and Ross wish to be nonnaturalists and avoid subjectivism, they must have just as much commitment to the supernatural as Plato or Moore does.

A second problem for Reid and Ross's variety of intuitionism is that claiming that moral judgments are synthetic a priori is a cheap way to evade the subjectivists' challenge. In philosophy, as in everyday life, the claim that we just "know" things without being able to say how we know is usually a copout. For example, Kant claimed that he could "intuit" that the propositions of Euclidian geometry and "Every event has a cause" were necessary truths for any world humans could experience. Far from being a priori knowable, these claims are probably not even true. Likewise, the claim that moral judgments such as "One should keep one's promises" (Ross's example) are intuitable, synthetic a priori is pure bluff. As soon as a critic asks why it is true, the intuitionist runs out of things to say.

7. *Kant's Theory*

Like Reid and Moore, Kant believes that some moral principles are synthetic a priori truths. As seen in chapter 6, the most important are these. The Categorical Imperative says: "Act only according to that maxim by which you can at the same time will that it should become a universal law" (Kant, 1959, 39). The Principle of Ends maintains: "Act so that you treat humanity, whether in your own person or in that of another, always as an end and never as a means only" (Kant, 1959, 47). Kant believes that any person who tries to be moral must assume these principles, just as anyone who experiences nature must assume the principle that every event has a cause.

Kant's metaethical theory is difficult to classify. Because Kant says that the principles of morality are not dependant on ordinary human desires and feelings, but are truths that any purely rational being (an angel or a Martian) must recognize, we could see him as an intuitionist like Reid and Ross. On the other hand, because Kant claims that the Categorical Imperative and the Principle of Ends are part of how *any* rational being looks at morality, we could see him as making a claim about the psychology of anyone who thinks about morality. This would allow us to see him as a universal subjectivist.

For our purposes, it is not important whether we classify Kant as an intuitionist or a universal subjectivist, for there are objections to Kant's view either way. Taken to be an intuitionist, Kant faces the objections just raised against Reid and Ross. To provide concrete support for his view, Kant is committed to the nonnatural existence of moral properties that ground our moral intuitions. We have seen with Reid and Ross that this is problematic. (Kant is already committed in the rest of his philosophy to hoping for the nonnatural existence of God and the soul, although he admits that these are not provable.) If we take Kant simply as asserting that moral judgments are knowable synthetic a priori *without* providing the metaphysical foundation of moral properties to support his claim, we should ask why we should believe Kant's claim is true? Taken as a universal subjectivist, Kant will face the objection that human moral judgments are not universally shared.

8. Naturalistic Objectivism

Naturalistic objectivism maintains that the truth conditions of moral judgments are *objective moral properties that exist in the natural world*—the world of space and time—rather than simply in our opinions about moral issues (subjectivism) or in nonnatural entities (nonnaturalistic objectivism). The picture of the natural world that includes persons' intentions and actions is more familiar than one that includes divine decrees, Platonic Forms, and Moore's nonnatural properties. So naturalism will seem a more plausible choice for many persons than the nonnatural theories. *Nondefinist naturalist objectivism*, which is more plausible than definist naturalism, maintains that although moral properties are identical to natural properties, moral *terms* are *not synonymous with* natural property *terms*.

Nondefinist naturalists offer various models of what moral properties are like. For example, just as fragility is a dispositional property of physical objects to break under stress, so goodness might be the dispositional property to increase human pleasure (Campbell and Pargetter, 1986). Naturalistic objectivists make claims such as: (1) "The highest good is what contributes to perfection of our uniquely human abilities." (2) "What is right is what is conducive to human flourishing." (3) "Goodness is the satisfaction of human needs." Pleasure, being conducive to flourishing, and satisfying human needs seem to be natural, unmysterious characteristics of persons and actions; thus, naturalism does not seem to commit itself to the existence of strange, nonnatural moral properties. Therefore, naturalistic objectivism appears to be an attractive theory.

A PROBLEM FOR NATURALISTIC OBJECTIVISM: SUBJECTIVISM MAY BE A BETTER NATURALISTIC THEORY

The great advantage of naturalist theories is that they avoid the objections religious authoritarianism and nonnaturalism face. Naturalistic objectivism postulates *fewer* entities, it postulates *no mysterious* entities, and it is *more understandable*. Unfortunately for the naturalistic objectivist, the last two factors—which show that naturalistic objectivism is preferable to nonnaturalism—may show that naturalistic subjectivism is preferable to naturalistic objectivism. Naturalistic subjectivism may be an *even better theory* than naturalistic objectivism. To examine this possibility, we need to compare subjectivism and naturalism.

SUBJECTIVISM

9. Subjectivism as a Better Type of Naturalism

Just as there are definist and nondefinist arguments for objectivism, there are definist and nondefinist arguments for subjectivism. *Definist subjectivists* believe that moral judgments such as "X is good" *mean* "I approve of X" or "My society approves of X," thereby making moral judgments into *psychological* or *sociological reports*. This definitional strategy is defective for the same reason other definist arguments are defective—the previously discussed open question argument. It is always an open question to ask: "Is what I approve of really good?" and "Is what my society approves of really good?"

This leaves *nondefinist subjectivism*, the view that *moral judgments have no truth conditions and merely express subjective feelings, but are not reports of those feelings.* According to nondefinist subjectivism, moral talk is not equivalent in meaning to talk about personal or social approval. According to this theory, persons who express moral judgments typically take themselves to be making moral statements that are either true or false, but their moral judgments are not true. Because nondefinist subjectivism is the only plausible variety of subjectivism, I'll just refer to it as "subjectivism." Subjectivism will be *naturalistic* if it claims that our subjective feelings occur in our physical bodies, rather than in a *nonnatural* nonphysical mind or soul. Because naturalistic subjectivism is the strongest variety of subjectivism, I shall examine that theory.

Naturalistic subjectivists claim that although persons have beliefs, opinions, feelings, and attitudes about moral topics, there are no moral properties. Subjectivists "relocate" moral properties by saying that moral properties do not exist outside our mental states. This *subjectivizing strategy* is probably the strongest argument for preferring subjectivism to naturalistic objectivism. This strategy will appeal to anyone who endorses a scientific realist view of physical objects, as discussed in section 4. If we like the metaphysical simplicity of "relocating" some or most of the commonsense properties of physical objects in the sensations of perceivers, we will be sympathetic to "relocating" moral properties into the minds of persons. The motivation is similar in each case: a simpler worldview and the avoidance of puzzles.

The scientific realist theory of physical objects gives a model of how persons can "recognize" the moral properties of agents and actions that *really are not there*. Our feelings of approval and disapproval toward agents and actions will be the results of how our perceptions of agents and actions affect our minds. This is analogous to our having color sensations caused by physical objects that are atoms swirling in empty space and are not themselves colored.

Here is a summary of the subjectivists' view:

(1) Reality consists of *things* (objects, events, and properties).
(2) There is no such *thing* as objective moral properties such as rightness or wrongness, good or evil. (What does exist is our beliefs, feelings, and attitudes about moral issues, all of which exist only in our minds.)
(3) Therefore, reality does not contain objective moral properties existing outside our minds, but instead only our beliefs, feelings, and attitudes about moral issues.

The crucial part of the subjectivist view is (2). Step (2) rejects the naturalistic identity theorist's claim that objective moral properties exist. To decide whether we should accept (2), we need to compare the identity theory against its subjectivist competitor, and decide which is better.

In his famous *argument from queerness*, J. L. Mackie (1977, 38–42) claims that realistic moral properties would fit onto physical objects in a bizarre, inscrutable way. Metaphysically speaking, it would be difficult to understand how realistic moral properties could exist alongside the familiar properties of physical objects that science assigns to them. And epistemically speaking, our ability to see or know realistic moral properties would require some strange method of perception that we have no reason to believe exists.

Let me support Mackie's basic argument for subjectivism by comparing subjectivism and naturalistic identity theories in detail. An obvious challenge for naturalistic identity theories is to answer a question that all identity theories must face: "What *makes* the identity true?" (Not: "Why do we *believe* it is true?") Why, for example, is the naturalistic property of developing my abilities identical to the moral property of being good rather than the property of being bad or indifferent? To see why this is a difficult question, contrast this case to one in which we *can* give an answer, for example, that blue is identical to my favorite color. We can explain why the identity holds by saying that we are thinking about the same thing in two different ways: "Blue" is simply a color term, while "my favorite color" is an autobiographical term. It just turns out that I prefer the color blue. (Blue may be my favorite color because my first bicycle was blue.) Note that the historical explanation, if true, *completely* explains the identity at stake.

This theme is repeated in other examples of property identities. We can explain the identity of temperature and the mean kinetic energy of molecules by telling a story in which a commonsense property (temperature) is held to be identical to a theoretical property of physics (mean kinetic energy). The same sort of story can be told for lightning and electrical discharges from clouds, genes and DNA molecules, and so on. The identity statement is less easily known in the scientific examples than in the case of blue and my favorite color. But the *identity claim* is no more puzzling. In these cases of identity, there is a fully understandable explanation that tells *why* the identity holds.

But when the objectivist says that a moral property (such as goodness) is identical to some naturalistic property (such as producing pleasure), there is no clear explanation of why the moral property and the naturalistic property are the same. The problem is that the objectivist is trying to identify as *one* what appear to be *two different types of entities*: a normative property that is basically action motivating and a descriptive property that simply exists. This is not to claim that moral properties *cannot be* identical to descriptive properties, but it does show that subjectivism is easier to understand than the objectivist's identity theory.

In sum, although identity theories and subjectivist theories both avoid postulating nonnatural entities, subjectivism avoids the additional puzzle: How can the moral be identical to the natural? If moral properties are "relocated" in the psychological states of persons who make moral judgments as subjectivism holds, the question does not arise. The identity at stake becomes that of identifying two types of *nonmoral* properties. If we did not have the subjectivizing option open to us, then we might have to bite the bullet and conclude that a naturalistic identity theory is the best we can do. But, because the subjectivizing option is available, the naturalist cannot argue this way.

10. A First Problem for Subjectivism: Subjectivism Appears Contrary to Ordinary Language

A common objection to subjectivism is that most moral judgments have the grammatical structure of descriptive statements. For example, "Jealousy is a bad emotion" has the same subject-predicate structure as "Solar energy is a nonpolluting source of power." Both *appear* to pick out an object and assign to it a property. Thus, moral judgments look as if they assign moral properties and have truth values. Moreover, moral judgments serve in logical inferences *as if* they were truth valued. Consider: "If killing is wrong, then capital punishment is wrong," "Killing is wrong," "Therefore, capital punishment is wrong." This appears to be a modus ponens argument, because the sentences in it have the grammar of truth-valued propositions.

Subjectivists known as *noncognitivists* respond to this objection by providing accounts of the meaning of moral language designed to show that moral judgments are not really subject-predicate statements. *Noncognitivism holds that analyzing the meaning of moral judgments shows that, contrary to appearances, moral judgments do not assign moral properties.* Noncognitivists such as A. J. Ayer (1952), Charles Stevenson (1944), and R. M. Hare (1952) argue that moral judgments are not descriptive assertions, but are instead expressions of emotion, commands, or prescriptions. Ayer, for example, thinks that saying that X is morally wrong really means "X—booh!" Because "X—booh!" is neither true nor false, it cannot take any objective moral property as a truth condition.

One difficulty with noncognitivist theories is that they misrepresent the meaning of moral language. After all, moral language is used by persons who assume that moral properties are objectively real. When persons say, for instance, that certain actions are wrong, they *mean* that those actions are really wrong—they do not intend merely to express their disapproval of them. Persons who assert moral judgments *intend* to express objective moral truths; but *speakers' intentions determine the meaning of moral language*. Therefore, moral judgments are subject/predicate statements that claim that certain things are really right and wrong. They are not disguised expressions of emotion, commands, or moral recommendations. Noncognitivist analyses of moral language, thus, fail as accounts of what moral language means.

There is a second problem. Even if noncognitivism were a plausible theory of the meaning of moral language, it would not provide much support for subjectivism. If subjectivists hope to prove their ambitious metaphysical theory, they need stronger ammunition than just premises about *the meaning of moral language*. For even if those premises were true, moral objectivists would be able to respond by saying: "I accept your noncognitivist account of what moral language means; nonetheless, objective moral properties still exist." No premises about the meaning of moral language could disprove the existence of moral properties, because language is one thing and reality is another.

Despite these two problems, there is good news for subjectivism. Subjectivists do not *need* to provide noncognitivist analyses of moral language to succeed; subjectivists should wash their hands of noncognitivist accounts of moral language. Instead, subjectivists should reply to the objection from ordinary language this way. First, concede that moral judgments: (a) have a subject-predicate structure; (b) are intended to refer to objective moral properties; and (c) cannot be given a noncognitivist interpretation. Second, distinguish between metaethics (the debate between objectivism and subjectivism) and the philosophy of language (the attempt to analyze meanings). Third, because of the second point, deny that the first point has *any* weight in supporting objectivism. In sum, subjectivists do not need to offer analyses of moral language in noncognitivist terms. They should quit trying.

11. A Second Problem for Subjectivism: Subjectivism Seems to Lead to Moral Nihilism

Moral nihilism (sometimes called "amoralism") is the view that no values are better or worse than any others and that there is no right and wrong. Thus, moral nihilism is a complete rejection of normative ethics. The preacher in John Steinbeck's *The Grapes of Wrath* expressed moral nihilism this way: "There ain't no sin, and there ain't no virtue. There's just stuff people do" (1939, 32). As noted in the previous chapter, the great Russian novelist Dostoevski worried that if there is no God, then all is permitted.

The fear that subjectivism leads to moral nihilism haunts subjectivism. Abhorrence of nihilism drives some philosophers to adopt objectivism, not because they believe they have a good argument for it, but because they wish desperately to avoid nihilism. But the question is: Is the threat of moral nihilism an objection to subjectivism?

First, we might wonder whether this sort of motivation is very philosophical: Should philosophers construct their theories with an eye toward what they *want to be true*, rather than "follow the argument wherever it leads," that is, toward what is most likely to *be true*? As noted in chapter 1, some philosophers think that they should build their philosophical theories to support beliefs they already hold *before* they begin to philosophize. Others believe that philosophy should not give any beliefs preferential treatment. Neither side is likely to win this debate.

Second, we should ask whether, and in what sense, subjectivism might lead to moral nihilism. *Logically speaking*, subjectivism does not lead to nihilism, because subjectivism is a metaethical theory, whereas nihilism's claim that all actions are equally good is a claim in normative ethics. Metaethics addresses the metaphysical foundations of normative ethics, and one can build one's normative theories on either objectivist or subjectivist grounds. It is possible to build a nonnihilistic moral theory on a subjectivist metaethical view. Although some moral subjectivists are nihilists, many subjectivists reject nihilism. Hume, for example, was a subjectivist who believed that morals have no grounding other than our sentiments (especially sympathy), but he believed that we can build a utilitarian normative theory on that subjectivist foundation. Hume took morality very seriously, despite his moral subjectivism.

Psychologically speaking, persons with different temperaments will react in differ ways to subjectivism. For example, persons who think that subjectivism supports nihilism reason as follows. If there are no impersonal, objective standards that ground the difference between right and wrong, then metaphysically speaking, there *is* no right and wrong "out there" independent of our judgments. In this case, right and wrong are not "written on the walls of the universe." Persons who demand that morality have such a grounding outside human sentiment before they take it seriously will think that subjectivism jeopardizes morality.

This is only one possible response to subjectivism, however. Subjectivists might emphasize that morality, as Mackie puts it, is a *human invention*, rather than a *discovery* of something that is established by a reality that exists outside human minds. Going along with Mackie and Hume, subjectivists might regard morality as *a very important human invention*. After all, subjectivists believe that it is a matter of *decision* how we *should* respond to the metaethical theory of subjectivism. *If* we wish to adopt nihilism and say that all actions are equally good, there is nothing about the structure of reality to show that we have made a factual error. *But* if we decide to view morality seriously—even passionately—there is nothing about reality that says that our decision to do so is mistaken. In short, according to their own doctrine, subjectivists may go in either direction from the premise of subjectivism. They may decide that morality matters very much or very little. This is similar to the disagreement between strident and sheepish subjectivists discussed in chapter 8.

All we need to construct a theory of normative ethics is a norm. It does not matter whether the norm "comes from" an objective or subjective source. Whether we believe that the norm is created by God, exists as the Form of the Good as Plato did, or is the way most human beings feel about moral issues, we have to decide whether to follow that norm. Even if there is an Objective Morality Source, it remains up to us to *endorse* or *reject* that Objective Source's dictates. This is the lesson of our criticism of religious authoritarianism in the last chapter: Try as we may, we cannot escape from having to make moral choices. Even if we say "I didn't make the rules, my source did," we are still making a decision when we decide to follow the rules of the source.

Thus, we do not need moral objectivism to take morality seriously. I suspect that the belief that moral objectivism is needed is largely due to: (1) confusing morality and the prudence of trying to placate an Objective Morality Giver; and (2) a yearning for some cosmic stamp of approval to be placed on right and wrong. These are familiar thoughts, but they are scarcely necessary. Simon Blackburn makes this point with biting sarcasm:

> It might be that there are people who cannot "put up with" the idea that values have a subjective source. . . . But this will be because such people have a defect . . . in their sensibilities—one that has taught them that things do not matter unless they matter to God, or throughout infinity, or to a world conceived apart from any particular set of concerns or desires, or whatever. One should not adjust one's metaphysics to pander to such defects. (Blackburn, 1993, 157)

Finally, we should remember that subjectivism comes in universal and mixed varieties. For those thinkers who want extra grounding for moral judgments, universal subjectivism gives more support than mixed subjectivism does. By appealing to near-universal moral sentiments of human beings, universal subjectivism gives persons who are serious about morality a way to insist that morality is not simply a matter of personal whimsy: Our feelings are correct if and only if they agree with the sentiments of normally evolved human beings. Universal subjectivism, thus, shows that morality *does not need to be objective to be nonarbitrary*. Adopting universal subjectivism may reduce the motivation to claim that morality "must" reside outside human feelings as the only alternative to the view that otherwise morality is simply a matter of personal taste.

12. A Third Problem for Subjectivism: Extreme Cases

Moral objectivists sometimes support their position by citing extreme cases in which anyone other than a sociopath would have strong moral feelings. For instance, an objectivist might ask whether it is *just a matter of opinion* whether it is morally wrong to burn babies with cigarette butts. Because it sounds outlandish to say that this is "just a matter of opinion," the objectivist seems to gain the upper hand over the subjectivist.

This advantage is illusory. Rather than giving in, the subjectivist should say that it *is not* simply a matter of opinion that cruelty is bad in the way that it *is* a matter of opinion whether peas taste good. The subjectivist should say that our feelings about cruelty are a very important feature about us. As noted by Hume, Mackie, and Blackburn, the subjectivist does not have to think that morality is frivolous business. Nonetheless, the subjectivist should say that *im-*

portant feelings are still *feelings*, just as an important tennis match is still a tennis match.

Moral objectivists who try to make capital from the fact that humans have strong moral feelings about extreme cases overlook an obvious difficulty. If objectivism is true of the *extreme* cases such as intentional cruelty, then objectivism also should be true for *less extreme* cases. There is no reason why moral objectivism should hold in only the extreme cases, but not the rest. Instead of reminding us only of cases in which we widely agree, objectivists should mention cases in which persons disagree.

Objectivists need to explain how there *can* be objective answers to disputed cases: capital punishment, the allotment of scarce medical resources, abortion, physician-assisted suicide, or even whether it is OK to play dirty if one's opponent does. In principle, the moral objectivist is committed to saying that there is a right and wrong answer to *all* moral dilemmas, including those where utility and the rights of individuals clash. The objectivist also needs to say that there are moral truths in cases in which morality conflicts with the creation of intrinsic goodness, for instance, the example from chapter 6 in which you can compose a masterpiece only if you break a promise to pick up a friend at the airport. The objectivist should also explain how there could be objective evaluative truths in the rest of value theory, such as questions about intrinsic value and even aesthetic judgments. Until the objectivist can do this, citing extreme cases has only rhetorical, but no logical, force.

A FINAL ASSESSMENT OF THE DISPUTE BETWEEN THE OBJECTIVISTS AND SUBJECTIVISTS

I have argued that nondefinist subjectivism appears to be more likely to be true than any of the objectivist theories examined. This conclusion is quite tentative, as all philosophical conclusions must be. Further examination of the issue could make things look very different. Nonetheless, for a complete philosophical worldview, we need a view of metaethics, even if we are not confident that our view is correct.

We have seen that there are universal and mixed varieties of nondefinist subjectivism, and the question remains of which is more likely to be true. The question of how widely moral feelings are shared—like questions about *all* human psychological traits—is an empirical one that is not to be decided by philosophers' arguments. So I shall not propose an argument to prove which is correct. I can consider what the implications of the two views would be *if* they turn out to be true. Let us close by considering this question.

From a purely metaphysical perspective, it does not matter whether universal or mixed subjectivism is true—both theories maintain that there are no moral properties and no moral truths that possess an objective grounding outside human minds. Both views are subject to the implication cited in chapter 6 regarding moral relativism: If morality is at most only shared moral feelings determined by the way human beings are, then cross-cultural value judgments cannot be objectively true. We would be unable to say that from a cosmic perspective that beings who evolved to feel no benevolence or sense of fairness are objectively morally worse than we are. This is because according to subjectivism there is no cosmic perspective. They would just be *different*. Any variety of subjectivism has this consequence.

Nonetheless, the difference between universal and mixed subjectivism *can* matter psychologically to us when we do *normative ethics*—if we think universal subjectivism supports moralizing better than mixed subjectivism does. The claim "*We humans* find it immoral to do things to other persons what we would not like done to ourselves" is psychologically more powerful than saying "*I* find it immoral." Indeed, for some persons, saying this may be just as persuasive as saying that such actions *are* immoral in some God-given or Platonic sense. When it comes to morality, an overwhelming human consensus in favor of a certain moral view may be all we require.

Guide Questions

1. What is the difference between normative ethics and metaethics? (172–73)
2. What is a descriptive statement? An evaluative statement? (173)
3. According to the definition of "truth condition," a false statement such as "Asia is a country" can have a truth condition. How is this possible? (173)
4. What is the main question of metaethics? (173–74)
5. What is the difference between the *meaning* of a word and its *referent*? (174)
6. In what sense do definist identity theorists engage in "overkill"? (175)
7. What is the difference between metaethics and the epistemology of ethics? (175–76)
8. What is the key difference between moral objectivism and moral subjectivism? (176–77)
9. Explain the analogy between moral objectivism in metaethics and direct realism in the problem of the external world. (177)
10. Explain the analogy between moral subjectivism and scientific realism. (177–78)
11. What issue separates universal subjectivists from mixed subjectivists? (178)

12. What is the basic claim of definist religious authoritarianism? (179)
13. Express the open question argument against definism in modus tollens form. (179–80) (Modus tollens is described in chapter 2.)
14. How does the open question argument refute definist religious authoritarianism? (180)
15. What is Plato's objection to all forms of religious authoritarianism? (181)
16. What is the difficulty of trying to base the objectivity of morality on the subjectivity of God? (181)
17. What is the general thesis that Platonic and non-Platonic moral intuitionism share? (181–82)
18. The second objection to Platonic intuitionism claims that being told that actions are good because they participate in the Form of the Good is *puzzling*. Why? (183)
19. The third objection to Platonic intuitionism is that Plato's theory makes the moral character of actions depend on the wrong sort of factor. Explain. (183–84)
20. What is one difficulty with Moore's view that moral properties are simple, nonnatural properties? (184)
21. In what way are the views of Ross and Reid just as questionable as the views of Plato and Moore? (184)
22. What does Kant mean when he says that moral judgments are synthetic a priori? (185)
23. What does nondefinist naturalistic identity theory say? (186)
24. What major advantage does naturalistic metaethical theories have over nonnatural metaethical theories? (186)
25. What is the theory of nondefinist subjectivism? (187)
26. What is the subjectivizing strategy of the subjectivist? (187)
27. Why do the subjectivists think that their theory is less puzzling than the objectivists' identity theory of moral properties? (188–89)
28. In what sense does Mackie believe that realistic moral properties would be "queer"? (188)
29. In what way do subjectivists think their theory is simpler than objectivist identity theories? (188–89)
30. What does it mean to say that subjectivism appears contrary to ordinary language? (189)
31. Why is noncognitivism an unrealistic theory of what moral language means? (189)
32. Why do the subjectivists not need to worry whether noncognitivist theories of moral language succeed or fail? (190)
33. Why do some objectivists fear that subjectivism will lead to *moral nihilism*? (190)

34. In what sense does subjectivism lead to moral nihilism? In what sense does it not lead to moral nihilism? (191)
35. What does it mean to say that morality does not have to be objective to be important? (191–92)
36. Explain why the objectivist's talk about extreme case has more *rhetorical*, rather than *logical*, force? (192–93)
37. In what way can adopting universal subjectivism be helpful to our practice of normative ethics? (193–94)

Review Questions for Examinations

1. Define: "descriptive statement," "evaluative statement," "meaning," "referent," "truth condition," "truth value," "definist identity theory," "nondefinist identity theory," "open question argument," "noncognitivist."
2. Explain these theories: moral skepticism, moral nonskepticism, moral subjectivism, moral objectivism, moral naturalism, moral supernaturalism, universal subjectivism, mixed subjectivism, religious authoritarianism, intuitionism, naturalism, moral nihilism.
3. Classify the following statements as either definist or nondefinist:
   (a) "Right" means "whatever is sanctioned by law."
   (b) "X is good" means "I like X."
   (c) Right actions are those that produce beneficial results.
   (d) To say "X is morally permissible" is to say "X furthers human flourishing."
   (e) Although "wrong" does not mean "produces disutility," wrong actions are always disutile.
4. Classify the following statements as either expressing objectivism or subjectivism:
   (a) "Goodness is a simple, nonnatural property."
   (b) "Virtue and vice are simply sentiments of the human heart."
   (c) "X is right" means "X helps humans evolve as a species."
   (d) "Moral language does not describe facts, but serves only to make commands."
   (e) "God establishes the difference between right and wrong."
5. What is the difference between moral skepticism and moral nihilism in theory? What is the difference from a practical standpoint?
6. What is the metaphysical difference between the theories of objectivism, universal subjectivism, and mixed subjectivism? What is the difference from a practical standpoint?
7. What are the strongest points in favor of moral objectivism? What are the strongest points in favor of moral subjectivism?

Discussion Questions

1. This chapter emphasizes the difference between the philosophy of language question "What do moral judgments mean?" and the metaethical question "Are moral judgments objectively true or false?" According to the chapter, which thinkers are helped when we understand this difference: the objectivists or subjectivists?
2. The contemporary American philosopher John Searle believes it is possible to validly deduce a moral judgment from descriptive premises. Searle believes that (e) is a moral judgment that can be deduced, step by step, from the descriptive statement (a). What do you think of Searle's famous deduction of an "ought" statement from an "is" statement:
   (a) Jones uttered the words "I hereby promise to pay you, Smith, five dollars."
   (b) Jones promised to pay Smith five dollars.
   (c) Jones placed himself under (undertook) an obligation to pay Smith five dollars.
   (d) Jones is under obligation to pay Smith five dollars.
   (e) Jones ought to pay Smith five dollars. (1969, 177)
3. Consider the following statement: "To determine the difference between right and wrong, simply ask yourself what is right." Add details to this statement that would make it an expression of *moral subjectivism*. Then add details that would make it an expression of *moral objectivism*.
4. At the end of the chapter on normative ethics we considered a mixed utilitarian/Kantian theory. In this chapter we did not consider a mixed objectivist/subjectivist theory. Was this an oversight? Explain.

FOR FURTHER READING

Dawkins, Richard. 1976. *The Selfish Gene*. New York: Oxford University Press. A brilliant account of the evolutionary (sociobiological) basis of morality by a prominent biologist. Moderately difficult.

Double, Richard. 1991. *The Non-Reality of Free Will*. Chapter 7. New York: Oxford University Press. Argues for mixed subjectivism. Moderately difficult.

Frankena, William. 1973. *Ethics*. Chapter 6. Englewood Cliffs, NJ: Prentice-Hall. A very clear explanation of the main theories.

Harman, Gilbert. 1977. *The Nature of Morality*. New York: Oxford University Press. A powerful, beginning-level argument for subjectivism.

Mackie, J. L. 1977. *Ethics: Inventing Right and Wrong*. New York: Penguin. The classic modern argument for subjectivism. Moderately difficult.

Plato. *Ethyphro*. (1994). In Walter Kaufmann and Forrest Baird, eds., *Philosophical Classics: From Plato to Nietzsche.* Englewood Cliffs, NJ: Prentice-Hall. An entertaining dialogue between Plato's hero, Socrates, and Euthyphro, a young man who thinks he knows what morality is. A classic refutation of nondefinist religious authoritarianism and a good introduction to Plato.

Pojman, Louis. 1995. *Ethics: Discovering Right and Wrong*. Chapter 9. Belmont, CA: Wadsworth. A highly readable introduction to metaethics from a theistic, objectivist perspective.

Chapter 8
The Free Will Problem

INTRODUCTION

Before coming to philosophy we typically believe that most persons, most of the time, choose their actions freely and at those times are morally responsible for their behavior. For example, we usually think that convicted murderers are not only legally responsible for their crimes, but are *blameworthy* as well. In addition, when we look at our actions and character traits with pride or shame, we assume that *we* are morally responsible for them. Thus, holding others and ourselves responsible is a large part of the way we see persons. But to be morally responsible for our actions and our characters, it seems that we need to be *free* in choosing them. It is unfair to hold persons morally responsible if they did not choose freely. Thus, the truth of our assumption that we are morally responsible seems to depend on the existence of free choices. In the free will problem philosophers ask whether we can enjoy a degree of freedom in our choices that makes us morally responsible for our behavior and justifies expressing resentment, blaming, and punishing.

1. The Key Definitions

To say that persons are *morally responsible* for their actions is to say that persons *deserve* praise or blame for them. If persons are morally responsible, then it would be morally right to give them either positive or negative treatment for their good or bad actions. Moral responsibility is different from *legal responsibility*, which is accountability according to a law. Moral responsibility is different from *causal responsibility*, which is being the cause of something happening. Moral responsibility is also different from the everyday notion of "being responsible," which simply means being reliable or at least being assigned roles we are *supposed* to fill reliably.

To blame persons (which includes expressing negative attitudes toward them and punishing them) treats them worse than not blaming them. For this reason we seem to be justified in blaming persons only if those persons act from *free will*. ("Free will" is an old-fashioned term for "the faculty" of making *free choices*.) If persons do not act from free will, then blaming them seems unfair. Because being morally responsible requires making free choices, if no one's choices are free, then no one is morally responsible. The best way to define "free choices," therefore, is "choices that are enough under our control for us to be morally responsible for the actions they produce."

Making a choice is *creating an intention to perform an action*. For example, if a friend asks you whether you want to have lunch at McDonald's or Burger King, you choose when you decide on one or the other. Given this definition, choices may be caused or uncaused. If a choice is caused, then given the chooser's state of mind at the moment of choice, it has to occur. If a choice is uncaused, then given the chooser's state of mind at the moment of choice, the choice occurs, but does not *have* to occur.

To say that one event *causes* another event is to say that given the first event occurs, it is physically necessary that the second event occur. For instance, the falling of one domino causes the falling of the next domino. To claim that *determinism* is true is to claim that *all* events are caused to occur. "All events" includes events involving physical objects such as billiard balls, events in outer space, events within the atom, and, most importantly, every choice that persons make—including choices that occur in our nonphysical minds (souls), if we have them. Determinism is the view that every event that happens is physically necessary, given the laws of nature and the condition of the world in the past. Although we can *imagine* events occurring differently than they did, it is physically (or really) impossible that things could have occurred differently. According to the determinist, there is only one physically possible history to reality—the one history that actually has occurred and will occur.

Although textbooks often portray determinism at large as crucial to the free will issue, what philosophers really care about is whether a tiny subset of all events is caused, namely, human choices. If some event that occurs in outer space or inside an atom is uncaused, this will have no bearing on the free will question unless that uncaused event has something to do with choices. Could the Big Bang's being caused or uncaused matter to your free will and moral responsibility? This is a reason to not call the free will problem the *problem of free will and determinism*.

2. Questions and Theories in the Free Will Problem

The six major theories in the free will problem are: *libertarianism, hard determinism, soft determinism, free-will-either-way theory, no-free-will-either-way theory,* and *subjectivism*. We shall examine these at length in the next section. The six theories can be understood by seeing where each stands on the existence of *uncaused* choices, the existence of *free* choices, and the *logical relationship* between free choices (and moral responsibility) and determinism. Here are the four questions:

1. *Are all human choices caused*? If we answer "yes," we are *determinists*, at least regarding human behavior, if not all events in the cosmos. If we answer "no," we believe that *not all* choices are caused and we are *indeterminists*.
2. *Do we ever have free will, that is, do we ever make choices that are enough under our control to make us morally responsible*? If we answer "yes," we are *free-will realists*. To be a realist about a supposed entity (thing) is to think that the entity exists beyond our attitudes and beliefs about it. If we answer "no," we are *free will nonrealists*. To be a nonrealist about an entity is to think that the entity does not exist.
3. *Can caused choices be free*? If we answer "yes," we are *compatibilists*. If we answer "no," we are *incompatibilists*.
4. *Can uncaused choices be free*? If we answer "yes," we are libertarians, hard determinists, or free-will-either-way theorists. If we answer "no," we are soft determinists or no-free-will-either-way theorists. These theories are explained in the next section.

SIX THEORIES

3. Libertarianism

Libertarians are incompatibilists who believe that we sometimes choose freely and at those times are morally responsible for our behavior. Libertarians believe that because caused choices cannot be free, we exercise free choice only when we make uncaused choices. A libertarian free choice is two-way in the following sense: If we choose to do A, we could have chosen to do not A, and if we refrain from A, we could have chosen to do A, *given exactly the same circumstances*. An uncaused choice could have been otherwise than the way it was even though everything in the chooser's mind remained exactly the same.

Roderick Chisholm expresses libertarianism this way:

> Let us consider some deed, or misdeed, that may be attributed to a responsible agent: one man, say, shot another. If the man *was* responsible for what he did, then, I would urge, what was to happen at the time of the shooting was something that was entirely up to the man himself. There was a moment at which it was true, both that he could have fired the shot and also that he could have refrained from firing it. And if this is so, then, even though he did fire it, he could have done something else instead. (1982, 24–25)

Peter van Inwagen expresses libertarianism this way:

> When I say of a man that he "has free will" I mean that very often, if not always, when he has to choose between two or more mutually incompatible courses of action—that is, courses of action that it is impossible for him to carry out more than one of—each of these courses of action is such than he can, or is able to, or has it within his power to carry it out. (1983, 8)

Van Inwagen provides an example of what this would be like. Sometimes while stealing money a thief remembers the face of his dying mother as he promised her he would lead an honest life. Just once when this happens the thief decides not to complete the crime and "this decision was undetermined." By this van Inwagen means:

> there are possible worlds in which things were absolutely identical in every respect with the way they are in the actual world up to the moment at which our repentant thief made his decision—worlds in which, moreover, the laws of nature are just what they are in the actual world—and in which he takes the money. (1983, 128)

There are two types of views about how uncaused, libertarian free choices might occur. *Event-causation libertarianism* holds that free choices occur in part due to our reasons and in part due to uncaused events in choosers' minds. These uncaused events might be the unpredictable events of contemporary quantum physics—things such as the emission of a beta particle from a radioactive atom or the quantum leap of an electron from one orbit around its nucleus to another. Such subatomic indeterminism might conceivably be amplified so that it makes our choices in our brains undetermined. (A normal adult brain contains 10 billion neurons. One neuron contains 10 billion atoms.) On the other hand, the uncaused events might occur in nonphysical minds.

The event-causation libertarian Robert Kane thinks that quantum indeterminism might contribute to uncaused free choices. Kane imagines a case in which a libertarian agent faces a moral struggle trying to decide whether to select altruistic option *A* or selfish option *S*. The option she selects depends on the amount of effort she can exert to select *A* over *S*. And the amount of effort she exerts depends at least in part on indeterministic brain events that trace to amplified undetermined quantum events in the atoms in her brain. As a result, whether she selects *A* or *S* is not determined.

Agent-theory libertarians believe that looking at causation as a relation that holds only between events makes libertarianism unattractive. Instead, they postulate an additional kind of causal relation called "agent causation." Whereas event causation holds between two events (e.g., one mental event causing another), agent causation holds between a *thing* and an event (e.g., an agent and a mental event). According to agent-theory libertarians, free choices are made by an *agent*, a special kind of metaphysical entity that chooses indeterministically. Indeterminism results because the agent is an "unmoved mover" that makes choices without being caused to do so. (Aristotle's Unmoved Mover caused everything else in the world to move, but itself was not caused to move.) Here is how Richard Taylor expresses agent theory:

> [T]his conception of activity, and of an agent who is the cause of it, involves two rather strange metaphysical notions that are never applied elsewhere in nature. The first is that of a *self* or *person*—for example, a man—who is not merely a collection of things or events, but a substance and self-moving being. . . . Second, this conception of activity involves an extraordinary conception of causation, according to which an agent, which is a substance and not an event, can nonetheless be the cause of an event . . . without anything else causing him to do so. (1974, 55–56)

4. Hard Determinism

Hard determinists believe that: Free choices are incompatible with our choices being caused and all our choices are caused, so none of our choices are free (and we are never morally responsible). What is "hard" about hard determinism is its conclusion: no free will and no moral responsibility. Most hard determinists are sorry to reach this conclusion, but accept it because they believe that the two premises that prove it are true.

The hard determinist Baron d'Holbach ('DOLE BOCK) (1723–1789) finds our belief in free will ironic:

> Man's life is a line that nature commands him to describe upon the surface of the earth, without his ever being able to swerve from it, even for an instant. He is born without his consent; his organization does in nowise depend upon himself; his ideas come to him involuntarily; his habits are in the power of those who cause him to contract them; he is unceasingly modified by causes, whether visible or concealed, over which he has no control, which necessarily regulate his mode of existence, give the hue to his way of thinking, and determine his manner of acting. He is good or bad, happy or miserable, wise or foolish, reasonable or irrational, without his will being for any thing in these various states. Nonetheless, in despite of these shackles by which he is bound, it is pretended he is a free agent. (1978, 404–5)

The hard determinists' view that no one is ever free or morally responsible for anything has serious results for how we view ourselves and others. If no one is morally responsible, then logically we ought to give up all beliefs and practices that require moral responsibility for their justification. For example, hard determinism says that we need to give up blaming persons and all ideas of *retribution* (rightful payback for misdeeds). On this view, we can no longer justify punishing criminals on the grounds that criminals *deserve* punishment—the justification of punishment would have to rely entirely on *consequentialist reasons* such as deterring crime or rehabilitating criminals. (See chapter 6 for a discussion of consequentialism in ethics.) Hard determinists disagree about how many of the attitudes we hold toward other persons—gratitude, resentment, indignation, and perhaps even love and friendship—we should surrender. Some hard determinists think we should not view our own *actions* with pride or shame, and that we should take a similar view toward our *character traits*, such as our degree of diligence required to complete a difficult task or our degree of honesty in the face of temptation.

5. Soft Determinism

Soft determinists believe that all choices are caused, but that many of our choices are free. This entails that some of our caused choices are free. So free will and moral responsibility are held to be compatible with our choices being caused. Many soft determinists are not interested in claiming that *all events* in the cosmos are caused, but only that *choices* can be both caused and free. For this reason, thinkers who are traditionally called "soft determinists" are also called "compatibilists."

Soft determinists claim to combine the best aspects of libertarianism and hard determinism. They endorse free will, as the libertarians do, thereby agreeing with common sense about moral responsibility. They believe that all choices are caused, as the hard determinists do, thereby agreeing with most psychologists and philosophers. The soft determinists' main task is to dispel the incompatibilist worry that we cannot be morally responsible for caused choices.

Here is a way to see what soft determinists need to show. Any theorist who believes that we make both free and unfree choices needs to be able to distinguish the two. If some of our choices are free and others are unfree, there must be something that makes the difference. The hard determinists avoid the problem by saying that because all choices are caused, they are *all* unfree. The libertarians have their answer: Our caused choices are unfree and only uncaused choices are free. Soft determinists cannot use the hard determinists' formula, because soft determinists believe there are some free choices. Soft determinists cannot use the libertarians' formula, because they believe all our choices are caused. Therefore, the soft determinists need a different criterion for distinguishing the free from the unfree.

Traditional compatibilism's solution was that freedom is the ability to act as one wishes. Because acting as we wish is compatible with our choices being caused, these compatibilists see freedom as possible within a determined universe. Here is how three famous British thinkers presented this compatibilist idea. Thomas Hobbes (1588–1679) argued:

> [H]e is free to do a thing, that may do it if he have the will to do it, and may forbear if he have the will to forbear. And yet if there be a necessity that he shall have the will to do it, the action is necessarily to follow; and if there be a necessity that he shall have the will to forbear, the forbearing also will be necessary (1841, 42).

John Locke expresses compatibilism this way:

> [S]o far as a man has a power to think or not to think, to move or not to move, according to the preference or direction of his own mind, so far is a man *free*. Wherever any performance or forbearance are not equally in a man's power, wherever doing or not doing will not equally follow upon the preference of his mind directing it, there he is not *free*. . . . So that the *idea of liberty* is the *idea* of a power in any agent to do or forbear any particular action, according to the determination or thought of the mind, whereby either of them is preferred to the other. (1974, II, XXI, 8)

David Hume also sees freedom as the ability to make our actions match our desires:

> [W]hat is meant by liberty when applied to voluntary actions? We cannot surely mean that actions have so little connection with motives, inclinations, and cir-

> cumstances that one does not follow with a certain degree of uniformity from the other, and that one affords no inference by which we can conclude the existence of the other. For these are plain and acknowledged matters of fact. By liberty, then, we can only mean *a power of acting or not acting according to the determinations of the will*; that is, if we choose to remain at rest, we may; if we choose to move, we also may. (1955, VIII, pt. I, 104)

The basic soft determinist idea is that although all choices are caused, there are two *kinds* of causes. I call these "freedom-enhancing causation" and "freedom-destroying causation." When we enjoy *freedom-enhancing causation*, our desires determine our choices and we choose as we wish. Our freedom is enhanced by such causation, because causation enables us to do what we want. When we are the victims of *freedom-destroying causation* we are forced to choose in ways we do not want to choose. Soft determinists believe that various factors count as freedom destroying causation: external compulsion, such as being locked in a room or being threatened, and internal compulsion, such as drug addiction or kleptomania. Soft determinists differ among themselves on what sort of factors to count as freedom-destroying determinism. Hobbes, Locke, and Hume counted only the more overt kinds of external compulsion as freedom-destroying. Contemporary compatibilists provide more sophisticated criteria for distinguishing between freedom-enhancing and freedom-destroying causation.

Harry Frankfurt (1982) distinguishes between our *first-order desires* (e.g., our desire to smoke cigarettes or eat hamburgers) and our *second-order desires* (our approval or disapproval of our desire to smoke cigarettes or eat hamburgers). According to Frankfurt, we are not necessarily free whenever our choices correspond with our first-order desires. For example, if I am addicted to smoking and wish that I were not, then I am unfree in my smoking, even though I have a first-order desire to smoke. To be free, Frankfurt says, we need to be able to make our choices correspond with our *second-order evaluations of our first-order desires*. So if I disapprove of my desire to smoke and am able to make my disapproval control my behavior by choosing not to smoke, then I enjoy free will.

Gary Watson makes a similar point by distinguishing between things we desire without valuing them and things we desire and value. Watson says that free choices are the choices we make on the basis of desires that we value. Agents choose freely when they bring their actions into line with their valuational system:

> The *valuational system* of an agent is that set of considerations which, when combined with his factual beliefs (and probability estimates), yields judgments of the form: the thing for me to do in these circumstances, all things considered, is *a*. To ascribe free agency to a being presupposes it to be a being that makes judgments of this sort. (1982, 91)

Soft determinism offers this challenge: So long as you are choosing as you want (Hobbes, Locke, Hume) and as you reflectively think is best (Frankfurt, Watson), what *more* could you want by way of free will? Do you want your desires, beliefs, and values *not* to cause your choices? Would you like to be in a situation where you want to choose X and end up choosing Y? How could the possibility that your choice might go awry *improve* your freedom?

Think of the freedoms we prephilosophically believe are important. Consider the First Amendment freedoms of speech, religion, and assembly. Consider the personal rights we take for granted: the right to believe what we want, select a lifestyle, make purchases, or dress the way we want. All these freedoms are soft deterministic freedoms, because they can be satisfied if we experience freedom-enhancing causation in a deterministic world. You want to start your own newspaper, you may. You want to believe that the Loch Ness monster exists, you may. You want to shave your head, you may. None of these freedoms requires that we make uncaused choices.

Finally, contrast the factors that expand our freedom with those that reduce it. Factors that increase our freedom include health, physical skills, intelligence, imagination, knowledge, vigor, a willingness to think for oneself, money, and social status. Factors that limit our freedom include illness, physical disabilities, stupidity, lack of imagination, ignorance, lethargy, conformism, poverty, and a lack of social status. None of these factors—positive or negative—depends on whether our choices are caused or uncaused. The soft determinists' point again is that we can have all the things that help us increase our freedom even if each of our choices is caused.

6. Free-Will-Either-Way Theory

The *free-will-either-way theory* is largely unrecognized in the history of philosophy, because most philosophers are either soft determinists, libertarians, or hard determinists. It is nonetheless easy to see how one might adopt the free-will-either-way theory: Simply agree with the soft determinists that *caused* choices can be free *and* agree with the libertarians and hard determinists that *uncaused* choices can be free. Thus, free-will-either-way theorists do not worry about determinism. For any choice that is caused, these thinkers believe that it can be free provided it is caused in a way that meets an acceptable soft determinist criterion of free will. For any choice that is uncaused, it can be free if it meets an acceptable libertarian criterion. Accordingly, we can be free either way.

7. No-Free-Will-Either-Way Theory

The *no-free-will-either-way theory* is the reverse of the free-will-either-way theory. This theory uses as premises the negative claims of the soft determinists on the one hand and the libertarians and hard determinists on the other. Suppose we accept the soft determinists' claim (in section 12 below) that uncaused choices could not be free, because they would be chancy and out of our control. If a choice that we make is not caused by the state of mind we are in when we make the choice, in what sense did *we* control the choice that occurred? Suppose also that we accept the libertarian/hard determinist claim (in section 11 below) that caused choices could not be free, because our choices could not have been otherwise than they were. Putting these two premises together, we would conclude that whether our choices are caused or not, they cannot be free. So, irrespective of the issue of determinism, we cannot have free will.

It might seem to be a contradiction to claim that neither caused nor uncaused choices can be free, but this is not true. What follows from "If C then U" and "If not C then U" is simply "U." Consider these premises: "If you are six feet tall, then you cannot jump thirty feet into the air" and "If you are not six feet tall, you cannot jump thirty feet into the air." What follows is that you cannot jump thirty feet into the air. The no-free-will-either-way theory was hinted at by Peter Strawson (1982).

Here is another way to argue for the no-free-will-either-way theory. Galen Strawson (1986, 28–29) argues that being truly responsible for our behavior is logically impossible:

(1) To be responsible for our choices, we must be responsible for the psychological states that go into our choices.
(2) To be responsible for these psychological states, we must responsibly choose them.
(3) To choose our psychological states responsibly we must use some principles for choosing them *and* we must be responsible for having those principles.
(4) To be responsible for our principles of choice, we must consciously choose our principles by following some higher-level principles of choice. And so on.
(5) Therefore, to be responsible for our choices, we must complete an infinite regress of choices of principles of choice.
(6) It is logically impossible to complete an infinite regress.

In sum, Strawson believes that to be responsible we would have to choose how we wish to be, but we must already exist in order to make that choice. We can never get outside ourselves and choose how we shall be. Thus, whether our choices are caused or not, freedom and moral responsibility are impossible.

8. Subjectivism

Subjectivism holds that *talk about free will and moral responsibility is simply the expression of our feelings and has no basis in facts lying outside those feelings.* Subjectivism in the free will problem is similar to moral subjectivism mentioned in chapter 6 and examined at length in chapter 7. Moral subjectivists hold that to talk about right and wrong is to vent positive and negative attitudes that are neither true nor false. On this view, there is no objective fact that would make it incorrect to endorse any action as right or condemn any action as wrong: Rightness and wrongness are attitudes persons feel about actions that themselves are neither right nor wrong.

Subjectivists in the free will problem hold that when we call choices "free" (enough under our control for us to be *morally responsible* for them), we are expressing our moral attitudes, which do not correspond to objective facts. If moral judgments in general are neither true nor false, it follows that statements such as "Caused choices are compatible (or incompatible) with free will and moral responsibility" are neither truth nor false. They would be merely emotional responses to determinism. According to subjectivists, incompatibilists simply show their subjective dread of determinism, whereas compatibilists reveal their subjective fondness of determinism. Thus, subjectivists believe that the other five theorists are wrong to think that "free will" makes enough objective sense to enable us to talk about the compatibility *or* incompatibility of free will and caused choices.

SUMMARY OF THE SIX THEORIES

Here is a chart recapping how the six theories answer the four questions. "D/C" means "We don't care" and "Huh?" means "This question makes no sense."

	Lib	HD	SD	FWEWT	NFWEWT	Subj
Are all choices caused?	No	Yes	Yes	D/C	D/C	D/C
Do we ever have free will?	Yes	No	Yes	Yes	No	Huh?
Can caused choices be free?	No	No	Yes	Yes	No	Huh?
Can uncaused choices be free?	Yes	Yes	No	Yes	No	Huh?

Here are some things to notice about the chart. First, the libertarians, hard determinists, and soft determinists take a stand on whether all human choices are caused. These thinkers believe that we need to decide this question to decide whether we have free will. The free-will-either-way theorists, the no-free-will-either-way theorists, and the subjectivists do not. These thinkers do not think that we have to decide whether all choices are caused before we can reach a conclusion about the existence of free will.

Second, the hard determinists and soft determinists equally believe that *all* choices are caused. They both believe that there is only one possible history to reality, again, at least regarding choices. Hard and soft determinists differ only regarding the implications determinism has for free will and moral responsibility, but not on whether determinism is true. *To think that soft determinists believe that some choices are caused and some are uncaused is a serious mistake.*

Third, the libertarians, hard determinists, and no-free-will-either-way theorists accept *incompatibilism*. They agree that: *If all choices were caused, then we could not have free choices.* The libertarians think that because we have free choices, at least some of them must be uncaused. The hard determinists believe that because all choices are caused, no one makes free choices. So the hard determinists use the conditional premise above in a modus ponens argument against free will, whereas the libertarians use the conditional premise in a modus tollens argument against determinism. I call this type of disagreement: "One person's modus ponens is another person's modus tollens."

Whereas the libertarians and the hard determinists choose between accepting determinism or free will, the soft determinists argue that this is a *false dilemma* by accepting *both* determinism and free will. The soft determinists and the free-will-either-way theorists are *compatibilists,* who believe that caused choices can be free. The subjectivists answer "Huh?" to the questions about the possibility of caused and uncaused being free, because they do not think that "free" is objectively meaningful.

Fourth, although the libertarians, soft determinists, and free-will-either-way theorists are free will realists, they accept free will for very different reasons. The libertarians, who are incompatibilists, believe we have free will only because our free choices are *uncaused*. The soft determinists, who are compatibilists, believe we have free will *and* our free choices are *caused*. Free-will-either-way theorists believe that persons can choose freely whether their choices are caused or not.

Fifth, the hard determinists, no-free-will-either-way theorists, and the subjectivists are free will nonrealists, but for different reasons. The hard determinists believe that determinism eliminates free will. The no-free-will-either-way theorists believe that whether our choices are caused or not, we are unfree. The subjectivists believe talk about free will is confused.

THE FOUR QUESTIONS CONSIDERED

To decide which free will theory we think is best, we need to decide where we stand on the four questions in the chart in the last section. If we are able to reach verdicts on all four questions, we will decide which theory we think is most plausible. If we can reach verdicts on only some of the questions, we will at least know what theories we think are live candidates and which we reject.

9. Are All Choices Caused?

Libertarians, soft determinists, and hard determinists believe that to decide whether we are free, we need to decide whether our choices are caused.

Although all choices might be caused even if determinism is false, if determinism is true, then all human choices are caused. The truth of determinism is a sufficient condition for all choices being caused. For this reason, a great deal of the historical debate over the free will problem has focused on the overall doctrine of determinism. I begin this section by examining arguments concerning determinism and then move to arguments concerning the narrower thesis that all *choices* are caused.

WHAT DETERMINISM IS

The German libertarian Johann Gotlieb Fichte ('FICK TA) (1762–1814) presents a poetic description of a deterministic worldview:

> I behold plants, trees, animals. To each individual I ascribe certain properties and attributes by which I distinguish it from others; to this plant, such a form; to that plant, another; to this tree, leaves of one shape; to that tree, leaves of another. . . .
>
> Why had Nature, amid the infinite variety of possible forms, assumed in this moment precisely these and no others?
>
> For this reason: that they were preceded precisely by those conditions which did precede them, and by no others; and because the present could arise out of those and out of no other possible conditions. Had anything in the preceding moment been in the smallest degree different from what it was, then in the present moment something would have been different from what it is. And from what cause were all things in that preceding moment precisely such as they were? For this reason: that in the moment preceding that, they were such as they were then. And this moment again was dependent on its predecessor, and that on another, and so on into the past without limit. . . .
>
> Nature proceeds throughout the whole infinite series of her possible determinations without pause; and the succession of these changes is not arbitrary, but follows strict and unalterable laws. Whatever exists in Nature, necessarily exists as it does exist, and it is absolutely impossible that it should be otherwise. I enter within an unbroken chain of phenomena in which every link is determined by that which has preceded it, and in its turn determines the next; so that, were I able to trace into the past the causes through which alone any given moment could have come into actual existence, and to follow out in the future the consequences which must necessarily flow from it, then, at that moment, and by means of thought alone, I could discover all possible conditions of the universe, both past and future—past, by explaining the given moment; future, by predicting its consequences. (1956, 7–10)

Should we accept this flowery vision? To decide this we need to become clear about what the doctrine of determinism is *not*.

An important preliminary is that determinism is not *fatalism*. Fatalism is *the doctrine that our choices will not influence our lives, that our fates are sealed regardless of how we try to avoid them.* Fatalists may be determinists or indeterminists, theists or atheists, free will realists or nonrealists. Many ingenious arguments have been offered to support fatalism: fatalism due to God's foreknowledge, fatalism due to interventions in human affairs by the gods, fatalism due to the fact that statements describing future events are true now, and arguments that involve subtle maneuvers in symbolic logic. I do not find any of these arguments persuasive, but the thing to notice is that determinism is not the same thing as fatalism. Fatalism, which is the counterpart to the psychological concept of *learned helplessness* (Seligman, 1970), maintains that our choices do not matter. Determinism says that our choices *do* matter. Our choices dictate how our lives shall be. It is just that our choices are caused, and those causes were caused, and so on.

The next preliminary is that determinism does *not* entail that we can predict the future. Determinism says that every event is the necessary result of laws that govern all events and the condition of the universe immediately before the event. This might seem to entail, as Fichte noted, that if someone did know all the laws of nature (including the laws regarding the supernatural, if there is a supernatural) and had a complete description of the condition of reality at any one moment, then that being could *pre*dict the future and *retro*dict that past. Although Fichte's idea is basically right, it needs two qualifications.

Determinism is a metaphysical claim about what is true, whether anyone *knows* it is true or not. Prediction is an epistemological feat that we may or may not manage. Many events that are determined are not predictable simply because they are complicated. For example, we know that rolling a pair of fair dice will produce a 7 more often than a 12, but we cannot predict with certainty what number will come up on any single roll. If I drop a piece of chalk onto the floor from four feet I am not able to predict whether it will break or not, despite the fact that the chalk's breaking or not breaking is determined. Thus, the concept "certain" is ambiguous. The concept might refer to an event's being certain *in itself* (*metaphysical certainty*), or it might refer to *our state of confidence* about the event (*psychological certainty*). So, not all metaphysically certain events are ones about which we are psychologically certain. The most we can say is that if determinism is true then all events are *in principle predictable,* but not necessarily *actually predictable.*

Even this needs qualification. Determinism entails that events are in principle predictable *only if the predictors do not interact with what they are predicting.* Suppose, for example, that you know that there are ten factors that cause my choices. Then you can predict my choices if you know these ten factors. But suppose you interact with me *by telling me your prediction.* There is now an eleventh factor that may influence my choice, namely, your prediction. I might decide to falsify your prediction by changing my mind or cross you up by choosing what you originally predicted. So your initial prediction made on the basis of the ten factors—which would have been accurate had you *not* told it to me—is no longer sure to be accurate; now there is an additional factor that you did not take into account. Suppose you respond by figuring out how I will choose on the basis of all eleven factors and make your prediction accordingly. Then, by hypothesis, this prediction will be accurate, but, again, only if you do not tell me what it is. If you do, that will contribute a twelfth factor to the determination of my behavior. And so on. The point is that determinism entails that events are predictable *only in principle* AND *only if the predictors do not interact with the subjects they predict.*

DOES "ALL EVENTS ARE CAUSED" TAKE A TRUTH VALUE?

Philosophers have offered two reasons for thinking that (D) "All events are determined" is not a statement that is either true or false. First, some philosophers argue that (D) should be understood as a nontruth-valued prescription, because assuming determinism prods scientists to keep looking for the unknown causes of phenomena rather than to quit looking and say that the phenomena in question have no causes. So the apparently truth-valued statement "All events are caused" really means the nontruth-valued command "Let's always look for causes."

Second, strictly speaking, determinism is neither provable nor disprovable. We can never be certain that *every* event is *caused*, because the next event we examine might be uncaused. We can never be certain that *any one individual event* is *uncaused*, because maybe it has a cause that we have failed to find. Because determinism can be neither proved nor disproved, some philosophers conclude that "All events are caused" must not be a truth-valued claim, but only a recommendation for sustaining scientific inquiry.

The premises of both arguments are true, but they do not show that "All events are caused" is neither true nor false. Regarding the first argument, the assumption of determinism *does* serve a helpful role in scientific inquiry, but so do other truth-valued hypotheses. Consider the assumption "A high percentage of murders are committed by spouses." Despite the fact that assuming this serves to help police detectives to suspect spouses in murder investigations, the statement is either true or false. Regarding the second argument, although determinism cannot be proved or disproved, that provides no reason to think that determinism is neither true nor false. Consider an analogy: The fact that we cannot prove the existence or nonexistence of God gives no reason to suppose that "God exists" does not have a truth value.

THREE ARGUMENTS FOR DETERMINISM

Although the truth or falsity of determinism is an empirical (a posteriori) question that cannot be settled by philosophical speculation, this has not kept philosophers from providing arguments for determinism. The first argument is that determinism appears to be increasingly supported by the progress of science. The earliest natural science was astronomy, with the Greek philosopher/scientist Thales predicting a solar eclipse in the seventh century B.C. During the rise of modern science beginning in the sixteenth century, physics and chemistry became sciences. In the nineteenth and twentieth centuries biology and psychology became sciences. Science proceeds by discovering causal laws that predict and explain the phenomena under its scope. Thus, it seems that as science grows and the technology based on it increases, the inductive argument for determinism becomes stronger. It is easy to imagine that a fully complete scientific knowledge will strongly support determinism.

This is not to say that science has *proved* determinism. As noted, the universal claim that *all* phenomena are caused cannot be proved. Moreover, although unexplained phenomena are typically assumed to have causes, it would be dogmatic to assume that they *must*. The idea of uncaused events is strange, but it is not unthinkable. Quantum mechanics, the dominant twentieth-century theory of matter at the level of the atom, holds that many events *in principle* cannot be predicted exactly but only probabilistically. Many thinkers interpret this to mean that events at the quantum level are uncaused.

The second argument is that determinism is assumed not only in science, but in everyday thought. If we throw a piece of chalk into the air 100 times, we expect it to fall toward Earth 100 times, unless some force other than gravity acts on it. If we put bread dough in the oven, we expect that it will become bread, not chocolate cake. To borrow an example from Cornman, Lehrer, and Pappas, if our new car won't start one morning, we refuse to accept our mechanic's judgment that there is no cause for its failure to start, no matter how knowledgeable we think the mechanic is (1987, ch. 3). The point is that at least for the behavior of the normal-sized objects of everyday life, we assume that determinism holds. It is only natural to expect that the events we experience in everyday life are caused.

A third argument for determinism lies in a rhetorical question (a statement phrased as a question) that was the title of a popular song: "Do you believe in magic?" If events are not caused to happen, then why do they occur? Even if gods were as numerous and active as primitive persons believed, gods' production of natural events (earthquakes, floods, tornadoes) would *still* be causation—albeit supernatural causation. If events occur neither due to natural causes *nor* supernatural causes, then it seems that they happen for no reason at all—"by magic." This is possible, but it does not seem very plausible.

REGARDLESS OF DETERMINISM PER SE, ARE ALL CHOICES CAUSED?

Although these are suggestive reasons for believing that *all events* are caused, they scarcely *prove* it. This failure does not necessarily hurt the hard and soft determinists, however, because they need to argue only that *all choices* are caused. We need to ask, therefore, whether there are strong reasons to accept the narrower thesis that all choices are caused. I shall examine this question by first looking at commonsense arguments for the thesis and then by looking at scientific arguments for it.

A familiar, but dubious, argument for thinking that all choices are caused is the *motive argument*. According to this view, conscious choices are always determined by our strongest motives, which are sometimes called "our effective desires." And our strongest motive at any time will be a determined result of the various psychological states that produce them: our likes, dislikes, fears, hopes, beliefs, and values. "The will," which is simply our ability to choose, is pushed or pulled to choose as it does by the sum of the psychological states of the chooser. Finally, those psychological states were determined by our heredity and environment. Baron d'Holbach expresses the argument this way:

> This will is necessarily determined by the qualities, good or bad, agreeable or painful, of the object or the motive that acts upon his senses, or of which the idea remains with him, and is resuscitated by his memory. In consequence, he acts necessarily, his action is the result of the impulse he receives either from the motive, from the object, or from the idea which has modified his brain, or disposed his will. When he does not act according to this impulse, it is because there comes some new cause, some new motive, some new idea, which modifies his brain in a different manner, gives him a new impulse, determines his will in another way. (1978, 404–5)

One might object: What about times you choose not as you want, but *from prudence*, as when you hand over your wallet to a mugger? According to the motive argument, your strongest motive—all things considered—*must* have been to give your wallet to the mugger. Otherwise, you would not have done so. Another objection is that we sometimes choose *from duty*, not according to what we most want. Robert Blachford anticipates this point:

> A young woman gets two letters by the same post; one is an invitation to go with her lover to a concert, the other is a request that she will visit a sick child in the slums. The girl is very fond of music, and is rather afraid of the slums. . . . But she goes to the sick child and she forgoes the concert. Why? Because her sense of duty is stronger than her self love. . . . We may say that the girl is free to act as she chooses, but she *does* act as she has been *taught* that she *ought* to act. This teaching . . . controls her will. (1982, 105)

The problem with the motive argument is that it *assumes* rather than *proves* that each step between heredity/environment, the creation of our effective desires, and our choices is deterministic. Although this assumption is probably true, it is really no stronger than the do-you-believe-in-magic argument cited above. Thus, it begs the question against libertarians like Chisholm, van Inwagen, and Kane, who hope that uncaused choices *might* occur.

A more compelling argument for the determinism of choices comes from brain science. All the evidence we have about the production of human behavior indicates that it is caused by the central nervous system, our brains in particular. (See chapter 5.) Some dualistic interactionists such as the French philosopher René Descartes believe that persons possess nonphysical minds that make choices in nondeterministic ways. But there is no evidence that we have nonphysical minds, nor that if we did, that they would be indeterministic. (If the nonphysical mind *did* interact with the brain, there would be as much reason to think that the interaction would be deterministic as indeterministic.) Likewise, agent-theory libertarians have speculated that unmoved agents produce indeterministic choices, but there is no evidence that agents in this sense exist.

An adult human brain is a three-pound physical object that, so far as we know, operates according to electrical and chemical laws. Although it is *possible* that some brain processes are indeterministic, there is no evidence for this. The brain seems just as deterministic as our other organs. If there is indeterminism at the level of the atoms, it does not seem to affect the functioning of the brain any more than it affects the functioning of our livers or kidneys. Putting these two premises together yields a moderately strong argument for the determinism of behavior:

(1) Human behavior is a product of the brain.
(2) The brain is a determined system.
(3) Therefore, human behavior is determined.

INDETERMINIST ARGUMENTS

The Objection from Quantum Physics. As noted, event-causation libertarians such as Kane believe that indeterminism within the atom may be amplified to contribute to uncaused choices in the brain at times of conflicting motivation. Kane is right to think that this could happen, and that if it did happen it might yield indeterminism in our choices. Nonetheless, there are three objections to the use of quantum mechanics to support libertarianism.

First, although the majority of physicists take the unpredictability of certain quantum events to show that these events are not caused, the unpredictability might simply be a matter of our lack of precise knowledge of what is happening, and not be an indicator of genuine indeterminism. Although many scientists are quick to conclude what reality is like from limitations in our knowledge, we should not forget the difference between two issues: the way reality is (a metaphysical issue) and what we know about reality (an epistemological issue).

Second, although amplifications of indeterminism from single subatomic events to brain events is possible, a far more probable result is that any indeterminacies that occurred inside the atom would *cancel each other out rather than be amplified*. An adult human brain consists of 10 billion cells, and each cell consists of 10 billion atoms. So it is far more likely that any indeterminacies in the atoms would even out rather than be amplified to create undetermined brain events. According to the British physicist Sir Arthur Eddington, it is theoretically possible for all the particles of a billiard ball to go on a spree simultaneously and for the ball to float up to the ceiling, but the probability of that happening is so small that even if he saw it, he would not believe it.

The third point (which we examine in section 12) says that even if brain activity were undetermined due to amplified quantum indeterminacies, uncaused choices would not help to give us the sort of free will needed for moral responsibility. Uncaused choices would be random and not controlled by persons. So, even if the libertarian can argue for uncaused choices, those choices might be *worse* for our freedom than caused choices and certainly would not be *better*.

The Argument from Introspection. A classic argument for uncaused choices is based on our introspective feeling that we often can choose either of two ways. (*Introspection* means "looking into our mental states.") For instance, I can hold my hand in front of me, decide that in ten seconds I shall elect to move it either to the right or left, and then after ten seconds move it one of the two ways. Now, although I move my hand one way, it *seems* to me that I could have moved my hand in the other direction—*given the exact state of my mind when I decided*. Therefore, I seem to have introspective evidence that determinism is false, because I seem to know that both what I *did* choose *and* what I *did not but could have chosen* were physically possible. Some libertarians take this sort of example as proof that we make uncaused choices.

This argument for indeterminism is worthless. It runs afoul of the epistemological lesson from chapter 3 that phenomenological feelings by themselves *never* provide evidence that things are the way we feel they are. In every case in which a phenomenological *f*eeling (F) provides evidence for the way something *is* (I), the theory (I) must be a better explanation for (F) than all competing theories. Phenomenological reports are data that need explanation, and the hypothesis that they are true cannot be assumed to be a better explanation than the hypothesis that they are false. Feeling that we make uncaused choices does not provide evidence that we make uncaused choices, because we would feel as if we make uncaused choices even if our choices are caused. The easiest way to see this is to suppose, for the sake of the illustration, that determinism is true. Nonetheless, in our hand-moving experiment we would still *feel* as if we could have moved our hand in either way. But, by hypothesis, we could not. Therefore, our introspective feeling of making uncaused choices does not provide evidence that we make uncaused choices.

Determinism is just as good an explanation as indeterminism is for our feeling that we make uncaused choices.

Here is a more dramatic example. Suppose you go to a hypnotist in the morning to help you quit smoking. While you are hypnotized, the hypnotist suggests to you that at 3:00 P.M. that day, wherever you find yourself, you will feel a strong desire to cluck like a chicken. That afternoon you are in your English class and glance at your watch. Suddenly it seems like a very good idea to cluck like a chicken and you elect to do so, to the amusement of your classmates. Here it *seems* to you that your choice is uncaused, but the choice was caused by the hypnotist. Generalizing from this example, for all we can tell, any choice that seems uncaused could be caused by unknown factors.

10. Are We Ever Free and Morally Responsible?

The most common reason cited for believing in moral responsibility is that it is common knowledge. Van Inwagen claims "we have a perfectly good, in fact, an unsurpassably good, reason for believing in free will. For surely we cannot doubt the reality of moral responsibility" (1983, 206). We know that *other persons* are morally responsible by the way we look at them. To think that Adolf Hitler is a villain and Mother Theresa is a hero is to believe that each bears moral responsibility. We know that *we* are morally responsible by looking into our own hearts—by feeling pride and shame about our own behavior.

Although popular, this is not a strong argument. According to the approach to philosophy used in this book, our *beliefs* that we and others are morally responsible must be treated as data that stand in need of explanation. We cannot take such beliefs at face value. For example, moral subjectivism (discussed in chapter 7) holds that our beliefs that certain *actions* are right or wrong are best explained by citing psychological facts about our moral training and do not need to be explained by saying that actions are objectively right or wrong (Harman, 1977, ch. 1). Similarly, a free will subjectivist can say that our belief that persons are morally responsible is best explained by citing psychological facts about our moral training and does not need to be explained by saying that we *really are* morally responsible. Hard determinists and no-free-will-either-way theorists can say the same thing. Therefore, introspection provides no evidence that we are morally responsible.

Here is a different way to see the point. Feeling morally responsible no more proves that we are morally responsible than feeling free proves that we are free. In the hypnotism example given in the last section, you feel free but really are not. Now, suppose that your deciding to cluck like a chicken causes your English professor to suffer a heart attack. You may feel morally responsible, but you would be mistaken, because you did not exercise free will.

Here are two pragmatic maneuvers offered by free will realists. The first is a moral argument. Realists might concede that although we cannot give *good theoretical evidence* for believing in free will, we *morally ought to believe* in it anyway. The American William James provided an argument for believing in indeterministic free will that was similar to his Will-to-Believe argument regarding the existence of God discussed in chapter 9: Because we cannot prove that free will does not exist, and because believing in it is so useful to us, we may believe in free will *because* it is useful. James says that because determinism (an unprovable theoretical thesis) conflicts with free will and moral responsibility (things he needs to believe in to be the sort of person he wants to be), he has no hesitation in rejecting determinism (1962). The German Immanuel Kant (1724–1804) also thought that free will cannot be proved, but urged us to believe it on faith so that we might fulfill those moral duties that require free will. If we did *not* believe in free will and moral responsibility, Kant feared, we would lead immoral lives.

The problem with such arguments for free will and moral responsibility is that they acknowledge precisely what the free will nonrealists (hard determinists, no-free-will-either-way theorists, and subjectivists) assert: that we have no evidence for the existence of free will. The nonrealists think that as philosophers we should believe only those things for which we have evidence. For them, no evidence, no belief. It is not that they deny thinkers like James and Kant *the right* to construct their metaphysical theories with an eye toward what would make us better persons. The nonrealists insist, though, that this just is not *their* way of approaching philosophy.

A second pragmatic theme, developed by Peter Strawson (1982), claims that because we cannot *help* acting as if persons are free and morally responsible, there is no point to thinking they are not. According to Strawson, our normal reactions toward persons such as feeling gratitude and resentment are not things that we could ever give up. If it is impossible to give up holding persons responsible, then there is no need to justify our practice of holding persons responsible by providing a theory of free will. We should believe in free will without worrying whether we can provide a philosophical justification for it.

Strawson may be resisted on two counts. First, claiming that persons cannot live without holding each other morally responsible is an a posteriori claim that cannot be proven by philosophers' armchair speculations. In his novel *Walden Two* the behaviorist psychologist B. F. Skinner (1948) sketches a behaviorally engineered utopia where persons who are brought up believing in determinism give up the idea of moral responsibility. Maybe Strawson's speculation is right, and maybe Skinner's speculation is right, but we should not accept either without serious scientific investigation.

Second, even if Strawson's speculation were true, it would not matter to our attempt to build the most accurate picture of reality, the nonrealists' primary interest. Suppose that you were psychologically built so that you could never avoid believing a falsehood: that Elvis is really alive or that the New York Mets will win the next World Series. This quirk about you would not prove anything about the existence of Elvis or the future success of the Mets. Likewise, even if we cannot help believing in free will and moral responsibility, that would provide no evidence that they exist.

11. Can Caused Choices Be Free?

Compatibilists (soft determinists and free-will-either-way theorists) believe that a choice can be both caused and free, whereas incompatibilists (libertarians, hard determinists, and no-free-will-either-way theorists) believe that choices cannot be both caused and free. A good way to examine the disagreement is to look at classic incompatibilist arguments and then see whether the compatibilists can offer a satisfactory reply.

THE CASE FOR INCOMPATIBILISM

One incompatibilist argument is to take a clear example in which causation takes away our freedom, and then argue that all causation is likewise harmful to us. Consider the plight of addicts who wish not to take heroin, but are unable to resist their addictions. It is reasonable to say that their addictions, which have a chemical basis in their bodies, destroy their freedom by causing them to take the drugs. Now suppose that determinism is true, or at least, that all choices are caused. *If* this is true, then *everyone's* choices possess the same degree of inevitability that drug addicts' choices display. Given the state of persons' bodies, we *cannot not* make the choices we make. Therefore, if addicts' caused choices are unfree, then *everyone's* caused choices are unfree.

A second argument for incompatibilism may be expressed this way:

(1) If all choices are caused, then no one could have chosen differently.
(2) If no one could have chosen differently, then no one is free or morally responsible.
(3) Therefore, if all choices are caused, then no one is free or morally responsible.

One way to see the force of this argument is to imagine yourself in prison waiting to be executed for a crime. While waiting through years of unsuccessful appeals, you begin to read science and philosophy, and you gradually come to believe in hard determinism. As a hard determinist you are appalled at the unfairness of your impending execution: "Given determinism is true, I could not have chosen otherwise than I did. If the total history of the world were rerun 1 million times, I would have committed murder 1 million times. It is unfair to take revenge on me for something that was bound to happen."

Incompatibilists have other ways to get us to accept this second argument.

If determinism is true, then there theoretically could be a "Book of Life" somewhere that describes all things that will ever happen to us on Earth (Goldman, 1968). Another variant is to imagine God's complete foreknowledge of everything you will ever choose. Finally, in his "Consequence Argument" van Inwagen argues that determinism prevents choices from being "up to us":

> If determinism is true, then our acts are the consequences of the laws of nature and events in the remote past. But it is not up to us what went on before we were born, and neither is it up to us what the laws of nature are. Therefore, the consequences of these things (including our present acts) are not up to us. (1983, 56)

A third argument for incompatibilism emphasizes that common sense holds that causation makes choices unfree. Consider a thought experiment provided by William Halverson (1981, 247–48). Two criminals, Fred and Sally, commit a crime. Fred is the product of a terrible environment: He was abandoned by his parents, abused as a child, grew up in poverty and crime, and received no love or moral instruction. Sally grew up in an affluent, upstanding, supportive family and was never abused. Although both are equally guilty under the law, most persons would blame Sally more for committing the crime than Fred. Why? The incompatibilist thinks that most persons accept incompatibilism: We recognize the causation of Fred's behavior by his poor environment, and we blame him less because of it. But with Sally, we assume that her behavior is *uncaused*, and, thus, do not soften our view of her responsibility. (The incompatibilist completes the thought experiment: If we were to come to believe that all of Sally' choices were caused, we would not blame her, either.)

THE COMPATIBILISTS' REPLY TO THESE ARGUMENTS

The basic compatibilist answer to all these arguments has to be: So long as we choose as we want with self-conscious deliberation, the fact that our choices are caused is irrelevant to our freedom. Because we examined this view in the soft determinism section, I shall provide only one more point in its behalf.

Consider the following thought experiment. Imagine that on Earth and on its molecule-for-molecule duplicate, Twin Earth, there are two persons who are qualitatively indistinguishable in every way (including the states of their Cartesian minds, if they have them), call them "Jim" and "Twin Jim." Jim and Twin Jim have led identical lives—they have made identical choices for identical reasons. But some of Jim's choices are undetermined, libertarian choices, whereas all of Twin Jim's choices are determined. Now, if incompatibilism is correct, then Jim is sometimes morally responsible, but Twin Jim never is.

But how can that be? They have done all the same things for the same reasons—they are qualitatively indistinguishable physically, intellectually, emotionally, and so on. If we tell Jim and Twin Jim about the existence of the other, neither can tell who he is—whether he is Jim on libertarian Earth or Twin Jim on determined Twin Earth. Therefore, if Jim and Twin Jim differ regarding freedom or moral responsibility, these characteristics seem odd. Freedom and responsibility would depend not on the *internal character* of the mental states of Jim and Twin Jim, which are, after all, indistinguishable, but on the degree of *physical necessity* of them. Compatibilists think this looks very strange.

12. Can Uncaused Choices Be Free?

Soft determinists and no-free-will-either-way theorists answer "no" to this question. Libertarians, hard determinists, and free-will-either-way theorists answer "yes." One way that the soft determinists and free-will-either-way theorists present their point is to argue that free agents can *control* their choices only if determinism is true. For instance, R. E. Hobart argues that if "the self" experiences undetermined volitions, then

> The self, considering the alternatives beforehand, is not in a position to say, "If I feel thus about it, this volition will take place, or if I feel otherwise the contrary will take place; I know very well how I shall feel, so I know how I shall will." The self now existing has not control over the future "free" volition, since that may be undetermined, nor will the self's future feelings, whatever they may be, control it. Hence the sense expressed by "I can," the sense of power inhering in one's continuous self to sway the volition as it feels disposed, is denied to it. All it is in a position to mean by "I can" is, "I do not know which will happen," which is not "I can" at all. (1966, 77)

Even the libertarian Roderick Chisholm sees uncaused events as problematic for control:

> Perhaps there is less need to argue that the ascription of responsibility also conflicts with an indeterministic view of action—with the view that the act, or some event that is essential to the act, is not caused at all. If the act—the firing of the shot—was not caused at all, if it was fortuitous or capricious, happening so to speak out of the blue, then, presumably, no one—and nothing—was responsible for the act. (1982, 27–28)

A. J. Ayer expresses the point in terms of rationality:

> [I]f it is a matter of pure chance that a man should act in one way rather than another, he may be free but can hardly be responsible. And indeed when a man's action seems to us quite unpredictable, when, as we say, there is no knowing what he will do, we do not look upon him as a moral agent. We look upon him as a lunatic. (1954, 17)

Hobart and Ayer believe that uncaused choices would hurt rather than help our freedom and responsibility. Here is a way to appreciate their argument. If the existence of breaks or gaps in the causation of our behavior would be helpful for our freedom, then there must be some place where such gaps would be helpful. (If having $1,000 is a good thing, then there must be *a place* where it would be good to have $1,000—in one's wallet or bank account.) It follows, therefore, that if there is no place where indeterminism is helpful to our freedom, then uncaused choices cannot help us to be free and morally responsible.

If we trace human behavior from hereditary and environmental factors through our choices and actions, there seem to be five places where indeterminism might occur. First, the hereditary and environmental factors themselves might be uncaused. Second, the hereditary and environmental factors might influence our mental states (our beliefs, desires, and values) only in indeterministic ways. Third, our earlier mental states might not cause our subsequent mental states. Fourth, our mental states at the time we make choices might not cause those choices. Fifth, our choices might not cause our actions.

Compatibilists argue that in each of these possible locations, undetermined gaps either would be no help to our freedom or would make us less free. Let us consider the five locations in turn. First, suppose that some hereditary and environmental factors are not caused. This would mean that strictly speaking our behavior is undetermined; if the events of the universe were rerun 100 times over, our behavior would not necessarily be the same each time. But this would not enhance our free will and moral responsibility, because we can have no control over the hypothesized undetermined environmental and hereditary factors. We cannot choose our heredity, and we cannot get outside our environment to pick that either. So we cannot control either. Indeterminism in our heredity and environment would not help our freedom.

Second, suppose we postulate a gap in causation between heredity and environment on the one hand and our mental states on the other. To be rational and free, we need to be responsive to the factors influencing us. It is no help to our freedom if we acquire beliefs, desires, and values that are not caused by heredity and environment, for then our mental states are not accurate responses to who we are and how the environment influences us. If we see a predator charging at us, we do not *want* indeterminism to result in our perceiving the predator as harmless or our endocrine systems responding with gladness.

Third, consider the gap that might be postulated to hold between our mental states at earlier and later times. If our mental states at Time 1 (along with hereditary and environmental factors) do not cause our mental states at Time 2, then we have lost rather than gained control of our mental lives. Why bother to collect true beliefs about physics or history if your subsequent beliefs are subject to change in an uncaused way? Likewise, why try to develop today a certain type of moral character if your desires and values are subject to change without cause? To the extent that our mental states at Time 1 do not cause our mental states at Time 2, intellectual and moral learning would be impoverished.

There is a single theme that connects the objections to trying to increase our freedom by "locating" indeterminism at any of the first three locations. Incompatibilists want free agents to have *the ability to choose otherwise at the instant of choice*. As Chisholm noted above, incompatibilists want us to be able to choose, for example, either to commit murder or to refrain from committing murder given one single mental condition that immediately precedes our choice. It will not satisfy the incompatibilists to learn that we might choose either way depending on the outcome of some uncaused event that happens *before* our choice—whether in our heredity or environment, our earlier mental states, or our mental states that immediately precede choice. Incompatibilists would think that such indeterminism would still leave us unfree, because *we* would not be in control of the undetermined event. So, incompatibilists want to locate the indeterminism at either location four or five.

Locating indeterminism at point five—the gap between our choices and our actions—could not help our free will, because it would serve only to make our choices less effective. Free agents *need* their choices to determine the actions they perform. It would reduce our control if our choices do not dictate the actions we perform. Imagine that your choice to greet a friend were immediately followed by your action of assaulting him.

Thus, the only place left for incompatibilists to locate indeterminism is between our present mental states and our choices. This location has the advantage of being the right place to locate the indeterminism according to the incompatibilists. The trouble is that the less our choices are caused by our mental states, the less we control them. Given one set of beliefs, desires, and values, we might make the obvious choice or one that makes no sense at all. Consider an analogy. Given exactly the same stroke that you make in putting a golf ball under identical conditions, the ball sometimes rolls ten feet and sometimes rolls forty feet. In this case, you are not in control of how far the ball travels: How far the ball goes is not up to you. Likewise, to the extent that *our state of mind* does not cause what choice occurs, *we* do not control our choices. Given the same psychological profile of beliefs, desires, and values, we might as easily choose battery-acid flavored ice cream as butter-pecan. We would be victimized by indeterminism, not made free.

THE CASE FOR SUBJECTIVISM

So far, I have assumed that each of the four major questions takes a "yes" or "no" answer. On this assumption, one of the first five theories must be true, even if we are unsure which it is. But philosophy teaches us to question assumptions. Subjectivism, the sixth theory, is the result of rejecting the assumption that each question has an answer.

Let us reconsider questions (3) *Can caused choices be free*? and (4) *Can uncaused choices be free*? I am often inclined to accept negative answers to both (3) and (4). Incompatibilists seem correct to reject the freedom of caused choices, which, after all, could not have been different than they were. Thus, I often agree with the libertarians and hard determinists in answering "no" to (3). Compatibilists also seem correct when they say that locating indeterminism within our choice-making process would reduce our freedom. Thus, I often agree with Hobart and Ayer in answering "no" to (4). Nonetheless, sometimes I agree with the positive accounts of free choice given by the compatibilists such as Hobbes and Frankfurt. This gives a "yes" answer to (3). I also sometimes agree with libertarians in giving a "yes" answer to (4).

By having my opinions move in these different directions I seem to be contradicting myself, but am I? Not necessarily. It is possible that the *apparently* contradictory theories of incompatibilism and compatibilism are "equally true." The only way that this would be possible is if "free choice" can have no objective reference. This would mean that free will and moral responsibility would exist only in the eye of the beholder. This is the theory of subjectivism.

Here is an analogy to explain subjectivism. If we ask different baseball fans what a good baseball game is, we will get different answers. Some purists think that a good baseball game is a pitchers' duel that ends up with a score of 1–0. Others disagree, preferring high-scoring games with lots of home runs. Others will not mention ideal scores, but emphasize different variables—stolen bases, dramatic rallies, good fielding plays, even nice weather, or "any game my team wins." "Baseball subjectivists" believe that no one *can* have the correct answer as to what a good baseball game is. There is no reason to think that, for example, 1–0 games are objectively or *really* better than 20–16 games, or vice versa. Contradictory opinions are equally correct, which is to say that no opinion can be objectively correct or incorrect.

To claim that these conflicting opinions are equally correct means that it is logically impossible for goodness to be a real characteristic of baseball games. Logically, a single baseball game cannot possess the contradictory characteristics that good baseball games are thought to have. For instance, one game cannot have the characteristics of a 1–0 and a 20–16 final score. Goodness can be assigned to baseball games themselves only on pain of contradiction, which entails that goodness *cannot* be a characteristic of the games. The goodness of baseball games lies only in the subjective attitudes of persons who respond favorably toward the objective features of the games.

Free will subjectivists believe that "free choice" is like "good baseball game." Our acceptance and rejection of (3) and (4) depend on our changeable, subjective opinions about what factors make our choices "good enough" to make us morally responsible. To ask whether caused choices can be free is to ask whether a choice can be good enough to make us responsible if we theoretically can trace its causes back to the laws of nature and events occurring before the chooser was born (van Inwagen's consequence argument). When we frame the question in this historical perspective, it is very attractive to say "no" to (3). To ask whether an undetermined choice can be free is to frame matters so that we think about the perils of indeterminism, bringing to mind examples of choices that are not under the control of the chooser (the gap argument). When we are impressed that such cases are destructive to freedom, we say "no" to (4).

Nonetheless, there is no reason why we cannot give high marks to caused and uncaused choices. If we focus on the internal rationality of choices, the fact that they are caused seems irrelevant to their freedom (Frankfurt). This is to say "yes" to (3). If we do not demand that free choices be so rigidly connected to what went before, we have no difficulty saying that uncaused choices may be free (Kane). This is to accept (4).

Therefore, we have perfectly good reasons to answer both "yes" and "no" to (3) and (4). The subjectivist concludes from this that the freeness of choices is not a characteristic that exists in the choices. All that the freeness of choices amounts to is the question of how we feel about or *grade* choices. The grades we give do not correspond to a characteristic of the choices themselves, but depend on our opinions and feelings about the actual characteristics of choices. Our opinions and feelings on this score are moved by a disorganized variety of factors that are not dictated by the choices themselves. Instead they involve such subjective factors as our personal histories, our temperaments, philosophical schooling, ideologies, and other idiosyncratic elements.

WHERE SUBJECTIVISM LEADS

If we adopt subjectivism about free will and moral responsibility, we still need to decide whether to *treat* persons as morally responsible for their behavior. (This issue corresponds to the question of which view in normative ethics we should adopt if we accept moral subjectivism.) We might adopt *sheepish subjectivism*, which holds that our expressions of moral responsibility are severely undermined by the fact that there is no truth to the question whether free will and moral responsibility really exist. Sheepish subjectivists shy away from strong attitudes regarding moral responsibility due to their belief that there can be nothing in the nature of the cosmos that dictates that we *ought* to have those attitudes. Thus, sheepish subjectivism sees the attitudinal nature of free will and moral responsibility as reason to give up the strong attitudes the free will realists wish to justify.

On the other hand, we could adopt *strident subjectivism*. Strident subjectivists endorse the institutions of praise, blame, the expression of negative attitudes, and recrimination with full force—despite the fact that they think that free will and moral responsibility are simply matters of subjective attitude. Strident subjectivists say that subjectivism is compatible not only with applying a weak sense of responsibility, but with applying the strongest possible sort that underwrites punishment and blame. After all, there is no logical or moral inconsistency in holding that: (1) the free will problem is just a matter of nontruth-valued attitudes; *and* (2) persons are morally responsible and subject to reactive attitudes in the strongest sense.

Strident subjectivists admit, however, that the sheepish subjectivists—who choose to renounce such feelings because subjectivism is true—also have a legitimate point. Subjectivism's own principles allow subjectivists to be either strident or sheepish. Indeed, one might even vacillate between strident and sheepish subjectivism every other time one thinks about the free will problem. According to subjectivists, the choice is ours.

Misconceptions about the Free Will Problem

Each of the following is a possible confusion about the free will problem. Explain why each is a mistake.

1. Fatalism requires the existence of a great fate-maker who governs our fates.
2. If determinism is true, we do not make choices.
3. If determinism is true, we cannot influence our lives.
4. If determinism is true, there is no point to punishing criminals.
5. Determinists cannot say that some persons have stronger will power than others.
6. Determinism requires that God exists.
7. Determinism requires that God does not exist.
8. Soft determinists believe that only some events are caused.
9. The only way to believe that free will exists is by accepting libertarianism.
10. The only way to deny that free will exists is by accepting hard determinism.
11. Libertarians believe that all our choices are free.
12. We can tell by inspecting our minds (introspection) whether we: (a) have free will, (b) are morally responsible, (c) make uncaused choices.

Guide Questions

1. What connection do philosophers see between free will and moral responsibility? (199–200)
2. What does "moral responsibility" mean? (200)
3. What is the difference between caused and uncaused choices? (200)
4. Which thinkers believe that all human choices are caused? (200)
5. What are the six major free will theories? (201)
6. What are the four questions whose answers distinguish the four major theories? (201)
7. What is the basic libertarian view about free choices? (201–2)

8. How do agent-theory libertarians and event-causation libertarians differ? (202–3)
9. What are basic tenets of hard determinism? (203)
10. Why are soft determinists also labeled "compatibilists"? (204)
11. How did traditional compatibilists such as Hobbes, Locke, and Hume characterize freedom? (205–6) How do contemporary compatibilists such as Frankfurt and Watson characterize freedom? (206–7)
12. How can compatibilists cite the U.S. Constitution to argue for compatibilism? (207)
13. What separates the free-will-either-way theory from the no-free-will-either-way theory? (207–8)
14. What is the basic idea held by free will subjectivists? (208–9)
15. What are the four questions that constitute the free will problem? (209)
16. Which thinkers believe that persons sometimes have free will and moral responsibility? (209)
17. Why is it a mistake to believe that soft determinists think that some events are caused and others are not? (209–10)
18. On what point do the compatibilists and incompatibilists disagree? (210)
19. Which thinkers believe that there is no answer to whether caused or uncaused choices can be free? (210)
20. Who are the free will realists? Who are the free will nonrealists? (210)
21. What is the basic idea behind Fichte's description of determinism? (211)
22. How is fatalism similar to learned helplessness? (211–12)
23. Why does determinism not entail that *we* can accurately predict the future? (212–13)
24. Provide two reasons why some philosophers have thought that "All events are caused" is neither true nor false? (213)
25. What is the point of the example in which the new car will not start? (214)
26. Why do determinists believe that to be an indeterminist is to believe in magic? (214)
27. Explain d'Holbach's motive argument. (215)
28. Explain the determinist's argument from brain science. (216)
29. How do some libertarians such as Kane argue that indeterminism in quantum physics could help us make free choices? What are three objections to this? (216–17)
30. Explain the argument from introspection. (217)
31. What is the most common argument for the existence of moral responsibility? (218)

32. Explain the incompatibilist's analogy between determinism and drug addiction. (220)
33. What is the point of the incompatibilist's example of a determinist waiting to be executed? (220)
34. Explain the point of the compatibilist's example of Jim and Twin Jim. (221–22)
35. Summarize the basic argument given by thinkers such as Hobart and Ayer, who believe that uncaused choices cannot be free. (222)
36. Explain the gap argument. (223–24)
37. Why do subjectivists believe we cannot provide objective answers to the four questions that constitute the free will problem? (225–26)
38. What factors might lead a subjectivist to adopt *sheepish subjectivism*? *Strident subjectivism*? (226–27)

Review Questions for Examinations

1. Define these terms: "moral responsibility," "causal responsibility," "legal responsibility," "free will," "choice," "cause," "determinism," "fatalism," "freedom-enhancing causation," "freedom-destroying causation."
2. Explain these free will theories: libertarianism, hard determinism, soft determinism, free-will-either-way theory, no-free-will-either-way theory, subjectivism, compatibilism, incompatibilism.
3. Why do hard and soft determinists not really need to care whether determinism is true? Why do free-will-either-way theorists, no-free-will-either-way theorists, and subjectivists not care whether determinism is true?
4. Logically speaking, what does it mean to say that one person's *modus ponens* is another person's *modus tollens*?
5. What is the difference between event-causation libertarianism and agent-theory libertarianism?
6. In what way do some libertarians see moral struggles as important to our free will?
7. What are the consequences for morality if one accepts hard determinism?
8. How do compatibilists distinguish between caused choices that are free and caused choices that are unfree?
9. What is the basic reason for accepting compatibilism?
10. How is the no-free-will-either-way theory different from hard determinism?
11. Explain why determinism is different from fatalism.
12. What is the logical connection between determinism and our ability to predict the future?
13. Provide three arguments for determinism. Provide two arguments that all *choices* are caused. How would the indeterminist resist these arguments?

14. Explain how the indeterminist uses quantum physics to argue for libertarianism. Give three objections to using quantum physics to support libertarianism.
15. What is the indeterminist's argument from introspection? What is the weakness in this argument?
16. What are two pragmatic arguments for believing that we are free and morally responsible?
17. Give three arguments to support incompatibilism. What is the compatibilist's reply to all three arguments?
18. Explain the gap argument that uncaused choices cannot be free.
19. Explain the analogy the subjectivist sees between "free choice" and "good baseball game."
20. Explain the difference between *sheepish subjectivism* and *strident subjectivism*.

Discussion Questions

1. Given that there are three types of responsibility—causal, moral, and legal—there can be eight possible combinations in which we are responsible or not responsible. Map out those ways by drawing a tree graph of "yes" and "no" answers and provide an example to illustrate each of the eight ways.
2. Is it easier to tell whether a person is causally, morally, or legally responsible for an action? Explain.
3. Consider the following thought experiment. You are a judge with sole discretion on how to punish a convicted murderer. You know that if you give the murderer the maximum sentence (life in prison), the murderer will become eligible for parole in twenty years, and the probability that she will murder again when released is 0.5. There is another way for you to handle the sentence, however. If you give the murderer a harmless injection, the murderer will never commit murder again and will entirely forget that she committed the murder for which she was convicted. (As the judge in the case, you can discredit the evidence against the murderer, so that no one will believe that she is guilty. Instead, you can make another guilty murderer appear guilty for this crime also.) If you believe in free will realism, which sentence should you prescribe? If you believe in free will nonrealism, which should you prescribe?
4. The libertarian Isaiah Berlin gives the following description of free will:

> I wish my life and decisions to depend on myself, not on external forces of whatever kind. I wish to be the instrument of my own, not of other men's, acts of wills. I wish to be a subject, not an object; to be moved by reasons, by conscious purposes, which are my own, not by causes which affect me, as it were, from outside. . . . I wish, above all, to be conscious of myself as a thinking, willing, active being, bearing re-

> sponsibility for my choices and able to explain them by reference to my own ideas and purposes. (Quoted in Lindley, 1986, 6)

Question: Could the things Berlin wants exist in a determined universe? Give reasons for thinking both "yes" and "no."

5. Consider this argument for fatalism:
   (1) If I am going to die in an auto accident, then since I am going to die, I shall die whether I wear my seat belt or not.
   (2) If I am not going to die in an auto accident, then since I am not going to die, I shall not die whether I wear a seat belt or not.
   (3) Therefore, either way, it does not matter whether I wear a seat belt or not.

   This argument appears to be both valid and sound, but it is not. Can you see what is wrong with it?

6. Suppose that tomorrow a group of the world's most distinguished physicists announced that they have proven that determinism is true for all events in the cosmos. Assume they are correct. (1) Would you conclude that you have never made a *choice*? (2) Would you conclude that you have never made a *free choice*? (3) Would you be dismayed?

7. Evaluate this argument that God's existence requires that all choices are caused:
   (a) Suppose God exists.
   (b) If God exists, then God knows all facts, including the truth or falsity of *S*: "Jones will choose to eat lunch at Burger King on January 2, 2020."
   (c) *S* is either true or false.
   (d) If *S* is true, then God knows *S* is true, and Jones cannot falsify *S* (because that would falsify God's knowledge).
   (e) If *S* is false, then God knows that *S* is false, and Jones cannot make *S* true (because that would falsify God's knowledge).
   (f) Therefore, Jones cannot choose otherwise than God knows he shall choose.
   (g) Therefore, because there is nothing special about Jones' case, no persons can choose otherwise than God knows they shall choose.

8. Evaluate this argument that God's existence requires that some choices are uncaused:
   (a) Suppose God exists.
   (b) If God exists, then God is omniscient, omnipotent, morally perfect, and the creator of all things.
   (c) Suppose that all choices are caused.
   (d) Some choices produce evil in the world.
   (e) Therefore, God is the ultimate cause of some evil in the world.
   (f) Therefore, God is not morally perfect.

(g) Step f contradicts step b.
(h) Therefore, c must be false: at least the choices that cause evil must not be caused; they must be uncaused choices. God is not causally responsible for evil choices.

9. Does having moral principles increase or decrease one's free will? Explain.

FOR FURTHER READING

Dennett, Daniel. 1984. *Elbow Room*. Cambridge, MA: MIT Press. A witty, easy-to-read defense of compatibilism.

Double, Richard. 1991. *The Non-Reality of Free Will*. New York: Oxford University Press. Argues that "free will" is a subjective and contradictory concept. Moderately difficult.

———. 1996. *Metaphilosophy and Free Will*. New York: Oxford University Press. Argues that the free will problem is unsolvable because of the undecidable nature of philosophical argumentation. Moderately difficult.

Honderich, Ted. 1993. *How Free Are You?* Oxford: Oxford University Press. A brief, readable, but erudite argument that we are not as free as we would like to be.

Kane, Robert. 1996. *The Significance of Free Will*. New York: Oxford University Press. A powerful argument for event-causation libertarianism. Moderately difficult.

Seligman, Martin. 1970. *Helplessness: On Depression, Development and Death*. San Francisco: Freeman. A leading psychologist's fascinating account of learned helplessness, the psychological counterpart to fatalism. Easy reading.

Skinner, B. F. 1948. *Walden Two*. New York: Macmillan. A highly entertaining novel by the foremost behavioristic psychologist of all time depicting a hard determinist utopia.

Taylor, Richard. 1974. *Metaphysics*. Englewood Cliffs, NJ: Prentice-Hall. Short, easy-to-read text by a prominent agent-theory libertarian. Good chapters on the free will problem and fatalism.

Waller, Bruce. 1990. *Freedom without Responsibility*. Philadelphia: Temple University Press. Highly readable argument in favor of freedom and against moral responsibility.

Chapter 9
THE EXISTENCE OF GOD

INTRODUCTION

One of the most important metaphysical questions for philosophers and non-philosophers is whether to include a supernatural supreme being (or beings) in our worldview. Regardless of how much science we know or think we know, we cannot have a complete picture of reality until we address this question. As persons, it is our right to ignore the question, or simply to assume we know the answer to it; but we cannot be completely *philosophical* until we address it. This chapter examines reasons for including God in our picture of what exists.

1. Philosophizing about Religion

Philosophy asks critical questions about the assumptions of religion. This is different from *theology*, which is *the noncritical interpretation of religion*. The foremost assumption of most religions is the topic of this chapter—the assumption that gods, or in Western culture, God, exists. Theology works from this standpoint: Given that God exists, how shall we explain the world in terms of God? Philosophy—at least the variety of philosophy that tries to construct the most-likely-to-be-true picture of reality—works from a different standpoint: Given what we know about the world, is it likely that God exists? This difference in approach between theology and philosophy is very distinct.

This philosophical approach is most striking if we pose the question about the existence of God this way. Would we find the various arguments for the existence of God logically persuasive if: (1) We did not already believe in God? or (2) We did not hope that the existence of God would provide some positive benefit for us? If we accept the arguments for the existence of God only because we already believe God exists, then those arguments are not themselves convincing to us. (Remember the discussion of convincingness from chapter 2.) The case is likewise if we accept the arguments only because we *want* to believe in the existence of God. One way to address the issue in a less emotional way is to ask whether the arguments for the existence of God would be logically persuasive in proving the existence of a God or gods of *some religion other than yours*. Posing the question this way provides some emotional distancing about a question that many persons find difficult to consider unemotionally.

Besides not being theology, the philosophy of religion is *neither the psychology of religion nor the sociology of religion*. Psychology and sociology address issues such as the motivation persons feel to adopt theistic belief and the purposes that religions serve in societies. The philosophy of religion is not a variety of armchair social science in which writers speculate on such questions about religion. This is not to deny that thinkers such as Karl Marx (1818–1883), Friedrich Nietzsche (1844–1900), and Jean-Paul Sartre (1905–1980) *have* speculated about the psychology and sociology of religion. Nor is it to deny that such speculations can produce interesting literature. It is to affirm the difference between philosophy and speculative social science.

The confusion of philosophical and psychological approaches to religion is fostered by the ambiguity of the question: (A) "Why does S believe religious assertion *p*?" The *philosophical* interpretation of this question is: (B) "What *evidence* does S have for believing *p*?" The *psychological* interpretation is: (C) "What *factors caused* S to believe *p*?" (B) has to do with *good reasons*, and (C) has to do with *motivating reasons*. Although good evidential reasons for beliefs sometimes constitute our motivating reasons, these concepts are different. For all but an ideally rational agent, there is seldom a perfect fit between the two. Philosophy, as a logical and epistemological discipline, asks questions about good evidence and leaves scientific questions about religion to disciplines better equipped to address them.

2. "God" the Word and God the Entity

The word "God" is a linguistic device that has three letters, a meaning or definition, and is used by speakers to try to refer to an entity (thing) God. This is like the distinction between the word "cats," which has four letters and is "stac" spelled backward, and the real things we refer to by using "cats." Words are devices we *use* to refer to and think about entities—which we usually think exist outside the mind.

Using this terminology we can characterize the three major positions on the existence of God. *Theists* (god-ists), who *believe that God exists*, believe that the word "God" refers to God. *Atheists* (non-god-ists), who *believe that there is no God*, believe that the word "God" does not refer to God. *Agnostics*, who *neither believe that God exists nor believe that there is no God*, do not believe that "God" refers to God *nor* believe that "God" does not refer to God. Defined as persons who believe neither in theism nor atheism, there are relatively few agnostics: infants, persons who have thought deeply about the existence of God and are entirely undecided, and those who have never thought about the issue at all or who are otherwise indifferent to it. This is a better description of the agnostic than saying that an agnostic does not *know* whether God exists, because theists and atheists do not know whether God exists.

"God," which is both ambiguous and vague, needs careful definition. A term is ambiguous when there is more than one distinct meaning commonly assigned to it. "Club" is ambiguous, because it means both "a sturdy piece of wood" and "a social organization." "God" is ambiguous because many persons have different ideas (definitions, meanings) of "God." Here are some that philosophers have used: "the LORD of the Old Testament," "the totality of things that exist," "ultimate caring," and "the Being than which None Greater can be Conceived."

A definition is vague if it cites characteristics that are imprecise or fuzzy. For example, many definitions say that God is eternal, but does this mean that God always has and always will exist in time or that God exists *outside* time altogether? Many definitions say that God is all-powerful, but does this include the power to perform logically contradictory tasks such as making $2 + 2 = 5$ or making a chair exist at the same place and time that it does not exist? Many definitions say that God is morally perfect, but it is unclear exactly what moral perfection is. To the extent that a defining characteristic of "God" is vague, the whole definition is vague.

In selecting a definition of "God" to use in this chapter, I am guided by two considerations. First, what definition of "God" is closest to the views held by the historically dominant theologians in Western culture? Because Judeo-Christian conceptions are the most common ones in the West, they will serve as the basis of our definition. Second, what definition of "God" is closest to those used by the Western philosophers who are best known for their proofs of God's existence—thinkers such as St. Augustine, St. Anselm, and St. Thomas Aquinas. These two questions are related—as is suggested by the fact that Augustine, Anselm, and Aquinas achieved sainthood in Christianity. These three were important philosophers and major figures in shaping Western theology. The definition I offer derives from both philosophical argumentation and traditional Christian theological thinking.

I define "God" as: "A being that is *omniscient* (all-knowing), *omnipotent* (all-powerful), morally perfect, the creator of all things, who has psychological states such as concern for His creations, but is not a human being—because God is nonphysical, that is, exists outside the natural world of space and time." There are other characteristics that are sometimes listed, such as being *immutable* (*unchanging*), having necessary existence, and being perfect in every way, but the first list of characteristics will suffice for our purposes.

This philosophical/theological definition of "God" is highly abstract. It lacks the detailed characteristics that are gotten from particular religious doctrines. In particular, this abstract definition is not one that we would derive from a *literal* (*word-by-word, fundamentalist*) *interpretation* of any major religious text. Augustine's recommendation 1,600 years ago, which was widely accepted by Christianity, was that religious texts need to be interpreted figuratively, rather than read literally. If we want to provide a more detailed picture of God, we must add to the basic definition details from a specific theology.

3. Ways to Argue for the Existence of God

By defining "God" in abstract terms, philosophers set the stage for the sort of arguments they will use to prove the existence of God. Because "God" is defined as nonphysical, there will be no possibility of direct observation of God—the nonphysical cannot be sensed, although the nonphysical may have *physical effects* that are sensed. For the same reason, atheists cannot argue from the premise that we cannot observe God to the conclusion that God does not exist. One should not expect to be able to observe a nonphysical being.

Once we get through some poor arguments for the existence of God based on simple logical confusions, we will see that there are three main types of philosophical arguments for the existence of God. The first type counts the hope that God exists as a reason for believing that God exists. The second type postulates the existence of God as the best explanation for observed facts about the world. These arguments try to prove the existence of God by using inference to the best explanation. These are *a posteriori arguments*, because they *rely on a premise that is justified by collecting evidence about the world*. I call such arguments for the existence of God "quasi-scientific hypotheses." Like scientific hypotheses, they postulate the existence of an unobserved entity to explain a fact that we think we know. Unlike scientific hypotheses, the entity they postulate is nonnatural—not located in space and time. Quasi-scientific hypotheses include everything from the traditional first cause and design arguments to arguments based on miracles and religious experience. The third type of argument tries to prove the existence of God by pure logic without using as premises any facts about the world. Such an argument is a priori, because none of its premises are justified by collecting evidence about the world. The ontological argument from Anselm is the most famous a priori argument for the existence of God.

4. Fallacies of Relevance

As we saw in chapter 2, not every argument with a true conclusion is a good argument. The arguments: (a) "Snow is white. Therefore, God exists." and (b) "Snow is white. Therefore, God does not exist." are both *terrible* arguments, despite the fact that one of their conclusions must be true. The argument "Continental drift occurred, because my five-year-old brother says it did" is a poor argument *for* the existence of continental drift, even though continental drift did occur and even if your brother tells you it did. Debate in all areas of philosophy, including the existence of God, is loaded with poor arguments for true conclusions. Remember: *Showing that an argument for X is weak is not the same thing as showing that X does not exist.* If it were—then because there can be poor arguments for the existence of God *and* poor arguments for the nonexistence of God as noted above—we could prove both that God does *not* exist and that God *does* exist.

Here are three attempts to argue for the existence of God that exemplify *fallacies of relevance* (*invalid arguments whose premises are irrelevant to establishing their conclusions*). An example of *the fallacy of popular belief* takes this form: "Many societies believe God exists. Therefore, God exists." This is a fallacy, because even if the premise is true, it provides no evidence for the conclusion. A logical analogy demonstrating its invalidity could be given by filling in its argument form with sentences that make the premise true and the conclusion false: "Many societies believe ______________. Therefore, ______________."

An example of *the fallacy of lack of proof to the contrary* takes this form: "One cannot disprove the existence of God. Therefore, God exists." Again, the truth of this premise is irrelevant to proving the truth of the conclusion. A logical analogy to demonstrate this could be made by filling in this form: "One cannot prove that NOT (______________). Therefore, (______________)."

A third fallacy of relevance that has no established name takes this form: "I'll believe any old thing I want to believe—it's my right. If I want to believe God exists, who are you to try to stop me?" This is confused, because no one denies persons *the right* to hold whatever metaphysical beliefs they wish. The problem is that wanting to believe a statement provides no evidence for thinking that it is true. For example, it is also one's right to believe that Cuba is in the Mediterranean Sea and that Coca-Cola is one of the items listed in the periodic table of elements, but having the right to hold a belief does not constitute evidence that the belief is true.

FAITH-BASED ARGUMENTS FOR THE EXISTENCE OF GOD

5. Wishful Thinking

The most straightforward argument based on faith maintains that God exists because we have faith that God exists. "Faith," as defined in chapter 1, is a term we use to express our *hope* that a statement is true when we have no *evidence* that it is true. ("What evidence do you have that the Phillies will win the World Series next year?" "None. But I have faith.") By definition, therefore, faith does not provide evidence for any conclusion. If your reason for believing that God exists is simply that you have faith, you have no evidence that God exists. I can just as well reply to you that God does *not* exist, because I have faith that there is no God. So, faith in *A* provides exactly as much evidence for *A* as faith in *not-A* provides for *not-A*: None. If you have *both* faith *and* evidence for your belief, then you need to present your evidence. Faith by itself is not evidence.

6. Textual Proof

Some theists say that the god or gods of their religion can be shown to exist, because their preferred religious texts describe their god or gods. This is sometimes called the "argument from textual proof." There are three variations of this view: (1) Theists may believe that God exists *simply* because the text says so. I call this the "pure faith interpretation." (2) Theists may take the religious text to be a history book that recounts the occurrences of a supernatural being. I call this the "religious-text-as-a-history-book interpretation." (3) Theists may take the religious text as providing evidence for the existence of God by presenting information that can be explained only by assuming that God exists. I call this the "inference to the best explanation interpretation." There are powerful objections to each version of the argument.

The objection to the pure faith interpretation is straightforward. Consider the concept "representational device," which was introduced in chapter 6. A *representational device* is *anything that we use to claim that something else is a certain way*. Representational devices include paintings, photographs, sentences written on chalkboards, newspaper advertisements, spoken statements, blueprints for buildings, and books. The thing to notice about a representational device is that the device is one thing and what it tries to represent is another. So there are always two possibilities: the representational device *accurately represents* what it tries to represent or the representational device is *inaccurate*.

Next, consider what I call "the problem of representation." The *problem of representation* is that *we can never tell solely from examining a representational device whether what it says is true or not*. So, for example, we can never tell by simply looking at an advertisement whether what it says about the product is true. We can illustrate this point with an experiment: Write the sentence "There are 45 chairs in this room" on the chalkboard, and peer at it as carefully as you can. See if you can tell whether that statement is true or false simply by looking at the statement and not looking to the room to determine its truth. Obviously, we cannot. Now extend the principle to texts: If we think that we can *ever* take *any* text as evidence for X *simply because it says X*, we run afoul of the problem of representation. This includes religious texts. Therefore, taking a religious text to show that God exists simply because it *says* God exists provides no evidence for the existence of God.

There are other difficulties with the pure faith version of the textual proof argument. If we adopt it, we would be logically committed to believing in the gods of all religions—not only the gods of the major religions, but those of all the innumerable minor religions with and without religious texts. (Why give preferential treatment to religions with written texts?) Worse, we would have to believe in logical contradictions, because some religions, like Judaism, are monotheistic (believe in one god), others, like Hinduism, are polytheistic (believe in more than one god), and still others, like Buddhism, are atheistic.

In the second version of the textual proof argument, advocates accept a religious text's claims not simply because the text makes them, but because they treat the religious text as a history book. Just as Western civilization texts describe Alexander the Great, so *Genesis* describes God. The trouble with this approach is that religious texts—though sometimes mentioning historical events in the *natural world*—cannot be taken as recording the history of the *supernatural*. The reason is that genuine history books do not record the supernatural; the supernatural explanations of historical events require an interpretation of the historical facts that goes beyond the realm of the historian. For example, history books tell us that Mohammed fasted a great deal, but they do not say that he communicated with God. The latter may be true, but even if it is, it is an interpretation that goes beyond the publicly observable facts that are the domain of the historian.

The third version of the argument—the inference to the best explanation version—claims that some data found in religious texts can be best explained by supposing that the humans who compiled the text received direct communications from God. For example, if a religious text accurately predicted congressional election results that occur in 2000 A.D., one might be tempted to say that this proves the existence of God—because there is no way this prediction could get into the text except by divine communication. The problem with this way of using religious texts to argue for the existence of God is that there are no predictions in religious texts that are specific enough to require a supernatural explanation. Some things predicted by religious texts (there will be wars, famines, plagues, and the rise and fall of nations) could be predicted by persons without divine communication. Moreover, in trying to find such data, we must be very careful about compiling presence/absence tables, as discussed in chapter 2, before concluding that there are any data that need to be explained. Otherwise we are like the readers of the supermarket tabloids who think that psychics have an uncanny ability to foresee the future when in fact they make *many* predictions each year, only a few of which turn out to be accurate.

These criticisms may not impress advocates of the textual proof argument if they are already convinced that their favorite text is accurate. Notice, however, that if an argument is attractive to us only because we *already* accept its conclusion, then the argument itself is not doing any logical work for us. We would be mistaking the fact that we already accept the conclusion for a reason for thinking the argument designed to *prove* the conclusion is a good one. In the terminology of chapter 2, such an argument is not *convincing*. As noted above, "Snow is white. Therefore, God exists" is not a good argument, even if its conclusion is true.

7. Pascal's Wager

Pascal's Wager was provided by Blaise Pascal (1623–1662), the French mathematician, scientist, and religious writer after whom the computer language Pascal was named. According to Pascal, although we cannot intellectually determine whether God exists, we can construct a persuasive argument regarding God's existence:

> If there is a God, He is infinitely incomprehensible, since, being undivided and without limits, He bears no relation to us. We are, therefore, incapable of knowing either what He is, or whether He exists. . . .
>
> "Either God is, or He is not." But which side shall we take? Reason can decide nothing here. . . . Yes, but you must bet. . . . Since you must choose, let us see which will profit you less. You have two things to lose: truth and good, and two things to stake: your reason and your will, your knowledge and your happiness. And your nature has two things to avoid: error and misery. . . . Let us weigh the gain and loss in calling heads, that God exists. . . .[I]f you win, you win everything; if you lose, you lose nothing. Do not hesitate, then; gamble on His existence. (1961, 156–57)

Pascal's Wager is an example of *cost-benefit analysis* in which we add the pluses and minuses of believing in God and weigh them against the pluses and minuses of not believing in God. I illustrate this with a presence/absence table:

		Metaphysical Possibilities		
		God Exists	Not(God Exists)	Sum
CHOICES	Believe God exists (Theism)	(1) True belief Infinite happiness gain	(2) False belief Zero happiness gain	Infinite happiness gain
	Not (believe God exists) (Agnosticism or Atheism)	(3) False belief Zero happiness gain	(4) True belief Zero happiness gain	Zero happiness gain

According to these values, the theistic choice has a better payoff than the nontheistic option. Note that atheists and agnostics are assigned the same values, inasmuch as Pascal thinks they both lose out on the rewards gained by believing in God. In the Wager, Pascal says that agnostics and atheists lose the reward of eternal bliss, but he does not explicitly say that they will suffer eternal damnation. If we were to enter this premise into the Wager, then the value assigned to position 3 would be even worse: Infinite gain in unhappiness. But that premise is not necessary for the Wager to look impressive: Whether we assign a negative value to position 3 or not, the Wager seems a good bet. If the possible payoff for believing in the existence of God is eternal bliss, then, mathematically, the possibility of infinite gain would make theism very attractive, irrespective of whether disbelief yields only a zero amount of happiness (extinction upon death) or great suffering (eternal damnation). Nonetheless, there are problems with Pascal's Wager.

First, religious persons might wonder whether the Wager's cost-benefit analysis—its calculation of what's-in-it-for-me—displays a suitably religious attitude. Second, one might object to Pascal's happiness value assignments. Some libertines may feel that theism has a considerable negative value that Pascal ignores, namely, the cost of surrendering their irreligious lifestyles if they elect to become believers. (Of course, Pascal could reply that even a slight loss in carnal pleasures on Earth is insignificant compared to eternal bliss in an afterlife.)

Third, Pascal's Wager emphasizes consequences in terms of our *happiness*, but discounts the value we may place on being good epistemic agents, as discussed in chapter 3. Pascal thinks that from a purely intellectual standpoint the best thing to do is to suspend judgment on God's existence. I go even further: From an epistemological perspective, *denying* the existence of God is an even better strategy than *suspending belief*. It is not a wise epistemic strategy to suspend belief about the existence of entities for which we have no positive evidence. Philosophers typically place great value on believing only propositions for which there is sufficient evidence. If suspension of belief (agnosticism) or disbelief in the existence of God (atheism) are stronger epistemic positions, then philosophically minded persons should count that fact, not ignore it.

Fourth, Pascal's Wager works only if we supply a specific interpretation of the mind of God to arrive at Pascal's numbers. On Pascal's view, believers receive infinite rewards (provided they do the other things required of them by Christianity) and atheists and agnostics do not. But how does Pascal know that *the God that really exists*—assuming God exists—has adopted that reward policy? Perhaps God rewards atheists and agnostics for carefully withholding belief, but *punishes* theists who believe without evidence! Maybe God is really a God-of-the-Epistemologists, who does not want us to believe on faith, rather than Pascal's God. In this case, it would be better cost-benefit analysis to *not believe* in the existence of God.

This leads to a fifth objection. Given the large number of gods adopted by the thousands of humanity's religions, how do we know which one to bet on, even if we assume that the God who exists will reward belief in the way Pascal says? If we bet on the wrong one, and the real God is jealous, we risk antagonizing the real god. Perhaps a more prudent strategy would be to suspend judgment on *any* specific god to avoid making the one (or ones) that exist angry?

Sixth, as Pascal noted, the Wager provides no evidence for the existence of God. Its conclusion is not that God exists, but rather that it is prudent to believe in God, *despite our lack of evidence.* So Pascal's Wager is not really an argument for the existence of God. Seventh, as Pascal also realized, belief is not as easily turned on as a faucet. Just try to believe that the textbook that you are reading right now is a 2,000-pound elephant. Even if we want to follow Pascal's reasoning for the sake of gaining the reward, if we do not already believe in the existence of God, we will not find it easy to start to believe.

8. James's Will to Believe

The American pragmatist philosopher William James claims that our interests as practical human beings should play a decisive role in the philosophical theories we adopt. In the free will problem James thinks that we should believe in libertarianism if it is important to us and we have no definite proof that it is false. The case is similar with the existence of God. James reasons that if believing in God is important to us, then we may believe that God exists, despite the fact that we have no evidence for God's existence.

Here is how James expresses his "Will to Believe" argument:

> *Our passional nature not only lawfully may, but must, decide an option between propositions, whenever it is a genuine option that cannot be decided on intellectual grounds: for to say, under such circumstances, "Do not decide, but leave the question open," is itself a passional decision—just like deciding yes or no—and is attended with the same risk of losing the truth. . . .* We see, first, that religion offers itself as a *momentous* option. We are supposed to gain, even now, by our belief, and to lose by our non-belief, a certain vital good. Secondly, religion is a *forced* option, so far as that good goes. We cannot escape the issue by remaining skeptical and waiting for more light, because although we do avoid error in that way *if religion be untrue*, we lose the good *if it be true*, just as certainly as if we positively chose to disbelieve. . . . To preach scepticism to us as a duty until "sufficient evidence" for religion be found, is tantamount therefore to telling us, when in the presence of the religious hypothesis, that to yield to our fear of its being error is wiser and better than to yield to our hope that it may be true. (Cited in Kahane, 1983, 18)

I analyze James's argument this way:

(1) Whenever we have a choice of whether to believe X and (a) the truth of X can be neither proved nor disproved, (b) the choice is *momentous* (very important) to us, and (c) the choice is *forced* (to delay making a choice is to lose out on the benefits of making a positive choice), then it is rational to decide to believe in X.
(2) Belief in God, at least for some persons, satisfies (a), (b), and (c).
(3) Therefore, at least for some persons, it is rational to decide to believe in God.

I mention quickly some of the objections to Pascal's Wager that also apply to James's argument. First, religious persons might wonder whether James's reasoning is sufficiently reverent. Second, James, like Pascal, puts human happiness over the epistemic goal of avoiding believing in things without sufficient evidence. Some persons may prefer to be good epistemic agents rather than to go with their passions. Third, James's argument will work equally well for any conception of God: Greek gods, Native American gods, Allah, and so on. James gives no way to select among them. Fourth, as with Pascal's Wager, the Will to Believe provides no evidence, but at best suggests a shrewd belief strategy.

James's argument has its own problems. First, James's argument displays more bluster than logic. James divides persons into two types: those who most want to believe truths, and those who most want to avoid falsehoods. James tries to persuade us to accept his argument by portraying the former persons as brave and admirable, and the latter as wimpy and whiney. But James's dichotomy is too simple. Good epistemic agents must have elements of *each* personality. If we care only about maximizing the number of true beliefs we hold, we could do so by believing everything we are ever told. But that is being *gullible*. If we care only about avoiding falsehoods, we could accomplish this by believing nothing. But this would bring action to a halt. So, we must try to strike a balance between the conflicting aims of maximizing true beliefs and minimizing false beliefs. Trying to figure out the most desirable ratio of true beliefs to false beliefs strikes me as an unanswerable evaluative issue: Is one true belief worth exactly one false belief? Is the ratio 1:2, 2:1, or so on? James's suggestion that theists have more gusto than his opponents clouds a thorny issue.

The second problem arises if we take James's reasoning to its logical conclusion. As noted, James restricts his Will to Believe argument to apply only to cases when the belief at stake cannot be refuted. But according to James's own reasoning, why should he place this restriction on his argument? From a purely epistemic viewpoint, the best strategy seems to be to deny that entities exist unless there is at least more than 50 percent positive evidence for them. After all, we do not believe that invisible gremlins exist simply because we cannot *prove* that there are none. The burden of proof is always on the side that says that an entity exists. Therefore, if James says that we may believe in God without any positive evidence, he is placing our desires over our epistemic competence. But if he does this, then, perhaps he should say that we may believe in entities *no matter how much evidence there is against their existence*. But if James were to admit this, then the Will to Believe reduces itself to absurdity. It would give too much license to engage in wishful thinking and should be rejected.

A POSTERIORI ARGUMENTS FOR THE EXISTENCE OF GOD

Several arguments conclude that the existence of God is the *best explanation* for facts and presumed facts: that morality is objective, that miracles occur, that we have certain religious experiences, that events are happening in the universe, that the universe exists at all, and that there is order in the natural world. In these examples of inference to the best explanation, the postulation of God is a *quasi-scientific hypothesis*: *the hypothesizing of a supernatural (nonphysical) being to explain something in the physical world*. This is different than a *scientific hypothesis, the hypothesizing of a natural (physical) being to explain some thing in the physical world*. The arguments in this section treat the existence of God as a quasi-scientific hypothesis.

9. Moral Arguments

Moral arguments use premises concerning morality to argue for God's existence. The *moral objectivism version* is this:

(1) There exists an objective difference between right and wrong actions.
(2) Only God could create the objective difference between right and wrong actions.
(3) Therefore, God exists.

Both premises can be resisted. Regarding the first premise, as we saw in chapter 7, moral objectivism is debatable. It is difficult to understand what it means to say that the difference between right and wrong lies objectively outside human moral sentiments. Regarding the second premise, also as noted in chapter 7, the idea that God could *create* the difference between right and wrong (as opposed to God's making it prudent for us to act in certain ways) is difficult to understand. Theists could reply by saying that they have faith in premises (1) and (2), but this would only illustrate that this version of the moral argument is nothing more than wishful thinking.

A second version of the moral argument—the *"precondition of morality"* argument—was given by Kant:

(1) Only belief in God—who is assumed to reward moral behavior in an afterlife—will motivate human beings to live morally.
(2) Therefore, we need to postulate the existence of God as a precondition of moral life.

Here are three problems with this version of the moral argument. First, its premise may be true for some persons, but it is false for others. Human beings have acted morally long before religions existed, and long before the rise of fairly recent monotheistic religions such as Judaism, Christianity, and Islam. Although religion has had morally beneficial effects in human history, it has also had morally harmful effects: the Crusades, the Inquisition, the burning of "witches," and innumerable other holy wars and religious persecutions. Atheists and agnostics, as well as theists, have been both moral paragons and moral villains. So religion and morality do not always correspond.

Second, suppose it *were* true that a significant number of persons need to postulate the existence of God to live morally. This might not be a compelling reason to believe in God even for those persons. We can sensibly ask whether we should postulate the existence of God on *moral* grounds if we do not have sufficient *epistemological* grounds for the postulation. This is similar to an earlier objection to Pascal's and James's arguments: Even if it is wise from the perspective of maximizing one's happiness to bet on the existence of God, perhaps as thoughtful persons we should prefer to believe that entities exist only if we have evidence that makes them more likely to exist than not. Even if morality needs to assume the existence of God, perhaps—all things considered—we should go with our best epistemic efforts.

Third, Kant's version of the moral argument, like Pascal's Wager and James's Will to Believe argument, does not conclude that God exists, but that we ought to *believe* that God exists. Kant understood that his argument is not evidence for the existence of God. Indeed, Kant is famous for his arguments that the existence of God cannot be proved. So Kant's version of the moral argument is not an argument for the existence of God in the way that the following arguments in this chapter are.

10. Miracles

The argument from miracles cites remarkable events as evidence for believing that God exists as the cause of them. Some of the miracles cited come from various religions: the burning bush that was not consumed in Genesis, Jesus' turning water into wine in the *New Testament*, or religious persons bleeding from their wrists and heads on Good Friday (the stigmata). Other examples include events from everyday life: persons surviving falls from airplanes in flight or inexplicably recovering from life-threatening illnesses.

To address the miracles argument we need to choose between two definitions of "miracle." If we define "miracle" as "an unusual event caused by God," then if we accept the premise that a miracle occurred, we would have to accept the existence of God. The argument would look like this:

(1) Miracle M happened.
(2) By definition, all miracles are caused by God.
(3) Therefore, God exists.

If we use this definition of "miracle," then the critics of the miracles argument will reject the first premise. Just because we acknowledge that something unusual happened, we would have no conclusive reason to believe that it was a miracle in the sense that it was *caused by God*. This suggests that it would be better to adopt a more neutral definition: "miracle" means "a highly unusual event," without including in the definition the claim that miracles are caused by God. Using this definition will permit critics to agree that some remarkable events occur without thereby having to concede that God exists. The debate now will be over whether those events were caused by God. Using the second definition of "miracle," the advocate of the miracle argument needs to offer the argument as an inference to the best explanation:

Data:	Some highly unusual events occurred.
	↑
Best explanation:	God caused them.

Some persons think that any highly unusual event—such as a terrible automobile accident where a passenger is unhurt—requires an explanation by citing God. To think that such "coincidence-miracles" (Cornman, Lehrer, and Pappas, 1987, ch. 5) require an explanation citing God misunderstands probability. In the natural world, events that are barely possible in the short run are certain to happen eventually. This is what it *means* to say that an event is improbable, but possible. Such events do not require explanations citing divine agency, but only the relevant physical factors that establish their degree of probability. Otherwise we would need to invoke the supernatural all over the place—to explain why long shots win at the race track and baseball pitchers sometimes throw no-hitters. What *might* require a supernatural explanation is what Cornman, Lehrer, and Pappas call a "violation-miracle"—an event that violates a law of nature. If an event breaks a physical law, then perhaps the best explanation is that God caused the event.

There are several difficulties with reports that violation-miracles occur. First, reports of violation-miracles are often explainable in psychological terms: The subjects were psychologically primed to "see" things that did not occur, the subjects misperceived what they did see, the subjects hallucinated due to fasting, drugs, and fatigue, the subjects purposely lied about what they saw, or the reports were embellished after the fact by other persons who relayed the reports. Second, we have no reliable scientific evidence that any event has ever violated a law of nature. There are no violation-miracles that can be documented by being repeated under controlled conditions. Third, a general challenge offered by Hume goes this way: A reported miracle is either a genuine violation of a natural law or it is not. On the one hand, if the reported miracle *is not*, it can be naturalistically explained and provides no evidence that God exists. (Perhaps we were incorrect about what we *thought* was a law of nature and we now have to revise our view of what the law is.) On the other hand, if the reported miracle *is* a violation of natural laws, then

> as a firm and unalterable experience has established these laws, the proof against a miracle, from the very nature of the fact, is as entire as any argument from experience can possibly be imagined. . . . The plain consequence is . . . that no testimony is sufficient to establish a miracle unless the testimony be of such a kind that its falsehood would be more miraculous than the fact which it endeavors to establish. (Hume, 1955, 122–23)

In other words, if we claim that a violation miracle has occurred, we must face the challenge that it is always more reasonable to conclude that *we* are mistaken than to conclude that our testimony is strong enough to show that a law of nature has been violated. Although we might be wise to accept this challenge if violation miracles were documented and our perceptual abilities were more reliable than they are, given what we know about the world and ourselves, we are unwise to accept the challenge.

Most of us vaguely acknowledge Hume's point by being skeptical of the miracles of other religions. Although some theists are willing to accept the testimony of violation miracles designed to prove the existence of *their* gods, few accept the violation miracles that are offered to prove the existence of the gods of *other* religions. Why should the violation miracles of our religions be acceptable and those of other religions be mere superstitions? It seems that the argument from miracles shows bias in favor of our own religions.

11. Religious Experience

"Religious experience" is ambiguous in the same way that "miracle" is. "Religious experience" might mean: (1) "a direct experience of a religious entity." "Religious experience" might also mean: (2) "an experience that someone *takes to be* of a religious entity." If we use the first definition, then it will validly follow from the premise that someone has a religious experience that God exists:

(1) Person P has religious experience R.
(2) By definition, anyone who has a religious experience has a direct experience of God.
(3) Therefore, person P has a direct experience of God.

If we elect to use definition (2), the advocate of the experience argument will need to use inference to the best explanation:

Data: Person P has religious experience R (P *takes* R to be of God).

↑

Best explanation: Person P has a direct experience of the existence of God.

If we use definition (1), then critics of the argument will object that we have no reason to believe that persons have religious experiences in that defined sense, that is, of directly experiencing God. If we use definition (2), critics of the argument will say that although persons *do* have religious experiences, the experiences do not prove the existence of God, because they are better explained by natural causes. From a logical point of view, the difference in definitions does not help one side or the other. But using the second definition avoids the confusion of thinking that belief in God is justified *simply because* someone has a certain experience. So I shall use the second definition of "religious experience" and the corresponding inference to best explanation form of the argument.

Some examples of religious experiences include hearing what seems to be the voice of God, seeing religious visions, and having feelings of oneness with God when one looks at the stars. Such experiences often are highly persuasive to the subjects who have them, but two questions arise: (1) Should *the subjects themselves* take their religious experiences as evidence for the existence of God? (2) Should *other persons* who learn of subjects' religious experiences take them as evidence for the existence of God? Even if an experience provides evidence for the person who has it, that person's report to another person who does not have the experience might not serve as evidence to the other person. In my view, the important question is whether religious experiences provide evidence for the existence of God *even for those persons who have them*. I shall examine two ways one might think religious experience shows the existence of God.

Some persons who like the argument from religious experience are *mystics* who *deny that we should even use the rationalist approach of asking what the best explanation of their religious experiences might be*. According to mystics, it does not *matter* if there are competing explanations of religious experiences besides saying that one has experienced God. There is something about religious experience that is unique and "self-validating" (proves itself to be true). If you have it, then you know that you are experiencing God, and there is no room for question. This point of view is sometimes expressed in the cliche, "If you have to ask, you'll never know."

The mystical position cannot withstand scrutiny. If we distinguish between *subjective* (existing in us) *issues* and *objective* (existing outside us) *issues*, as we did in chapter 4, we see that subjective feelings or beliefs cannot guarantee that the corresponding objective belief is true. My thinking I see an apple does not guarantee that I am seeing an apple, no matter how psychologically certain I am. Likewise, believing that Sally loves me does not guarantee that she does. Mystics, it turns out, are not interested in the theory of knowledge. They want us to assume that subjective experiences prove objective facts simply due to the *internal quality of the experience*, without questioning whether the experience can have that internal quality without coming from God.

Nonmystical defenders of the argument from religious experience *are* willing to enter the debate with critics over whether their religious experience justifies belief in God. Some nonmystics adopt a *burden-of-proof strategy*. Although religious experiences are not self-validating, they give evidence according to this principle: "If one person says *X*, then other persons should believe *X* unless there is a good reason to reject the claim." So, although my saying that the apple is green is not self-validating, other persons should accept my word simply because I said it—provided there are no reasons to think I am lying or colorblind. The nonmystic says that religious experience has just as much credibility as claims about physical objects or claims about the past based on our memories.

Trying to put the burden of proof on the critic of the religious experience argument is a clever maneuver by the advocate, but critics should refuse the burden for two reasons. First, if we accept the burden-of-proof argument, then logically we have to accept the existence of every religious entity that anyone claimed to have experience of: Hindu deities, Roman gods, and the gods of primitive religions. But if the monotheistic religions such as Judaism, Christianity, and Islam are correct, then these other gods do not exist. So using the burden-of-proof argument would lead to endorsing the existence of other gods, which the monotheistic religions deny exist. This means that only polytheists could use the burden-of-proof argument.

Second, the burden-of-proof argument is a poor strategy for building a most-likely-to-be-true picture of the world. If we accept testimony whenever we cannot show good reason to reject it, we will overpopulate our worldview with all sorts of zany entities from Bigfoot to the Loch Ness monster to every variety of space alien. If one replies that there *is* good reason to reject the testimony of persons who claim to experience these things—namely that we have no evidence that they exist except the testimony—then critics of the religious experience argument will say that the same applies to claims to experience God. Therefore, if we are interested in painting the most-likely-to-be-true picture of the world, we should not use either the mystical or nonmystical versions of the argument from religious experience. Anyone is welcome to decide that the role of philosophy is to support religion, and accordingly to endorse the argument from religious experience because it is helpful for religious purposes. This leads to the question that we addressed in chapter 1: What do we think philosophy is *for*?

If we think that philosophy is for devising the most-likely-to-be-true answers to philosophical questions, then the theistic explanation of religious experiences must compete with natural (mostly psychological) explanations before we can accept the argument. This means that other factors need to be considered: First, many religious experiences have come to persons who are under extreme psychological strain: those who have fasted, experienced sensory deprivation, had life-threatening dangers or other psychological traumas, and consumed various drugs and hallucinogens. Second and similar to the first, one can intentionally bring about religious experiences by ingesting drugs, by going into meditative trances, and by praying. Near-death experiences, which many persons consider religious, can be brought about in the laboratory by injecting subjects with curare, a chemical South American natives use on their poison darts. Third, religious experiences are relative to one's own religion—we have experiences of the deities in our own religions, not others, whereas persons from other religions have experiences in their religions, not ours. This suggests that religious experiences depend on learning, which makes their explanation in psychological terms more likely. These points do not show that those who have religious experiences do not experience their gods, but along with the first two objections, they suggest that natural explanations of religious experiences strongly compete with theistic explanations.

12. The First Cause Argument

In just a few pages in his thirteenth-century masterpiece, *Summa Theologica*, St. Thomas Aquinas (1225–1274) produced five famous arguments for the existence of God, known as "The Five Ways." The *first cause argument* is Thomas's Second Way:

> In the world of sensible things we find there is an order of efficient causes. There is no case . . . in which a thing is found to be the efficient cause of itself; for so it would be prior to itself, which is impossible. Now in efficient causes it is not possible to go on to infinity because . . . if in efficient causes it is possible to go on to infinity, there will be no first efficient cause, neither will there be an ultimate effect . . . which is plainly false. Therefore, it is necessary to admit a first efficient cause, to which everyone gives the name of God. (1948, 25–26)

The most natural interpretation of this argument is this:

(1) There are events that occur now in the natural world.
(2) Every event in the natural world requires a cause other than itself. [Every event has a cause, and nothing can cause itself, for that would require it to exist before it exists.]
(3) Therefore, there must be a series of causes tracing backward into the past (from 1 and 2)
(4) It is impossible for a series of causes to go backward in time infinitely. [If there is no *first* cause, then there could be no *second* cause, and so on. Thus, the events that occur in the natural world today would not occur.]
(5) Therefore, there must have been a first cause of the events occurring now in the natural world.
(6) This first cause is God.

The first cause argument relies on the same intuition as do some other arguments for the existence of God. Aquinas's First Way—the *argument from motion*—argues that the motion we observe today must be traceable to an initial motion originator. This idea of an Unmoved Mover had been given by Aristotle 1,600 years earlier. The same sort of premise is also at work when we emphasize not *events* or *motion*, but matter or matter/energy. Surely, many persons think, the physical material of the universe must "have come from something"—it could not have *always* been there. I call this argument the "matter-must-have-come-from-somewhere argument" or the "matter argument." Arguments of this type can seem very persuasive. Because they all rest on the basic idea that "everything must have come from something," if we discredit the first cause argument, we discredit the motion and matter arguments also.

CRITICISMS OF THE FIRST CAUSE ARGUMENT

First, the argument involves a commitment to *determinism*—the view that every event has a cause, or at least that every event in the natural world has a cause. If we accept the physical possibility that some events in the natural world might be uncaused (not caused by themselves, but without causes altogether), then we reject step two and stop the argument from getting started.

Second, step four's claim that it is impossible that an infinite series of causes goes backward in time is doubtful. A series of causes going backward infinitely would simply be a series in which, no matter how far back you trace the series, that event has a cause. This idea is not odd if we consider a series of integers. By starting with any whole number and counting backward by subtracting one, there will never be a smallest number beyond which we cannot count. The idea that the series of natural events that we observe today should trace back without beginning is actually a *logical consequence* of believing in determinism: If we believe in determinism, then we should conclude that the series of causes *has* to go backward infinitely. Unless some qualification is provided—such as one stating that all natural events have causes, but supernatural events do not—it is logically inconsistent to claim both that determinism is true *and* that there must have been a first cause. So, as given above, the first cause argument literally contradicts itself.

Third, the premise that a series of events cannot go backward infinitely in time seems to violate *the Principle of Conservation of Energy/Mass*, which says that *energy (and mass) can neither be created nor destroyed, but only changed in form.* If the Conservation Principle is true, then given any state of the *cosmos* (*universe*) where energy exists, we can infer that into the future *and* into the past *there must be* states where energy exists. An infinite series of events is thereby ensured.

Defenders of the first cause argument might admit that they do not really believe in determinism or the Conservation Principle, because they think that *there has to be* a first cause that is an exception to determinism and conservation. Instead, they might think that determinism and conservation are *mostly* true, but that they cannot be true for all events, because the idea of an infinite series of physical causes strikes them as incomprehensible. Common sense seems to support the defenders of the first cause argument on this point, because most persons hold a simplistic model of the physical world. The first cause argument, the motion argument, and the matter argument share this naive way of seeing the world. It *is* tempting to look at the world as if its "natural condition" is to be completely still (the first cause and motion arguments) or to not have any matter in it at all (the matter argument). When we do this, we see motion, events, and even the existence of matter as "unnatural" and therefore as requiring a supernatural explanation. Hence, the postulation of a nonphysical God seems needed.

But there is no reason why we have to say that the "natural" state of the cosmos is to be completely at rest or nonexistent. Newton's law of inertia states that bodies in motion stay in motion and bodies at rest stay at rest, unless acted on by external forces. Neither motion nor rest has a special status over the other. Therefore, we can just as easily adopt a model of the cosmos that holds that things were always in motion, where events always occurred, and where matter and energy have always been in existence—all without the need for a supernatural cause. Instead of seeing the events in the world on the model of a series of falling dominoes, which prompts us to ask what tipped over the first domino, we can see events on the model of an electron spinning around the nucleus of an atom—as always in motion.

A fourth criticism is that the first cause argument cannot prove that there is a *single* first cause rather than *many*. Even if we believe that an infinite series of causes backward in time is impossible, the first cause argument proves only that each event can be traced to one first cause or another, not that each event traces back to *one single* first cause. As Bertrand Russell puts it, the fact that every person has *a* mother goes no way toward proving that they all have *the same* mother.

A fifth criticism objects to the move from (5) to (6). Even if we conclude there was a first cause, why say that it was God in the sense in which we have defined "God"? A first cause of all events in the cosmos is not necessarily omnipotent, omniscient, morally perfect, nor need it exist outside space and time.

A REVISED FIRST CAUSE ARGUMENT

Given these difficulties for the first cause argument, it is only fair to ask whether a more sophisticated version can succeed. Recognizing that the traditional first cause argument makes religion compete against science, advocates of the revised argument try to reinterpret the original argument so it is *compatible* with science, but still requires the postulation of God to explain some facts about the cosmos. In this way, advocates of the revised argument hope to make the first cause argument consistent with determinism and the conservation of energy. The revised argument relies on two themes: (1) seeing God as *an explainer* of events in the universe rather than *a cause* who interacts with the universe; and (2) emphasizing *the Principle of Sufficient Reason*, which maintains that for every fact, there is a true explanation of why it is a fact.

Here is how the revised argument proceeds. Assume that the series of physical causes and effects is infinite into the past, as the critics of the first cause argument assert. Therefore, (1) there is no first event in time, (2) there is no time that God set the cosmos into motion, and (3) God did not create the matter of the cosmos. Nonetheless, God—being eternal—has existed as long as the cosmos has. Most important, God is *the explanation* of why events are happening in the cosmos, why motion occurs, and why matter exists. Saying that there is an infinite series of events backward in time would not provide an explanation for why anything exists at all, but postulating God provides an explanation: God wanted there to be a cosmos. Thus, God is seen not as a competitor to a scientific story about the cosmos, but as a needed explanation of *why* the scientific story is true. In this sense, God answers the question: "Why is there something rather than nothing?"

This revised argument is doubtful. Once we quit seeing God as the actual first cause of events, it is difficult to understand in what sense the postulation of God *explains* events. For example, if citing my throwing a stone explains why a window breaks, it is only because my throwing the stone *caused* the window to break. If God does not cause the first event, how is God the explanation? Saying God oversees the cosmos may be gratifying to believe, but it does not seem that we can argue for the existence of God as a first cause unless we assign to Him a genuine causal role. And to do that takes us back to the original first cause argument.

13. The Contingency Argument

The contingency argument (sometimes called the "cosmological argument") is Aquinas's Third Way. It maintains that a physical universe consisting solely of *contingent things* (*things that go in and out of existence*) could not continue to exist by itself, but needs to be sustained by God. Left to its own devices, the entire cosmos would go out of existence. (My term for the dramatic event when all contingent entities go out of existence is the "Cosmic Catastrophe.") Therefore, the fact that there is a universe at all proves that God, the *necessary thing*, must have preserved it. Here is how Aquinas expresses the contingency argument:

> We find in nature things that are possible to be and not to be, since they are found to be generated, and to be corrupted, and consequently, it is possible for them to be and not to be. But it is impossible for these always to exist, for that which can not-be at some time is not. Therefore, if everything can not-be, then at one time there was nothing in existence. Now if this were true, even now there would be nothing in existence, because that which does not exist begins to exist only through something already existing. Therefore, if at one time nothing was in existence, it would have been impossible for anything to have begun to exist; and thus even now nothing would be in existence—which is absurd. Therefore, not all beings are merely possible, but there must exist something the existence of which is necessary. (Aquinas, 1948, 26)

I interpret this as a reductio ad absurdum argument that tries to reduce atheism to absurdity:

(1) Assume that atheism is true, that is, that the physical universe consisting of contingent things is the only thing that exists.
(2) Assume that time goes back infinitely into the past.
(3) Assume that there is a large, but finite, number of contingent things in existence.
(4) Assume that over infinite time, every mathematically possible event will occur. (Whatever is mathematically possible is physically possible, and what is physically possible will eventually occur.)
(5) Then, at some time in the past all the contingent things in the universe would have ceased to exist. (The Cosmic Catastrophe would have occurred.)
(6) Then, nothing would exist now. (Because something cannot come to exist from nothing.)
(7) But something does exist now.
(8) Therefore, atheism is false. The physical universe consisting of contingent things is not the only thing that exists. A necessary being (God) exists.

The key to the argument is step 5. Why should Aquinas think that over infinite time, if there were only a finite number of contingent things in existence and no God to sustain them, there would have been a Cosmic Catastrophe? Step 5 is quite reasonable once we assume steps 2, 3, and 4. One way to see Thomas's reasoning is through an analogy. Represent two contingent things by two fair coins, and let heads stand for existence and tails stand for nonexistence. Toss the coins simultaneously and record how they land. We can expect that, on average, one fourth of the time they will both land tails, representing by our analogy that two contingent things do not exist. Repeat the process for five contingent things. Here we will have to toss the five coins thirty-two times on the average, but, again, we can be sure that eventually we will get a combination with all tails. This is the analogue to saying that the five contingent things have ceased to exist. The point is that if there are a finite number of coins to flip and an infinite amount of time to perform an infinite number of flips, you can be certain that the "losing combination" of all tails is bound to occur. Indeed, it *already* would have had to have come up *an infinite number of times*, because if time is infinite into the past, an infinite number of trials has already occurred. We cannot answer Aquinas's argument by suggesting that the Cosmic Catastrophe is physically possible, but simply has not occurred yet. Given the analogy, we see that it has to have already occurred.

Here is another way to appreciate the move to step 5. Writing in the 1200s—more than 500 years before the laws of conservation of energy and mass were known—Aquinas thought that physical objects come into and go out of existence *completely*. For many medieval thinkers, physical objects depended for their continuance at every second on the active power of God. For Aquinas, God played the role of conserving the existence of physical objects that is played by the conservation laws of physics in contemporary science.

CRITICISMS OF THE CONTINGENCY ARGUMENT

Understanding why Aquinas endorsed the move to step 5 suggests a way to rebut it. The problem is step 4. Instead of simply talking as Aquinas did about contingent (possible) and necessary things, suppose we distinguish between *logically* necessary and contingent events, and *physically* necessary and contingent events. *Logically necessary events* are *events that have to happen in every possible world*, whereas *logically contingent events* are *events that happen in some possible worlds but not others*. *Physically necessary events* are *events that have to happen in the real world due to the laws of nature*, whereas *physically contingent events* are *events whose happening or not happening in the real world is not guaranteed by the laws of nature*.

Using this distinction, we can say that although the Cosmic Catastrophe is *logically possible* (*can be imagined in some possible worlds*), it is *not physically possible* (*cannot ever happen in the real world, given the laws of physics*). For example, although it is logically possible that an ant might turn into a computer, it is not physically possible. It can never really happen—even given an infinite amount of time. Therefore, we do not have to accept step 4's claim that every mathematically possible event, including the Cosmic Catastrophe, will eventually occur. Because the contingency argument depends on the idea that without God's intervention the cosmos would have gone out of existence, resisting step 4 undermines the entire argument.

As noted, the first cause and contingency arguments are *Quasi-Scientific Hypotheses*: attempts to use Inference to the Best Explanation of some data about the natural world to prove the existence of God. The first cause argument relies on the fact that events are happening now. According to Aquinas, the explanation that God was the first cause is more plausible than the competing explanation that events have been occurring infinitely into the past. But if we reinforce the non-Thomistic explanation with our knowledge of the conservation of energy/mass, then that explanation looks better than Aquinas's. It postulates fewer unneeded entities, and it avoids the puzzle of how a supernatural being could affect the natural world. Although God's first causing of the events of the cosmos is a *possible* explanation, it scarcely seems *the best* one.

In the contingency argument that fact to be explained is that physical objects (logically contingent things) exist. Aquinas, believing that physical objects with no way to sustain themselves would go out of existence, thinks that God must be postulated as the best explanation for why contingent things continue to exist. But if we add to the non-Thomistic explanation the premise of the conservation of energy/mass, the explanation in terms of physical laws looks to be a better one than Thomas's postulation of God. Given that energy/mass is conserved, there never was a *physical possibility* of a Cosmic Catastrophe occurring, although it is *logically possible*. Here, again, the critic's alternative explanation has obvious advantages over Aquinas's. It avoids the postulation of unneeded entities, it avoids the puzzle of supernatural/natural interaction, and, unlike Aquinas's explanation, there is independent reason for believing that it is true, because the conservation laws are supported experimentally.

A REVISED CONTINGENCY ARGUMENT

Some advocates of the contingency argument respond to these criticisms in the same way that advocates of the first cause argument offer their revised argument. Here again, the revisionist might appeal to: (1) the idea of God as an explainer of the cosmos rather than a sustainer who interacts with it, and (2) the Principle of Sufficient Reason, which claims that every fact has an explanation.

An advocate of the revised contingency argument might argue that although a Cosmic Catastrophe is not a physical possibility (and therefore that God's existence need not be postulated to explain why it never happened), we need to postulate God's existence to explain something else: why there is any cosmos at all, rather than nothing. Even if the physical cosmos is self-sustaining and eternal, that does not explain its very existence. Only citing God provides the sufficient explanation of why there is something, rather than nothing.

This revision, like the revised first cause argument, avoids proposing quasi-scientific hypotheses to explain physical facts that are better explained by scientific hypotheses. This is a wise strategy for the theist. The history of Western civilization suggests that when the supernatural competes against the natural, the supernatural usually loses. Nonetheless, this revision seems no more plausible than the original contingency argument. First, using the Principle of Sufficient Reason launches an *infinite regress* (an unending series). If we try to provide a true explanation for every fact, then given that explanation is asymmetrical (if A explains B, B cannot explain A), we are bound to fail. There *has* to be some unexplained fact. If we ask "why?" of every explanation we receive, our questioning goes on without end.

What theists who use the Principle of Sufficient Reason to argue for God's existence really have in mind is a restricted version: Everything about *the physical world*—including the fact that there is a physical world at all—needs an explanation, but *God's existence* does not. Use of such a principle is cheating. If we really believe in the Principle of Sufficient Reason, we will ask *why God exists*. If we are willing to accept as an answer the statement that God "just does," then logically, if not psychologically, we should also be willing to accept the same type of answer as to why the cosmos exists: The cosmos just does.

Second, the claim that postulating God *explains* the existence of the world once we accept a scientific account is doubtful. As noted regarding the revised first cause argument, understanding why things are the way they are requires citing a causal relationship between the data to be explained and the explanatory entity postulated. If God is not the active sustainer of the physical cosmos, then it is difficult to see in what sense God *explains* why the cosmos stays in existence. When we reduce the role of the theistic postulation from that of a quasi-scientific hypothesis to one that is compatible with science, there is no *explanatory need* to postulate God. The claim that God is somehow responsible becomes an expression of emotion, but it does not mean what we ordinarily mean when we say that X explains Y.

14. The Argument from Design

The argument from design (also known as the "teleological argument") cites the orderliness found in the natural world as grounds for concluding the existence of God as the designer of that order. The best known versions of the design argument rely on an analogy between the orderly products of human intelligence and the orderliness of nature. In *Dialogues Concerning Natural Religion*, Hume, perhaps the most famous critic of the design argument, expresses the argument this way:

> Look round the world: Contemplate the whole and every part of it: You will find it to be nothing but one great machine, subdivided into an infinite number of lesser machines. . . . All these various machines, and even their most minute parts, are adjusted to each other with an accuracy, which ravishes into admiration all men, who have ever contemplated them. The curious adapting of means to ends throughout all nature, resembles exactly, though it much exceeds, the productions of human contrivance; of human design, thought, wisdom, and intelligence. Since therefore the effects resemble each other, we are lead to infer, by all the rules of analogy, that the causes also resemble; and that the Author of nature is somewhat similar to the mind of man; though possessed of much larger faculties, proportioned to the grandeur of the work, which he has executed. (1947, 143)

A generation after Hume, the English theologian William Paley (1743–1805) gave the design argument its most famous formulation:

> In crossing a heath, suppose I pitched my foot against a *stone*, and were asked how the stone came to be there, I might possibly answer, that for anything I knew to the contrary it had lain there forever; nor would it, perhaps, be very easy to show the absurdity of this answer. But suppose I had found a *watch* upon the ground, and it should be inquired how the watch happened to be in that place, I should hardly think of the answer which I had given before. . . . Yet why should not this answer serve for the watch as well as of the stone; why is it not as admissible in the second case as in the first? For this reason, and for no other, namely, that when we come to inspect the watch, we perceive—what we could not perceive in the stone—that its several parts are framed and put together for

a purpose, *e.g.*, that they are so formed and adjusted as to produce motion, and that motion so regulated as to point out the hour of the day; that if the different parts had been differently shaped from the way they are, or placed after any other manner or in any other order than in which they are placed, either no motion at all would have been carried on in the machine, or none which would have answered the use that is now served by it.

[F]or every indication of contrivance, every manifestation of design which existed in the watch, exists in the works of nature, with the difference on the side of nature of being greater and more, and that in a degree which exceeds all computation. I mean, that the contrivances of nature surpass the contrivances of art, in the complexity, subtlety, and curiosity of the mechanism; and still more, if possible, do they go beyond them in number and variety; yet in a multitude of cases, are not less evidently mechanical, not less evidently contrivances, not less evidently accommodated to their end or suited to their office, than are the most perfect productions of human ingenuity. (1963, 9–13)

I express the argument from design in three ways: as an analogy, as an inductive argument with premises and conclusion, and as inference to the best explanation. As an analogy, the argument from design claims that human *artifacts* (*manufactured items*) such as a watch are related to human designers as orderly nature is related to God-the-designer-of-nature:

We observe:	A watch	Orderly nature
We infer:	A watch-designer	God-the-designer-of-nature

We might also express the design argument as inductive reasoning with two premises and two conclusions:

(1) Nature is to a large extent orderly.
(2) All order requires an orderer that produces the order.
(3) Therefore, nature had an orderer.
(4) This orderer is God.

Finally, we might express the design argument as an example of inference to the best explanation:

Data: Much of the world around us is orderly.
↑
Best explanation: God designed the order.

CRITICISMS OF THE ARGUMENT FROM DESIGN

Some questions will reveal weaknesses in the design argument. First, what should we make of the claim that nature is *orderly*? To address this, we have to decide what we mean by "orderly." Suppose we say that a process is orderly if and only if it is regular and predictable. According to this definition, much of what happens in nature is orderly (for example, the revolution of the planets around the sun, animals reproducing offspring of their own kind, the four seasons). According to this definition, other things that happen in nature are not orderly: the explosion of stars (supernovas), genetic mutations, cancer, earthquakes, and tornadoes. On the whole, it seems that much of what happens in nature is orderly—orderly enough to require some explanation. This point supports the design argument so far.

Second, we should ask whether we can think of any examples of order that we have *no reason to think* were caused by purposive planning? If we can think of examples in which order exists without planning, then the order of nature will look less like the artificial orderliness of human artifacts and the argument will be weakened. Consider the fact that animals reproduce animals of their own species. Dogs give birth to dogs, not cats. Spiders reproduce spiders, not birds. There is no reason to think that dogs or spiders consciously plan to reproduce offspring of their own kind. The laws of nature—the laws of biology in particular—guarantee it. We can generalize this moral to the rest of the biological world: Biological order is produced by the laws of biology; we have no need to explain it by citing conscious design.

Viewed in terms of inference to the best explanation, our second question leads to the objection that the laws of nature produce a *better explanation* for the orderliness we find in the universe at large and the plants and animals on Earth. A big part of this is given by the process of *natural selection* (loosely called "evolution") as described by the English biologist Charles Darwin (1809–1882). According to Darwin, species change their characteristics over great periods of time due to unpredictable genetic mutations that occur in offspring. Most mutant offspring are poorly suited to their environments and die off. But those that are better suited to their environments than are their parents tend to survive and reproduce offspring that carry their genetic variations. Given the age of Earth (which was vastly underestimated until the start of the twentieth century), organisms had time to change through the process of natural selection so that many of them *looked* as if they were consciously designed for their environments: giraffes developed long necks, rabbits became camouflaged to blend into their surroundings, certain mammals took to the seas and became whales and dolphins, and certain reptiles became capable of flight (became birds). The biological account needs supplementation by a naturalistic account of how the evolutionary process got started on Earth—how one-celled organisms began to live on Earth. This requires a description of the formation of

Earth and the rest of the astronomical story of the cosmos. (For a persuasive account see Dawkins, 1976, 15–16.)

At this point it is helpful to look at the design argument in terms of a competition between two explanations of the orderliness that exists in nature: the God-designed-nature hypothesis versus the scientific account provided by the laws of physics and biology. Which explanation is more likely to be true? First, natural selection is the explanatory basis of contemporary biology. Although biologists disagree about specifics, there is an overwhelming consensus that natural selection explains why plants and animals are the way they are. We have *independent evidence that natural selection occurs*: We know that species adapt to changing environments. For example, during the industrial revolution in England, a species of moths changed their color when the trees they lived in became sooty from pollution caused by coal burning. We have no independent evidence that God designs things. Second, there is no philosophical puzzle about how physical organisms can adapt to their environments. It is a puzzle to understand how a nonphysical being could affect the physical world.

Third, the scientific hypothesis explains some data that the theistic hypothesis does not: why some animals are poorly suited to their environments. According to natural selection, species will do the best job they can to survive, but their success is limited by the harsh realities of the world. In the worse case, species become extinct. Biologists say that the vast majority of species that ever lived on Earth have become extinct. If an all-powerful, all-knowing designer designed the species, why would so many of them fail to survive?

In other cases, animals may survive, but their adaptation is far from ideal. Harvard biologist Stephen Jay Gould (1980) cites the case of the panda's thumb: the giant panda's "thumb" is not a genuine, moveable thumb, but merely a growth of cartilage that the panda uses in stripping bamboo shoots for food. Now it would be much more useful if the panda had an all-purpose thumb like primates, with which it could both strip bamboo shoots *and* serve other functions. But it does not have a better "thumb." Why not? Gould says that natural selection explains this: This is the best the panda could do, given its genetic endowment. Pandas simply could not develop primate-style thumbs. The theistic hypothesis, however, leaves it a puzzle why the panda does not have a better thumb. God, being omnipotent and omniscient could have provided better for the panda, but did not. The same question that arose over extinction arises here: Why does God provide better for some species than others?

A fourth criticism of the design argument comes from Hume. Even if we accepted the design argument despite the problems just cited, we would still have to ask whether the argument proves the existence of *God*, the supreme being defined in section 2. What characteristics would the designer of the cosmos have to have? Would it be the creator of the universe? Not necessarily. Persons who design ships or watches simply work with pre-existing materials; they do not create the wood or steel. Would the designer be perfect in every way: omniscient, omnipotent, morally perfect, and exist outside space and time? Persons who design artifacts have none of these qualities. Would the designer of the cosmos have to be a single being? Persons who design artifacts usually do so in teams, so perhaps the universe was designed by a committee. Would the designer have to still be in existence? Human designers die after they complete their works. In sum, even if we thought that the argument from design supports the existence of a designer of the nature, that designer would not have to look much like the God that Paley wants to prove.

A REVISED ARGUMENT FROM DESIGN

At this point some defenders of the design argument will say that although natural selection produced the orderliness of nature, *only God could make the laws of nature that produce natural selection*. So God must be hypothesized to explain *that* order. Like the revisions to the first cause and contingency arguments, this revision tries to amend the original argument so that it no longer pits religion against science. God still has a role to play, despite the admission that the orderliness of nature is due to the laws of nature.

There are two problems with this reply. First, the revision is weaker than the original argument. We have no more reason to think that God "designed" the laws of nature than we do to think that God directly designed the plants and animals. At least Paley could appeal to the analogy of a person designing a watch; we have no examples of *anyone* designing the law of gravity or "$E = MC^2$." The only "evidence" that God designed the laws of nature is that the laws produced order and intelligent beings. But that does not prove anything about a supernatural designer. If there is no supernatural designer, then we are lucky that the laws of nature produced *us*—instead of just one-celled organisms or entirely nonliving matter. But if we acknowledge the laws of nature, we will view this occurrence as determined, just as we view any other physical process. Carl Sagan (1979, 315) estimated that, given the laws of nature and the way that matter is spread out in our part of the cosmos, there should be 1 million civilizations within the Milky Way galaxy alone that are advanced enough to have radio astronomy. So any of those statistically improbable ("lucky") organisms could with equal justice think that the laws of nature were rigged just to produce *them*. It is a common vanity of human beings to suppose that anything special (for good or for bad) that happens to them was designed for them. But this vanity does not constitute evidence for the existence of a being who rigs the laws of nature.

Second, persons who like the revised design argument misunderstand what the argument from design is supposed to show. The argument from design is supposed to *give evidence for* postulating the existence of God. Once the argument from design is criticized by showing that science is a better explanation, it is *cheating* to use the assumed existence of God to defend the argument from that criticism. It is true that the existence of God can always be added onto any scientific explanation of anything. The question regarding evidence, though, is whether the addition of God is *necessary* to explain the phenomena in question. The theistic hypothesis does not seem necessary to explain the laws of nature. Thus, the revision has no evidential weight, but is only a reminder that God *might* exist. Critics of the design argument never denied this.

AN A PRIORI ARGUMENT FOR THE EXISTENCE OF GOD: THE ONTOLOGICAL ARGUMENT

The a posteriori arguments for the existence of God use the postulation of God as a quasi-scientific hypothesis to explain some facts (or presumed facts) about the world. The ontological argument, given by the Italian native St. Anselm (1033–1109), who became Archbishop of Canterbury in England, is unique because it argues for the existence of God from a *definition* of "God": "the being than which none greater can be conceived." Because the ontological argument uses no premises regarding the world, its success does not depend on the world being in any certain way or even whether the world exists at all. According to Anselm, God can be proved by pure reason—that is, a priori. Although many famous philosophers attacked the argument (Aquinas, Kant, Bertrand Russell), philosophers widely disagree about what exactly is wrong with it. And among philosophers who think that there is a good philosophical argument for the existence of God, the ontological argument probably has as many supporters as any other argument.

To understand Anselm's argument we need to define three terms. "The being than which none greater can be conceived" is a term for the supreme being that Anselm tries to prove exists. Because Anselm's argument relies on the idea that this being is so supreme than nothing greater can even be *thought*, the ontological argument will not work to prove the existence of a god that is less than the greatest imaginable. So theists who hold lesser concepts of God than this cannot use the ontological argument. "To exist in the understanding" means "to exist in the mind as a thought." Any idea that we have exists in our understanding, or, in terms used in chapter 4, *exists subjectively*. So, for example, both Superman and Bill Clinton exist in the understanding. For an entity "to exist in reality" means "to exist in its own right, *not merely in someone's understanding*." In terms used in chapter 4, to exist in reality is to exist *objectively*. So Bill Clinton exists in reality as well as in the understanding, but Superman does not. According to Anselm, God exists in both the understanding and in reality. Things that exist in reality may be either physical or nonphysical. It is a mistake to think that "existing in reality" means "being physical." Anselm will argue that God exists both *in the understanding* and *in reality*—but *not physically*.

Here is how Anselm expresses the argument:

> [W]hatever is understood, exists in the understanding. And assuredly that, than which nothing greater can be conceived, cannot exist in the understanding alone. For, suppose it exists in the understanding alone: then it can be conceived to exist in reality; which is greater.
>
> Therefore, if that, than which nothing greater can be conceived, exists in the understanding alone, the very being, than which nothing greater can be conceived, is one, than which a greater can be conceived. But obviously this is impossible. Hence, there is no doubt that there exists a being, than which nothing greater can be conceived, and it exists both in the understanding and in reality. (1962, 8)

I express Anselm's argument in two ways. The simplest version explicitly emphasizes Anselm's basic belief that existence in reality is a *great-making characteristic* (*something that makes you greater than you would be if you did not have it*). (Philosophers sometimes express this idea by saying "existence is a perfection.")

(1) By definition, the being than which none greater can be conceived has all great-making characteristics.
(2) Existence in reality is a great-making characteristic.
(3) Therefore, the being than which none greater can be conceived has existence in reality.

Here is a way of seeing Anselm's argument as a modus tollens argument that I extract from a version given by Cornman, Lehrer, and Pappas (1987, ch. 5). I simplify Anselm's language by using the expression "the greatest conceivable being" in place of "the being than which none greater can be conceived." Both premises are supposed to be true by definition:

(1) If the greatest conceivable being exists only in the understanding and not in reality, then it is possible that there exists a being that is *greater* than the greatest conceivable being (namely, one that exists both in the understanding *and* in reality).
(2) Not (it is possible that there exists a being that is greater than the greatest conceivable being).
(3) Therefore, not (the greatest conceivable being exists only in the understanding and not in reality)—that is, God exists.

CRITICISMS OF THE ONTOLOGICAL ARGUMENT

The first criticism of the ontological argument asks whether the term "the being than which none greater can be conceived" has any meaning. Many perfectly grammatical expressions turn out after analysis to make no sense: "the largest possible number," "the only married bachelor in town," "the 350-degree circle." Perhaps a being can *always* be conceived to be greater, just as we can always conceive of a larger number by adding one. If the expression "the being than which none greater can be conceived" has no meaning, then Anselm's argument cannot get started.

Second, a famous criticism of the ontological argument is the logical analogy given by a contemporary of Anselm, the monk Gaunilo. Gaunilo asked Anselm to consider someone who tried to prove by a similar line of reasoning to Anselm's that an island that has all possible perfections must exist. Surely, Gaunilo claimed, any argument that tries to prove the real existence of a most perfect island from our idea of a most perfect island would be unsound. By analogy, because Anselm's argument has the same unsound structure as a proof of the existence of the most perfect island, Anselm's argument is also unsound.

Anselm could reply that the ontological argument works for only *perfect* beings—which requires them to be nonphysical—and therefore, that Gaunilo's analogy is not apt. It is certainly difficult to decide who has the better side on this question. But even if Gaunilo is right in saying that the ontological argument would be as defective as a "proof" of the most perfect island, Gaunilo's logical analogy does not pinpoint what is wrong with Anselm's argument. A decisive criticism of the ontological argument should indicate what is wrong with it.

Here is a third criticism. In both of its versions, the ontological argument relies on the assumption that having existence in reality makes an entity better than it would be if it existed only in the understanding. Immanuel Kant (1965, 500–507) challenges this assumption with his famous reply that "existence is not a predicate." Kant claims that having existence in reality is *not* a characteristic that we assign to entities as we do characteristics such as being omnipotent, omniscient, or morally perfect. Kant gives the example of comparing one hundred real dollars with one hundred imaginary dollars. The real dollars do not contain one *more* coin; it is just that one group exists and the other does not. Likewise, a supreme being that exists in reality is not *greater* than an entity that exists only in the understanding—by saying it exists in reality we have not assigned to it any different characteristics. Therefore, according to Kant, Anselm cannot claim that a greatest conceivable being with real existence is greater than a greatest possible being that exists only in the understanding. Without this assumption, the ontological argument fails.

Here is a fourth objection that agrees with Kant's criticism, but tries to undermine the ontological argument in a more radical way. Anselm compares two possible entities—a greatest conceivable being that exists only in the understanding and a greatest conceivable being that exists both in the understanding and in reality. Once we accept Anselm's contrast between these two entities, it *is* tempting to think that the second entity is greater than the first. So, to think that the *greatest* conceivable being might exist only in the mind does seem logically contradictory. But if we reject Anselm's way of setting up the problem, we can prevent the argument from getting started. Here is how we could rewrite the ontological argument in order to undermine it:

(1) Instead of saying "the greatest conceivable being exists in the understanding," let us say "we are thinking in ways that try to represent a greatest conceivable being." (After all, there is not an odd, *possible* being "existing" in our minds; we are merely thinking in a certain way.)
(2) On the one hand, there may exist in reality an entity to which our thinking corresponds. In this case, our thinking truly represents a greatest conceivable being.
(3) On the other hand, there may exist in reality no being to which our thinking corresponds. In this case, our thinking fails to represent a greatest conceivable being. (Notice: It is no contradiction to say this.)
(4) Either way, whether our thinking matches an entity outside our minds or not depends on whether that entity exists, not on anything about the concept "the greatest conceivable being."

THE CASE FOR ATHEISM

No one can prove the nonexistence of *any* logically possible entity. We can prove that round squares and married bachelors do not exist, but this is only because such entities logically cannot exist. We know that nothing can be a round square or a married bachelor, *using the terms as we mean them today.* (It is possible to change the meaning of the relevant terms, for example, mean by "married" what we mean by "unmarried," but this would not change the fact that what we mean today when we say "married bachelors" cannot exist.) It is, thus, impossible to *prove* that the Loch Ness monster and Bigfoot do not exist. For all our failure to find such beings, they might still exist. This is even more clear for proposed *nonphysical beings* such as God. Our inability to prove God exists (or even to provide any positive evidence for the existence of God) does not *prove* that God does not exist. So, atheism is not provable.

Nonetheless, we may be able to devise an argument to show that atheism is *more likely to be true* than theism. The most direct way to attempt this is to present a naturalistic picture of what exists that explains everything that the theistic hypothesis explains *without* postulating the existence of God. Here is one way to sketch that picture.

To a large extent, the history of humanity illustrates the gradual reduction in the role persons have assigned to all forms of the supernatural in their attempt to understand the cosmos. Primitive persons placed gods everywhere: to explain the rising of the sun, the changing of the seasons, the blowing of the winds, and coming of droughts. As religions became monotheistic—in only the last three thousand years of human history—humans reduced the number of gods they postulated. Through the Middle Ages in Europe, supernatural beings were still assigned the role of explaining some very broad natural phenomena, as we saw in the first cause, contingency, and design arguments. But as modern physics and biology developed, humans learned that there are simpler and more testable ways to explain motion, the persistence of matter, and order in the biological world than by postulating God's agency. By the end of the 1800s a fully naturalistic picture emerged that eliminated the need to postulate the existence of God to explain any natural phenomena.

Thus, the most straightforward atheistic move is to construct a naturalistic worldview as a competitor to theistic ones. Theistic hypotheses can always be added onto any scientific picture, as noted in discussing the traditional versions of the first cause, contingency, and design arguments. But the key point is that the supernatural explanations are not *needed* to account for natural phenomena. For example, although we *can* say that a piece of chalk that we drop is carried to the floor by invisible, nonphysical gremlins, there is no need to say it once we know Newton's law of gravitation. It also helps the argument to explain the psychological mechanisms that lead persons to theistic hypotheses in the first place. This is attempted by social scientists and speculative thinkers, especially Sigmund Freud (1856–1939).

Atheists can offer a slightly different argument not to prove that God does not exist, but to prove that persons who wish to construct a most-likely-to-be-true theory of the world ought to deny that God exists. This argument relies on the theme of the last two paragraphs and uses *Occam's Razor* (*the principle that we should not multiply entities in our theories beyond what is necessary to explain the data*):

(1) For any proposed entity X, if we have no more evidence that X exists than evidence that X does not, then from an epistemological point of view we should deny X exists. (Occam's Razor)
(2) No argument for the existence of God gives any more evidence that God exists than evidence that God does not exist.
(3) Therefore, from an epistemological point of view we should deny God exists.

Premise (1) seems both commonsensical and philosophical. A good epistemic agent, as noted in chapter 3, is one who tries above all else to accept views if and only if they are likely to be true. Accordingly, the burden of proof is always on the person who says that a thing exists. If it is not at least slightly more than 50 percent likely that something exists, then we should say that it does not exist. Otherwise, our picture of the world would be cluttered with things we have no positive reason to believe in, simply because we cannot disprove their existence.

Premise (2) displays my verdict on the theistic arguments examined in this chapter: None of the arguments gives a better than 50–50 edge to the theistic hypothesis. This is a tentative judgment, as all philosophical judgments must be. Perhaps if we thought more carefully about one of the arguments, we would decide that it does provide greater than 50 percent evidence for the existence of God. Or perhaps someone will devise an entirely different, epistemologically persuasive argument. Nonetheless, the point of the argument remains clear: The burden of proof is on the theist to prove the existence of God, not on the atheist to disprove it.

It might be tempting to try to build a hybrid argument for the existence of God by combining several of the arguments that individually fail. So, for instance, if we think that the design argument is 30 percent likely to be sound, and the ontological argument is 25 percent likely to be sound, we might add the arguments together and conclude that the existence of God is 55 percent likely. But this would be mistaken. By the same reasoning we could show that in the design argument the atheistic hypothesis is 70 percent probable, and in the ontological argument atheism is 75 percent probable, so the atheistic thesis is 145 percent probable. So, we could "prove" atheism is true just as readily as we can prove theism is true—which shows that we cannot use this sort of reasoning at all. Several bad arguments do not add up to make one good argument. If it did, we could prove anything by simply putting together enough bad arguments.

The conclusion of my argument from Occam's Razor does not assert that God does not exist, so even if the argument is sound, it does not prove God does not exist. The argument is not trying to prove that, but only that atheism is a good bet *for those persons who want to build a most-likely-to-be-true worldview.* In this sense my argument is like Pascal's Wager and James's Will to Believe: Here is a good strategy for you to follow *if* you hold certain desires.

Note finally that the atheistic argument contains the qualification "from an epistemological point of view." There is no reason why any person—even a philosopher—has to adopt the epistemological point of view for every philosophical issue. As noted in chapter 1, philosophers disagree concerning what they want to accomplish by doing philosophy. Some want to adopt the epistemological view for all problems at all times, no matter what. Other philosophers want philosophy to serve other goals they hold dear: to create inspiring literature, to make the world a morally better place, or even to support religion. I do not claim to *refute* these other desires for philosophy, but I do praise the liberating effect of pursuing philosophy with the sole aim of discovering what is most likely to be true. Scientists aim to find truth in their specific domains. What more ennobling ambition could philosophers have than to seek truth in a complete view of reality?

Guide Questions

1. What is the difference between the philosophy of religion and theology? (234)
2. Explain the difference between the philosophical and psychological interpretations of "Why does S believe *p*?" (234–5)
3. What is the difference between "God" and God? (235)
4. In what way is the concept "God" ambiguous? Vague? (235)
5. What is the definition of "God" used in this chapter? (236)
6. What are the three main *types* of argument for the existence of God? (236–37)
7. Provide a logical analogy to show that the fallacy of popular belief is a fallacy. Provide one for the fallacy of lack of proof to the contrary. (237)
8. "By definition, faith does not provide evidence." What does this sentence mean? (238)
9. What are the three versions of the argument from textual proof? (238)
10. How does the pure faith version of the argument from textual proof run afoul of the problem of representation? (238–39)
11. What difficulty arises if we accept any of the versions of the argument from textual proof only because we already believe in the existence of God? (240)
12. In two sentences, why does Pascal think that theism is a good bet? (241)
13. What criticism of Pascal's Wager can be made from the perspective of our *epistemic agency*? From the perspective that we must know the mind of God? (242)
14. In two sentences, express James's Will to Believe argument. (243)
15. What problem is there with adopting the epistemic strategy of trying to hold as many true beliefs as we can? Of avoiding as many false beliefs as we can? (243–44)
16. What does it mean to say that an argument for the existence of God postulates the existence of God as a *quasi-scientific hypothesis*? (244)
17. What is the difference between the *moral objectivism* version and the *precondition of morality* version of the moral argument? (245)
18. What are the two versions of the argument from miracles? (246–47)
19. What is the difference between *coincidence-miracles* and *violation-miracles*? (247)

20. What are the mystical and nonmystical versions of the argument from religious experience? (249–50)
21. Explain the burden-of-proof strategy used by the nonmystic? What are two objections to this strategy? (249–50)
22. Express the first cause argument in two sentences. (251)
23. What does it mean to say that it is a logical consequence of determinism that natural events trace infinitely into the past? (252)
24. How can we use Newton's law of inertia to deny that the "natural" state of the cosmos is to be at rest? (253)
25. Express the contingency argument in two sentences. (254)
26. Explain why someone might think that if God did not exist, then the universe certainly would have gone out of existence. (255)
27. How does using the concept of an event being *logically possible*, but *physically impossible* provide a way to criticize the contingency argument? (256)
28. How might someone use the *Principle of Sufficient Reason* to argue for the existence of God? (257) What is the weakness with this maneuver? (257–58)
29. What does it mean to say: "The curious adapting of means to ends throughout all nature, resembles exactly, though it much exceeds, the productions of human contrivance"? (258)
30. Explain the argument from design as an inference to the best explanation. (259)
31. How does the idea of natural selection pose an alternative explanation to the one given by the design argument? (260–61)
32. How does the maladaption of species pose a problem for the design argument? (261)
33. Explain the revised argument from design. How may it be criticized? (262–63)
34. What is it to exist in the understanding? To exist in reality? (263–64)
35. Why did Anselm think that it is absurd to think of God as existing only in the understanding? (264)
36. How did Kant object to the ontological argument? (265)
37. Even if atheism is *true*, it is not *provable*. Why not? (266)
38. How do atheists use Occam's Razor to construct an argument that we should conclude that God does not exist? (267–68)

Review Questions for Examinations

1. Define these concepts: "theist," "atheist," "agnostic," "vague," "ambiguous," "omnipotent," "omniscient," "a posteriori," "a priori," "quasi-scientific hypothesis," "scientific hypothesis," "fallacy of relevance," "representational device," "problem of representation," "contingent things," "necessary things," "cosmic catastrophe," "principle of conservation of

energy/mass," "principle of sufficient reason," "natural selection," "Occam's Razor."

2. Explain these arguments for the existence of God: popular belief, lack of proof to the contrary, it's-my-right-to-believe-what-I-want, textual proof, Pascal's Wager, the Will to Believe, the moral argument, the argument from miracles, the argument from religious experience, the first cause argument, the contingency argument, the argument from design, the ontological argument.
3. Provide at least one criticism of each of the minor arguments and two for each of the major arguments.

Discussion Questions

1. Philosophers examine other issues concerning religion besides the existence of God. How would you answer these questions?
   (a) Is there anything that an omnipotent being cannot do?
   (b) Is there anything that an omniscient being cannot know? (For example, can God know what you are going to choose tomorrow?)
   (c) Can words that are used to describe God mean the same thing as when they are used to describe humans?
2. Which of the arguments in this chapter for the existence of God is the strongest? The weakest? Explain.
3. Consider the following analogy offered by Richard Taylor (1974, 113–14):

   > Suppose while riding on a railway train you look out of the window and see a group of white stones arranged in such a way as to seem to spell-out the words, "The British Railways Welcomes You to Wales." Suppose also that you take these stones as your sole evidence that you have just entered Wales. Then you are rationally committed to believing that these stones were placed there purposely by some entity that wants you to believe the message. By analogy, if we take *our senses* to reveal the way the physical world really is, then we are logically committed to believing that our senses were deliberately designed by some entity that wants us to believe what our senses tell us. So, if we take our senses as revealing the nature of the external world, we are logically committed to believing that some sense-designer designed our senses for that end.

   Which argument from this chapter does this look like? Is it a strong argument?
4. The question "Why is there something rather than nothing?" works both for and against the theist. How?
5. Evaluate the following argument:
   (1) If we believe in the existence of *one* God without evidence, then we can believe in *any plurality* of gods without evidence.

(2) If we can believe in any plurality of Gods without evidence, then we have no rational way to decide *how many* gods to believe in.
(3) If we have no rational way to decide how many gods to believe in, then it is irrational to believe in any gods at all.
(4) Therefore, if we believe in the existence of *one* God without evidence, then it is irrational to believe in any gods at all.

6. Which of the arguments for the existence of God given in the chapter clearly treat God as a quasi-scientific hypothesis? Which clearly do not? Are there any borderline cases?

7. For the following argument, if we assume that the premise is true, which conclusion is the most likely to follow? If you can think of a better conclusion than (a), (b), or (c), supply your own:
1. Premise: The existence of God (as described by my religion) would have greater benefits for me than the nonexistence of God.
2. Therefore: (a) God exists.
Therefore: (b) Probably, God exists.
Therefore: (c) I shall believe God exists.
Therefore: (d) ______________.

8. Norman Kretzman (1966) offers a valid deductive proof that the qualities of being omniscient (all knowing) and immutable (unchanging) are logically contradictory, so God cannot be both omniscient and immutable. Therefore, if a perfect being is understood as a being that is both omniscient and immutable, it cannot exist. Kretzman's basic idea is that an immutable being could not know what time it is:
(1) A perfect being is not subject to change. (by definition)
(2) A perfect being knows everything. (by definition)
(3) A being that knows everything knows what time it is. (because time is real)
(4) A being that knows what time it is is subject to change. (because to know what time it is, one has to constantly update one's belief about what time it is)
(5) Therefore, a perfect being is subject to change. (from 2–4)
(6) Therefore, a perfect being is not a perfect being (from 1 and 5)
(7) Therefore, there is no perfect being. (from 6)
Are Kretzman's premises all true? Is the argument convincing?

FOR FURTHER READING

Cornman, James, Keith Lehrer, and Gorge Pappas. 1987. *Philosophical Problems and Arguments*. Chapter 5. Indianapolis: Hackett. Detailed analyses of many arguments for the existence of God. Includes the problem of evil. Moderately difficult.

Gould, Stephen Jay. 1980. *The Panda's Thumb*. New York: Norton. A fascinating account of natural selection by a prominent biologist. Moderately difficult.

Leslie, John, ed. 1990. *Physical Cosmology and Philosophy*. New York: Macmillan. Contains excellent recent papers by philosophers and physicists on whether the cosmos was "fine-tuned" to allow intelligent life to evolve. Very difficult.

Robinson, Timothy, ed. 1996. *God*. Indianapolis: Hackett. A wide-ranging collection of short readings from philosophers and theologians. Selections vary in degree of difficulty.

Ruse, Michael, ed. 1989. *Philosophy of Biology*. New York: Macmillan. A collection of excellent recent papers by philosophers and biologists on the design argument. Difficult.

Sagan, Carl. 1977. *The Dragons of Eden*. New York: Ballantine. A highly entertaining discussion of cosmology and biology by a Cornell astro-physicist and producer of the television documentary series *Cosmos*. Easy to read.

Smith, Huston. 1991. *The World's Religions*. San Francisco: Harper. Informative best-selling account of the major religions from a sympathetic perspective. Easy to read.

Swinburne, Richard. 1996. *Is There a God*? Oxford: Oxford University Press. Fascinating short book by a foremost theist. Includes a chapter on the problem of evil. Easy to read.

Chapter 10
THE PROBLEM OF EVIL

INTRODUCTION

Regarding the problem of evil (also known as "the problem of suffering"), philosophers ask whether we can reconcile the belief in the existence of a Supreme Being with the amount of suffering that exists in the world. David Hume expresses the problem this way: "Is God willing to prevent evil, but not able? then is he impotent. Is he able but not willing? then is he malevolent. Is he both able and willing? whence then is evil?" (Hume, 1947, part X, 198). Is it reasonable to believe that if God has absolute power, knowledge, and goodness, God would create *this* world, rather than a *better* world or maybe no world at all? Would a world created by such a being contain the amount and degree of suffering that exists on planet Earth? If *we* were to create a world for human beings, wouldn't we provide for them better than God provides for us? Moreover, if God punishes sinners, can such retribution be just, given that God created the sinners in the first place?

The problem of evil can be both a philosophical puzzle and an emotional issue. Many thinkers have a stake in finding an answer that satisfies them temperamentally. For example, many theists hope to understand why a God they worship would permit suffering. Some theists want so much to find reasons to exonerate God (excuse God from blame) that they cannot bring themselves to question those reasons. Other theists and many atheists have an emotional investment in the opposite direction and applaud any argument critical of God, whether it is logically cogent or not. None of these attitudes reveal the temperament of the critical thinker discussed in chapter 1. For anyone who finds it difficult to examine the problem of evil dispassionately, here is a method that might help: Think about the God under consideration not as the God of your culture, but as the God of the Martians, and pretend that the world being discussed is Mars (which has just as much suffering as Earth).

1. The Problem of Evil as a Logical Inconsistency

One way to understand the problem of evil is as a *logically inconsistent set of statements*, this is, as a *group of statements that (logically) cannot all be true.* Consider this example: (a) Bjorn Borg was a Swede. (b) Bjorn Borg was a Wimbledon champion. (c) No Swedes were ever Wimbledon champions. This set is logically inconsistent, because if any two of the statements are true, the third has to be false. If we were to believe all three statements we would contradict ourselves—at least one of the statements *has* to be false. Moreover, we can know this by considering the logic of the three statements. We cannot figure out a priori *which* statement is false, but on the basis of logic alone we can see that at least one of them must be false. So if we want to avoid holding contradictory beliefs, we should not accept (a), (b), *and* (c).

The problem of evil can be expressed as an inconsistent set of six statements:

(1) God (a supreme being existing outside space and time who planned and created the cosmos) exists.
(2) God is omniscient (knows all truths—past, present, and future).
(3) God is omnipotent (can perform all acts that do not involve a logical contradiction).
(4) God is morally perfect (which entails that God wants there to be no unnecessary suffering).
(5) If statements 1–4 are all true, then there is no unnecessary suffering.
(6) There is unnecessary suffering.

To see that these six statements are logically inconsistent, notice that the first five statements logically entail by modus ponens: (5A) "There is no unnecessary suffering." But (5A) contradicts (6): "There is unnecessary suffering." So logically we cannot accept all six statements. We need to find at least one statement we think is false. The problem of evil amounts to the question: Which statement should we reject? Given that not all six statements can be true, which one is the most likely to be false?

2. Definitions of Terms

Philosophers of religion have provided fascinating examinations of the various characteristics of God. For the purposes of this chapter, however, I want to emphasize only the concept of "omnipotence." To say that God is omnipotent means that God can do anything—even if it violates the laws of nature—as long as it is not logically contradictory. (Some religious thinkers argue that God can perform even contradictory acts, like creating a square circle, but this view would not help defend God in the problem of evil. So I ignore it here.) The important thing to note is that an omnipotent being is not bound by the laws of nature. After all, as the omnipotent creator of the cosmos and its laws, God has enough power to violate the laws He created; the laws of nature simply represent the way God has made nature operate up until now. An omnipotent being could suspend the law of gravity, turn predators into herbivores, and cause bullets in midflight to vanish into thin air.

Here are some other definitions we will need. A defense of God in the problem of evil is known as a "theodicy," and a defender of God is called a "theodicist." Persons who believe that God exists are called "theists." Those who deny that God exists are called "atheists." "Evil" is defined in terms of "good"; evil is anything that makes the world less good. It may seem unilluminating to define "evil" in terms of "good," but this is what we should expect from our examination of definism in the metaethics chapter: Moral terms cannot be defined by nonmoral terms. We can make up for this lack of an informative definition, however, by providing examples of evils.

Evils are usefully divided into two kinds. *Natural evils* are instances of suffering that are not caused by agents' malicious intentions. Natural disasters such as floods, hurricanes, and earthquakes count as natural evils. So do accidents, diseases, and the diminution of our powers as we age. *Moral evils* (nonnatural evils, man-made evils) are evils that are caused by agents' malicious intentions. Moral evils include murder, assault, rape, arson, racial and sexual discrimination, wars, and genocide. Some evils are difficult to classify (a house fire that might have been caused by lightening or by arson), whereas others are combinations of both (a famine that is traceable to drought and to greedy socio/economic decisions by humans).

3. Legitimate Solutions

Because the problem of evil is generated by accepting six statements, rejecting any of the six will solve the problem. Consider the statement that God exists. If anyone rejects this statement, as atheists do, the problem of evil disappears for that person. With no God to prevent evil from occurring, there is no reason to think that evil would not occur. Natural and moral evil, for atheists, are normal things that are to be expected.

Consider statements (2) and (3). If we deny that God is omniscient, we can avoid the inconsistency. The explanation of evil would be that God does not know that evil occurs or does not know how to prevent it. This would provide a legitimate solution. This possible answer shades into the next one: We could deny that God is omnipotent. On this view, God did the best He could, but was unable to overcome evil. Historically, this view has been accepted by many famous thinkers. Plato conceived of a god as a limited being who did the best job he could in designing the world out of imperfect matter, but was simply unable to make the world come out better. The English philosopher John Stuart Mill and the American philosopher/psychologist William James also thought that God was less than omnipotent. Among some theologians, the theory of Manichaeanism (MAN A KEY ISM) has long attributed evil to the power of Satan, whom God was unable to control. Although rejecting (2) or (3) would solve the problem from a logical point of view, most theodicists would be unhappy to take that route, because they are unwilling to surrender God's omniscience or omnipotence.

Another possible way to solve the logical problem is to reject (4), God's moral perfection. This might seem to be a promising way out: The religious texts of the three major Western religions (Judaism, Christianity, and Islam) portray God as often vengeful and unsympathetic to the suffering of humans and beasts. Nonetheless, few theodicists reject (4), because, as with (2) and (3), they do not want to give up any of God's great qualities.

Another way to avoid the problem is to reject the conditional statement (5), which says that if God exists and is omniscient, omnipotent, and morally perfect, then there is no unnecessary suffering. Although in most discussions (5) is assumed without being explicitly stated, it is important to be aware of it. Without (5) the other five statements are *not* logically inconsistent. Theodicists who attribute moral evil to humans' misuse of their libertarian free will (explained later in the chapter) might resist (5).

This takes us to (6), the most popular target of the theodicists. Theodicists typically argue that, contrary to appearances, all the suffering that occurs *is* necessary in the sense that its existence contributes to some greater good that would be impossible otherwise. Much of this chapter will be devoted to the theodicists' various attempts to reject (6).

4. Evasions

The above solutions are serious answers, because they recognize the logical problem created by the six inconsistent statements, state exactly which statement they think is false, and say why. These solutions are also serious in that they take suffering as a *moral* problem needing a sincere explanation. Some evasions are cop-outs that try to get around the problem without bothering to come to grips with the issue—without saying which statement we should reject and why. Other evasions fail to take the moral dimension of the problem of evil seriously. Here are three examples of the first sort and two of the second.

The first evasion is to say that God's logic is not our logic, God is omniscient but we are not, so we should not even try to figure out the problem of evil. On this view, there is no point to trying to figure out which statement to reject, because we are not smart enough to do so. Against this, we admit that humans are not omniscient; but it does not take an omniscient mind to recognize a logically inconsistent set of statements when one sees one. The problem of evil, like any scientific or philosophical problem, is one that *humans* need to figure out using *our minds* to the best of our abilities. If we quit trying to figure out the solution, we surrender our attempt to think for ourselves. If we give up on this issue because we are not omniscient, why not give up everywhere else too?

Moreover, persons who give this evasion usually take it as an exoneration of God from blame for evil, and this is a mistake. The conclusion that God *can be* exonerated in the problem of evil does not follow from the premise that we are not omniscient, any more than the conclusion that God *cannot* be exonerated follows from that premise. So this evasion could not be of any logical help in the defense of God. It would at most make persons feel better by creating a *smoke screen* (a diversion that obscures the real issue in question), so that they could ignore the problem.

The second evasion is an appeal to faith: "I have faith that God is exonerated in the problem of evil." If what we mean by "faith" is "belief without evidence," then having faith cannot address the question of which of the six statements to reject. If one side says he has faith that the problem of evil is no problem for God, the other side can say with as much evidence (none) that she has faith that the problem of evil *is* a problem for God. Faith cuts no ice either way.

A third evasion is to refuse to address the problem of evil by asking what "right" we have to question God's goodness: After all, what does *God* owe *us*? (Compare this to the *Old Testament* reply God makes to Job when Job asks God why he is being punished.) This rebuttal misses the point. To address the problem of evil is to try to understand a troubling philosophical and personal question. We do not need a "right" to seek answers, we need only inquiring minds.

A fourth evasion was offered by the Dutch philosopher Spinoza (1632–1677) who argued that there are no unnecessary evils, because, when viewed correctly, there are no evils at all. For Spinoza, things are good and evil only relative to our limited perspectives, but they are not really good or bad. So kindness is not good, and malice is not bad. The problem with this move is that the problem of evil is a *moral problem—a problem about whether certain bad things (evils) can be justified*. If we deny that good and evil exist as Spinoza does, we are no longer talking about the problem of evil. This evasion also is insensitive to suffering.

A final evasion says that God will make it up to us in the end, no matter how much we suffer and however unfairly we are treated (M. Adams, 1990, 219). The problem is that this move is too easy. It exaggerates the value of the payoff so that no matter how much evil occurs, we can overwhelm it with one fell swoop. In addition, like Spinoza's reply, this reply shows insensitivity to the seriousness of suffering.

THE BEST OF ALL POSSIBLE WORLDS

In his play *Candide*, the French Enlightenment thinker Voltaire (1694–1778) parodies the German philosopher Leibniz by having the character Dr. Pangloss respond to all catastrophes by saying that they are all part of the best of all possible worlds. Leibniz's claim that this world—with all its suffering—is really the best world that could *possibly* exist sounds ludicrous, but Leibniz produced a powerful argument for it:

> [T]he infinite wisdom of the Almighty allied with his boundless goodness has brought it about that nothing better could have been created, everything taken into account, than what God has created. As a consequence all things are in perfect harmony and conspire in the most beautiful way. . . . Whenever, therefore, some detail of the work of God appears to us reprehensible, we should judge that we do not know enough about it and that according to the wise who would understand it, nothing better could even be desired. (Leibniz, 1965, 123–24)

Here is Leibniz's reasoning. When selecting a world to create, God had before His mind all of the infinitely many *logically possible* worlds that He *could* create. (God also had the option of creating no world.) Being omniscient, God knew everything that would happen in each one of those worlds if He actualized it. Being omnipotent, God had the power to create any possible world, which included many with very different laws of nature than our world has, and many without laws of nature at all. Being morally perfect, God wished to choose the morally best world from among all the possible worlds. Moreover, God chooses freely, which means God chose the best, *because* He recognized it to be the best. To choose from a "liberty of indifference" in which multiple options are equally attractive would be to choose unfreely—for God or humans. (Using a term introduced in chapter 8 and used later in this chapter, Leibniz is a *compatibilist*.)

Given all these facts, what type of world would God select? Obviously, the *best* of all logically possible worlds. In other words, this actual world *must* be the best of all possible worlds that God could create, given Leibniz's premises about God. Therefore, all natural and moral evil *is* necessary in the sense that it is part of the best of all possible worlds. There can be no unnecessary suffering in the world God selected. Suffering, though evil in itself, contributes to the greater perfection of the whole world. Leibniz says that if we took the big picture, we would realize that the evil of the world makes the entire world better in the way that a few planned discordant notes in a symphony make the whole work more beautiful. Thus, statement (6) of the problem of evil is false, and the contradiction is avoided.

Leibniz emphasized that "the best of all possible worlds" is not the same idea as "an absolutely perfect world." This world has more than enough evil to convince Leibniz that it is not perfect. But we can be sure, according to Leibniz's logic, that although not perfect, this world is better than any other that God could have chosen to take its place. Given his premises about God, this world *must* be the best, despite the suffering. As Leibniz said, this means that any other possible world that might *appear* to be an improvement over the actual world (for example, a possible world where the Holocaust never occurred) would *really* be worse than this one, all things considered. If that other possible world really would have been better, then God would have created *that* world instead of our own.

We can express Leibniz's reasoning as a valid modus ponens argument:

(1) If this world was chosen by God (defined as Leibniz does), then this has to be the best of all possible worlds, and there is no unnecessary suffering.
(2) This world was chosen by God (defined as Leibniz does).
(3) Therefore, this has to be the best of all possible worlds.

I think premise (1) is acceptable. Given Leibniz's conception of God, it seems highly likely that such a being would have to create the best of all possible worlds. The problem for Leibniz concerns (2). How can Leibniz support the claim that this world was chosen by any god at all, let alone by a being possessing all the remarkable characteristics that Leibniz assigns to God? Leibniz uses familiar arguments to try to prove the existence of God, including the argument that there must be an explanation for everything including the existence of the cosmos (the Principle of Sufficient Reason). But as we saw in the last chapter, such arguments are questionable. In addition, suppose someone were inclined to accept such arguments. These arguments would not prove the existence of the *morally perfect* God that Leibniz needs for his theodicy. It is even more difficult to prove the existence of a morally perfect god than it is to prove the existence of a god per se.

Here is another way to see the weakness in Leibniz's argument. We can take its first premise, add to it the denial of Leibniz's conclusion, and validly deduce that its second premise is false. Throughout this book I call this sort of reversal "one person's modus ponens is another's modus tollens:"

(1) If this world was chosen by God (defined as Leibniz does), then this has to be the best of all possible worlds, and there is no unnecessary suffering.
(2′) NOT (this is the best of all possible worlds, and there is no unnecessary suffering).
(3′) Therefore, NOT (this world was chosen by God [defined as Leibniz does]).

The modus tollens argument is valid (see chapter 2), and it shares the first premise of the modus ponens argument. To decide which argument we prefer, therefore, we need to compare the plausibility of (2) in the modus ponens argument against that of (2′) in the modus tollens argument. We have seen that (2) is extremely difficult to support, but (2′) looks easier to support. Would not the world have been better if the Holocaust never happened, if persons and animals never choked to death while eating, and if all animals fed on vegetation and none preyed on other animals? Wouldn't the world be better if it had even *a little less* natural and moral evil? Can we really view all the natural and moral evils of the world as just "little disharmonies" that make the symphony of the whole world better?

I believe that the critic's modus tollens version seems stronger than Leibniz's modus ponens version, at least to persons who do not think they already have a proof of God's existence as omniscient, omnipotent, and morally perfect. But the theodicist has a possible reply: Although it *seems* obvious that there could be a better world, we cannot *know* that there could be a better world. To say that this is not the best of all possible worlds, we would have to be able to specify down to the minutest detail what a better world would be like. Theodicists say that the *burden of proof* is on their opponents to specify a complete alternative world that is better than the actual world before they can say that the actual world is not the best possible world. But we (and any finite being) cannot do that: We are unable to envision a complete world at all, let alone a world better than our own. For example, if there had been no Holocaust, maybe there would have been an even worse calamity, as difficult as that is to imagine. If persons do not choke to death while eating, perhaps worse fates lie in store for them elsewhere. And so on.

There are two weaknesses with this attempt by the theodicists to place the burden of proof on their opponents. First, it is an *appeal to ignorance*, another informal fallacy. To argue that because we do not know that X is false (that this is *not* the best of all possible worlds), we have reason to believe that X is true (that this *is* the best of all possible worlds) is poor critical thinking. After all, in everyday life, we reject appeals to ignorance. Suppose your child complains, "You cannot blame me for coming home late from school: You cannot prove that I was not abducted by space-aliens." Would you accept this argument? Then why should we accept an appeal to ignorance in the problem of evil? Should we accept less rigorous standards of reasoning about God than we do in everyday life?

Second, appeals to ignorance "work" just as well in reverse, which means that they do not really work at all. If we are entitled to say that this is the best of all possible worlds until we can prove that it is not the best, then we are equally entitled to say that this is the *worst* of all possible worlds until we can prove that it is not the worst. But we cannot prove that this is not the worst possible world, any more than we can prove that this is not the best. So if the theodicists' argument were cogent, we could equally "prove" that this is the worst of all possible worlds. (Worse yet, we could "prove" both that this is the best of all possible worlds *and* that this is the worst of all possible worlds.) What logical grounds are there for using the appeal to ignorance to support the theodicists' conclusion rather than to support the opposite conclusion?

I conclude that Leibniz's argument that this *must* be the best of all possible worlds is unpersuasive. This is not to deny that this *might be* the best of all possible worlds. After all, it is possible that a Leibnizian God created the world. If a Leibnizian God created the world, then this probably is the best of all possible worlds—even if we do not have any epistemic reason for believing it is. So we cannot *prove* that this is *not* the best of all possible worlds. But as we have seen in this book, decisive proofs of philosophical conclusions are almost never available. Instead, we must try to reach the most reasonable conclusions we can using our intellectual abilities the best we can. Leibniz's argument does not appear to meet that standard.

EVIL AS A NECESSARY PART OF ANY WORLD

Leibniz's argument *deduced* that evil *must* be ineliminable, because God chose the best possible world. Arguments that evil is necessary *offer reasons* for thinking that evil is ineliminable. We shall look at three versions of this argument: (1) that if there were no evil, then there could be no good, (2) that the orderliness of the world (which is a great good) requires evil, and (3) that evil is a means to producing greater goods that could not exist otherwise.

5. Without Evil, There Could Be No Goodness

This argument tries to prove that it is logically necessary that if good exists, then evil has to exist also. Logically, there could be no good without evil. This is supposed to be a logical truth like the fact that there could be no squares if there were no four-sided figures, and there could be no brothers if there were no siblings.

J. L. Mackie (1982, 151) suggests a rebuttal to this argument that we can develop with a thought experiment. Let us compare "good" and "evil" with another part of contradictory concepts, "red" and "nonred." Suppose that on Sunday 90 percent of the world's physical objects are red and 10 percent are nonred. Then, gradually, the percentages change. On Monday 93 percent of all physical objects are red, and only 7 percent are nonred. On Tuesday 96 percent of the physical objects are red, and only 4 percent are nonred. On Wednesday 99 percent of physical objects are red, and only 1 percent are nonred. The difference between red and nonred objects still exists, it is just that the percentages have changed. Finally, on Thursday, the remaining 1 percent of physical objects become red. Would it follow that all of a sudden there are *no* red physical objects? Of course not. To complete the analogy, replace "red" with "good" and "nonred" with "evil." If goodness were to entirely replace evil, goodness would still exist, just as red would in the thought experiment. Therefore, evil is not logically necessary for goodness to exist.

The theodicist might respond that even if goodness logically can exist without evil, the presence of evil is necessary if persons are to *recognize* goodness. After all, in the thought experiment, once everything becomes red, persons might forget what nonred things look like, and, thus, might not realize what red is. Perhaps our *knowledge of goodness* is so important that it justifies the existence of evil.

There are several problems with this reply. First, as Mackie notes, at most this recognition argument would justify only a tiny amount of evil, not the vast amount of evil that exists in the world. A speck of evil is all one would need to make the discrimination between good and evil. So the recognition point cannot justify very much evil. Second, there are morally better ways for us to get the idea of evil than through actual suffering. When Hollywood directors make a war movie, they do not actually slaughter thousands of actors to create a realistic effect: They simulate it. By analogy, we could get the idea of evil from novels, poems, plays, and movies. Or God could implant in our minds an innate idea of what evil is. Third, however much real evil was needed for us to recognize the difference between good and evil, there is the question of whether that knowledge is worth the price. This question seems especially relevant when we remember that evil is not evenly distributed. Some persons and beasts suffer much more than others: Why should some pay such a high price for the "education" of others? Is it fair that the victim suffer for the education of the attacker or that children die premature deaths for the edification of their parents?

6. Evil Is Necessary for the Orderliness of the World

Some theodicists emphasize that God cannot be expected to constantly intervene to prevent evil every time it occurs. It is a great benefit to humans that there are laws of nature, rather than having a disorderly world that we could neither predict nor understand. But these laws of nature guarantee that there will be natural disasters like floods, tornadoes, and droughts, as well as disease, pain, and animal suffering. Even though we sometimes wish that the laws of nature did not apply to us (when we fall off a ladder or develop arthritis), it would be much worse to try to live in a world that did not have laws of nature. We must learn to take the bad with the good.

The first objection to this argument is that God is not limited by the laws of nature in the way that finite beings are. Not only could God violate the laws of nature at any moment (for example, prevent the assassin's bullet from hitting Martin Luther King), but God could have created complete worlds with entirely different laws of nature. As Hume (1947, pt. XI, 205–6) notes, rather than designing humans and animals to notice unsafe stimuli by feeling pain, God could have designed them to recognize these by a *diminution of pleasure*. This would have worked just as well, especially given that an omnipotent being could guarantee that it worked as well. If God is omnipotent, He was not limited by His choosing the laws of nature; so we cannot defend God in the problem of evil by saying that He cannot help the way nature operates.

Hume provides a second objection. God could disrupt a law of nature without persons realizing that He has done so. There are so many things that happen due to unknown causes that God could intervene in these events without our knowledge. Such interventions would not disturb our understanding of nature. For example:

> Good princes (might) enjoy sound health and long life: Persons born to power and authority, be framed with good tempers and virtuous dispositions. A few such events as these . . . would change the face of the world; and yet would no more seem to disturb the course of nature or confound human conduct, than the present economy of things, where the causes are secret, and variable, and compounded. (Hume, 1947, pt. XI, 206–7)

Hume suggests a third objection that can be understood in terms of cost-benefit analysis. To the degree that it *is* good that God does not interfere with the laws of nature, does that good (the benefit) always outweigh the corresponding evil that could be prevented by God's interference (the cost)? Even if it is better that God not interfere with the laws of nature in *most* cases, wouldn't it be morally best for God to intervene in some extreme cases? For example, the slightest interference in the uniting of the egg and sperm that produced Adolph Hitler could have prevented Hitler from ever being born. Might not a violation of the laws of nature be justified in some special cases?

7. Evil as an Instrument to Produce Greater Goods

It is a fact of life that some goods cannot be obtained without the existence of certain evils. Surgery is not pleasant, but it is sometimes needed to alleviate worse suffering. No one runs a four-minute mile without enduring pain not only during the run itself, but also in the long training required for it. Few persons are successful in their livelihoods without a great deal of hard work, to say nothing of the many failures and frustrations they encounter along the way. Having a serious emotional relationship with another person takes hard work. So we cannot deny that some pains are instruments to greater goods or, at least, to avoiding worse evils. This is the basis of a theodicist reply: *Some evils are permitted by God because they are needed as instruments to produce greater goods.*

Although this reply has many applications, there are two reasons why it does not prove as much as theodicists wish. First, in the above examples in which evil in a necessary instrument to producing good, evil is only *physically* necessary, not *logically* necessary. To take surgery as an example, human surgeons have to cut into human flesh to perform an appendectomy, because they have no other way to perform the operation. But it would be an immoral surgeon who cut into a patient if she *were* able to perform the needed task without cutting. Human beings are restricted by physical necessity, but God is not. God is like a surgeon who can remove one's appendix without cutting the abdominal wall. So we cannot exonerate God in the problem of evil in the way we can exonerate surgeons—by saying that God is limited by physical necessity. Such a defense by the theodicist surrenders God's omnipotence.

Second, although evil sometimes leads to a greater good, evil more frequently leads to no compensating good or even to greater evil. For example, growing up in an environment where one is unsafe, unloved, and not respected sometimes produces personalities that are strong and compassionate. But more often, such environments produce adults who transmit the disadvantages of their environments to others, especially their own children. Very often, poverty leads to poverty, ignorance leads to ignorance, violence leads to violence. Thus, although some evils lead to greater goods, other evils crush or warp the human spirit. It seems unlikely that evil as an instrument for producing good can justify a very large percentage of evils.

THE VIRTUE (SOUL-MAKING) DEFENSE

Theodicists could agree with all that has been said so far but respond that their opponents have misunderstood the real point of evil. The goodness that God wishes to maximize is not a favorable balance of pleasant experiences over unpleasant ones. Such a world would be an appropriate one for lower creatures or even for humans who have already reached moral perfection, but not for human moral development. God sees the purpose of human life on Earth not to seek happiness, or even to avoid suffering, but, using John Hick's term, for the purpose of "soul-making." God wants humans to become *worthy* in God's eyes: "(H)uman goodness slowly built up through the personal histories of moral effort has a value in the eyes of the Creator which justifies even the long travail of the soul-making process" (Hick, 190, 169). Evil is placed on Earth so that persons can develop their moral characters by responding to it. Heaven is without evil, but Heaven is a reward for dealing with the suffering experienced on Earth in a way that makes one *worthy* to get to Heaven.

Hick argues that morality could not develop in the absence of suffering, because no one would ever be hurt by our immorality: "If to act wrongly means, basically, to harm someone, there would no longer be such a thing as morally wrong action" (Hick, 1990, 179). Generosity and courage could not develop unless there are persons who need help and dangerous situations that test our courage. Truthfulness would never develop in a world where lying produced no evil. Even the love between marriage partners could not fully develop, because such love depends on the couple's facing together the adversities (evils) of life.

I believe the virtue defense is much more interesting than the earlier argument that evil always leads to a greater good. It is easy to confuse the two, but they are quite different. The argument that evil always leads to a greater good makes the implausible claim that *each bit of evil* always promotes goodness in the long run. This is similar to the naive belief that no matter what happens, everything will come out all right in the end. The trouble is that this is a doubtful a posteriori (empirical) claim. For example, hatred usually leads to more hatred.

The virtue defense does *not* say that evil is justified, because each bit of evil leads to a greater good. Hick, for example, can admit that suffering often breaks persons' characters, rather than builds them. Many (most?) souls are lost in the struggles against evil. Thus, Hick's claim is not that each bit of evil produces more goodness individually, but that the soul-making accomplishments of *those who succeed* outweigh the cost of the suffering on Earth, including the evil that befalls *those who fail* at soul-making. This makes Hick's version of the virtue defense a moral claim, rather than an empirical claim, and harder to criticize.

Nonetheless, objections can be raised. First, the virtue defense will seem extremely harsh to soft-hearted persons. Is the value of soul-making really great enough to outweigh the massive suffering faced on Earth? From the perspective of cost-benefit analysis, does the purported value of soul-making make up for all the suffering? Does the end justify the mean? Even if soul-making is a noble end, can it justify, for example, the suffering of children? (See Dostoevski, 1950, bk. V, ch. 4, for a moving argument that it does not.)

Second, there is a question of fairness. Remembering that only some persons succeed at soul-making, does that justify the suffering of the others? In objection II of his *Theodicy* (Baird and Kaufmann, 1997, 262), Leibniz suggests that the glory of the few who get to Heaven might outweigh the eternal suffering of the damned. Is this fair?

Third, if God wants morally trained persons, He could have made us all morally trained without the struggle. Why is it so important that we undergo the painful process? Would not a world where everyone already had moral virtue be a better world than a world full of evil, with humans stumbling about trying to deal with it, a few succeeding and many failing? If theodicists reply that the process is *intrinsically valuable* (good just for its own sake), this would seem to be admitting that they have no real answer.

Fourth, as Mackie (1982, 153–55) notes, the virtue defense puts a higher positive value on virtues like compassion than it places a negative value on the suffering of those for whom we feel compassion. Is this really plausible? Would it be a good thing for *you* to kick someone in the shins (a lower grade of suffering) so that *I* could feel compassion for her (a higher grade of goodness)? Isn't this what *God* does according to the virtue defense?

Fifth, there exist massive, uncontrolled amounts of suffering that do not seem to be justified by the virtue defense. Consider, for example, a baby born with AIDS or animal suffering (discussed later in the chapter). These seem to make no significant contribution to the moral development of virtue in humans or animals. Even Hick admits that the virtue defense justifies only small, carefully placed bits of human suffering, but not the massive, haphazard quantity of real suffering on Earth: "[I]nstead of serving a constructive purpose pain and misery seem to be distributed in random and meaningless ways, with the result that suffering is often undeserved and often falls upon men in amounts exceeding anything that could be rationally intended" (Hick, 1990, 186).

There is a final objection to the virtue defense based on *belief-desire psychology*. Belief-desire psychology holds that our behavior is produced by our beliefs and our desires. For example, we run out of a burning building when we *believe* the building is on fire and we desire to avoid fire. It is not necessary for the building to really be on fire for us to flee the building. We act bravely when we *believe* we are in danger and we resist our fear. We act compassionately toward a person when we *believe* that the person is suffering and we attempt to reduce the suffering.

It follows from belief-desire psychology that to exercise our moral virtues, we need only to *believe* that we are in situations that require them. Dire situations do not really have to exist. God could have given everybody all the opportunities for soul-making that they have in the real world by providing a different world with vastly fewer evils. All God needed to do was make persons *believe* that there is suffering, danger, adversity, and so on. This would require some trickery by God, but it would be similar to the virtuous trickery of Hollywood directors who do not actually have the actors in war movies killed.

THE FREE WILL DEFENSE

A principal theodicist attempt to explain moral evil is the free will defense. The free will defense claims that it is highly desirable that persons exercise free will (make free choices). But for us to make free choices, those choices must be undetermined (uncaused by any preceding conditions). Because a free choice is not determined by anything, it is not under the control of God. God wants humans to use their free will wisely, but it is inevitable that some free choices will produce moral evil. Thus, God is not responsible for the evils that result from persons' free choices. God's only options were to make a world where persons choose freely (and, thus, sometimes wrongly) or to make a world with no free persons at all. Between these two possibilities, God chose the better option: a world with freedom and moral evil rather than the world with no freedom and no moral evil.

Here is the free will defense explicitly stated:

(1) It is a great good that persons make free choices.
(2) Free choices are undetermined by anything, including God's omnipotent creation of all persons.
(3) Undetermined choices necessarily produce moral evil sometimes.
(4) Therefore, the great good of making free choices necessarily results in moral evil sometimes.
(5) The goodness of making free choices outweighs the badness of the evil that sometimes results from them.
(6) Therefore, the goodness of making free choices exonerates God from any blame for the evil that free choices produce.

We should note that there are different ideas of what free choices are. In chapter 8, I defined "free choices" as "choices that are enough under our control to make us morally responsible for the actions they produce." *Libertarians* believe that free (morally responsible) choices must be *undetermined*. That means that they are not caused to occur by previous conditions, including the choosers' state of mind at the time of the choice. In other words, libertarians believe that we can be free and morally responsible for choices only if those choices are not determined. Step (2) of the free will defense relies on the libertarians' theory of free choice.

But, as also noted in chapter 8, there is a competing view of what free choices are. *Compatibilists* believe that free choices *must* be determined by previous conditions, and these previous conditions must include a voluntary and rational evaluation by the chooser of the choice to be made. Compatibilists believe that we make free choices in a determined cosmos when we voluntarily choose actions that we rationally think are best. Thus, compatibilists believe that persons can be free and morally responsible for choices that trace back to events that occurred before they were born. So, theistic compatibilists such as Leibniz believe that persons often choose freely, despite the fact that all their choices were ultimately determined by God's creation of the cosmos.

The first objection to the free will defense is that it relies on the libertarian conception of what free choices are. For it is only libertarian free choices—not compatibilist free choices—that God is powerless to control. If God determined (and foresaw) all of the events in the cosmos when He selected the world, as Leibniz held, then by that choice He also determined *all human (free and unfree) choices*. According to theistic compatibilists, God selected ("predetermined") all the free choices by all persons when He selected our world. So God knew what evil persons would do, and He could have prevented it by selecting a different world. This is why Leibniz uses the best of all possible worlds defense, rather than the free will defense.

As noted in chapter 8, there are serious objections to the libertarian view of free choice. For example, if a choice is not determined by the chooser's state of mind at the moment of choice, how could the chooser *control* the choice enough to be morally responsible for it? As the compatibilist Leibniz says in *Theodicy* (objection III), it would be unfair for God to punish persons who sinned involuntarily, but determinism does not say that persons always choose involuntarily (Baird and Kaufmann, 1997, 263–64). Because the free will defense works only if we adopt a libertarian view of free choice, this is a serious problem. Perhaps the compatibilist view of free choice is better.

Second, even if we accept the libertarian conception of free choice, assigning libertarian free will to persons may reduce two of God's definitional characteristics: His omnipotence and perhaps His omniscience. If we exonerate God from responsibility for the moral evil humans do because He could not control human choices, then there are some events that are literally out of God's control. So the idea of God as selecting everything that happens in the world must be surrendered. This why many theists avoid using the free will defense. It can also be argued that if humans make libertarian free choices, then God does not even *know* what humans will choose until they make those choices. If this is true, then God would not be omniscient.

Third, the free will defense implicitly assumes a *false dichotomy* between two worlds: (1) a world with libertarian freedom and moral evil, or (2) a world with no libertarian freedom and no moral evil. But even if we accept the libertarian view of free will, God would have more than just these two options. God would not have to choose between letting *all* persons exercise their libertarian free will no matter how much evil it produces and making *all* persons unfree. There are some evils that are so great that it seems morally obligatory to stop them, even at the expense of someone's freedom. For example, if God could have prevented Stalin's massive executions of Russian dissenters by taking away some of Stalin's libertarian free will, would not that have been better than allowing both Stalin's free will and the executions?

Fourth, the free will defense is designed to exonerate God from blame for moral evil, but it does not seem to touch natural evil. How can free choice justify the suffering of animals in the wild, birth defects, natural disasters, and accidents? Some theodicists appeal to specific theological doctrines at this point, but besides the fact that we could never know these doctrines are true, there is a question of whether they are morally acceptable. For example, some theodicists say that natural evil is a result of Adam and Eve's misuse of their free will in original sin. But this reply suggests that it is fair to punish the children for the misdeeds of their parents, which looks patently unfair. According to Alvin Plantinga, St. Augustine, an important philosopher and one of the founders of Christianity, thought that natural evil is due to Satan's misuse of his free will (Adams and Adams, 1990, 107): Satan produced natural evil by his immoral free choice. But this reply, too, looks unfair. Why should other beings suffer for Satan's misuse of his free will?

Fifth, the free will defense assumes that if we assign the blame for moral evil to humans, then we can exonerate God from blame. This assumption can be questioned by considering a thought experiment. Suppose you own in your backyard an Olympic-size swimming pool with a high diving platform. You place a high fence around it, topped with barbed-wire and broken glass, and post signs forbidding trespassing. Nonetheless, every time you are away from your home, local teenagers get drunk, climb the fence, and dive off the platform. And, like clockwork, every few weeks one of them accidentally hits his or her head on the platform and drowns in your pool. No matter how often you warn them (and prosecute them for trespassing when you catch them), you cannot prevent the local youths from sneaking into your pool and periodically killing themselves by diving from the platform. What should you do?

Here are two possible responses. First, you could say that because you have tried to keep the trespassers out, *you* are not responsible for the deaths that result. The deaths are unfortunate, but they are not your fault. So you might continue to try to prevent the youths from sneaking into your pool and feel confident that you have done your moral best. And when the youths continue to die, you can remind yourself that it is not your fault. Second, if you *really* want to prevent the deaths, you could take further steps: Dismantle the high board, and, if that fails to prevent the drownings, fill in the swimming pool altogether. This second option would be extremely morally conscientious of you. (Moral philosophers call such acts "supererogatory.") But if you really care about the deaths, and are not satisfied to simply blame the teenagers for the problem, you would have to consider seriously the second option.

This example suggests that sometimes placing blame on A is not enough to exonerate B from responsibility. Blaming the teenagers does not necessarily exonerate you from all blame. By analogy, even if we can correctly assign blame to humans for moral evil, that does not necessarily exonerate God from all responsibility. Like the swimming pool owner who refuses to drain the swimming pool, God may be partly to blame for human sinning, even if humans are largely to blame. Sometimes there is enough blame to go around for all sides.

ANIMAL SUFFERING

We have examined four major types of theodicist strategies: (1) This *must* be the best of all possible worlds. (2) Evils, taken individually, are instruments to greater goods. (3) Evil, collectively, is justified by the soul-making process. (4) Evil is necessary if we are to have libertarian free will. Many philosophers believe that one or more of these replies succeed. I have argued that none of these replies deals successfully with human suffering—either natural evil or moral evil. I believe that the inadequacy of theodicist arguments is even more apparent when it comes to the suffering endured by nonhuman animals or beasts.

There is strong evidence that animals other than humans experience pain from disease, starvation, and injury. There is suggestive evidence that beasts experience unpleasant psychological states such as frustration, terror, and even depression. These claims are best supported for other mammals due to the great behavioral and anatomical similarities between humans and mammals. But the similarities extend down the phylogenetic scale to birds, reptiles, and perhaps animals with even less complex nervous systems.

In addition, suffering among animals is not an exception, but the rule. Most animals have natural predators who live by eating them. Most animals die young and, except for pets, almost none live long enough to "die of old age." The English philosopher Thomas Hobbes said that the lives of humans living without a strong ruler to ensure law and order were "nasty, brutish, and short." This describes the lives of most animals who have ever existed on this planet.

Why would an omniscient, omnipotent, and morally perfect creator make the lives (and deaths) of beasts so full of pain? The vast majority of animal suffering is the result of the laws of nature rather than human cruelty, so we cannot say that the majority of animal suffering is due to humans misusing their free will. (Most beasts who lived on Earth did so before humans evolved on the planet.) Theodicists do not claim that animal suffering is for the purpose of building *the animals'* souls. It is sometimes said that animal suffering is a necessary part of the ecosystem ("food chain"): If animals did not eat each other and die of starvation, they would overpopulate the world. This is true, but an omnipotent God is not limited by the laws of biology. God could have made all animals herbivores who live by eating vegetation, not other animals. God could have made animals reproduce at much lower rates. Then, if God wanted to replace existing animals with new ones, he could make old animals painlessly vanish into thin air—not have them starve to death or be eaten by predators. In sum, it appears that God could have done much better for the animals than He did.

I think that theodicists have to appeal to implausible premises to respond to this challenge. The French philosopher René Descartes provided an irrefutable, but unlikely, theory that theodicists could use: Animals, lacking nonphysical minds, are not capable of feeling pain. Animals are simply "machines" that cannot suffer. An equally irrefutable, but hard-hearted, claim could be offered by the *speciesist* (a person who discounts the well-being of all creatures other than humans): "Even if they suffer, animals simply do not count. After all, they are *only animals*; humans are God's chosen creatures."

I conclude this section by looking at animal suffering from the perspective of *inference to the best explanation*, a reasoning device used throughout this book. Discounting Descartes's position, let us take as a datum the fact that there is great suffering among beasts. Let us assume also that the suffering is due to the biological laws governing animals in the wild. Consider two possible explanations for why animals suffer. One explanation is that the biological laws were purposely designed by a morally perfect, omniscient, omnipotent God who wanted to produce the best of all possible worlds. The second explanation is that the biological laws were not designed by such a God. In the second case, either the laws were not purposely designed at all, or, if they were, the designer of the biological laws is not a morally perfect, omniscient, and omnipotent God. Which explanation makes the datum more less surprising? Which explanation seems more likely to be true? If we select the second, we are saying that the existence of animal suffering gives some evidence to think that nature was not designed by a being that is morally perfect, omniscient, and omnipotent.

A PROBLEM OF GOODNESS?

As is customary, in this chapter we have distinguished between natural evils and moral evils. We have seen that the compatibilist and libertarian theodicists disagree over the best way to defend God regarding moral evil. To simplify the remaining discussion, let us consider only *natural evils*, a topic on which compatibilists' and libertarians' different views about free will and moral evil do not matter. I shall argue that theodicist defenses of natural evil face a final objection.

If we think about the problem of evil long enough, the question is bound to occur: If natural evil were really as great as the theodicists say, then why didn't God provide *more* of it? Thus, the theodicist faces a *Problem of Goodness*: *Given that evil is really good, why is there not more*? This is the counterpart to the problem of evil, which asks why there is not less evil. To this challenge, the theodicist must reply that because God is omniscient, omnipotent, and morally perfect, the actual amount of evil in the world must be *exactly* the correct amount. As noted in the discussion of the Best of All Possible Worlds reply, a little more or a little less evil would make the world worse.

Now, here is the problem. Theodicist explanations of why evil is necessary are *not* restricted so that they apply only to the *exact actual amount* of natural evil that exists in the real world. Instead, they are perfectly general explanations that, if cogent, *would* justify *indefinitely more or indefinitely less* evil than exists in the real world.

Suppose that in the history of the world *twice* as many humans and beasts choked to death while eating as actually happened. If that had happened, then the theodicists could just as well use their arguments to say that *that* was exactly the right amount of accidental choking (for the purposes of creating goodness or for soul-making). Suppose, on the other hand, that in the history of the world only *half* as many humans and beasts choked to death while eating. Then the theodicists could just as sensibly say that *that* was just the right amount of accidental choking. So whether much more or much less evil occurred, the theodicist could use the same reasoning to justify it. And any "solution" that would "work" equally well, no matter how much evil there is, cannot work at all. Call this the *Principle of Explaining Evil* : *Any solution that works to exonerate God of all possible evil is not a satisfactory solution to the problem of actual evil.*

Here is some support for this principle. The philosopher of science Karl Popper (1902–1994) distinguishes between scientific and pseudo (phony) scientific theories in this way: A scientific theory must be in principle *falsifiable* in the sense that there *could* be some possible observations that would help to disconfirm or discredit it. If a theory cannot be discredited by any possible data, then it is not a serious scientific theory, but a pseudo theory. For example, the theory that metals conduct heat at different rates of speed due to the different personality traits of undetectable gremlins living inside the metals is a pseudo theory, because no possible observation could ever discredit it.

By analogy, the theodicists' arguments explaining natural evil in terms of creating goodness or soul-making are all-purpose arguments for which we could never find disconfirming evidence. No matter how much or how little evil occurs, those arguments could still "explain" it away. This means that these arguments are like pseudo-scientific theories and should be rejected.

Guide Questions

1. Explain the idea of a logically inconsistent set of statements? (275)
2. What six statements constitute the problem of evil? (275)
3. What is the connection between omnipotence and the laws of nature? (276)
4. Explain the difference between natural evils and moral evils. (276)

5. Why do some theists refuse to explain evil by saying that it is due to Satan? (277)
6. Which of the six statements that constitute the problem of evil do most theodicists say is false? (277)
7. Give one reason not to try to solve the problem of evil by saying that we cannot understand God's logic? (278)
8. Give one objection to Spinoza's solution to the problem of evil. (278–79)
9. What is Leibniz's argument that God must have created the best of all possible worlds? (279)
10. Provide one objection to Leibniz's argument. (279–80)
11. In what sense might theodicists try to place the *burden of proof* on their opponents on the question of whether this is the best of all possible worlds? (281)
12. What is the point of the example in which all of the physical objects on Earth gradually become red? (283)
13. What is the point of the example of directors making war movies? (283)
14. Explain the theodicists' argument that evil is necessary for the world to be orderly? (284)
15. What point was Hume making when he suggested that good princes might enjoy sound health and long lives? (284)
16. How does the opponent of the theodicist compare God to a surgeon who can remove one's appendix without cutting, but cuts anyway? (285)
17. What are some virtues that Hick thinks could not exist without evil? (286)
18. Explain the difference between the virtue defense and the argument that evil always leads to a greater good. (286)
19. How does the virtue defense face an objection regarding fairness? (286–87)
20. How does *belief/desire psychology* pose a difficulty for the virtue defense? (287–88)
21. Explain the free will defense in two sentences. (288)
22. How are the two conceptions of free will important to the free will defense? (288–89)
23. How may the free will defense be criticized as presenting a *false dichotomy*? (289)
24. Explain the relevance of the swimming pool example to the free will defense. (290–91)
25. What difficulty does animal suffering pose to the theodicist? (291)
26. Explain the analogy between Popper's account of pseudo-scientific theories and the *Principle of Explaining Evil*. (293)

Review Questions for Examinations

1. Define these terms: "theist," "atheist," "theodicist," "omniscience," "omnipotence," "natural evil," "moral evil," "logically possible," "physically possible," "free will," "libertarian free will," "compatibilist free will."
2. What are these informal fallacies: false dichotomy, appeal to ignorance, smoke screen.
3. Express the problem of evil as a logical inconsistency. What is so bad about believing a logical inconsistency?
4. Explain these theodicist arguments: the best of all possible worlds, evil is a necessary part of any world, the virtue (soul-making) defense, the free will defense.
5. Explain these criticisms of the theodicist: animal suffering and the problem of goodness.

Discussion Questions

1. The philosopher B. C. Johnson provides the following objection to the theodicists based on moral urgency:

   > Theodicists say that God put natural evil on Earth to create *moral urgency* (so persons would respond to it). This entails that if natural evil dropped below a certain point, God morally should add more natural evil to the world to bring the world up to the needed level needed for maximum moral urgency. But the idea of God being morally obliged to add more suffering to the world is absurd. Therefore, the theodicist position is absurd.

   How might the theodicist reply to this objection?
2. There is a theodicist argument that stems back to Plato, which was endorsed by Augustine and several prominent theodicists:

   > Evil is not real, it is just the limitation of (or lack of) goodness. For example, ignorance is a lack of knowledge and poverty is a lack of wealth. Because evil is not really there, it cannot be blamed on God. God is responsible only for what exists, not for what does not exist.

   How might one object to this argument?
3. In this chapter we saw that inference to the best explanation can be used against the theodicist. Can you think of any data that are best explained by the hypothesis that this world *has been designed* by a morally perfect, omniscient, omnipotent creator?
4. Evaluate this challenge to the theodicist posed by B. C. Johnson:

   > God does not try to stave-off natural evil (for example, to save persons from a forest fire) when He sees it. But a morally conscientious human

bystander would try to help. So, God is not as morally commendable as a morally conscientious human being.

5. J. L. Mackie suggests this objection to the libertarians' free will defense.

   > Even if libertarian free will were better than compatibilist free will, God could have adopted this strategy: Permit persons to make libertarian choices, but whenever a choice is morally bad, intervene to prevent the evil it would cause. Persons would still be left with their libertarian free will, moral evil would be prevented, and persons would soon learn that they should not make immoral choices (because their immoral choices would never yield their intended results).

   What is the best theodicist response to this argument?
6. In this chapter we have examined several theodicist strategies: this must be the best of all possible worlds, evil is a necessary part of any world, the virtue defense (evil contributes to soul-making), and the free will defense. Which of these defenses works best for these evils: premature death due to illness, birth defects, environmental pollution, political dictatorships, jealousy, malnutrition, global warming, AIDS, senile psychosis, strokes.

FOR FURTHER READING

Adams, Marilyn and Robert Adams, eds. 1990. *The Problem of Evil*. Oxford: Oxford University Press. A collection of some of the most influential recent discussions of the problem of evil discussion, including the works by M. Adams, Hick, and Mackie cited in this chapter. Difficult.

Hume, David. 1947. *Dialogues Concerning Natural Religion*. Indianapolis: Bobbs-Merrill. Part X is Hume's classic discussion of the problem of evil. The rest of the book contains Hume's treatments of the proofs of the existence of God, including his famous discussion of miracles. Interesting to read. Moderately difficult.

Leibniz, Gottfried Wilhelm. 1997. *Theodicy*. In Forrest Baird and Walter Kaufmann, eds., *Modern Philosophy*, Upper Saddle River, NJ: Prentice-Hall. A short but powerful defense by one of the great historical philosophers. Moderately easy to read.

Peterson, Michael, ed. 1992. *The Problem of Evil*. Notre Dame: University of Notre Dame Press. A comprehensive anthology that contains selections from nonphilosophers (*Book of Job*, Dostoevski, Camus) and philosophers. Twenty–four-page bibliography. Ranges from easy to difficult.

Chapter 11
A Total Picture

PHILOSOPHY AS WORLDVIEW CONSTRUCTION

A person who holds the view of philosophy exemplified in this book—Philosophy as Worldview Construction—wishes to accept only those philosophical beliefs and theories with the greatest probability of being true relative to the other things one thinks are true. To achieve that end, such a thinker is committed to the methodology of critical thinking described in chapters 1, 2, and 3. In my view, critical thinkers accept claims only on evidential grounds, regardless of whether those claims are attractive on any other grounds. According to this way of approaching philosophy, it does not matter whether our philosophical theories support other intellectual endeavors, common sense, or religion, whether they contribute to morality or other valuable aims, or whether the story we tell is artistically interesting. Persons who hold the Philosophy as Worldview Construction metaphilosophy may or may not value these other aims, but, by definition, they never let these aims interfere with the aim of trying to provide the most-likely-to-be-true answers to philosophical questions.

A driving motivation behind Philosophy as Worldview Construction is *the desire to achieve consistency across all areas of human thought*. Philosophers who endorse the Worldview metaphilosophy think we should make equal demands for evidence for *all* types of beliefs, whether philosophical beliefs or beliefs from everyday life. This means that Worldview thinkers demand just as much evidence for a belief they find uplifting, beautiful, or useful as they do for a belief they find depressing, ugly, or useless.

Consider an analogy. Most of us think it is a virtue of a legal system to require equal evidence against persons charged with crimes regardless of their race, sex, or economic status. We think it is an error—moral, logical, or both—to apply inconsistent standards to defendants. Worldview thinkers believe this is also the case for our beliefs. For example, if in everyday life we let wishful thinking lower our standards of evidence for beliefs we want to be true (commit the fallacy of wishful thinking), then we are prone to be duped by medical quackery such as the belief that laetrile is effective in combatting cancer when all the evidence shows that it is not (Gilovich, 1991, ch. 8). By analogy, why should we let nontruth-seeking goals have *any* part to play in our philosophical theorizing—*if* our goal is to produce a worldview that is most likely to be true? Why should we be less ardent truth seekers in philosophy than we are in everyday life? If consistency is a virtue, then we should demand equal evidence in all areas of our lives *and* for all philosophical beliefs.

Ralph Waldo Emerson wrote in "Self-Reliance" that "a foolish consistency is the hobgoblin of little minds." This remark is sometimes misunderstood to make Emerson seem as if he were criticizing logical consistency. In fact, Emerson meant by "foolish consistency" the sort of phenomenon that contemporary psychologists call "belief-perseverance bias"—our natural tendency to try to keep our beliefs insulated from disconfirmation. Emerson meant that when evidence shows that one of our beliefs is false, we should admit it, rather than remaining attached to the discredited belief. For Emerson, we display a foolish consistency when we remain wedded to a belief simply because we do not like to admit that we are wrong.

To the extent that we lessen our adherence to the metaphilosophy of Worldview Construction, we risk falling into the trap Emerson warned us against: If we say that philosophy is for underpinning faith or promoting morality, we insolate certain beliefs from criticism. We would be deciding to give certain beliefs preferential treatment not because they have been found more likely to be true than their denials, but simply because we *want* them to be true. This is wishful thinking, once again. Worldview thinkers admit that it is possible to lead one's life believing only those facts one *has* to believe, and believing everything else because one *wants* to. But this is not the way Worldview thinkers choose to go.

A WORLDVIEW

Philosophers hold many worldviews. Here is the one that emerges from this book. Given the Worldview Construction metaphilosophy adopted in chapter 1, logic, critical thinking, and epistemology (chapters 2 and 3) constitute the methodology for addressing philosophical questions. Two of the most important epistemological tools are inference to the best explanation and Occam's Razor. Inference to the best explanation allows entities into our worldview if they best explain *other entities* that we already believe exist. Occam's Razor dictates that we not add anything to our worldview that is *not* needed to explain the things we already believe exist. Because the ultimate data that we have to admit are our sensations, everything let into our picture of the world is ultimately justified by its role in explaining our sensations. (This is a thought expressed by Quine, 1960.) So if we are justified in saying that physical objects, other minds, nonphysical minds, God, or objective free will and moral values exist, we are justified only because postulating them creates a picture of the world that best explains our sensations.

The picture arrived at in this book is naturalistic. Naturalism maintains that everything that exists is located in space and time. Thus, in the mind/body problem, persons are seen as physical beings, their mentality being the operations of their nervous systems. Regarding the existence of God, atheism is the winner, because there is no need to include the existence of a nonphysical Supreme Being to explain the things we already must acknowledge. Regarding the existence of the external world, inference to the best explanation and Occam's Razor support scientific realism. Scientific realism holds that the commonsensical properties of physical objects such as color, solidity, and sharp edges exist only subjectively in our minds, not in the objects themselves. Physical objects in themselves are held to be only atoms and empty space.

Scientific realism's subjectivism regarding the commonsense properties of physical objects links metaphysics and value theory, because subjectivism in metaphysics provides a model for subjectivism in value theory. Subjectivism in metaethics holds that right and wrong and good and evil consist of *human sentiments* or *feelings* about right and wrong and good and evil. Moral subjectivism acknowledges that moral sentiments are extremely important to us, but insists that morality is subjective in the sense of existing only in our minds, not in some objective way outside human sentiment. This moral subjectivism applied to the free will problem maintains that "free" in the sense that it is supposed to sanction moral responsibility is merely in the eye of the beholder, no less than "good" and "evil."

In sum, the picture of the world that emerges in this text portrays all of reality as physical, with no supernatural components. Human beings are complex, marvelous biological organisms; so far as we know, humans are the most intelligent creatures that exist. Human mentality is produced by our remarkable three-pound brains, which allow us to think about free will, morality, the existence of the supernatural, and our own mortality. Because of our big brains, we humans are able to reflect on ourselves and even raise the question of whether there is a point to our existence.

THE MEANING OF LIFE

The idea of life having a meaning or purpose is paradoxical. On the one hand, most of us want there to be a meaning to life in the sense of a larger purpose that our lives are designed to serve. *Objectivists* say there *is* a meaning to human life, whether anyone recognizes it or not. (In this sense, objectivists about the meaning of life are like objectivists in metaethics who say that there are moral truths whether anyone recognizes them or not.) Objectivists look outside themselves for meaning—to God, interpersonal relationships, community, history, political movements, or ideology. By being a part of a larger whole, objectivists hope to find meaning for their own lives. This is why naturalistic worldviews seem unattractive to theologically oriented objectivists: The idea that persons on Earth are the biological results of the laws of physics in a Godless cosmos seems to drain meaning from their lives.

Objectivism looks attractive at first blush, probably because we like the idea of our lives having a solid foundation of meaning that does not depend on us. This is reassuring, because if our meaning does not *depend* on us, then we do not have to face the task of making it. Worries begin to arise, however, when we realize that being told "the" meaning of life is such and such proves psychologically satisfying to us only if we *endorse* that meaning ourselves. Human beings have the ability to look at any proposed candidate for the role of the meaning of life and protest: "So what? The existence of God, other persons, history, or ideological causes means nothing to *me*." For any fact the objectivists offer as "the" meaning of life, critics can look at that proposed meaning and deny that it gives *their* lives meaning. On the other hand, we can take any activity, whether others find it meaningful or not, and *make* it the meaning of *our* lives. Persons find the strangest things valuable and meaningful.

These last two points suggest that although we would like there to be an objective meaning to life lying outside our own making, by the very definition of "meaning," there cannot *be* any such thing. This is the subjectivist view. *Subjectivists* say that there can be no meaning to life in the objectivist's sense, because "meaning" is a psychological concept. According to the subjectivists, *we* provide meaning in our lives. Like it or not, we are "doomed" to provide whatever meaning our lives have, just as we are "doomed" to determine what things we think are valuable.

To see why subjectivism about the meaning of life is plausible, compare two possible scenarios. In World 1 there *is* an answer to the meaning of life in the objectivist sense, but none of the persons in that world accept that answer. Suppose, for the sake of this example, that we stipulate that the meaning of life is to worship God. To call this "objective" is to say that the meaning of human life is to worship God whether any person realizes it or not. Now suppose that all the persons in World 1 are presented with this objectively true answer, but each one refuses to acknowledge it. Some of these persons are atheists, others are theists of different religions who accept the answers to the meaning of life that their ("wrong") religions propose, whereas still others are skeptics who suspect that the whole idea of an objective meaning of life makes no sense. For the persons in World 1, worshipping God would not provide meaning to their lives.

In World 2, there *is no* answer to the meaning of life in the objectivist sense, and all persons are subjectivists who believe that persons alone create whatever meaning their lives have. Moreover, they all go on to decide on various goals for their lives that they *take* to make their lives meaningful. Some elect to make the meaning of their lives reside in their interpersonal relationships, others in their jobs, still others in developing their intellects. The lives of the persons in World 2 will be more meaningful to them than are the lives of the persons in World 1 who have an objective meaning, but fail to acknowledge it.

Thus, it seems that the *subjective belief in meaning* rather than the *objective existence of meaning* produces *real meaning*. Strange as it sounds at first, real meaning—not an abstraction, but that which gives purpose to our lives—is subjective, not objective. (Compare: *Real pain* is the sensation we feel rather than an actual injury we do not feel.) This suggests that the meaning of life is not an objective thing, but something that exists only to the extent that persons create it themselves. Although we want there to be an objective meaning to life that is not our own invention, that is impossible. Meaning is created from within, it is not given from the outside. If this is so, then naturalism does not necessarily take away the meaning of our lives, but only if we decide it does.

It is our prerogative to respond to the subjectivist conclusion with despair or to embrace it joyfully. The nineteenth-century American novelist Henry Adams writes that learning that the universe will eventually become lifeless left him with an overwhelming sense of the meaninglessness of life. The French writer Albert Camus writes that the mythical character Sisyphus, who was doomed by the gods to eternally push a boulder up a mountain, was happy because he was able to self-consciously recognize his unfortunate plight. These examples show that persons have the ability to find meaning or meaninglessness in practically any fact—the fact that we are aware of our plights or the thought that human life will perish long after we die. This is, again, analogous to moral subjectivism. We may elect to be saddened by the thought that morality is subjective to human sentiment, or we may feel ennobled by the thought. Once again, the choice is ours.

Discussion Questions

1. Consider the following possible answers to five of the problems examined in this book. *External world*: direct realism, scientific realism, and phenomenalism. *Mind/Body Problem*: materialism, dualism, idealism. *Metaethics*: objectivism and subjectivism. *Free Will Problem*: hard determinism, soft determinism, libertarianism, Free-Will-Either-Way Theory, No-Free-Will-Either-Way Theory, and subjectivism. *Existence of God*: theism and atheism. Selecting one theory as an answer to each of the five problems, is there any combination that fits together especially well? Are there any combinations that do not fit together at all? Which combination do you think is most likely to be true?
2. Suppose I am a theist who believes in libertarian free will. What position will I need to take in epistemology? Suppose I am a scientific realist regarding the nature of the external world. What options are open to me regarding the existence of God and metaethics?
3. It seems sensible for an employer or a family member to say to you: "This is your duty, whether you recognize it or not." Could a similar judgment be

made about the meaning of one's life: "This is the meaning of your life whether you realize it or not"? Why or why not?

4. A classic statement that it is always immoral to believe on insufficient epistemic grounds was given by the British mathematician and philosopher W. K. Clifford:

> Belief, that sacred faculty which prompts the decisions of our will, and knits into harmonious workings all the compacted energies of our being, is ours not for ourselves, but for humanity. It is rightly used on truths which have been established by long experience and waiting toil, and which have stood in the fierce light of free and fearless questioning. . . . It is desecrated when given to unproved and unquestioned statements, for the solace and private pleasure of the believer; to add a tinsel splendor to the plain straight road of our life and display a bright mirage beyond it; or even to drown the common sorrows of our kind by a self-deception which allows them not only to cast down but also to degrade us. . . . [I]t is wrong always, everywhere, and for any one, to believe anything on insufficient evidence. (1877, 170–75)

   If one takes Clifford's epistemological position, what sort of worldview will one be likely to reach? Is Clifford's position an acceptable one? What factors should we use to decide the second question?

FOR FURTHER READING

Double, Richard. 1996. *Metaphilosophy and Free Will*. Argues that the conclusions philosophers reach on the free will problem—and by extension, other philosophical problems—are dictated by their having different goals in doing philosophy. Moderately difficult.

Gilovich, Thomas. 1991. *How We Know What Isn't So*. New York: Free Press. A fascinating exploration of recent findings in psychology dealing with human reasoning. A lively, enjoyable invitation to consistency in critical thinking across all domains of our thought.

Nagel, Thomas. 1979. *Mortal Questions*. New York: Oxford University Press. Insightful essays into questions of meaning by a prominent contemporary philosopher. Moderately difficult.

Westphal, Jonathan and Carl Levenson, eds. 1993. *Life and Death*. Indianapolis: Hackett. Contains nineteen short selections on the meaning of life from philosophers such as Plato, Aristotle, Nietzsche, and Wittgenstein and literary figures such as Shakespeare, Tolstoy, and Simone Weil.

Philosophical Quotes

Aristotle, *Nicomachean Ethics*, bk. II, sect. 6 (4th century B.C.)

Virtue is concerned with emotions and actions; and in emotions and actions excess and deficiency miss the mark, whereas the median is praised and constitutes success. . . . Consequently, virtue is a mean in the sense that it aims at the median. This is corroborated by the fact that there are many ways of going wrong, but only one way which is right.

A. J. Ayer, *Language, Truth, and Logic*, ch. 1 (1935)

Our charge against the metaphysician is not that he attempts to employ the understanding in a field where it cannot profitably venture, but that he produces sentences which fail to conform to the conditions under which alone a sentence can be literally significant.

George Berkeley, *Principles of Human Knowledge*, sects. 92. and 94 (1710)

The doctrine of Matter . . . [has] been the main pillar and support of Scepticism . . . Atheism and Irreligion. . . . The existence of Matter, or bodies unperceived, has not only been the main support of Atheists and Fatalists, but on the same principle doth idolatry likewise in all its various forms depend. Did men but consider that the sun, moon, and stars, and every other object of the senses are only so many sensations in their minds, which have no other existence but barely being perceived, doubtless they would never fall down and worship their own *ideas*, but rather address their homage to that ETERNAL INVISIBLE MIND which produces and sustains all things.

Albert Camus, *The Myth of Sisyphus* (1955)

There is but one truly serious philosophical problem, and that is suicide. Judging whether life is or is not worth living amounts to answering the fundamental question of philosophy. All the rest . . . comes afterwards.

W. K. Clifford, "The Ethics of Belief" in *Lectures and Essays (vol. II)* (1877)

Men speak the truth to one another when each reveres the truth in his own mind and in the other's mind; but how shall my friend revere the truth in my mind when I myself am careless about it, when I believe things because I want to believe them, and because they are comforting and pleasant? Will he not learn to cry "Peace" to me, when there is no peace? By such a course I shall surround myself with a thick atmosphere of falsehood and fraud, and in that I must live. It may matter little to me, in my cloud-castle of sweet illusions and darling lies; but it matters much to Man that I have made my neighbors ready to deceive. The credulous man is father to the liar and the cheat. . . .

To sum up: it is wrong always, everywhere, and for any one to believe anything upon insufficient evidence.

Confucius, *Analects*, bk. 15:18 (5th century B.C.)

The superior man is distressed by his want of ability. What the superior man seeks is in himself. What the mean man seeks is in others.

Rene Descartes, *A Discourse on Method Part I* (1637)

Good sense is of all things in the world the most equally distributed, for everybody thinks himself so abundantly provided with it, that even those most difficult to please in all other matters do not commonly desire more of it than they already possess.

Epictetus, *The Encheiridion*, sect. 41 (1st century A.D.)

It is a mark of an ungifted man to spend a great deal of time in what concerns his body, as in much exercise, much eating, much drinking, much evacuating of the bowels, much copulating. But these things are to be done in passing; and let your whole attention be devoted to the mind.

Epicurus, *Letter to Menoecens* (c. 300 B.C.)

So death, the most terrifying of ills, is nothing to us, since so long as we exist, death is not with us; but when death comes, then we do not exist. It does not then concern either the living or the dead, since for the former it is not, and the latter are no more.

G. W. F. Hegel, *Philosophy of Right* (1821)

What is rational is real and what is real is rational.

Martin Heidegger, "What Is Metaphysics?" (1949)

The nothing noths.

Thomas Hobbes, *Leviathan*, pt. I, ch. 13 (1651)

[D]uring the time men live without a common power to keep them all in awe, they are in that condition which is called war; and such a war, as is of every man, against every man. . . . Whatsoever therefore is consequent to a time of war, where every man is enemy to every man; the same is consequent to the time, wherein men live without other security, than what their own strength, and their own invention shall furnish them withal. In such condition, there is no place for industry; because the fruit thereof is uncertain: and consequently no culture of the earth; no navigation, nor use of the commodities that may be imported by sea; no commodious building; no instruments of moving, and removing, such things as require much force; no knowledge of the face of the earth; no account of time; no arts; no letters; no society; and which is worst of all, continual fear, and danger of violent death; and the life of man, solitary, poor, nasty, brutish, and short.

David Hume, *An Inquiry Concerning Human Understanding* (1748)

When we run over libraries, persuaded of [my] principles, what havoc must we make? If we take in our hand any volume of divinity or school metaphysics, for instance let us ask, *Does it contain any abstract reasoning concerning quantity or number?* No. *Does it contain any experimental reasoning concerning matter of fact and existence?* No. Commit it then to the flames, for it can contain nothing but sophistry and illusion.

William James, *Pragmatism*, Lecture 5 (1907)

[O]ur fundamental ways of thinking about things are discoveries of exceedingly remote ancestors, which have been able to preserve themselves throughout the experience of all subsequent time. They form one great stage of equilibrium in the human mind's development, the stage of *common sense.* Other stages have grafted themselves upon this stage, but have never succeeded in displacing it. Let us consider this common-sense stage first, as if it might be final.

Immanuel Kant, *Foundations of the Metaphysics of Morals* (1785)

Nothing in the world—indeed nothing even beyond the world—can possibly be conceived which could be called good without qualification except a *good will.* Intelligence, wit, judgment, and the other talents of the mind, however they may be named, or courage, resoluteness, and perseverance as qualities of temperament, are doubtless in many respects good and desirable. But they can become extremely bad and harmful if the will, which is to make use of these gifts of nature and which in its special constitution is called character, is not good. . . . The good will is not good because of what it effects or accomplishes or because of its adequacy to achieve some proposed end; it is good only because of its willing, i.e., it is good of itself. . . . Even if it should happen that, by a particularly unfortunate fate or by the niggardly provision of a stepmotherly nature, this will should be wholly lacking in power to accomplish its purpose, and if even the greatest effort should not avail it to achieve anything of its end, and if there remained only the good will (not as a mere wish but as the summoning of all the means in our power), it would sparkle like a jewel in its own right, as something that had its full worth in itself.

W. Leibniz, *A Vindication of God's Justice.* sect. 46 (1710)

[T]he infinite wisdom of the Almighty allied with his boundless goodness has brought it about that nothing better could have been created, everything taken into account, than what God has created. As a consequence all things are in perfect harmony and conspire in the most beautiful way. . . . Whenever, therefore, some detail of the work of God appears to us reprehensible, we should judge that we do not know enough about it and that according to the wise who would understand it, nothing better could even be desired.

John Locke, *An Essay Concerning Human Understanding*, bk. II, ch. 1, sect. 2 (1688)

Let us then suppose the mind to be, as we say, white paper, void of all characters, without any ideas; how comes it to be furnished? Whence comes it by that vast store which the busy and boundless fancy of man has painted on it with an almost endless variety? Whence has it all the materials of reason and knowledge? To this I answer, in one word, for *experience*; in that all our knowledge is founded, and from that it ultimately derives itself.

Karl Marx, *Economic and Philosophic Manuscripts* (1844)

The alienation of the worker . . . is expressed according to the laws of political economy as follows: the more the worker produces, the less he has to consume; the more values he creates the more worthless and unworthy he becomes; the better shaped his product, the more misshapen is he; the more civilized his product, the more barbaric is the worker; the more powerful the work, the more powerless becomes the worker; the more intelligence the work has, the more witless is the worker and the more he becomes a slave of nature.

John Stuart Mill, *On Liberty*, ch. 1 (1859)

[T]he sole end for which mankind are warranted, individually or collectively, in interfering with the liberty of action of any of their number, is self-protection. . . . His own good, either physical or moral, is not a sufficient warrant. He cannot rightfully be compelled to do or forbear because it will be better for him to do so, because it will make him happier, because, in the opinions of others, to do so would be wise, or even right. There are good reasons for remonstrating with him, or reasoning with him, or persuading him, or entreating him, but not for compelling him, or visiting him with any evil, in case he do otherwise.

New Testament, John 8:32

[T]he truth will set you free.

Friedrich Nietzsche, *Beyond Good and Evil*, sect. 259. (1886)

Here one must think profoundly to the very basis and resist all sentimental weakness: life itself is *essentially* appropriation, injury, conquest of the strange and weak, suppression, severity, obtrusion of peculiar forms, incorporation, and at the least, putting it mildest, exploitation. . . .

William of Occam, *Scriptum in Librum Primum Sententiarum* (13th century)

Plurality should not be posited unnecessarily.

Plato, *Phaedo*, 66, e (4th century B.C.)

[I]f we are to have clear knowledge of anything, we must get rid of the body, and let the soul by itself behold objects by themselves.

W. V. O. Quine, *Word and Object*, ch. 1, sect. 6 (1960)

To call a posit a posit is not to patronize it. A posit can be unavoidable except at the cost of other no less artificial expedients. Everything to which we concede existence is a posit from the standpoint of a description of the theory-building process, and simultaneously real from the standpoint of the theory that is being built. Nor let us look down on the standpoint of the theory as make-believe; for we can never do better than occupy the standpoint of some theory or other, the best we can muster at the time.

John Rawls, *A Theory of Justice*, ch. 1, sect. 3 (1971)

This original position is . . . a purely hypothetical situation characterized so as to lead to a certain conception of justice. Among the essential features of this situation is that no one knows his place in society, his class position or social status, nor does any one know his fortune in the distribution of natural assets and abilities, his intelligence, strength, and the like. I shall even assume that the parties do not know their conceptions of the good or their special psychological propensities. The principles of justice are chosen behind a veil of ignorance. This ensures that no one is advantaged or disadvantaged in the choice of principles by the outcome of natural chance or the contingency of social circumstances. . . . I shall maintain instead that the persons in the initial situation would choose two rather different principles: the first requires equality in the assignment of basic rights and duties, while the second holds that social and economic inequalities, for example inequalities of wealth and authority, are just only if they result in compensating benefits for everyone, and in particular for the least advantaged members of society.

Jean Jacques Rousseau, *The Social Contract*, bk. I, ch. VIII (1762)

The passage from the state of nature to the civil state produces a very remarkable change in man, by substituting justice for instinct in his conduct, and giving his actions the morality they had formerly lacked. . . . Although, in this state, he deprives himself of some advantages which he got from nature, he gains in return others so great, his faculties are so stimulated and developed, his ideas so extended, his feelings so ennobled, and his whole soul so uplifted, that, did not the abuses of this new condition often degrade him below that which he left, he would be bound to bless continually the happy moment which took him from it for ever, and, instead of a stupid and unimaginative animal, made him an intelligent being and a man.

Bertrand Russell, *Religion and Science*, ch. VII (1935)

From a scientific point of view, we can make no distinction between the man who eats little and sees heaven and the man who drinks much and sees snakes. Each is in an abnormal physical condition, and therefore has abnormal perceptions.

Jean-Paul Sartre, *Existentialism Is a Humanism* (1945)

What is meant here by saying that existence precedes essence? It means that, first of all, man exists, turns up, appears on the scene, and, only afterwards, defines himself. If man, as the Existentialist conceives him, is indefinable, it is because at first he is nothing. Only afterward will he be something, and he himself will have made what he will be. Thus, there is no human nature, since there is no god to conceive it. Not only is man what he conceives himself to be, but he is also only what he wills himself to be after this thrust toward existence. Man is nothing else but what he makes of himself.

Wilfrid Sellars, *Empiricism and the Philosophy of Mind*, sect. 41 (1963)

[T]he common sense world of physical objects in Space and Time is unreal . . . there are no such things. Or, to put it less paradoxically, that in the dimension of describing and explaining the world, science is the measure of all things, or what is that it is, and of what is not that it is not.

Baruch Spinoza, *Ethics* (1675)

With regard to good and evil, these terms indicate nothing positive in things considered in themselves, nor are they anything else than modes of thought, or notions which we form from the comparison of one thing with another. For one and the same thing may at the same time be both good and evil or indifferent. Music, for example, is good to a melancholy person, bad to one mourning, while to a deaf man it is neither good nor bad.

Ludwig Wittgenstein, *Philosophical Investigations*, pt. II, sect. I (1953)

A dog believes his master is at the door. But can he also believe his master will come the day after tomorrow?

Glossary of Philosophical Terms

Act utilitarianism (Case-by-case utilitarianism) The theory that an act is morally right if and only if it brings about greater utility for everyone affected than any other possible action in that specific situation.

Adverbial theory of sensations Holds that sensations are sensory processes, not objectified things. For example, when we see a speckled hen we do *not* have an image in our minds of a speckled hen with a certain number of speckles. Instead, there is only a process or event happening to us that we call "sensing-speckled-hen-ly."

Aesthetics The philosophical examination of art and beauty. *Aesthetic Subjectivists* think that beauty exists only "in the eye of the beholder." *Aesthetic objectivists* think that aesthetic characteristics are real qualities of objects, although it may require a sophisticated observer to be able to recognize them.

Agnostic A person who neither believes God exists nor believes God does not exist.

AI functionalism The doctrine that mentality is brought into existence whenever a sufficiently complex computer program is run, regardless of whether the program is run by a biological organism or a machine.

Altruism Taking the welfare or rights of others into account when we decide what to do.

Ambiguous terms Terms having two or more distinct meanings.

Analogies Lines of reasoning that assert that the relationship between two things is similar in some important way to the relationship between two other things.

Analytic statements A statement whose truth or falsity depend solely on the meanings of its words.

Anecdotal evidence Evidence derived from small, vivid samples. One commits the *Fallacy of Anecdotal Evidence* when one ignores scientifically collected evidence in favor of anecdotes.

Antecedent The "if" part of a conditional statement.

A posteriori (empirical) statements Statements that are justifiable only after observation.

A priori statements Statements that are justifiable without relying on observation.

Argument A line of reasoning in which one or more premises are offered to support a conclusion.

Argument form The skeleton of an argument with its nonlogical words omitted. A *valid argument form* is a structure in which no matter what statements are used to fill it in, there can be no instance when all the premises are true and the conclusion is false. In an *invalid argument form*, there is at least one way of filling it in with all true premises and a false conclusion.

Argument from analogy Argues that if other bodies behave the same way that my body does when *I* have mental states, those other bodies possess mental states similar to mine.

Argument from design (Teleological argument) Argues that the orderliness of nature is best explained by postulating God as the orderer.

Argument from miracles Argues that miracles are best explained by postulating God as the cause.

Argument from motion Argues that the motion we observe today is best explained by postulating God as the motion-starter.

Argument from religious experience Argues that God exists because we have experience of God.

Argument from textual proof Argues that a supernatural being exists because a religious text says so.

Artifacts Designed products of human intelligence.

Artificial intelligence (AI) The building of artifacts that possess genuine mentality and do not merely simulate mentality.

Atheist A person who believes there are no gods.

Autonomy Self-rule.

Belief-acquisition account of perception Holds that we perceive physical objects when physical objects cause us to have true beliefs about the characteristics they really have.

Belief-desire psychology (folk psychology) The explanation of behavior in terms of beliefs and desires.

Burden of proof In a debate, having to prove that one's position is correct or lose the debate.

Burden-of-proof strategy Convincing one's opponents in a debate that they must prove their point and that you do not need to prove yours.

Categorical imperative Kant's moral principle "Act only according to that maxim by which you can at the same time will that it should become a universal law."

Causal definition of knowledge Holds that we know some proposition *p* if and only if *p* is true, we believe *p*, and *p* is causally related to the fact that *p* in an appropriate way.

Causal theory of perception Holds that we perceive physical objects only when physical objects affect our senses.

Cogito Descartes's argument "I think, therefore, I am."

Coincidence miracle A highly unexpected event that does not violate a law of nature such as being the sole survivor in the crash of an airliner.

Compatibilism Holds that determinism and free choices (moral responsibility) can both exist.

Conclusion The statement one is trying to prove when giving an argument.

Conditional statement An if-then statement that says that if one thing is true, then another thing is true.

Consequent The "then" part of a conditional statement.

Consequentialism (teleology) The view that what is morally obligatory is entirely a function of what has the best consequences.

Contingency argument (Aquinas's Third Way) Argues that a physical universe consisting solely of *contingent things* could not continue to exist by itself, but needs to be sustained by God. Sometimes called the "cosmological argument."

Contingent things Things that go in and out of existence.

Convincing argument An argument that takes its audience on a gradual "logical journey" *from* premises that the audience accepts *to* a conclusion that the audience finds to be made more believable by the premises.

Cosmic catastrophe According to the contingency argument, the dramatic event when all contingent entities go out of existence that would have happened if God did not prevent it.

Cosmos (Universe) The totality of physical things.

Cost-benefit analysis The mathematical weighing of the probable expense of an action against the probable benefit to determine whether the expected benefit outweighs the cost.

Counterexample A case cited to show that a definition or general claim is incorrect.

Critical thinking Thinking that criticizes (analyzes and evaluates) all beliefs, including one's own.

Deductive reasoning Reasoning that tries to produce a valid argument. When we argue deductively, we *intend* to make the logical structure of our argument so strong that it is logically impossible for our conclusion to be false if all the premises are true.

Definist identity theory Holds that two apparently different entities are really the same entity by arguing that the *words* that refer to the entity have the same meaning.

Definist subjectivism Holds that moral judgments such as "X is good" mean "I approve of X" or "My society approves of X."

Descriptive statements Statements that are either true or false and require no evaluation on the part of the person who expresses them.

Determinism The view that all events are caused to occur.

Dilemma The argument form that holds that if we assume *A then B*, *C then D*, and *A or C*, we may validly deduce *B or D*.

Direct (Commonsense, Naive) realism Holds that physical objects possess all the types of characteristics that common sense assigns to them, including colors, odors, tastes, and sounds.

Dispositions Tendencies to act in various ways.

Distributive justice The fairness of dividing goods among persons.

Dualism The mind/body theory that persons consist of nonphysical minds and physical bodies.

Dualistic interactionism The variety of dualism that holds that nonphysical minds and brains causally influence each other.

Dualistic parallelism The variety of dualism that holds that nonphysical minds run parallel to our brains without interacting with them.

Egoism Holds that we have no moral obligation to act unselfishly.

Eliminative materialism The view that human beings possess no mental states. Includes behaviorism and neurophilic eliminative materialism.

Empiricism Holds that all knowledge of what exists is a posteriori.

Empiricist criterion of evidence Holds that A is evidence for B only if (1) A and B have been observed together, or (2) "A" and "B" are connected in meaning.

Epiphenomenalism The variety of dualism that holds that brains affect minds, but minds do not affect brains.

Epistemic agents Persons who attempt to know some fact or facts.

Epistemic reasons for a belief One's reasons that increase the probability that one's belief is true.

Epistemology (theory of knowledge) The branch of philosophy that asks whether we know things and, if so, how?

Evaluative statements Statements that require an evaluation on the part of the person who expresses them.

Explanatory constructs (posits) Postulations designed to explain some phenomena. Used in inference to the best explanation.

External world Everything that exists outside one's own mind.

Faith Belief without evidence.

Fallacy An invalid argument.

Fallacy of affirming the consequent Invalid argument form that concludes from *A then B* and *B*, therefore, *A*.

Fallacy of appeal to ignorance Arguing that because we do not know that X is false, we have reason to believe that X is true.

Fallacy of begging the question Assuming in an argument what we need to prove.

Fallacy of denying the antecedent Invalid argument form that concludes from *A then B* and *not A*, therefore, *not B*.

Fallacy of lack of proof to the contrary Arguing that X is true because X has not been disproved.

Fallacy of popular belief Arguing that X is true because X is widely believed.

Fallacy of relevance Using a premise to argue for a logically unrelated conclusion.

Fallacy of smoke screen A diversion that obscures the real issue in question.

False dichotomy Claiming that only two alternatives exist when there are in fact more than two.

Fatalism Holds that our choices will not influence our lives and that our fates are sealed regardless of how we try to avoid them.

Fecundity The potential of a pleasure or pain to produce more pleasures or pain.

First cause argument Argues that the fact that events are happening now is best explained by postulating God as the first cause.

Free choices Choices that are enough under our control for us to be morally responsible for the actions they produce.

Freedom-destroying causation Compatibilism's idea of being determined to act contrary to our wishes.

Freedom-enhancing causation Compatibilism's idea of our desires determining our behavior, thereby enabling us to do what we want and contributing to our freedom.

Free will An old-fashioned term for "the faculty" of making free choices.

Free will defense A theodicist explanation of moral evil in terms of the importance that persons have libertarian free choices.

Free will subjectivism Holds that there can be no such thing as objective free will in the sense that grounds moral responsibility.

Free-will-either-way theory Holds that *caused* choices can be free and that *uncaused* choices can be free.

Functional definition A definition of a concept by citing the task performed by the entity it designates.

Greatest happiness principle Utilitarianism's claim that what is morally right is what maximizes pleasure and minimizes pain.

Hard determinism A variety of incompatibilism that holds that because all our choices are caused, none of our choices are free and we are never morally responsible.

Hedon A unit of pleasure or pain.

Hedonistic factors Factors that contribute to the pleasure/pain value of our actions. According to Jeremy Bentham (1748-1832), these include intensity, duration, probability, purity, and fecundity.

Holocaust The Nazi attempt to destroy the Jewish race before and during World War II.

Hypothesis A proposed explanation for some data. See *inference to the best explanation.*

Hypothetical syllogism The argument form that says if we assume *A then B* and *B then C*, we may validly deduce *A then C*.

Incompatibilism Holds that determinism and free choices (moral responsibility) cannot both be true.

Indeterminism The view that not all events are caused.

Induction (by enumeration) Concluding that because each member of a known sample of group G has a characteristic C, an unexamined member of G will have C also.

Inductive reasoning When we argue inductively, we intend to produce a strong argument, without trying to produce a valid argument. See *deductive reasoning.*

Inference to the best explanation A reasoning device that infers the existence of unobserved entities or unknown facts if they best explain some known data.

Infinite regress An unending series.

Instrumental value States of affairs that are worthwhile because they contribute to some further end.

Intrinsic value States of affairs that are worthwhile in themselves.

Introspection Examining the way one's mental states seem to be.

Intuitionism Holds that moral truths are synthetic a priori and are knowable by "intuition."

Invalid argument An argument that does not have a valid argument form, that is, where every form it satisfies is an invalid argument form.

Justification Epistemic reasons for a belief.

Justified, true belief definition of knowledge We know proposition p if and only if p is true, we believe p, and we can provide adequate evidence that p is true.

Knowledge argument (for phenomenalism) Argues that if we adopt either direct or scientific realism, we will be committed to skepticism about the nature and existence of physical objects. Therefore, to avoid skepticism, we should adopt phenomenalism.

Law of identity Holds that A is the same entity as B if and only if A and B share exactly the same internal characteristics.

Libertarianism A variety of incompatibilism that holds that we sometimes make uncaused choices and at those times we may be free and morally responsible for our behavior.

Logic The branch of philosophy that analyzes the strength of arguments and argument forms.

Logical analogy A clearly invalid argument that has the same argument form as an argument we wish to criticize.

Logical contradiction A claim that the same statement is both true and false.

Logically contingent statements Statements that are true in some imaginable worlds but false in others.

Logically inconsistent sets of statements Groups of statements that (logically) cannot all be true.

Logically necessary statements Statements that have to be true or have to be false in every imaginable world.

Logically possible world An imaginable way that the world could be, whether it is physically possible or not.

Magical theory of perception Holds that we know what physical objects are like without relying on a causal process. See *causal theory of perception*.

Making a choice Creating an intention to perform an action.

Manichaeanism (MAN A KEY ISM) The theological view that attributes evil to the power of Satan, whom God was unable to control.

Materialism The mind/body theory that persons are entirely physical beings.

Matters of fact According to Hume, statements that are synthetic, a posteriori, and logically contingent.

Meanings of words Dictionary definitions.

Metaethics The branch of philosophy that considers the objectivity of our judgments concerning moral obligation and intrinsic value.

Metaphilosophy A view of what philosophy is and what philosophy should try to accomplish.

Metaphysics The branch of philosophy that asks what exists.

Methodological behaviorism The approach in psychology of trying to understand human and animal behavior without referring to mental states.

Mind A thinking thing or center of consciousness.

Mind/body argument (for phenomenalism) Argues that physical objects are really nonphysical because sensations are nonphysical, sensations causally influence human bodies, and nonphysical things cannot affect physical things.

Mind/body problem The question of the ontology of persons' minds: Are minds brains or nonphysical minds?

Mixed deontological/utilitarian theories Theories of moral obligation that combine deontological and utilitarian principles.

Mixed subjectivism Holds that basic moral feelings are *not* shared widely by persons, but vary greatly from person to person.

Modus ponens The argument form that holds that if we assume *A then B* and *A*, we may validly deduce *B*.

Modus tollens The argument form that holds that if we assume *A then B* and *not B*, we may validly deduce *not A*.

Monism The view that reality is either all physical or all nonphysical. Specified to the mind/body problem, monists are either materialists or idealists (phenomenalists).

Monotheistic religions Religions that hold that only one god exists.

Moral argument (for the existence of God) Argues that God's existence either best explains the objectivity of morality or needs to be postulated to provide persons with the motivation to be moral.

Moral autonomy Analyzing moral issues and deciding for yourself what you think is best.

Moral (Nonnatural, Man-made) evils Evils that are caused by agents' malicious intentions.

Moral intuitions Reflective judgments about normative questions, for instance, judgments about whether a certain action would be morally permissible or whether certain activities are intrinsically worthwhile.

Moral nihilism ("amoralism") Holds that no values are better or worse than any others and that there is no right and wrong.

Moral objectivism Holds that moral judgments are made true by something beyond the moral opinions of persons.

Moral obligation What we owe other beings in terms of their rights or well-being-apart-from-rights.

Moral responsibility To be deserving of praise or blame.

Moral subjectivism Holds that there is nothing beyond the moral opinions of persons that makes moral judgments true.

Motive argument (for the determinism of choices) Argues that choices are always determined by our strongest motives, which are the determined results of our likes, dislikes, fears, hopes, beliefs, and values.

Natural evils Instances of suffering that are not caused by agents' malicious intentions.

Natural selection The mechanism that drives evolution. As described by the English biologist Charles Darwin (1809–1882), the view that species change their characteristics over great periods of time due to genetic mutations in offspring.

Naturalistic objectivism Holds that the truth conditions of moral judgments are objective moral facts that exist in the natural world.

Necessary things Things that cannot help but to exist.

Neurons Brain cells. An adult human brain has about 10 billion neurons.

Neurophilic eliminative materialism Holds that mental states do not exist, but only brain states.

No-free-will-either-way theory Holds that we are unfree whether our choices are caused or uncaused.

Noncognitivism Holds that analyzing the meaning of moral judgments shows that, contrary to appearances, moral judgments do not assign moral properties.

Nonconsequentialism (Deontologism, Formalism) Theories of moral obligation that hold that the creation of intrinsic value is not the sole determinant of right and wrong.

Nondefinist identity theory Holds that two apparently different entities are really the same entity, but *not* by holding that the words that refer to the entity have the same meaning.

Nondefinist subjectivism Holds that moral judgments have no truth conditions and merely express subjective feelings, but are not reports of those feelings.

Nonepistemic reasons for a belief Reasons that motivate us to believe without increasing the probability that our belief is true.

Nonnaturalism (in metaethics) Holds that moral truth is grounded in the supernatural (not existing in space and time) realm.

Noneliminative (Identity) materialism Variety of materialism that holds that mental states exist and are identical to brain states.

Nonphysical Not extended in space, nor having any other physical characteristics.

Nonphysical mind A thinking thing (center of consciousness) that has no extension in space, and, thus, no other physical characteristics.

Nonretributive (Consequentialist) grounds for punishment Reasons for punishing designed to increase favorable outcomes, not for the sake of just deserts.

Normative ethics The branch of philosophy primarily concerned with moral obligation and intrinsic value in human action and character.

Objective statements Statements that depend for their truth on the way the world is and not on anyone's beliefs.

Occam's razor The principle that we should not multiply entities in our theories beyond what is necessary to explain the data. Provided by the English philosopher William of Occam (1285–1349).

Occasionalism The variety of dualistic parallelism that holds that God causes all physical and nonphysical events, thereby creating the illusion of causal interaction.

Omnipotent Being able to do anything that is logically possible, including the violation of the laws of nature.

Omniscient Knowing all truths, past, present, and future.

Ontogenesis The development of an individual organism.

Ontological Pertaining to existence.

Ontological argument An a priori argument designed to prove the existence of God solely from the concept "the being than which none greater can be conceived." Provided by St. Anselm (1033–1109).

Open-question argument (against definism) Argues that two expressions, "A" and "B," cannot be synonymous if anyone who knows the meanings of "A" and "B" can seriously wonder whether A is B.

Paranormal phenomena Purported events such as psychokinesis (moving material objects with our minds), precognition (knowing the future), seeing at a distance (clairvoyance), mind-reading, communication with the dead, out-of-body experiences, reincarnation, and faith healing.

Pascal's wager Argues that we should believe in the existence of God as the most prudential choice between atheism, theism, and agnosticism. Provided by Blaise Pascal, French mathematician and theologian.

Perfection A great-making characteristic. Something that makes one greater than one would be if one did not have it.

Personal identity The issue of what makes a person the same person over time.

Personal subjectivism ("Whatever-your-conscience-decides-is-right theory") Holds that each person's moral conscience creates the difference between right and wrong for that person and the way to find out the difference between right and wrong is by consulting one's conscience.

Phenomenal (phenomenological) quality The felt characteristics of our mental states, such as the hurtfulness of pains or the color of a visual image.

Phenomenalism The view that only nonphysical minds and their contents exist.

Philosophical behaviorism The view that mental states do not exist, only tendencies of creatures to behave in certain ways.

Philosophical egoism Holds that psychological egoism is true because persons always choose according to their strongest desires.

Phylogenetic scale The ranking of animals from simple to complex.

Physical Existing in space and time.

Physical symbol system hypothesis AI functionalist thesis advanced by computer scientists Allen Newell and Herbert Simon: "A physical symbol system has the necessary and sufficient means for general intelligent action."

Physically necessary events Events that have to happen in the real world due to the laws of nature, but do not have to happen in all imaginable worlds.

Physically possible world A way that the world could be that is consistent with the actual laws of nature.

Polytheistic religions Religions that hold that more than one god exists.

Postulate (posit) To hypothesize the existence of something.

Pre-established harmony The variety of dualistic parallelism that holds that God designed minds and bodies to run in parallel sequences.

Premises Statements that are intended to provide evidence for another statement (the *conclusion*).

Presence/absence table A four-celled grid that compares the presence and absence of two variables to determine whether there is any nonrandom correspondence between the two.

Principle of conservation of energy/mass Holds that energy (and mass) can neither be created nor destroyed, but only changed in form.

Principle of deductive closure Holds that if one knows *A* and one knows that *A entails B*, then one must know *B* also.

Principle of ends Kant's second great moral principle: "Act so that you treat humanity, whether in your own person or in that of another, always as an end and never as a means only."

Principle of explaining evil Holds that any solution that works to explain all *possible* evil is not a satisfactory explanation of the *actual* evil in the world.

Principle of sufficient reason Holds that for every fact, there is a true explanation of why it is a fact.

Problem of evil The attempt to resolve the contradiction between these six statements: (1) God exists. (2) God is omniscient. (3) God is omnipotent.(4) God is morally perfect. (5) If statements (1), (2), (3), and (4) are true, then there *is no* unnecessary suffering on Earth. (6) There *is* unnecessary suffering on Earth.

Problem of induction The difficulty in knowing that past regularities will continue in the future.

Problem of interaction The difficulty in understanding how physical and nonphysical things can affect each other.

Problem of representation The fact that we can never tell solely from examining a representational device whether what it says is true or not.

Propositional knowledge Knowledge that some statement (proposition) is true.

Prudential decision making Decisions made solely on the basis of what we take to be in our own best interest.

Pseudo-science Imitations of science such as astrology and ESP.

Psychological hedonism Holds that the motivation of all our actions is the attempt to gain pleasure and avoid pain.

Quantum mechanics The dominant twentieth-century theory of matter at the level of the atom that holds that many events *in principle* cannot be predicted exactly but only probabilistically.

Quasi-scientific hypothesis The postulating of a supernatural (nonphysical) being to explain some fact about the physical world. This is different than a *scientific hypothesis*, which hypothesizes a natural (physical) being to explain some fact about the physical world.

Realists Thinkers who believe that some entity exists.

Reductio ad absurdum The argument form that holds if we assume *A*, and with the aid of other true premises deduce a logical contradiction, we may validly conclude that *A* is false.

Referent(s) of a word The thing(s) the word refers to.

Relations of ideas According to Hume, statements that are analytic, a priori, and logically necessary.

Relativism The view that actions are right or wrong depending on whether they are approved of or rejected by a certain group of persons.

Relativity of perception argument (for scientific realism) Argues that because many of the apparent qualities of physical objects depend on the sensory apparatus of perceivers, to avoid being arbitrary, we should say that these qualities exist only in perceivers' minds.

Religious authoritarianism Holds that moral judgments are made true by the commands of a theological being or beings and that we learn the truth of moral judgments by finding out those commands.

Religious experience An apparent experience of God.

Representational device Anything that we use to claim that something else is a certain way. Representational devices include paintings, photographs, sentences written on chalkboards, newspaper advertisements, spoken statements, blueprints for buildings, and books.

Retribution Punishment on the grounds of just deserts.

Rhetorical statements Statements that are worded as questions. "Rhetoric" often carries the unfavorable connotation of "words without substance."

Rights (e.g., rights to life, liberty, the pursuit of happiness) Things that would be morally wrong for anyone to take away from a person.

Rule utilitarianism (Follow-the-rules utilitarianism) The theory that an act is morally right if and only if it follows a rule that would produce the most utility for everyone affected in that type of situation.

Rule worshipping Following a rule simply because it is a rule, not because following it maximizes the end the rule is designed to maximize.

Science-replaces-naive-common-sense argument (for scientific realism) Argues that what we have learned about the nature of physical objects from twentieth-century physics makes direct realism obsolete.

Scientific (Critical) realism Holds that physical objects are atoms flying around in empty space, and that physical objects lack most of the characteristics common sense assigns to them such as colors, shapes, and sharp edges.

Scientific instrumentalism Holds that physicists' theoretical entities such as atoms do not exist, but are merely fictions that are useful in helping us to predict the course of our sensations.

Sensations Sensuous mental states such as itches and pains, but also including the experienced input from our five senses.

Separability argument (for scientific realism) Argues that the only characteristics that belong to physical objects themselves are the characteristics we *cannot* imagine them *not* having.

Simplicity argument (for phenomenalism) Argues that once we accept the existence of an omnipotent God, physical objects become redundant, useless postulations with no necessary role to play in our worldview.

Skeptical hypothesis A thought experiment designed by a skeptic to challenge a knowledge-claim.

Skepticism The view that we lack knowledge of some statement or entire area of belief.

Slippery slope argument Argues because A clearly has property p and because there is a continuous gradation from A to Z, Z also has property p.

Soft determinism A variety of compatibilism that holds that all choices are caused, but that many of our choices are free.

Solipsism Holds that the only things that exist are one's own nonphysical mind and its contents.

Sound argument An argument that is valid and has all true premises.

Spatio-temporal Existing in space and time.

Straw man fallacy Arguing against a fictional opponent who is weaker than one's real foe.

Subjective statements Statements that depend for their truth on the beliefs of persons.

Substitution instance The result of correctly placing nonlogical terms into an *argument form*.

Summum bonum The highest good of human action.

Supererogatory actions Actions that surpass what is morally obligatory.

Synthetic statement A statement whose truth or falsity does not depend solely on the meanings of its words.

Theist A person who believes that God or gods exists.

Theodicy A defense of God in the problem of evil.

Theory An explanation for some data. See *inference to the best explanation*.

Thought experiment A hypothetical case designed to make us think about some issue.

To exist in reality To exist in one's own right, not merely in someone's understanding. Things that exist in reality may be physical or nonphysical.

To exist in the understanding To exist in the mind as a thought.

True belief A belief that corresponds to the way the world is.

Truth conditions of statements Those parts of reality that make true statements true and false statements false.

Truth-is-relative fallacy Believing that the truth or falsity of an objective statement depends on our belief.

Truth-valued statements Statements that are either true or false.

Twilight Zone realism Holds that physical objects really exist in physical space when they are perceived and would pop out of existence if they were ever unperceived. This is not phenomenalism.

Universal subjectivism Holds that basic moral feelings such as benevolence and fairness are almost universally shared by human beings.

Universalization test A test for immoral actions: If we cannot universalize our actions, then they are not morally permissible.

Vague terms Terms with fuzzy or imprecise meanings.

Valid argument An argument that has a *valid argument form*.

Veil of ignorance John Rawls's thought experiment for determining principles of justice: Imagine that you select the moral rules and practices of the society that you are going to live in, not knowing where you will be in that society.

Veil of sensations skepticism Holds that because we can never compare our sensations and physical objects, we cannot know what physical objects are like by relying solely on our senses.

Veridical perception Accurate perception.

Violation miracle An event that violates a law of nature.

Virtue (soul-making) defense A theodicist explanation of evil in terms of the contribution that evil makes to persons' moral development.

Well-being-apart-from-rights States of affairs that we believe are valuable for persons to experience, for instance, pleasure or the development of one's abilities.

Will to believe argument Argues that, given that the existence of God is neither provable nor disprovable, we should postulate the existence of God if that belief is important to us. Provided by William James (1842–1910), American philosopher and psychologist.

Glossary of Names

The following list includes only the names of the major historical figures cited in the text.

Anselm (1033–1109) Italian theologian and philosopher who became Archbishop of Canterbury and achieved sainthood. Best known for the a priori argument for the existence of God, the ontological argument.

Aquinas, Thomas (1224–1274) Systematic interpreter of Aristotle and the most important Catholic philosopher. Achieved sainthood. *Thomism* is an important school of philosophy even today. Provided the Five Ways (proofs of the existence of God).

Aristotle (384–322 B.C.) Student of Plato who wrote on logic, metaphysics, and ethics, as well as a wide range of nonphilosophical topics. Along with Plato, Kant, Hume, and Descartes, is one of the most influential philosophers.

Augustine (353–430) Prominent Catholic theologian and philosopher who achieved sainthood. Advocated the nonliteral interpretation of the Bible.

Ayer, A. J. (1910–1989) English philosopher largely responsible for making Logical Positivism known to British and American philosophers through his 1936 book, *Language, Truth, and Logic*.

Bacon, Francis (1561–1626) English statesman, philosopher, student of human nature, and advocate of scientific method.

Bentham, Jeremy (1748–1832) English moral and political philosopher. Major figure in utilitarianism.

Berkeley ('BAR KLEE), George (1685–1753) Irish Bishop best known for expounding idealism (phenomenalism) as the logical consequence of Empiricism.

Confucius (551–479 B.C.) Chinese moral philosopher and founder of the religion/philosophy, Confucianism.

Darwin, Charles (1809–1882) English physician and naturalist most famous for propounding the theory of evolution through natural selection.

Descartes (DAY 'CART), René (1596–1650) French philosopher and inventor of analytical geometry who made epistemology the pivotal issue for subsequent philosophers. Famous for the Evil Genius hypothesis, the *cogito*, and mind/body interactionism.

d' Holbach ('DOLE BOCK), Baron (1723–1789) French Enlightenment materialist, atheist, and hard determinist.

Dostoevski, Fyodor (1821–1881) Major Russian novelist who wrote about philosophical topics such as free will, morality, the existence of God, and the problem of evil.

Einstein, Albert (1879–1955) German physicist who fled the Nazis for America. Renown for the special and general theories of relativity. Activist against the development of nuclear weapons.

Epicurus (EPA 'CURE IS) (341–270 B.C.) Greek atomist, materialist, and hedonist who believed that free will results because the atoms of our minds sometimes "swerve" indeterministically.

Freud, Sigmund (1856–1939) Austrian founder of psychoanalysis, the variety of psychology that explains human behavior by postulating an unconscious mind in addition to the conscious mind.

Galileo Galilei (1564–1642) Italian astronomer, physicist, and scientific realist. Discovered that Jupiter has moons, thereby supporting a heliocentric picture of our solar system, rather than the Church-endorsed geocentric picture given by Aristotle.

Hobbes, Thomas (1588–1679) English political and moral philosopher who advocated materialism, atheism, moral subjectivism, and compatibilistic free will. Famous for his defense of strong political rule.

Hume, David (1711–1776) Scottish antimetaphysician and subjectivist moral philosopher. Famous for his skepticism about the external world based on skepticism about causation and induction.

Huxley, Thomas (1825–1895) English biologist, advocate of evolution, and proponent of epiphenomenalism.

James, William (1842–1910) American pragmatist philosopher and psychologist who believed that what is conducive to human interests is true and that human desires have a role to play in justifying our belief in God and libertarian free will.

Kant (CONT), Immanuel (1724–1804) German epistemologist, antimetaphysician, and moral philosopher who claimed to have been interrupted from his "dogmatic slumber" by reading Hume. Famous for the categorical imperative and the principle of ends.

Leibniz ('LIBE NITZ), Gottfried Wilhelm (1646–1716) German theistic philosopher and inventor of (one variety of) calculus. Offered a famous variety of parallelism (*pre-established harmony*) and claimed that this is the best of all possible worlds.

Locke, John (1632–1704) English epistemologist and political theorist. A moderate Empiricist who attacked innate ideas, but used inference to the best explanation to justify belief in physical objects.

Malebranche (MALL 'BRONCH), Nicolas (1638–1715) French philosopher who held occasionalism, the view that God constantly causes physical and nonphysical events to occur, creating the illusion that the physical and mental interact.

Marx, Karl (1818–1883) German economic theorist and political philosopher. One of the intellectual founders of contemporary communism.

Mill, John Stuart (1806–1873) Bentham's successor in utilitarianism who wrote extensively in political theory, scientific method, and theory of knowledge. Advocate of womens' rights and opponent of slavery.

Moore, G. E. (1873–1958) English moral philosopher and commonsense epistemologist. Held that goodness is a nonnatural characteristic that we can recognize by carefully examining good actions.

Newton, Isaac (1642–1727) English mathematician, physicist, and scientific realist who invented (one system of) calculus, formulated the laws of motion and gravity, and made major contributions to optics.

Nietzsche ('NEAT CHA), Friedrich (1844–1900) German philosopher and philologist famous for claiming that God is dead. Also famous for the view that the *übermensch* (overman) is "beyond good and evil."

Occam, William of (1285–1349) English theologian and logician famous for "Occam's Razor," the methodological principle not to multiply entities in one's theories needlessly.

Pascal, Blaise (1623–1662) French mathematician and religious thinker famous for the argument concerning God's existence known as "Pascal's Wager."

Popper, Karl (1902–1994) Influential philosopher of science and anti-authoritarian political thinker. Famous for claiming that science proceeds by trying to disconfirm its hypotheses rather than by trying to confirm them inductively.

Plato (429–347) Greek metaphysician, political philosopher, and moral philosopher. Famous for the doctrine of Platonism, the theory that general terms such as "goodness," "justice," and "knowledge" designate intangible Forms. Plato's doctrine of the immortal soul influenced Christianity.

Reid, Thomas (1717–1796) Scottish nonskeptical moral philosopher and epistemologist of common sense. Famous opponent of Hume.

Ross, W. D. (1877–1971) British moral philosopher and Aristotelian scholar famous for the doctrine that intuitions enable us to recognize *prima facie duties,* duties we have unless a stronger duty overrules them.

Russell, Bertrand (1872–1970) English mathematician, philosopher, and political activist acclaimed for his work in the foundations of mathematical logic. Also contributed to metaphysics, theory of knowledge, and philosophy of religion.

Ryle, Gilbert (1900–1976) English behaviorist philosopher who analyzed ordinary language to argue that talk about minds as thinking things involved a "category mistake."

Sartre, Jean-Paul (1905–1980) French novelist, playwright, and philosophical thinker who expounded *existentialism,* the doctrine that humans possess the radical freedom to create themselves: Human beings' "existence precedes their essence."

Skinner, B. F. (1904–1990) The most influential behaviorist psychologist of the twentieth century. Advocated materialism and hard determinism.

Socrates (470–399 B.C.) Peripatetic teacher of Plato who was the main character of many of Plato's dialogues. Famous for the "Socratic method," a style of teaching involving interactive discussions between teacher and pupil.

Spinoza, Baruch (1632–1677) Dutch rationalist, monist, and pantheist who claimed that God is the totality of existence.

Works Cited

Adams, Marilyn and Robert Adams, eds. 1990. *The Problem of Evil*. Oxford: Oxford University Press.

Alston, William and Richard Brandt, eds. 1978. *The Problems of Philosophy*. Boston: Allyn and Bacon.

Aquinas, Thomas. 1948. *Introduction to St. Thomas Aquinas*. Anton Pegas, ed., New York: Modern Library.

Armstrong, David. 1968. *A Materialist Theory of the Mind*. London: Routledge & Kegan Paul.

Ayer, A. J. 1952. *Language, Truth, and Logic*. New York: Dover.

———. 1954. "Freedom and Necessity." In Ayer's *Philosophical Essays*. London: Macmillan.

Baergen, Ralph. 1995. *Contemporary Epistemology*. Fort Worth, TX: Harcourt Brace.

Baird, Forrest and Walter Kaufmann, eds. 1997. *Modern Philosophy*. Upper Saddle River, NJ: Prentice-Hall.

Bentham, Jeremy. 1970. *The Principles of Morals and Legislation*. Darien, CT: Hafner.

Berkeley, George. 1965. *Berkeley's Philosophical Writings*. New York: Macmillan.

Blackburn, Simon. 1993. *Essays in Quasi-Realism*. New York: Oxford University Press.

Blatchford, Robert. 1982. "The Delusion of Free Will." In E. D. Klemke, A. David Kline, and Robert Hollinger, eds., *Philosophy: The Basic Issues*. New York: St. Martin's Press, 103–9.

Brehm, Jack and Arthur Cohen. 1962. *Explorations in Cognitive Dissonance*. New York: Wiley.

Campbell, John and Robert Pargetter. 1986. "Goodness and Fragility." *American Philosophical Quarterly* 23, 155–65.

Campbell, Keith. 1980. *Body and Mind*. Notre Dame, IN: University of Notre Dame Press.

Carnap, Rudolf. 1959. "Psychology in Physical Language." In A. J. Ayer, ed., *Logical Positivism*. New York: Macmillan, 165–98.

Chisholm, Roderick. 1982. "Human Freedom and the Self." In Gary Watson, ed., *Free Will*. New York: Oxford University Press. 24–35.

———. 1989. *Theory of Knowledge*. Englewood Cliffs, NJ: Prentice-Hall.

Churchland, Paul. 1984. *Matter and Consciousness*. Cambridge, MA: MIT Press.

Clifford, W. K. 1877. "The Ethics of Belief" in Clifford's *Lectures and Essays*, vol 2. New York: Macmillan.

Cornman, James, Keith Lehrer, and George Pappas. 1987. *Philosophical Problems and Arguments*. Indianapolis: Hackett.

Curd, Martin. 1992. *Argument and Analysis: An Introduction to Philosophy*. St. Paul: West Publishing Company.

Davis, Thomas. 1987. *Philosophy: An Introduction through Original Fiction, Discussion, and Readings*. New York: Random House.

Dawkins, Richard. 1976. *The Selfish Gene*. New York: Oxford University Press.

Dennett, Daniel. 1978. *Brainstorms*. Montgomery, VT: Bradford Books.

———. 1984. *Elbow Room*. Cambridge, MA: MIT Press.

Descartes, René. 1972. *The Philosophical Works of Descartes*. Cambridge: Cambridge University Press.

d'Holbach, Baron. 1978. "Of the System of Man's Free Agency." In William Alston and Richard Brandt, eds., *The Problems of Philosophy*. Boston: Allyn and Bacon, 403–13.

Dostoevski, Fyodor. 1950. *The Brothers Karamazov*. New York: Modern Library.

Double, Richard. 1991. *The Non-Reality of Free Will*. New York: Oxford University Press.

———. 1996. *Metaphilosophy and Free Will*. New York: Oxford University Press.

Doyle, Arthur Canon. 1927. *The Complete Sherlock Holmes*. New York: Doubleday.

Eddington, Arthur. 1963. *The Nature of the Physical World*. Ann Arbor: University of Michigan Press.

Fichte, Johann. 1956. *The Vocation of Man*. Indianapolis: Bobbs-Merrill.

Fodor, Jerry. 1975. *The Language of Thought*. New York: Crowell.

Frankena, William. 1973. *Ethics*. Englewood Cliffs, NJ: Prentice-Hall.

Frankfort, Harry. 1982. "Freedom of the Will and the Concept of a Person." In Gary Watson, ed., *Free Will*. New York: Oxford University Press, 81–95.

Galileo. 1960. *The Controversy of the Comets of 1618*. Philadelphia: University of Pennsylvania Press.

Giere, Ronald. 1994. *Understanding Scientific Reasoning*. Fort Worth: Holt, Rinehart, and Winston.

Gilovich, Thomas. 1991. *How We Know What Isn't So*. New York: Free Press.

Glover, Jonathan. 1990. *Utilitarianism and Its Critics*. New York: Macmillan.

Goldman, Alvin. 1968. "Actions, Predictions, and Books of Life." *American Philosophical Quarterly 5*, 135–51.

Gould, Stephen Jay. 1980. *The Panda's Thumb*. New York: Norton.

Graham, George. 1993. *Philosophy of Mind: An Introduction*. Oxford: Basil Blackwell.

Halverson, William. 1981. *A Concise Introduction to Philosophy*. New York: Random House.

Hare, R. M. 1952. *The Language of Morals*. Oxford: Oxford University Press.

Harman, Gilbert. 1977. *The Nature of Morality*. New York: Oxford University Press.

Hempel, Carl. 1949. "The Logical Analysis of Psychology." In Herbert Feigl and Wilfred Sellars, eds., *Readings in Philosophical Analysis*. New York: Appleton-Century-Crofts.

Henry, Carl. 1957. *Christian Personal Ethics*. Grand Rapids, MI: Eerdmans.

Hick, John. 1990. "Soul Making and Suffering." In Marilyn and Robert Adams, eds., *The Problem of Evil*. Oxford: Oxford University Press.

Hobart, R. E. 1966. "Free Will as Involving Determinism and Inconceivable Without It." In Bernard Berofsky, ed., *Free Will and Determinism*. New York: Harper & Row, 63–95.

Hobbes, Thomas. 1841. *The English Works of Thomas Hobbes*. London: John Bohr.

Hofstadter, Douglas and Daniel Dennett, eds. 1981. *The Mind's Eye*. Toronto: Bantam Books.

Honderich, Ted. 1993. *How Free Are You?* Oxford: Oxford University Press.

Hume, David. 1947. *Dialogues Concerning Natural Religion*. Indianapolis: Bobbs-Merrill.

———. 1955. *An Inquiry Concerning Human Understanding*. Indianapolis: Bobbs-Merrill.

———. 1968. *A Treatise Concerning Human Understanding*. Oxford: Oxford University Press.

James, William. 1897. "The Will to Believe." Many editions.

———. 1962. "The Dilemma of Determinism." In James's *Essays on Faith and Morals*. New York: World Publishing Company, 145–83.

———. 1963. *Pragmatism*. New York: World Publishing Company.

Kahane, Howard. 1983. *Thinking about Basic Beliefs*. Belmont, CA: Wadsworth.

Kane, Robert. 1994. *Through the Moral Maze: Searching for Absolute Values in a Pluralistic World*. New York: Paragon House.

———. 1996. *The Significance of Free Will*. New York: Oxford University Press.

Kant, Immanuel. 1959. *Foundations of the Metaphysics of Morals*. Translated by Lewis White Beck. Indianapolis: Bobbs-Merrill.

———. 1965. *Critique of Pure Reason*. Translated by Norman Kemp Smith. New York: St Martin's Press.

Klenk, Virginia. 1994. *Understanding Symbolic Logic*. Englewood Cliffs, NJ: Prentice-Hall.

Kretzman, Norman. 1966. "Omniscience and Immutability." *Journal of Philosophy 113*, 409–21.

Kripke, Saul. 1972. "Naming and Necessary." In Donald Davidson and Gilbert Harman, eds., *Semantics of Natural Language*. Boston: Reidel, 253–355.

Leibniz, G. F. 1965. *Monadology and Other Philosophical Essays*. Indianapolis: Bobbs-Merrill.

———. 1997. *Theodicy*. In Forrest Baird and Walter Kaufmann, eds., *Modern Philosophy*. Upper Saddle River, NJ: Prentice-Hall.

Leslie, John, ed. 1990. *Physical Cosmology and Philosophy*. New York: Macmillan.

Levenson, Carl and Jonathan Westphal, eds. 1994. *Reality*. Indianapolis: Hackett.

Lewinsohn, Peter, Walter Mischel, William Chaplin, & Russell Barton. 1980. "Social Competence and Depression: The Role of Illusory Self-Perceptions." *Journal of Abnormal Psychology 89*, 203–12.

Lindley, Richard. 1986. *Autonomy*. Atlantic Heights, NJ: Humanities Press.

Locke, John. 1974. *An Essay Concerning Human Understanding*. New York: Dutton.

Mackie, J. L. 1977. *Ethics: Inventing Right and Wrong*. New York: Penguin Books.

———. 1982. *The Miracle of Theism*. Oxford: Oxford University Press.

Martin, Robert M. 1992. *There are Two Errors in the the Title of this Book : A Sourcebook of Philosophical Puzzles, Paradoxes, and Problems*. Peterborough, Ontario: Broadview.

Mill, John Stuart. 1981. *Utilitarianism*. Indianapolis: Bobbs-Merrill.

Moore, Brooke and Richard Parker. 1995. *Critical Thinking*. Mountain View, CA: Mayfield.

Moore, G. E. 1903. *Principia Ethica*. Cambridge: Cambridge University Press.

Moser, Paul and Arnold vander Nat, eds. 1995. *Human Knowledge: Classical and Contemporary Approaches*. New York: Oxford University Press.

Nagel, Thomas. 1979. *Mortal Questions*. Cambridge: Cambridge University Press.

———. 1986. *The View from Nowhere*. New York: Oxford University Press.

New Testament. Many editions.

Newell, Allen and Herbert A. Simon. 1981. "Computer Science as Empirical Inquiry: Symbols and Search." In John Haugeland, ed., *Mind Design*. Montgomery, VT: Bradford Books, 35–66.

Nisbett, Richard and Lee Ross. 1980. *Human Inference: Strategies and Shortcomings of Social Judgment*. Englewood Cliffs, NJ: Prentice-Hall.

Old Testament. Many editions.

Paley, William. 1963. *Natural Theology*. Indianapolis: Bobbs-Merrill.

Parfit, Derek. 1984. *Reasons and Persons*. Oxford: Oxford University Press.

Pascal, Blaise. 1961. *Pensées*. Baltimore: Penguin Books.

Peterson, Michael, ed. 1992. *The Problem of Evil*. Notre Dame: University of Notre Dame Press.

Plato, *Euthyphro*. 1994. In Walter Kaufmann and Forrest Baird, eds., *Philosophical Classics: From Plato to Nietzsche*. Englewood Cliffs, NJ: Prentice-Hall.

Pojman, Louis. 1995. *Ethics: Discovering Right and Wrong*. Belmont, CA: Wadsworth.

Popper, Karl. 1965. *Conjectures and Refutations*. New York: Basic Books.

Puccetti, Roland. 1981. "The Case for Mental Duality." *The Behavioral and Brain Sciences* 4, 93–123.

Quine, W. V. O. 1960. *Word and Object*. Cambridge, MA: MIT Press.

Rawls, John. 1971. *A Theory of Justice*. Cambridge, MA: Harvard University Press.

Reid, Thomas. 1978. *Essays on the Active Powers of Man*. In William Alston and Richard Brendt, eds., *The Problems of Philosophy*. Boston: Allyn and Bacon, 161–169.

Robinson, Timothy, ed. 1996. *God*. Indianapolis: Hackett.

Rorty, Richard. 1971. "Mind-Body Identity, Privacy, and Categories." In David Rosenthal, ed., *Materialism and the Mind-Body Problem*. Englewood Cliffs, NJ: Prentice-Hall, 174–99.

———. 1979. *Philosophy and the Mirror of Nature*. Princeton: Princeton University Press.

Ross, W. D. 1930. *The Right and the Good*. Oxford: Clarendon Press.

Ruse, Michael, ed. 1989. *Philosophy of Biology*. New York: Macmillan.

Russell, Bertrand. 1966. "Pragmatism" and "William James's Conception of Truth." In Russell's *Philosophical Essays*. New York: Simon & Schuster.

Ryle, Gilbert. 1949. *The Concept of Mind*. London: Hutchinson.

Sagan, Carl. 1977. *The Dragons of Eden*. New York: Ballantine Books.

———. 1979. *Broca's Brain*. New York: Ballantine Books.

Santayana, George. 1896. *The Sense of Beauty*. New York: Scribner's.

Sartre, Jean Paul. 1956. *Being and Nothingness*. New York: Philosophical Library.

Schlick, Moritz. 1939. *Problems of Ethics*. New York: Dover.

Schlick, Theodore and Lewis Vaughn. 1995. *How to Think about Weird Things: Critical Thinking for a New Age*. Mountain View, CA: Mayfield.

Searle, John. 1969. *Speech Acts*. Cambridge: Cambridge University Press.

———. 1984. *Minds, Brains, and Science*. Cambridge, MA: Harvard University Press.

Seligman, Martin. 1970. *Helplessness: On Depression, Development and Death*. San Francisco: Freeman.

Sellars, Wilfrid. 1963. *Science, Perception and Reality*. New York: Humanities Press.

Shulman, Max. 1964. *The Many Loves of Dobie Gillis*. New York: Bantam.

Skinner, B. F. 1948. *Walden Two*. New York: Knopf.

Smart, J. J. C. and Bernard Williams. 1973. *Utilitarianism: For and Against*. Cambridge: Cambridge University Press.

Smith, Huston. 1991. *The World's Religions*. San Francisco: Harper.

Sober, Elliott. 1991. *Core Questions in Philosophy*. New York: Macmillan.

Sorenson, Roy. 1992. *Thought Experiments*. New York: Oxford University Press.

Steinbeck, John. 1939. *The Grapes of Wrath*. New York: Modern Library.

Stevenson, Charles. 1944. *Ethics and Language*. New Haven: Yale University Press.

Strawson, Peter. 1982. "Freedom and Resentment." In Gary Watson, ed., *Free Will*. New York: Oxford University Press. 59–80.

Strawson, Galen. 1986. *Freedom and Belief*. Oxford: Oxford University Press.

Swinburne, Richard. 1996. *Is There a God*? Oxford: Oxford University Press.

Taylor, Richard. 1974. *Metaphysics*, 2nd ed. Englewood Cliffs, NJ: Prentice-Hall.

Unger, Peter. 1975. *Ignorance: A Case for Skepticism*. Oxford: Oxford University Press.

———. 1996. *Living High and Letting Die: Our Illusion of Innocence*. New York: Oxford University Press.

van Inwagen, Peter. 1983. *An Essay on Free Will*. Oxford: Oxford University Press.

Waller, Bruce. 1990. *Freedom Without Responsibility*. Philadelphia: Temple University Press.

Watson, Gary. 1982. "Free Agency." In Gary Watson, ed., *Free Will*. New York: Oxford University Press.

Westphal, Jonathan and Carl Levenson, eds. 1993. *Life and Death*. Indianapolis: Hackett.

Zimbardo, Philip and Michael Leippe. 1991. *The Psychology of Attitude Change and Social Influence*. New York: McGraw Hill.

INDEX